Environmental Problems of the Greeks and Romans

Ancient Society and History

J. DONALD HUGHES

Environmental Problems of the Greeks and Romans

Ecology in the Ancient Mediterranean

Second Edition

Johns Hopkins University Press
Baltimore

9 8 7 6 5 4 3 2 1

The first edition was published as *Pan's Travail: Environmental Problems of the Ancient Greeks and Romans.*

Johns Hopkins University Press
2715 North Charles Street
Baltimore, Maryland 21218-4363
www.press.jhu.edu

Library of Congress Cataloging-in-Publication Data

Hughes, Donald J., 1932–
    Environmental problems of the Greeks and Romans : ecology in the ancient Mediterranean / Donald J. Hughes. — Second edition.
        pages cm. — (Ancient society and history)
    Includes bibliographical references and index.
    ISBN-13: 978-1-4214-1210-8 (hardcover : alk. paper)
    ISBN-13: 978-1-4214-1211-5 (pbk. : alk. paper)
    ISBN-13: 978-1-4214-1212-2 (electronic)
    ISBN-10: 1-4214-1210-1 (hardcover : alk. paper)
    ISBN-10: 1-4214-1211-X (pbk. : alk. paper)
    ISBN-10: 1-4214-1212-8 (electronic)
    1. Human ecology—Greece—History. 2. Human ecology—Rome—History. 3. Greece—Civilization. 4. Rome—Civilization. 5. Greece—Environmental conditions. 6. Rome—Environmental conditions. I. Title.
    GF581.H85 2014
    304.2'80938—dc23
                        2013018546

A catalog record for this book is available from the British Library.

Photographs courtesy of J. Donald Hughes and Pamela L. Hughes except where noted otherwise. The final dates in parentheses represent, as closely as possible, the year the photograph was taken.

Special discounts are available for bulk purchases of this book. For more information, please contact Special Sales at 410-516-6936 or specialsales@press.jhu.edu.

Johns Hopkins University Press uses environmentally friendly book materials, including recycled text paper that is composed of at least 30 percent post-consumer waste, whenever possible.

Contents

Preface

During my earliest visits to Athens in 1959 and 1966, it was still possible to enter the Parthenon and to look out on the then-barren hills of Attica between the columns. As I stood there one time, I remarked to my wife Pamela, "I wonder if the ancient Greeks had any idea of what they were doing to the environment." The question continued to bother me, and I decided to try to find out the answer. I asked senior colleagues about it, and they warned me that I would not find any information along those lines. Still, as an experienced seasonal ranger in Yosemite and Grand Canyon, the idea struck me that there might have been something like national parks or wildlife refuges in the ancient world. They had numerous sacred groves—could these have served to protect trees and animals?

I was a student at the American School of Classical Studies at Athens, so two great libraries, including the Gennadeion across the street, were available to me, and I began to work my way through anything that seemed relevant to my questions, which soon broadened to include the environmental attitudes and actions of the Greeks, Romans, and Egyptians, and indeed the whole Mediterranean world. I began to see that modern environmental problems had precedents in antiquity, to one degree or another. Forests had been overused to the point where some of them disappeared. Animal species had been hunted and seen their habitats degraded to the point where they became extinct in certain areas. Poets complained about air and water pollution. Archaeology revealed piles of waste from mining and metallurgy. These are only a few examples that I brought together in my book *Ecology in Ancient Civilizations* (University of New Mexico Press, 1975). It was, I believe, the first book published specifically on the environmental history of the ancient world. George Perkins Marsh, in his pioneering work *Man and Nature* (1864), included a section on the environmental damage caused by the ancient Romans and its possible effect on the decline and fall of the Roman Empire. After that, a few succinct speculations appeared in the literature, but no extensive treatment of the subject was published until my book in 1975.

I continued my research and took a number of trips to Greece, Italy, Turkey, Egypt, Jordan, Israel, Spain, Portugal, and Mediterranean France. Libraries and museums in the United States, Europe, and Russia were of great help to me. I received a request from the Johns Hopkins University Press to prepare a new, reorganized study, which appeared in 1994 as *Pan's Travail: Environmental Problems of the Ancient Greeks and Romans*. The present volume is a second edition of that book, with new sections, chapters, illustrations, and the benefit of eighteen additional years of research, experience, and reflection. My areas of research are predominantly history, ancient literature, archaeology, scientific reports, and continued study of the landscape, including visits to significant sites. In recent years there has been a rapid increase of interest in ancient environmental history, with attendant publications that receive attention in this edition.

It may seem that awareness of environmental issues arose only in modern times, as the result of concern about problems such as pollution and the scarcity of natural resources. But environmental history has revealed that there were antecedents to these present-day conditions. The civilization of the ancient Mediterranean, and of Greece and Rome in particular, is of unique importance to later peoples who were inspired by it, such as the Europeans, the Arabs, and all the participants in the life and thought of the globe today. Gaining an understanding of ancient attitudes, actions, and relations to the natural environment will help us to understand the background of environmental issues in the present world.

Historians sometimes criticize environmental history of suffering from presentism. These critics note that being aware of environmental problems is an entirely a contemporary phenomenon. The word "environmentalism" did not emerge in general use until the 1960s, and environmental history became a recognizable subdiscipline only in the 1970s. The motive that led to environmental inquiry was a reaction to uniquely modern problems. So, is environmental history an untenable attempt to link late twentieth-century developments and concerns to past historical periods in which they were not operative, and certainly not conscious to human participants during those times? The problem with this criticism is that it is fundamentally an argument against history as an intellec-

View from inside the Parthenon on the Acropolis of Athens, with barren mountainsides visible between the columns. These mountains were deforested in ancient times. (1959)

tual endeavor that can be applied to the understanding of the present. Modern problems exist in their present forms because they are the results of historical processes. The relationship with nature was the earliest challenge facing human-kind. It would take a particularly egregious form of denial not to see a precedent for the market economy in the exchange of a tribal nomad's meat and skins for a village agriculturalist's grain and textiles. The Greek philosopher Plato described soil erosion, and the Roman poet Horace complained about urban air pollution. The study of past effects of environmental forces on human societies, and the impact of human activities on the environment, gives needed perspective to the dilemmas of the contemporary world.

An image that illustrates this relevance of the past is a view of the eroded slopes of Mount Parnes in Attica, not far from Athens. Of all the passages from ancient writers on the natural world, the most fascinating for modern environ-mental historians may be Plato's comment in the *Critias* on the consequences of deforestation in just such a place: "What now remains compared with what then existed is like the skeleton of a sick man, all the fat and soft earth having wasted away, and only the bare framework of the land being left." Mediterra-nean environmental history is in large part a history of deforestation and its consequences, although much more than that. Recent work in fields such as anthracology, palynology, and computer modeling of climate change provides new evidence supporting the judgment that ancient deforestation represents environmental damage that contributed to disruption of Mediterranean economies. Of course other factors were at work, too, notably agricultural decline.

Plato's quote above is valuable ancient evidence for ancient deforestation, but it has received seemingly endless commentary, some of it consisting of quibbles intended to explain it away. Although it occurs in a section about the lost continent of Atlantis, it is not at all mythical. Plato describes evidence present in his own time and place, and invites his audience to look at it: timber in standing buildings that had been taken from mountains left only with "food for bees" (flowering annuals and shrubs), and shrines marking springs that had dried up when the forests were removed. In his *Laws*, Plato advises planting trees to improve water supply.

If the past is not usable, then history is an enterprise in vain. The Greeks did not have science in the modern sense, as the scientific method, including observation and experimentation, was only partially achieved. But it would be gratuitous to ignore the steps they took in the direction of science. Aristotle's observation that animals seek out surroundings that are "appropriate" (*oikeios* in Greek) may, as Ernst Haeckel put it, be the root of the modern word "ecology." From earliest times, human societies have lived in interaction with, and in dependence on, the natural world that surrounds them and includes them. They had a dawning awareness of their situation, and expressed it in various ways. All this is a valid and rewarding subject for historical study.

Many institutions have provided aid and facilities for this study. I wish to thank especially the American School of Classical Studies at Athens, the Gennadeion Library, the Goulandris Natural History Museum, the Aristotelian University of Thessaloniki, the University of Denver (in particular the John Evans Professorship and the faculty research fund), the Denver Museum of Nature and Science, the Denver Art Museum, the Charles A. and Anne Morrow Lindbergh Foundation, the Princeton University Library, the Princeton Public Library, the U.S. National Archives, Fitzwilliam House and Cheshunt College at Cambridge, the University of Cambridge Library, the Bodleian Library at Oxford, the Royal Botanical Gardens at Kew, the Vatican Library, the Hermitage Museum at St. Petersburg, the Leibniz Institute for Regional Geography, the Institute of Geography of the University in Leipzig, and the Helmholtz Centre of Environmental Research in Leipzig and Halle.

Environmental Problems of the Greeks and Romans

One

Introduction: Ecology in the Greek and Roman World

The ancient Greeks and Romans faced a multitude of problems that the natural environment gave them. Droughts, floods, earthquakes, volcanic eruptions, wildfires, fluctuating temperatures, plagues, diseases of plants and animals—the list goes on— challenged them at different times. Such naturally occurring problems related to the environment have occurred since the first societies and continue today. But what about environmental issues caused by human activities, such as pollution of air and water, exhaustion of resources, energy use, deforestation, overgrazing, overfishing, overhunting, habitat loss, and the endangerment of animal species? At first consideration, it may seem that these challenges emerged only in the twentieth century, or at the earliest during the Industrial Revolution. But there is good evidence to show that most if not all of these problems existed in some form in the ancient world, although differing from their modern counterparts in intensity, magnitude, and range. Granted that human-caused environmental problems existed, were the Greeks and Romans aware of them? Did they reflect on them, seek their causes, and attempt to address them? Interestingly, the ancients made a start in these inquiries. Plato recognized that deforestation interfered with the water supply, and advised the conservation and plantation of trees to ameliorate that process.[1] Vitruvius recognized that pollution from smelting lead-silver ore was a danger to the health of workers, and Strabo noted that high chimneys could be built to disperse effluents.[2] In some of their biological writings, Aristotle and Theophrastus discussed notions that would today be called ecological. These and other examples are examined in this book.

The landscapes of Greece and Italy, and of the other countries once occupied by Greek colonists and the Roman Empire, have suffered from human occupation since ancient times. Visitors to those lands experienced in land-use management observed such damage as early as the mid-nineteenth century, starting with the versatile George Perkins Marsh, who ascribed the "decay of these flourishing countries" to "man's ignorant disregard of the laws of nature."[3] Similar comments were made by the ecologist Paul B. Sears and the soil conservationist Walter C. Lowdermilk in the early twentieth century.[4] All three of these perceptive scholars ascribed the decline of ancient civilizations to environmental problems such as deforestation, erosion, and agricultural exhaustion. Later, geographer Fairfield Osborn also detected in the decline of ancient societies "a contemporaneous deterioration of environment and peoples," of which "the causes were man-made, not natural."[5]

These modern authors wrote, for the most part, before extensive research had been done on environmental changes in the ancient world, but they did not ascribe all environmental degradation to antiquity. They recognized that the Mediterranean basin and neighboring lands have been subject to cycles of devastation and recovery, and that much of the evident damage was the result of modern mistreatment of the natural world. Their intuitive judgments constitute a hypothesis well worth investigating. The Greeks and Romans, like other ancient peoples, did degrade their environments, even if not to the extent of modern times, and it is not unreasonable to connect that process with the decline of classical civilizations.

Ruined cities surrounded by ruined land have long been common sights in the Mediterranean area. When I first visited Greece in the 1950s, I viewed the bare, desiccated slopes of Mount Hymettus between the Doric columns of the Parthenon. Plato first described deforestation in the same place, with resulting erosion and drying of springs, in the fourth century BCE.[6] Today the view is becoming less stark as trees planted on the mountain as part of reforestation projects grow larger, at low elevations if not higher. On the upper slopes of Hymettus there was so little soil remaining after centuries of erosion that in many places holes had to be dynamited in the limestone to allow the planting of pine seedlings. And these young trees have not fared well; many are dried out or dead because of insufficient soil and moisture. The scene of bare mountains rising above temples can be duplicated at other archaeological sites like the ancient Temple of Apollo at Corinth, where there has been little change in the view since antiquity.

All around the Mediterranean, ancient ports have been landlocked by erosional sediments, a fact mentioned by ancient writers. Ostia, the ancient port of the city of Rome, now has no direct access to the sea that was its lifeline; silt from the Tiber River filled its harbor basins. Successive emperors ordered the dredging of new basins, which one after another succumbed to alluvium. In the former Roman provinces of North Africa, the wide avenues and impressive buildings of populous cities such as Leptis Magna, Sabratha, and Thamugadi, which once exported wheat and olive oil, stand empty within a Saharan landscape that could not support such populations today without importing water. The irrigation systems of the Carthaginians and Romans, which made this arid region blossom, depended for their effectiveness on watersheds whose forests have disappeared. The Libyan government is now bringing sections of the desert under cultivation by mining the water that has been underground since the last ice age, but this fossil water will be exhausted in the foreseeable future, and another cycle of civilization may end because its environment will have been depleted. While it would be incorrect to blame the ancient Greeks and Romans for all the defects of the present-day Mediterranean lands, which have been subjected to successive pressures in medieval and modern times, in many instances ancient peoples initiated a process of wearing away the environment that had supported them. This environmental degradation was set in motion by economic, military, and religious factors, and it is important to examine the relationship between them; the causal factors operated in more than one direction, and environmental changes brought pressures on human societies.

The Role of Ecology in History

When Amphipolis, a northern colony of Athens, fell to Sparta during the war between the Greek city-states, "the Athenians were greatly alarmed . . . The chief reason was that the city was useful to them for the procurement of timber for ship-building."[7] This comment by Thucydides is one of countless references in ancient texts to the importance of nature in the course of human history. No ancient general could fight a war, no leader conduct diplomacy, no reformer advance a political program, without consideration of the land and its resources. A modern student of the ancient world who wishes to understand such motivations and actions must consider the environment within which they occurred. Robert Sallares said it well: "Any ancient historian who has not immersed himself or herself fully in the problems of ecology can have, at best, only an extremely limited comprehension of the course of history in Classical antiquity."[8] Humans are a species within an ecosystem, and the condition of the ecosystem

The marketplace of Leptis Magna, Libya, flourished under the Romans during the second century but was later abandoned to encroaching desert sands. Water supply was a problem here. (1970)

as it changes through time influences the direction and development of human affairs. Ecological analysis is therefore an important means of understanding human history.

Environmental history is the study of how humans have related to the natural world through time. As a method, it is the application of ecological principles to history. By definition, it requires familiarity with more than one of the artificial fields into which learning has been divided ever since Aristotle. Ecology is a natural science; history straddles the boundary between the social sciences and the humanities. In addition, to do environmental history properly requires knowledge in such fields as agriculture, archaeology, botany, climatology, economics, geography, geology, philosophy, technology, zoology, and the like, in addition to the search for useful synthesis.

The word "ecology" derives from the Greek *oikos*, meaning home or house, and by extension the whole inhabited Earth, and *logos*, meaning reason or study, a common suffix used to indicate a particular science. A survey of all surviving Greek literature shows that a word for ecology (which would have been *oikologia* or something like it) was not coined in ancient times, although important ecological ideas occur in the writings of philosophers such as Aristotle and Theophrastus, and their use of *oikeios* (appropriate) to indicate the relationship between a species and the environment where it characteristically flourishes comes close.[9] Ernst Haeckel receives credit for first using the word *oecologie* in 1866.[10] Haeckel was familiar with the classics and could have had in mind the ancient use of *oikeios*. As the study of the interrelationships of organisms with their living and nonliving environments, ecology can emphasize either a single species or the systems within which species live. Species ecology concentrates on the environmental relationships of one species. *Homo sapiens* can be the chosen species, and in that case the study can be called human ecology; environmental history is an application of human ecology in this sense, and that is what this book attempts to do for the ancient Greeks and Romans.

Systems ecology is the study of the relationships of all organisms within a defined area. Such an interacting group of organisms, with its environment, is called an ecosystem. An ecosystem can be as small as a pond or as large as the biosphere, the entire complex of the living Earth. In this book, the ecosystem chosen for study is the Mediterranean area, defined broadly both as a basin and a climatic zone, because it was the setting of most of Greek and Roman history. Historians, interested as they are in human culture, must never forget that on other levels processes are occurring that profoundly affect humankind.

Environmental history is significant because it gives perspective to the more traditional concerns of historians: war, diplomacy, politics, law, economics, technology, science, philosophy, art, and literature. Each one of these subjects is connected with nature, with the use and meaning of the natural environment. In this book, environment includes the Earth—its soil and mineral resources; its water, both fresh and salt; its atmosphere, climates, and weather; its living things, animals and plants from the simplest to the most complex; and the energy it receives from the Sun.

Ancient Environmental Problems

The fact that many of the problems of human ecology as they are now understood also existed in classical times should not come as a surprise. In this book I discuss the most important environmental problems that affected the Greeks and Romans: deforestation and overgrazing that removed vegetative cover; erosion of the land; destruction of wildlife; pollution of air, land, and water; warfare; depletion of resources; agricultural decline; and manifold urban difficulties such as food and water supply and sewage disposal. All these problems will be considered in the context of the natural environment of the Mediterranean basin. The city, for example, cannot be discussed in isolation from the countryside that it impacts and upon which it depends, because both are part of the same

5

ecosystem. For this reason, it is necessary to analyze the components and dynamics of the Mediterranean ecosystem, including natural disasters and climatic changes

The relationship of the Greeks and Romans with the natural environment was determined in part by their characteristic mental constructions of nature. The actions of people, after all, reflected their perceptions and values, even if many were confused about or in conflict with one another. Ancient attitudes varied from worship of nature to curiosity, desire for prudent use, and greed leading to wasteful exploitation. The Greeks and Romans were seldom deliberately destructive, and they often ameliorated the condition of the world in which they lived by planting parks and gardens and by protecting certain areas. At the same time, natural and economic forces could distort and overwhelm reason, custom, and religion. People were not, and are not, often aware of the long-term results of their actions on the natural world. Intending to sustain balance, they nevertheless upset it. If ancient people adversely affected the natural environment within which they lived—and they certainly did—it is reasonable to suspect that they may have helped to bring about the "decline and fall" of their own civilizations. In the summary, I expand the discussion of how the end of the Roman Empire, and of the ancient world in general, had an ecological dimension.

Sources of Evidence for Ancient Environmental History

The evidence on which this ancient environmental history depends comes from a wide variety of sources. Information can be derived from many different types of ancient literature, including both poetry and prose, and from papyri and inscriptions. Ancient Greek and Latin history, philosophy, drama, epic and lyric poetry, scientific and technical treatises, correspondence, and legal documents contain numerous references to environmental problems, although only a few include extensive discussions. The richness of this line of evidence is not as well known as it should be, since only a few modern historians of the ancient world have concerned themselves with it until recently. There are several important reasons why. One is the simple lack of evidence for some periods and places, especially from early times and less urbanized areas. Literature survives from the upper, educated class, from those who could write and whose texts were valued by later generations of literati. Another factor is that many descriptions of human interactions with the natural environment were written long afterward, lacking direct sources of information, and possibly corrupted by tendentious explanations that had arisen in the interim. It is also all too easy for a writer to imagine how he and his society might have reacted in a similar situation and to impute that reaction to people living under other circumstances and with different traditions and beliefs. This circumstance occurs with a historian writing in Roman times about classical Athens—Plutarch, for example—or with Christian writers like Eusebius or Sozomen writing about what they considered to be pagan antiquity. It can be a pitfall for historians writing in the present age, too, if we are not careful.

Archaeology is another important source of information on the ancient environment, particularly more recent classical archaeology. Earlier work in this field concentrated on the recovery of works of art and monumental architecture, but now, emulating work in other areas of the world, archaeologists in the Mediterranean have turned to ecological data. There is much more to be done. Studies of whole landscapes, including agricultural settlements, industrial sites, commercial ports, urban patterns outside the monumental centers of cities, and the systematic collection of animal and plant materials, have broadened the base for interpretation of the problems discussed in this book, and will undoubtedly continue to do so.[11]

A further significant category of evidence comes from scientific studies that provide information on environmental changes during the historical period. Paleobotany, paleoecology, paleoclimatology, and similar specialties have gained new tools in recent years and are making immense strides in understanding. Palynology, the study of pollen deposits, combined with radiocarbon and other methods of dating, has enabled the reconstruction of the succession of vegetation during ancient times at many points within the Mediterranean region. In the not-too-distant future, investigators will more closely correlate this information with historical events, and with the mass of data being gathered on past climatic changes. One hopes that in the future, conferences at which historians, archaeologists, and scientists in these fields can talk to each other and share their results across disciplinary lines will become more commonplace. For now, in some areas and in some spans of time there is sufficient evidence available to form a convincing picture of what was occurring, but for most times and places, too little is known. Additional study of this whole question will prove rewarding, adding important pieces to the puzzle of world environmental history, an understanding of which is crucial in providing perspective to today's ecological crisis. The purpose of this book is not to prove that environment determined the events of history, but to examine the ways in which human activities and the environment interacted in positive and negative ways.

Two

The Environment: Life, Land, and Sea in the Mediterranean

To understand Greek and Roman environmental problems, it is necessary to place them in the context of the special environment in which they occurred and with which they interacted. Fernand Braudel, in his magisterial study of early modern Mediterranean history, pointed out that the environment was not just a background for the human drama, but an actor—or a considerable number of the cast—in the play.[1] It is important to examine the constituent elements and dynamics of the environment, since they will be present and active throughout this study. As Braudel remarked, "Woe betide the historian who thinks that this preliminary interrogation is unnecessary, that the Mediterranean as an entity needs no definition because it has long been clearly defined [and] is instantly recognizable."[2] This comment is as applicable to the ecosystem as it is to geography. To know how human beings affect the world around them and produce environmental problems, one must understand ecological processes.

The main setting of the Greek and Roman civilizations was the Mediterranean basin, an area dominated by the sea that gives it its name.[3] It includes adjacent parts of Europe, Asia, and Africa. While this zone can be defined in several ways—culturally, historically, physiographically, climatically, and so on—for the present purpose it is best to regard it as a biogeographical region.[4] Greek civilization was almost entirely a Mediterranean phenomenon, although Alexander the Great and his successors temporarily extended it to the east as far as India and central Asia. The Romans, also a Mediterranean people, dominated a sig-

8

nificant area north of the Alps for a longer period of time. But the centers of both societies, and the bulk of their territories and populations, were always in the Mediterranean basin.

The Mediterranean area can also be described as an ecosystem, a changing community of animals and plants together with the physical surroundings on which they depend: the earth, water, atmosphere, and the fluctuating flow of energy. Human beings interact with, affect, and are affected by all the components of this ecosystem. The Mediterranean ecosystem contains many smaller communities of living organisms that can be considered, with their physical settings, to be separate ecosystems, but the entire region possesses enough common characteristics to make it a useful unit of study. It differs significantly from the three continents on which it impinges: Europe north of the Alps, Saharan Africa and farther south, and the vast landmass of Asia to the east. It is a region that has felt the impact of human actions as long and as extensively as almost any place on Earth.

Climate

When historical environmental changes occur, the question often arises as to whether they are the results of climatic alterations. The Mediterranean climate in particular affects many of the environmental processes discussed in this book. Climate gives the Mediterranean area its most recognizable character. Although the zone extends from the rainy Adriatic to the margins of the African desert, the general impression of the climate is agreeable: sunny and dry, but moderated by sea breezes. Visitors from less fortunate lands have often found it attractive, even seductive. The "land of the lotus eaters"[5] was, after all, a Mediterranean destination that travelers found too bountiful and luxurious to leave. Nonetheless, at certain times and in certain places the region can be dangerously hot, cold, or stormy, affecting human activities such as sea transport and agriculture.

The Mediterranean climate is unique among the Earth's climates.[6] It is relatively dependable, with two distinguishable seasons: a long, hot, dry summer extending from April to October, and a mild but sometimes rainy, windy winter the rest of the year. The summer is longer in the southern and eastern parts of the basin. People have deferred to the two faces of the year by making summer the time for travel, especially by sea—as well as the time for war—and the winter the season for peace, cultivation, and staying home.

Sunshine is a determining characteristic of the Mediterranean climate: the average number of hours of sunshine in Athens is 2,655 per year (in Berlin, it is only 1,614). Average rainfall is typically between 350 and 900 mm (15 and 35 in) per year, almost all of it falling in the winter. Still, the wet season is not constantly rainy, because most of the precipitation comes in a few heavy down-pours. On Malta, a total of 279 mm (11 in) of rain has been recorded in one day. The total amount varies greatly from year to year; one year may bring twice the normal amount, another only half. It also differs from place to place. Port Said, Egypt, in the dry southeast, annually averages 50 mm (2 in) of precipitation, while Crikvenica, Croatia, on the northern Adriatic coast, measures 4,600 mm (181 in), some of which falls as snow. Mountain ranges catch the moisture-laden winds that tend to blow from the west, producing orographic precipitation, leaving the eastern slopes in a dry "rain shadow." Corcyra, on the western edge of Greece, has an average of 1,320 mm (52 in) per year, while Larissa, east of the Pindus massif, receives only 500 mm (20 in). Mountains often breed thunder-storms in the summer, and flash floods can roll down otherwise dry riverbeds.

The nearness of the sea moderates the temperature in many places around the Mediterranean. The difference between the average temperature of the hottest and coolest months is often only 14°C (25°F), and between day and night about 8°C (14°F). In Palermo, Sicily, there is no month with an average temperature below 10°C (50°F), and near sea level anywhere in the Mediterra-nean, temperatures below freezing are rare. Summer temperatures of 27–32°C (80–90°F) in a maritime climate are fairly oppressive, so people often take an afternoon siesta in Mediterranean lands, but they frequently complain that the heat keeps them awake both then and at night. Winter snow is a brief novelty, except in the mountains. The higher one climbs, the colder it is likely to get, so shepherds in the mountains wear heavy cloaks with good reason. The tall-est peaks are snowcapped all winter, although usually not in summer; major glaciers occur only in the Alps and to the east in the Caucasus. There are a few glaciers in the Pyrenees, but there and elsewhere they are small and at present disappearing. We may assume that in ancient times they were larger; in summer, Roman nobles enjoyed ice from the Apennines.

Winds

The Greeks personified the winds and often portrayed them as winged figures: Boreas, the North Wind; Notos, the South; Zephyros, the West, and so on. They did not agree on their names or numbers; Athens's Tower of the Winds has re-liefs with the names of eight, but Aristotle distinguished twelve.[7] The character and prevalence of the winds varied from place to place.

In the summer, a cool air mass with high pressure prevails over western and central Europe, pushing winds of dry continental air across the Mediterranean Sea toward the Sahara and the deserts of Asia, where heated air rises. These winds are generally northwesterly, but northeasterly on the North African coast

The Tower of the Winds was built in Athens while Julius Caesar ruled Rome. The reliefs portray wind gods of eight directions. The building had a wind vane, sundials, and a water clock that rotated a circular map of the heavens. (2011)

and in the Aegean. In ancient Greece, they were called *etesian*, or annual winds. When not too strong, they assist sailing unless one happens to want to go to north, and they make it necessary to choose harbors that are sheltered from that direction. Summer winds can be dangerous; one July, sailing between Crete and Mykonos, I saw waves break over the bow of my cruise ship. Around large landmasses like Spain and Asia Minor, sea winds tend to blow inland, especially during the day, replacing heated air that is rising.

In winter, low-pressure cells form over the Mediterranean and move eastward with the global circulation of air at latitudes between 30 and 45 degrees north, and the jet stream shifts into the region, bringing westerly or southwesterly rain-bearing winds. Aristotle called Lips, the Southwest Wind, a "wet wind."[8] But the warmer air over the sea rises, and colder continental air rushes in from Europe in the form of dry northerlies that are often violent. Among local names for these winds are *mistral* in the Rhone valley, which can uproot trees, and *bora* along the Dalmatian coast. Similar downslope winds are called *favonio* in Italy, *lyvas* in Greece, and *terral* in southern Spain. Air attracted by the same lows from Africa in the form of the *sirocco* is much hotter, and bears a heavy load of sand and dust from the Sahara. It picks up moisture as it crosses the sea, and it can produce rain that is red from the dust. Where the continental air roars down the mountainside as a *föhn* (a dry wind that heats as it descends), a phenomenon common on the north side of the Atlas Mountains, it is reminiscent of a blast furnace.

Outdoor Life

The Greeks and Romans were fond of an active life lived out-of-doors. The Mediterranean climate is conducive to open-air activities for much of the year. The Athenian Ecclesia, or assembly, conducted its business outdoors, as did several other political bodies. Theaters had no roofs, and athletes competed nude in gymnasiums and stadiums. Temples had their altars outside, and airy colonnades surrounded the marketplaces. When the owners could afford it, houses were built around open courtyards that were arranged to be shaded in the summer and to take advantage of solar heat in the winter.

The Mediterranean light, given the lower levels of pollution in ancient times, was noted for its clarity and brilliance. This quality makes understandable the attention given to lines and shadows in architecture, such as the use of fluted columns and sculptured reliefs.

The Mediterranean Sea

Since the sea is the dominant geographical feature that ties the Mediterranean lands together and gives them a shared character, it is appropriate to discuss it before the land. The Mediterranean is the world's largest inland sea, with an area of 2.5 million km² (970,000 miles²), almost 3 million km² (1,143,000 miles²) if the Black Sea is included. It penetrates far into the landmasses of Europe, Asia, and Africa, forming islands, peninsulas, bays, inlets, straits, and isthmuses. There is an intimate interplay between sea and land; the Mediterranean area has a strongly littoral aspect. The sea extends 3,700 km (2,300 miles) from Gibraltar to the Levantine coast, with an average width of 800 km (500 miles) from north to south. Its presence at 30 to 45 degrees latitude, where similar climatic zones occur elsewhere in the world, is responsible for the great extent of the Mediterranean climatic zone. Mediterranean-type climates in California, Chile, South Africa, and Australia are limited by mountain and desert barriers.[9]

Compared with larger oceans, the Mediterranean is not extremely deep. Its average depth is about 1,500 m (5,000 feet), as against 3,800 m (12,500 feet) for the world's oceans. But it cannot be called a shallow sea; except in the Adriatic, its continental shelves are narrow, and the sea bottom has many ridges and chasms. The greatest depth, 5,120 m (16,797 feet), is in the Matapan Trench of the Ionian basin.

The Mediterranean is almost landlocked; its single natural connection with the rest of the world's oceans is through the Strait of Gibraltar, or Pillars of Heracles (Hercules), where the water is only 14 km (9 miles) wide and 365 m (1,200 feet) deep on average. An important result of this almost complete separation is the relative absence of tides within the Mediterranean Sea, since the gravitational pull of the Moon and Sun can act only on the comparatively small volume of water in the basin itself. The tidal range exceeds a meter (3 feet) only at Gibraltar itself and on the east coast of Tunisia, and the average throughout the basin is 10–15 cm (4–6 in).[10] For this reason, ports are accessible without major harbor works such as floating docks, and construction is possible relatively close to the shoreline—although floods are not unknown.[11] The connection to the outer sea is extremely important, however, because the rate of evaporation of water at the surface of the Mediterranean is exceptionally high, amounting to 1,450 mm (57 in) per year, the same as 113,000 m^3 (150,000 yards³) per second over the entire sea. Rainfall replaces only 27 percent of this loss, and rivers such as the Nile, Ebro, Rhone, Tiber, and Po supply an additional 6 percent. Another 6 percent comes from the Black Sea through the Bosporus and Dardanelles, leaving the preponderance, 61 percent of the Mediterranean's water budget, to be made up by the Atlantic. A surface current flows inward through the strait along the North African coast. Underneath, a smaller and slower current of heavier, saltier Mediterranean water flows into the Atlantic at a depth of about 300 m (1,000 feet). The high evaporation rate of the Mediterranean makes it much more saline than the oceans. It is not getting saltier, however, because the outgoing current carries an amount of salt equal to that being concentrated by evaporation. The water that enters the Mediterranean comes from near the surface of the Atlantic, which is warmer than the depths, and once inside the Mediterranean, it is further heated by the Sun. The sea is therefore the warmest large body of water at its latitude. In the mid-twentieth century, the average annual surface temperature was about 19.5°C (67°F). Since then, temperatures have been rising, likely connected with the global warming affecting the oceans worldwide, but which is exacerbated in the almost landlocked Mediterranean. Surface temperatures at the extreme can reach 31°C (88°F) in August in limited areas such as off the coast of Libya. Compared with the oceans, there is a minor temperature gradient between water near the surface and in the depths; the temperature of the deep

Mediterranean is 13°C (55°F). At times in geological history, the straits have closed and the sea dried up almost completely. Salt deposits on the sea bottom indicate that these processes last happened about six million years ago, when there were no human beings to witness it.

A layer of yellow-brown sediments about 9,000 feet deep covers the floor of the Mediterranean. These sediments are predominantly lime, with some clay and sand, intruded upon by extensive salt beds. Underlying these strata is another of blue mud. Fine riverine muds overlie the strata near river mouths, and their deposition is accelerated by erosion caused by human activities.

The Mediterranean Land

The Mediterranean basin has varied patterns of land, but in most places it is mountainous, with rugged and complex ranges. Between them are sheltered valleys and occasional alluvial plains. A typical feature of the landscape in this region is a sea backed by mountains. In many places, such as Mount Athos or the base of the Maritime Alps, mountainsides fall directly into the sea. The only extensive flat regions are found north of the Black Sea and along the dry eastern section of the coast of North Africa.

Mountains and Volcanism

The peaks themselves are not unusually high, but they are often bold and beautiful because their entire rise from sea level is visible. The highest mountain in Greece is Olympus, 2,917 m (9,568 feet) high. In Italy, Monte Corno in the Apennines is almost exactly as high, but Etna on Sicily rises to 3,322 m (10,902 feet), and Monte Viso, a high point of the Alps in Italy near the Mediterranean, reaches 3,841 m (12,602 feet). Spain has the Pyrenees in the north and the Sierra Nevada in the south, both of which exceed 3,300 m (11,000 feet) in elevation. The Middle Atlas Mountains of North Africa reach a similar height. Eastward are Mount Sinai in Egypt, 2,285 m (7,500 feet); Mount Lebanon, 3,088 m (10,131 feet); and the Taurus Range of southern Asia Minor, 3,734 m (12,251 feet). East of the Black Sea in Georgia (ancient Colchis) rises the highest peak of all in the region, Mount Elbrus in the Caucasus, 5,642 m (18,510 feet) high. But the number and extent of the mountains of the Mediterranean, not their elevation, are most impressive. Headlands on or near the sea might serve as landmarks for navigation, and temples built atop them, such as the Temples of Poseidon and Athena at Cape Sounion, enhanced them for that purpose.

The high relief of this zone is caused by the interaction between two huge continental masses, the northward moving African Plate and the Eurasian Plate.

The coastal landscape near Erice on Sicily, Italy, manifests the mountainous topography that typifies Mediterranean shores. (1992)

In their collision over a period of millions of years, smaller plates split off and squeezed between them, and mountains were thrust up as strata were folded and deformed. Most of the present mountains of the Mediterranean region rose in this process during the Tertiary Age of the Cenozoic Era. Earthquakes, often of disastrous intensity, can be expected from year to year. In this tectonically active region, the heated magma of the Earth's mantle sporadically finds its way to the surface and creates volcanoes. Etna, the highest Mediterranean volcano, has erupted frequently, "shooting hot, unapproachable floods of flame."[12] Others of note are Vulcano itself and the almost constantly active Stromboli, two islands in the Lipari group north of Sicily.[13] Vesuvius is famous for the ancient eruption that buried Pompeii and other neighboring towns, and is still intermittently active. Several of the Aegean islands are volcanic, including Melos, Lemnos, and Thera (Santorini). The latter had a catastrophic eruption, dating to around 1620 BCE, that destroyed most of the island. Through deformation and volcanism, many of the deposits of useful and valuable metals and minerals were formed.

The Temple of Poseidon, located on the crest of Cape Sounion, Attica, Greece, served as a landmark for approaching ships. (1959)

Rocks and Soil

The oldest rocks in the Mediterranean are huge fragments of the ancient continental plates, dating to the Precambrian Era. But by far the most prevalent and extensive strata are of sedimentary limestone originally laid down under the ocean, which in some places has metamorphosed into fine marble. Other formations such as sandstone, shale, conglomerate, and coal seams are found, along with ores containing metals like gold, silver, copper, lead, and iron.

Ancient writers, including Hesiod, Columella, and Pliny the Elder, considered the importance of soils to agriculture.[14] From surface rocks, the process of soil formation began with the aid of vegetation; there are areas of highly fertile soil in parts of the Mediterranean basin, but generally speaking soils are thin and poor compared with northern Europe. Because the predominant underlying rock is limestone, the soils tend to be calcareous. Because the climate is relatively dry, xeromorphic soils are prevalent. Since Mediterranean topography is generally mountainous, mountain soils that tend to be subject to erosion and relatively thinner and younger are important in almost every part of the basin. In most regions, the impact of human activity has disrupted the soil's structure. Even so, many Mediterranean soils, especially those in lowlands and coastal zones, are well suited for agriculture. Typical Mediterranean soils that form on limestone bedrock are *terra fusca* (black earth) and *terra rossa* (red earth). *Terra fusca* consists of sandy, darker soils, usually brownish in color, which develop under forest cover and are not acidic because limestone, which is calcium carbonate, acts as a buffer against acidity. *Terra rossa* gains its red color from iron oxide that is present as an impurity in the limestone, and tends to be rich in clay. It develops under maquis and garigue, and has been subject to more leaching by rainfall than *terra fusca*. The moister soils of the north tend to be darker in color. In the Balkans and across the northern shores of the Black Sea there are chernozems, or black soils rich in organic matter, that have developed under cool grasslands. Southern France has well-watered soils of ochre coloration. In much of Spain, where the rocks are siliceous and crystalline, the soils have a fine, sandy consistency. Along the desert margins on the south side of the Mediterranean, there are arid soils lighter in color. In the absence of vegetative cover, winds form dunes. Winds and rains carry away the lighter sand in many areas, leaving behind a desert pavement of rocks and pebbles. The opposite situation, namely saturation with water, occurs in the deltas of the large rivers such as the Nile, Po, Rhône, and Guadalquivir, where there is a heavy, silty soil, and where drainage is necessary for agriculture. Places with volcanic soils were noted for their richness; Theophrastus said that the soil of the volcanic island of Melos was "wonderfully productive, for it is good both for grain and olives, and fairly good for vines."[15] Except where erosion has occurred, and as long as water is available, Mediterranean soils tend to be well suited for agricultural purposes.

Living Communities: Plants and Animals

An amazing variety of living things flourishes in the Mediterranean ecosystem. Various parts of the basin support different communities of plants and animals and interact with one another.[16] Each community is adapted to its particular location and climate; as Strabo noted, humans and animals are shaped by the same climatic factors.[17] The number of Mediterranean plant species greatly exceeds that of the areas immediately to the north and south. Greece alone, for example, has more than 6,000 flowering plants, compared with 2,113 in Britain, which has twice Greece's land area. One reason for the diversity in the Mediterranean zone is that it escaped the glacial sheets of the Ice Age, which scoured northern Europe as recently as 11,000 years ago. As a result, the Mediterranean zone has an unusually high number of endemic species, or those that are unique to a defined geographic location, such as a location on a mountain, a soil type, or island. Estimates indicate about 12,500 endemic plant species, of which 44 percent are located in small regions, mostly on mountain ranges (Atlas, Sierra

Nevada, Pindos, Taurus, Lebanon, and Anti-Lebanon) and on islands (Corsica, Sardinia, Sicily, Crete, and Cyprus), including the Macaronesian Islands, the classical "Islands of the Blessed" (the Canaries and Madeira). Although these last-mentioned islands are in the Atlantic outside the Straits of Gibraltar, they share characteristics of the Mediterranean bioclimatic zone. Some of the species found there, and forest types such as the *laurisylva* (containing members of the laurel family), were formerly widespread around the Mediterranean basin but are now narrowly limited due to climate change and human activity.[18]

Plants

Plant life is the basic productive source of food and energy in the ecosystem; it is also an inspiration in art, literature, and the beginnings of science.[19] Mediterranean vegetation occurs in life zones whose limits correspond roughly to a combination of elevation and latitude. Each is affected differently by human activities. The lowest of the zones, from sea level to about 1,000 m (3,000 feet) elevation, contains vegetation typical of the Mediterranean coastal zone. Before human interference, this was for the most part a belt of forests dominated by pines and oaks, with dense stands of broadleaved trees near watercourses.

Also at this elevation occurs the most distinctive plant association of the present-day Mediterranean basin: maquis, a brushy cover of hardy shrubs that varies from sparse to impenetrable.[20] The bushes or small trees of which it is composed rarely exceed 8 m (25 feet) in height. Maquis often establishes itself after forest removal and can be a sign of previous deforestation or otherwise disturbed habitat, but in many districts it is the climax; that is, the biotic community that perpetuates itself under the prevailing conditions of soil and climate. The most prominent species are broad-leaved sclerophylls, which are evergreen trees with leaves adapted to drought by thick hairy, leathery, oily, or waxy coverings. Maquis plants also survive in dry conditions by having long root systems, high osmotic pressure, and the evergreen ability to utilize winter moisture. All the species possess adaptations that enable them to reestablish themselves after fire by recuperating rapidly, sprouting from buried root crowns, germinating from seeds that respond to heat or spread into a burned area on the winds or by other means, and finding in bare or scorched soil a congenial place to germinate.[21] Typical maquis plants are holm and kermes oak, juniper, arbutus, laurel, myrtle, tree heather, rockrose, broom, mastic tree, and rosemary.

In harsh locations, or after repeated destruction by clearing, browsing, or fire, maquis is replaced by garigue, or "rock heath," a tough, low community of shrubs that are often spiny.[22] It is rarely more than 50 cm (20 in) high, and therefore often lower than the rocks among which it grows. Among the more than 200 common garigue plants are many spice-producing herbs such as basil, garlic, hyssop, lavender, oregano, rosemary, rue, sage, savory, and thyme. Their pleasant odors waft far out to sea, especially during the spring flowering season.

Where the conditions are even more extreme or overexploited, not even garigue survives, and a winter grassland or "steppe" occurs.[23] It has many annual species that grow in the cooler, moister half of the year, as well as perennials that grow from rootstocks, tubers, or bulbs. Like garigue, the grassland blooms in spring before the desiccating winds of summer. Species that survive grazing do best here; most prevalent are asphodel, mullein, sea squill, thistle, and members of the buttercup, composite, grass, legume, lily, mint, mustard, parsley, pink, and rockrose families.

The deciduous forest zone occurs, where rainfall permits, above the coastal Mediterranean zone just described, extending upward to around 1,400 m (4,500 feet), and is sometimes called the upper Mediterranean zone. The dominant trees are deciduous oak, elm, beech, chestnut, ash, and hornbeam. These forests are seen most often in the mountains of the northern and western parts of the basin; elsewhere they have been eliminated by human use over the centuries, or in some districts this life zone may never have been present.

At even greater altitudes, the Mediterranean mountain zone, or coniferous forest zone, extends upward to the tree line, at about 2,200 m (7,200 feet) in the mountains on the northern side of the Mediterranean, and somewhat higher in the Atlas Mountains. In undisturbed conditions, a high forest of pines, silver firs, cedars, and junipers flourishes here, interspersed with open meadows. Here the famous cedar forests of the eastern and southern Mediterranean occur.[24] Precipitation is higher in this subalpine zone, taking the form of snow in the winter and thunderstorms in the summer. The growing season, which is limited by winter cold rather than dryness, takes place in the summer. Above the tree line is an alpine tundra of dwarfed plants and lichens. Tiny flowering plants are adapted to a short summer growing season, during which they must bloom and set seed quickly before frosts return. On the bare rocks of the summits, snow may persist until the hottest part of the summer.

To the south and east, deserts set the limits of the Mediterranean. Largest is the Sahara, which reaches the seashore in parts of Egypt and Libya. Elsewhere, there are the large Syrian and Arabian deserts, and a smaller one in central Turkey. Rainfall varies from 0 to 25 mm (1 in), and as a result there are stretches where no plants are visible, but plants have evolved survival mechanisms in marginal situations. Long root systems, reduced transpiration, short life cycles triggered by water, and devices to reduce palatability can be observed in various desert plants. The common genera of plants in the desert life zone are *Anabasis*, *Artemisia* (sagebrush), *Astragalus*, *Atriplex* (saltbush), *Centaurea* (thistle), *Convol-*

vulus (bindweed), *Ephedra*, *Halogeton*, *Haloxylon* (saxaul), *Origanum* (oregano, marjoram), *Retama* (broom), *Stachys* (betony), *Tamarisk*, *Varthemia*, and *Zygophyllum* (caltrop). In oases and along better-watered wadis (arroyos), including places where there is water not far below the surface, more hydrophytic plants can grow.

Animals

The dominant vegetation, or flora, in each of these zones supports an assemblage of animal life, or fauna, that is characteristic of that particular zone. Plants are the food producers of every ecosystem, and all animal life, including humans, depends on them. Some animals, the herbivores, consume plants directly, while others, the carnivores, prey on other animals. All animals and plants, before and after they die, may provide nutriment for decomposers such as bacteria, molds, and microscopic animals. Species do not extirpate one another when they eat each other; they maintain a fluctuating balance of numbers. Among the ancients, Plotinus recognized that predators and prey are equally necessary to biodiversity, the abundance of different kinds of life essential to the living world.[25] The variety of animals found in the aboriginal Mediterranean basin was even greater than that of plants, so that it is impossible to list them all. Just as people have changed plant communities in the basin, most notably by removing forests, they have also changed the distribution of animals by altering their habitat, reducing their numbers, causing extinction, and by deliberately or inadvertently introducing domestic or other exotic species.[26]

The primeval fauna of the Mediterranean were of the Palearctic type characteristic of Europe, with the addition of some species more representative of Asia and Africa. A number occurred only in the local area, although at a lower proportion than among plants. Some of the wild mammals of the Mediterranean were herbivorous relatives of domestic animals such as goats, sheep, cattle, swine, donkeys, and horses, although their initial domestication may have taken place in areas outside the basin. Other large herbivores like bison and deer ranged the forest. The hippopotamus was common in the Nile and other African and Asiatic rivers, and the desert margins had fauna with similarities to species found in present-day Kenya and Tanzania. Smaller plant eaters are ubiquitous, including rabbits, hares, mice, voles, porcupines, and squirrels. What ecologists call the next trophic level consists of animals that eat other animals: the carnivores and insectivores. The larger predators included lions, leopards, lynxes, hyenas, jackals, foxes, and wolves, present on the European side of the sea as well as the Afro-Asiatic. Omnivores such as the bear and Barbary macaque eat both animal and vegetable foods. There are smaller carnivores such as wildcats and weasels, and insectivores like the hedgehogs, shrews, and bats.

The Mediterranean ecosystem includes a variety of reptiles and amphibians. There are several kinds of tortoise, both herbivorous and insectivorous. Snakes of many species, both venomous and nonvenomous, prey mostly on small animals, helping to keep their numbers under control. Small lizards such as the insectivorous gecko and chameleon, including one poisonous species, can be found. The huge carnivorous crocodile sprawled on the banks of rivers in Africa and Palestine. Amphibians, including the frogs that Aristophanes made famous, toads, newts, fire salamanders, and others, as a rule are found near water and are insectivores.

The ancients were familiar with many species of birds and used them for divination, which indicates that they observed them carefully. Like other animals, birds can be herbivorous; some of them, like finches, pigeons, and sparrows, are seedeaters. Others are carnivorous, including eagles, owls, hawks, and other raptors. Some specialize in carrion: vultures, ravens, and magpies, for example. Great numbers of birds are insectivores, and this makes them important to the ecological balance; to list only a few, there are swallows, thrushes, warblers, nightingales, starlings, and crested hoopoes. The migratory habits of birds provide transfers of matter and energy into and out of the ecosystem at various times of the year. There are summer visitors (orioles and warblers), winter visitors (short-eared owls, gulls), commuters between the northern and southern Mediterranean (avocets, wrynecks), and year-round residents (buntings, wall creepers). The Mediterranean rock dove adapted to human buildings and spread around the world as the common pigeon.

A notably large fraction of the animals in the ecosystem is made up of insects, whether one considers the number of species, number of individuals, or total biomass. They perform many functions in ecological processes. Many of them—from bees, beetles, butterflies, and moths to the musical cicada, cricket, and locusts—eat plants. The cochineal scale insect, a parasite of the kermes oak, produced a useful red dye.[27] Insects that consume animal material include praying mantises, wasps, hornets, and some beetles. Literature pays attention with good reason to lice, fleas, flies, and mosquitoes, which include human blood in their diets. Various species of ants specialize in food sources; some are herbivorous, some carnivorous, and some practice mold agriculture or aphid pastoralism. Numerous insects, such as the dung beetle, assist in the process of decomposition.

Among other herbivorous arthropods are the wood louse and millipede. Centipedes, spiders, and scorpions are predominantly insectivorous. Snails and slugs, which are land mollusks, are destructive to plants but serve as food for predators, even humans at times. Annelids like earthworms also perform the helpful function of soil aeration and fertilization, although the ancients did not know it.

Aquatic Life

The different climates, water depths, degrees of salinity, and benthic (sea-bottom) forms of the Mediterranean Sea provide a variety of habitats for aquatic life. Here life depends on food producers such as algae and phytoplankton, and also on nutrients washed down from the land. More than 500 species of fish are found in the sea, along with algae, corals, shellfish, and sponges. Most sea life is found in the upper layers where light penetrates. The western basin has a greater variety of species than the saltier eastern one. The total quantity of marine organisms in the Mediterranean Sea is not particularly large compared to the oceans, however, either in number of species or in the total weight of living organisms per unit of volume of seawater, which is the result of several factors: high salinity, the barriers to entry from other seas, the relative lack of volume in river flow, the narrowness of the continental shelves that are nurseries of fish populations, and the fact that the weak temperature gradient in this relatively warm sea is not conducive to the cold vertical currents that favor the production of phytoplankton. It should not be supposed that Mediterranean fisherfolk found their work unprofitable. In ancient times fishing was an important economic activity, although catches were mostly destined for local markets. There were more than 120 species of economic importance, from sharks and rays to eels, sardines, and anchovies. Flounder and sole lurk on the sea bottom. Tyrian purple dye, made from the murex or rock whelk, was an important product shipped from the Phoenician coast. Large quantities of sponges, brought up by divers, were exported from Greece.

Mammals of the Mediterranean waters include whales, seals, and dolphins, all of which count as predators of other animal life of various sizes. Birds are well adapted to depend on the sea, whether frequenting the shore (snipes, sandpipers), the surface (gulls, terns), or diving under the surface (cormorants). There are numerous other seabirds, including grebes, pelicans, and puffins. Several species of sea turtles, which are marine reptiles, are found in the Mediterranean, too.

Saltwater animals are numerous, interesting, and some are considered delicacies and sought after by fisherfolk. There are crustaceans (barnacles, shrimp, prawns, lobsters, crabs); mollusks, including monovalves (limpets, tritons), bivalves (oysters, mussels, clams), and cephalopods (squid, octopus, nautilus);

echinoderms (starfish, urchins, sea cucumbers); and coelenterates (jellyfish, sea anemones, sponges, corals). The Greeks and Romans confused some coelenterates with plants. Rivers and lakes provided freshwater habitats for ecosystems composed of many species. The eels of Lake Copais were famous in the time before that large body of water was drained. Other fish in the lakes and streams include carp, perch, and catfish. Anadromous fish such as the salmon trout and sturgeon were known to spend most of their lives in the salt water, but ascended rivers to spawn. The hippopotamus and crocodile have already been mentioned; the Nile was a major ecosystem with many fish and, like other fresh waters, supported a huge population of aquatic birds, including ducks, geese, ibises, herons, and egrets.

Conclusion

The Mediterranean ecosystem is large, productive, and complex. Powered by the energy of a sun that is relatively seldom obscured, the yearly cycle of weather allows plants to grow, and they, depending on solar energy for photosynthesis, produce food for the whole interacting structure of the community of life. Its setting is a unique mixture of mountainous, unstable land and a tideless, omnipresent inland sea.

One can hardly imagine this cradle of civilizations without human inhabitants, but for most of its geological history, that was its condition. Then, for a long and formative time, the human species was simply one strand in the web of the ecosystem, held in delicate physical and biological balance with all the other strands. But humankind changed that relationship. The various activities adopted by the growing numbers of human beings—hunting, fishing, gathering, forestry, agriculture, pastoralism, mining, industry, and urbanism—began and accelerated the process of unbalancing the ecosystem. This process will be investigated in the following chapters.

Balance is, in the long run, essential to human survival. But balance need not mean the absence of change. The ecosystem is resilient and can absorb and adapt to various kinds and degrees of change. Its balance is not like that of a pyramid, solid and immovable. It is not the unstable balance of scales, where a weight added on one side must be compensated for by an equal weight on the other in order to keep the arm from swinging out of true. It is the living balance of an eagle in flight, which can compensate for changes in the currents of air by altering the position of its wings and tail. But even an eagle cannot survive a tornado.

Beyond limits that exist in the arrangement of nature, the ecosystem cannot maintain or recover its productivity and ability to support human activities. The

23

ancient Greeks and Romans reflected at times on those limits, without establishing exactly what they were. Neither has modern science, although it has come much closer. Sometimes the Greeks and Romans inadvertently exceeded the limits of the natural system that supported them, and they suffered as a result. It is in the interest of modern society to treat the experience of the ancients as a kind of experiment, to attempt to see what mistakes were made and what the results of those mistakes were, in order to understand not only the distant past but also the far more rapid, extensive, and dangerous experiment in imbalance upon which contemporary humankind has embarked.

Three

Ecological Crises in Earlier Societies

In light of the present state of knowledge of fossil and genetic evidence, it seems that the human species evolved outside the Mediterranean basin, most likely in either East or South Africa.[1] There, in an abundant ecosystem, early humans subsisted as omnivores, gathering useful plants, catching fish and crustaceans, and hunting mammals. Sometimes they were prey, too, but their ability to invent hunting tools eventually made it possible for them to kill the largest and most dangerous animals. They made hand axes from stones, and discovered the use of fire in cooking, keeping warm, and driving wild animals. They devised the spear and the spear-casting lever (atlatl), the fishhook, and later the bow and arrow, using materials such as wood, antlers, bone, and stone. This level of material culture is called Paleolithic (Old Stone Age). Humans brought this Paleolithic culture with them when they arrived on the margins of the Mediterranean Sea hundreds of thousands of years ago, and further developed it as they lived there through the long millennia of the Ice Age. This earliest way of life subsisted on hunting, fishing, and gathering. It endured for most of prehistory, indeed for more than nine-tenths of the time that humans have existed, and lay importantly as tradition, ritual, and custom below the civilized veneer of classical societies.

Culture and technology, which represent adaptations to the natural environment, undoubtedly became more complex and potent as time passed. They enabled humans to make sweeping changes in the ecosystem, even if they could not live outside it. Early humans were directly dependent on the natural environment for their daily food, drink, clothing, and shelter. Their total numbers and the size of their groups were therefore limited. Too many people could not crowd into a small territory without depleting the food supply and consequently either starving or being forced to leave. A natural balance was thus maintained between the number of humans and the carrying capacity of the local environment.

The Role of Tradition

This balance was also supported and maintained by an oral tradition, complete with stories embodying customary views of the world, creation, gods, animals, methods of hunting and gathering, and principles of family relationships, initiations, birth, and death. The broad characteristic outline of this tradition, even though these people had not as yet developed systems of writing, can be surmised through archaeology, the surviving evidence of their art, and comparative ethnography. Those who shared this tradition tended to look at the world as a place animated with spirits and spiritual power. This was true of living things like animals and plants, but also of rocks, springs, rivers, and mountains. These people regarded the universe as a sacred realm where everything was alive and conscious, including the Earth and the sky. They approached animals and plants respectfully, killing only when necessary, and honoring them with ceremonies even after they killed them. They treated themselves not as separate individuals, but as integral members of a tribal community, with the duty to provide it with food, to protect it against enemies, and to seek power for it from the spiritual side of nature through visions, disciplines, and the repetition of rituals. Certain tribal members revered for their closeness to other living creatures became shamans who identified with animals, wearing their skins, horns, and skulls, and danced with the movements of the animals they impersonated. All members of the tribe venerated tribal elders because they contained the memory, accumulated knowledge, and wise judgment of the community.

Through examining these traditional convictions, we uncover the community's ecological function, which helped the tribe adapt to the local environment and use it without destroying it. For example, hunters had an awesome respect for their prey, and a great degree of knowledge about them. Surviving carvings and paintings reflect the honor that hunters had for animals. The hunter got ready for a hunt by chanting, washing, and abstaining from food, sex, and the use of certain words such as the true name of the animal to be hunted. Then the hunter prayed to assure the animal that the tribe had great need for its flesh and would treat it with homage and gratitude, and to urge it to give itself willingly. The animal was stalked, slain with as little suffering as possible, and the dead body treated with ceremonies to honor it. Through these ceremonies, it was believed, the animal's spirit would consent to being reborn and killed again for the benefit of the tribe. There is evidence that some societies encouraged conservation to a certain extent, such as forbidding taking a mother bird together with its eggs or young.[2] Other rules cautioned the hunter not to kill more animals than were needed, not to waste meat, to leave at least one male and female so that an entire herd would not be destroyed, and not to kill the first animal seen of the species that the hunter was seeking. There was also a widespread belief that animals were protected by a watchful god, a Lord or Lady of Wild Animals, who would reward good hunters and punish reckless ones.[3] Comparable beliefs and methods were characteristic of gatherers in their treatment of plants. Many tribes maintained annual patterns of use that left parts of their hunting and gathering territories undisturbed for long periods, allowing the species there to recover.

Ecological Crises of the Paleolithic Age

Early hunters and gatherers were not wandering nomads in the usual sense of the term; most often they inhabited home territories whose topography, vegetation, and wildlife they knew well. Their subsistence, population, and health depended directly upon the condition of the local ecosystem. The hunting-gathering economy provided feedback in both the short and long term. Taking too many animals or plants of a critical species resulted in reduction of numbers or even extinction in the tribal hunting range, a memorable disaster for the tribe. Such events had occurred in the past history of every group, and they became part of their preserved traditions. Prohibitions against indiscriminate slaughter appeared and were strengthened as the eventual result of repeated experiences of this kind.

The Paleolithic period had its ecological crises, however. Despite traditions that taught rudimentary conservation, hunters and gatherers could not leave nature untouched. Cultural taboos would never have developed if mistakes had not been made, and in any case traditional teachings are notably resistant to change even when alteration in social, economic, and ecological conditions demands it. They persist even after they have become destructive. Hunting and domestication altered the zoological picture. The pressure of Stone Age hunting may have driven many of the larger animals of the Pleistocene period to extinction, or at least acted together with climate change at the end of the Ice Age to hasten their disappearance. Some of the animals that vanished from the Mediterranean ecosystem at that time were rivals of humans as predators, or predators upon humans, such as the cave bear and cave hyena. Others were huge herbivores like the mammoth and rhinoceros—good sources of food but not amenable to preservation through semidomestication, as the reindeer was. The present range of the domestic reindeer has climate and vegetation similar to the environment of more southerly parts of Europe during the glaciation. Their herders' way of life could easily have evolved from that of the Paleolithic hunters by a long process of association in which people came to control the movements of the herds and to protect them. The dog became the first true domesticate of these early times. Its wolflike ancestor was an animal that lived in packs, whose attachments shifted to human groups that adopted puppies.

Fire was "the first great force employed by man."[4] Hunters periodically set fire to forests, brushlands, and grasslands in order to drive animals and to encourage the growth of grass as a source of food for the grazing animals that were often their quarry. The practice resulted in the destruction of woodland and its replacement by grassland over large areas. But early hunters were aware of times and places to set fires so that they would be most suited to their purposes, and they sought to avoid harming their hunting territories. In areas that were not burned periodically, naturally occurring fire in the form of lightning could start firestorms, so judicious burning may have served as a preventive measure. Although hunters and gatherers made important impacts on ecosystems, they intended (and often succeeded) to maintain balance with them. They had little choice in the matter; if they damaged the local ecosystem, they would suffer, too.

The Invention of Agriculture: The Neolithic Age

The domestication of animals and plants caused such a radical change in humankind's relationship to the natural environment that it is justifiably called the "Agricultural Revolution," even though the process took thousands of years during the Neolithic period (New Stone Age). As a result, two new life styles appeared: the settled agricultural life of farmers and the pastoral way of herders.

Farming

Farming began independently at least twice in different parts of the lands neighboring the Mediterranean Sea. There is evidence of experimentation with planting and harvesting near pools of water left after the annual flood of the Nile in Egypt after 12,500 BCE, but this effort appears to have been abandoned by 9500 BCE.[5] Numerous farming villages appeared in the Levant and the northern margins of Mesopotamia between 7000 and 5000 BCE. There the major crops were barley, wheat, and legumes. Even before plant domestication, people in Palestine and elsewhere had used stone-edged sickles to reap wild grain. The early planters also used simple hoes and digging sticks, disturbing the soil to a certain extent.

In many ways the heritage of hunter-gatherers persisted in the new age. Hunting continued as a means of supplementing the food supply. The reverence formerly felt for wild species was maintained and extended to the domestic ones that had become the sustenance of life. In the large agricultural village of Çatal Hüyük in Anatolia, for example, murals of bulls in black and red decorated the walls, and the skulls and horns of bulls, covered by clay and painted with geometric designs, projected from the walls and floors.[6] Domestic sheep and goats were honored in art along with wild leopards and vultures. The Mother Goddess, enthroned between animals or shown in the posture of giving birth, her arms raised in benediction, may well have personified the fertile, life-giving grain. In agricultural societies studied ethnographically, grain was given the title of "Mother." Hunting rituals gave way in the calendar to festivals of planting and harvest. Farm animals were honored as prey species had been, particularly mighty ones like the bull, with its evident strength and fecundating potency. The act of slaughter for food became the supreme form of sacrifice.

The domestication of plants improved the dependability of the food supply and made a more concentrated population possible, but it also required a settled community to care for the growing crops. Much later, the Greek philosopher Theophrastus reflected on this development: "It is mankind, alone among all living things, to which the term 'domesticated' is perhaps strictly appropriate."[7] Humans began to build houses in villages, becoming more sedentary. Farmers selected seed after the harvest for planting in the following year, and in this way new varieties of food crops evolved. Material technology changed irrevocably; stone was worked into smaller and more finely shaped forms. Village dwellers invented pottery, useful for storage and cooking so long as it did not need to be carried very far; hunters would have rejected it because it was heavy and breakable.

With agriculture, human populations became larger and more concentrated, but they did not become healthier. Physical anthropologists have discovered that the farmers of the New Stone Age were shorter than the hunters of the Old Stone Age, suffered more from bad teeth and bones, caught more communicable diseases, and died at an earlier age on average. This was true both of men and women.[8] A choice had been made, no doubt unconsciously, in favor of supporting greater numbers of humans over improving the quality of life, at least as far as health and longevity are concerned. Anne and Paul Ehrlich suggested, "the agricultural revolution may prove to be the greatest mistake that ever occurred in the biosphere—a mistake not just for *Homo sapiens*, but for the integrity of all ecosystems."[9]

Pastoralism

Another way of life originated when some people, rather than following herds of grazing and browsing mammals just to hunt them, began with help from the already-domesticated dog to protect livestock from predators and to control their annual movements. Most herders were not nomadic wanderers but practiced transhumance, the alternate movement of herds to higher summer and lower winter ranges. Pastoralism developed first in the Near East with goats and sheep, and later with cattle, pigs, and donkeys.[10] These animals are all at home in ecotonal country where grassland, brushland, and forest interpenetrate. Weaving was a useful invention for clothes and also for material to make portable tents for shelter, replacing the animal skins used by hunters.

Ecological Crises of the Neolithic Age

Human ability to change and control the natural environment greatly increased with the invention of agriculture. One of the first challenges farmers encountered was finding soil suitable for cultivation. In limited areas, they could plant seed where flooding and mud deposition had left clear ground. But in most places, land that would support crops also supported wild vegetation until it was cleared. More and more land was opened for agriculture, which meant the breaking of grassland sod or the felling and burning of forests. When farmers burned to clear land, they observed that the ashes temporarily enriched the ground. Sometimes, as the soil lost its fertility, they shifted from one place to another. Forests also provided firewood and building materials, and forest stands closest to Neolithic villages were used up for these purposes. With the removal of plant cover came erosion, so that the hilly districts where farmers have practiced subsistence agriculture for 10,000 years or so are now desiccated, rocky, and almost denuded of useful herbage. These effects were slow and cumulative, and farmers who stayed permanently in the same area tried to find ways of countering them by caring for and restoring the earth. On hillsides, they built terraces to reduce erosion. They learned to let the land lie fallow for one or more years between crops. They discovered the use of manure and other fertilizers, and found that planting legumes enriches the soil for other crops. Neolithic farmers learned by trial and error, and managed to remain in balance with the changing environment for long periods of time.

Herders became a force that could destroy vegetation. They often started fires to open forests for their animals and to encourage the growth of grass. As soon as sheep were domesticated, overgrazing became a problem, as sheep eat grasses and herbs, roots and all, and their sharp hooves tear up the sod. Goats not only browse most kinds of shrubs, but also climb up into trees to eat the foliage, and they eagerly consume seedlings, thus preventing forest regeneration. Cattle munch all the palatable green things they can reach, including leaves on the lower branches of trees, and herders would lop off higher tree branches for them to eat. Baring the soil by overgrazing accelerated erosion. The movement to different pastures spread the damage, but made it less intensive. Balancing the destructive effects to a certain extent was the return of nutrients to the soil in the form of manure.

The people of the agricultural villages and pastoral herds were conscious of the passing of the seasons, and carefully watched the rising and setting of the Sun, Moon, and the brightest stars. The Mediterranean air was usually clear, and they spent long hours outside caring for their crops and keeping watch over their herds. Humans acknowledged their place in the processes of nature, and that they needed to cooperate with natural cycles if they wished to survive and prosper. Human numbers in the Neolithic period were relatively small, even if they were greater than they had been in the Paleolithic. It was still possible for people living close to natural cycles, dependent upon the annual crops and the increase of the herds, to maintain a balance with the ecosystems of which they were a part.

The Rise of Cities: The Bronze Age
Mesopotamia and the Levant

The first cities appeared in a large swath of the Near East that stretches from the Levantine (eastern) shore of the Mediterranean Sea to the head of the Persian Gulf, including the valleys of the Jordan, Orontes, Euphrates, and Tigris Rivers. Except for some montane margins and the Mediterranean coastal sections, this area would be desert were it not for the rivers and the irrigation they make possible. The so-called Urban Revolution that brought cities into existence was made possible by a changed relationship between human beings and the environment, marked by a more intensive agriculture using two new inventions: the plow and systematic, large-scale irrigation. The fertile, sandy soil of Mesopotamia was easily turned by the ox-drawn plow. The rivers provided the needed water, but their flow was so undependable that control by major irrigation works was necessary. This new agriculture enabled a much larger human population to live in expanded settlements, with many people no longer needing to work on the land, and specialized occupations flourished in the cities.

Building materials for urban centers were determined by their availability in the natural environment. In the Levant, there were mountains with abundant supplies of stone and timber. But many of the earliest cities arose in the

31

flat, alluvial land of Mesopotamia, where there was little stone or metallic ore, and few trees large enough to be useful for construction. Metal, stone, and wood were brought in by trade but were expensive, so native materials—reeds and, most abundant, clay—were used in ordinary construction. Urban dwellers raised mighty works of baked and unbaked clay bricks: temples, shrines raised on lofty ziggurats, palaces, and thick city walls. But the systems of canals that brought water to the fields constituted their most extensive and labor-consuming achievement. Such large-scale irrigation conquered sections of the land and won rich sustenance from its basic fertility. One Mesopotamian king felt justified in listing the construction of a new canal, along with the defeat of his enemies in battle, as a major event of his reign.

Copper and bronze metallurgy appeared as early cities developed, and the period (approximately 3000 to 1000 BCE) has been called the Bronze Age for that reason. Some of the earliest metal objects were formed from copper and copper alloys that occur naturally in metallic form around the Near East. In the search for additional supplies, metalworkers turned to smelting copper oxide ores, adapting techniques from pottery firing to obtain the high heat that was necessary. In the process, they discovered alloys of copper (called bronze of various kinds) that were superior in hardness and the ability to keep an edge. The preferred bronze was eventually an alloy of copper and tin. Since tin was the rarer of the two metals, it was often imported over long distances. Household utensils, decorative and ceremonial objects, and armor and weapons came to be made of bronze.

The attitude of city-dwelling people toward the natural environment shows a striking change from that of the hunter-gatherers, early farmers, and herders. It is as if the barrier of city walls and the rectilinear pattern of canals had divided urban human beings from wild nature and substituted an attitude of confrontation for the earlier feeling of cooperation. This attitude can be traced in Near Eastern literature from early Sumerian times down through Akkadian and Assyrian writings, which often use the image of battle to describe the new relationship with nature. In creation myths, Nature was represented as a female monster of chaos who was faced and overcome by a hero-god. It was only through the conquests made by the gods, and the constant labor of their human followers, that the natural chaotic state of the universe could be tamed and order established. The plan of the city, with its straight streets and strong walls, and the regular pattern of canals in the countryside, were believed to be earthly imitations of the heavenly order that the gods had established. The Mesopotamians admired the orderliness of the stars and planets, identifying them with their gods and developing astronomy and mathematics to a sophisticated level.

The *Epic of Gilgamesh*, perhaps the oldest extant long poem, reveals the urban

Mesopotamian sense of the distinction between the tame and the wild, between civilization and wilderness, and shows a new and hitherto unfamiliar attitude of hostility toward untamed nature. Enkidu, the hairy man of the wild, first appears in the poem as a friend and protector of beasts, but he is a nuisance and even a menace to townsfolk, releasing animals from the traps of the hunters and warning them away from ambushes. When he had been tamed, his former animal friends feared him and fled. Entering the city of Uruk, Enkidu met and struggled with King Gilgamesh, who became his close friend. Together they went on a quest for cedar wood in the far mountains. Mesopotamian tablets describe the journey of Gilgamesh, armed with his mighty axe, and his companion Enkidu to the mountains where they fought and killed Humbaba, the animal-god guardian of the cedar forest, and cut down the trees. The story is myth, but it reflects many historical truths. The forest mentioned is probably the cedars of Lebanon (the epic places it near the Euphrates), a source of timber for the tree-poor Mesopotamian plain subject to ancient deforestation. The forest was a sacred grove protected by the wild giant Humbaba, and his defeat and death at the hands of the two heroes was a symbol for the subjugation of the wilderness by the city. Gilgamesh promptly cut down the cedar trees and carried them off to Uruk to use in building a palace for himself. The proper effort of mankind toward wild things, in the view of the Mesopotamians, was to domesticate them. They did this with native animals such as the onager and the water buffalo, adding them to the cows, pigs, sheep, and goats already tamed by their ancestors. Animals that could not be domesticated were hunted mercilessly; Gilgamesh is said to have killed lions simply because he saw them "glorying in life."[11]

Environmental Problems of Mesopotamia and the Levant

Flooding was a continual danger for Mesopotamian cities; the Tigris and Euphrates Rivers rose over their banks unpredictably, destroying settlements and fields, which is one reason why these people regarded nature as chaotic. Cities accumulated mounds, rising above the plain and, if they were lucky, above the floods. The temple dwellings of the gods were raised high on platforms, and then even higher on the step-pyramids called ziggurats. The system of canals and dikes served both for irrigation and flood control. But the silt and mud carried by rivers and canals settled out rapidly. Constant dredging was needed to keep the canals flowing, and the excess material piled up along their banks until the canals were 10 m (30 feet) or more above the surrounding fields so that they could no longer serve to drain the land and were a danger during flood.

Salinization, the accumulation of salts in the soil as a result of water evaporation, is a danger wherever irrigation is practiced in dry climates, and it was

Sculpture of the hero-king Gilgamesh of Uruk, holding a lion, from the palace of Sargon II of Assyria (721 to 705 BCE), Khorsabad (Dur Sharrukin), Iraq. Now in the Louvre, Paris. (1998)

unfortunately prevalent in Mesopotamia. Irrigation water carried into low-lying areas was allowed to evaporate, and over the years in this land of low humidity and scanty rain, the salts accumulated. The conditions of poor drainage also made it difficult to correct the situation by leaching salt from the fields. Ground-water became increasingly saline. Farmers tried to adapt to the changing conditions by planting salt-tolerant barley instead of vulnerable wheat. In extreme cases, cultivated plants were unable to grow in salinized soil. Such areas had to be abandoned, while new sections were brought under irrigation and cultivation until they in turn suffered the same effects. A survey by Thorkild Jacobsen and Robert Adams found evidence of increased salinity and declining yields in southern Mesopotamia between 2400 and 1700 BCE, which they identified as contributing to the breakup of Sumerian civilization.[12]

The famous cities of ancient Mesopotamia are now desolate mounds in a desert environment, and photographs taken from space show that the fertile land occupies a remnant of its former extent. These effects are not the result of climate change or of warfare, although both have occurred through the centuries. Mesopotamia's clear relationship between man-made environmental degradation and cultural decline represents an ecological disaster caused by human actions.

Egypt

Egypt existed as an autonomous civilization from before 3000 BCE to after 1000 BCE, and during that period maintained a relatively consistent pattern in economy, government, religion, and ecological viewpoints and techniques. It is likely that the stability of Egyptian civilization was the result of the sustainability of Egypt's ecological relationships. Karl Butzer remarked, "it has become difficult to ignore the possibility that major segments of ancient Egyptian history may be unintelligible without recourse to an ecological perspective."[13] He added that the history of floodplain civilization in the Nile Valley offers a test case of human–land relationships. But a further observation must be made: the ecological attitudes and practices of the Egyptians were rooted in a worldview that affirmed the sacred values of all nature, and of land in particular.[14]

Although one of the first societies to develop cities, Egypt was predominantly agrarian rather than urban.[15] Agriculture remained the foundation of Egyptian civilization, and urban centers were not sharply separated from the rural landscape. Fortified walls were not the rule for Egyptian cities. Early art indicates that they existed in predynastic times, but with the unification of the Two Lands under the god-king (pharaoh), need for them disappeared except in frontier areas, and at times when central authority broke down. Thus it is agriculture that manifests the characteristic ecological relationships of Egyptian civilization.

Dependability of the Egyptian Environment

Egyptian agriculture was sustainable because of the annual flood of the Nile and the deposition of fertile alluvial soil containing phosphorus and other minerals and traces of organic debris brought down by the river from the mountains and swamps of lands farther south. Herodotus, observing that Egypt's soil had been formed by river sediment, pronounced Egypt the "gift of the Nile."[16] An early inscription said the Nile "supplies all the people with nourishment and food."[17] The climate was dependable, and although there was little rain, the river supplied needed water. Their environment encouraged the Egyptians to think of processes of nature as operating in predictable cycles. The Nile flooded its banks at the same time every year, bringing moisture and new soil to the fields. As Pliny the Elder remarked, "in that country the Nile plays the part of farmer."[18] The only fertile land was what the river watered in the long, narrow valley floor of Upper Egypt and in the broad, flat Nile Delta of Lower Egypt.

Of the world's great rivers used in early times for flood agriculture, the Nile was most regular, but not completely predictable.[19] Disasters occurred when a high flood washed away irrigation works, storage facilities, and villages, or when a low river failed to water or fertilize the black (cultivated) land adequately. Lapses in sustainability occurred when the Nile failed, and invaders often took advantage of weakness produced by flood or famine. Egyptian history is punctuated by difficult times when pharaonic governments collapsed, and researchers have correlated these "intermediate periods" with anomalies in the average level of Nile floods.[20] But traditional patterns of culture, including environmental relationships, reasserted themselves after these intervals with tenacity: "The Nile never refused its great task of revivification. In its periodicity it promoted the [Egyptians'] sense of confidence . . . True, the Nile might fall short of its full bounty for years of famine, but it never ceased altogether, and ultimately it always came back with full prodigality."[21] The natural regime provided the environmental insulation necessary for a sustainable society, but the positive efforts of the Egyptians were also necessary.

The Sacred View of Nature

Egyptian religion held as sacred the forces of nature that assured sustainability, and urged the people to cooperate with rather than to interfere with them. To Egyptians, the world was a place of system and regularity, qualities attributed to

The fertile "black land" of Egypt was watered by the annual Nile River flood and supported trees and rich crops. The Pyramids of Giza were constructed in the "red land" desert beyond. (1976)

Ma'at, goddess of balance. More than just a goddess, Ma'at embodied the order that harmonized apparent antitheses in nature. Gods and pharaohs alike were expected to act in accord with her principles. Egyptian creation myths display the idea that the world, with everything in it, is the expression of a creator, or creators, that acted in congruence with the harmony that Ma'at represents. The yearly Nile inundation reenacted creation, with the "primeval hillock" appearing to view above the sinking primordial waters. The first land emerging from the flood promised renewed life in the coming agricultural season.[22]

The orderly movements of the heavens were evident to the Egyptians, whose sky was so seldom clouded. Re-Harakhte, the Sun-god, appeared every morning and crossed the sky to his western harbor, and the movement of his path to north and south showed the passage of the year. The stars marked hours and seasons; when Sothis (Sirius), star of the goddess Isis, rose just before the Sun, it was a sign that flood time was at hand. As above, so below: the sky goddess Nut arched her body above her fertile consort, the male Earth-god Geb, in perfect balance. When the stars, the children of Nut, showed the proper season, then Geb's children, the plants, bore fruit. It is interesting to note the reversal of identifications common in other societies, where Earth is usually feminine and Sky masculine. The principle in Egyptian myth was a balance of sexual roles, not the dominance of either. Deities often occurred as balanced pairs of male and female, like Geb and Nut. Sometimes the pairs balanced two sides of the feminine, such as kind Hathor and angry Sekhmet, who could be transformed into each other; or two aspects of the masculine, such as Horus, hero-god of fertile land, and his counterpart, the desert-god Set, enemies whose battles ended in reconciliation and peaceful co-rule.

The land was a god, and therefore sacred, and all its aspects were gods. Osiris, widely worshipped, embodied vegetation. The annual cycle of flood, planting, harvest, and fallow was mythologically portrayed as his birth, growth, death, dismemberment, burial, and resurrection, so that every stage of the agricultural year repeated an event in the life of Osiris. Hapi was god of the Nile. Bringer of fertility, though male, he was portrayed with breasts to show his power to nurture. He was called "Father of the gods" because they depended on the Nile for offerings or existence. For example, Hapi suckled Osiris, helping to resurrect him in a myth standing for the reliance of vegetation on the Nile flood. So when the river rose to its appropriate level, people rejoiced at the advent of the god. In the words of a pyramid text, "They tremble, that behold the Nile in full flood. The fields laugh and the river-banks are overflowed. The gods' offerings descend, the visage of the people is bright, and the heart of the gods rejoices."[23] Farmers who cared for the earth carried on long-established traditions. It was believed that hoeing, properly done, was an act of veneration of the Earth-god. The round of the agricultural year had a numerous series of festivals honoring the recurrence of natural events. Originated by villagers in Neolithic times, these celebrations were later institutionalized. At the harvest festival of Min-Amun in Thebes, for instance, Pharaoh cut the first sheaf of wheat, and a bull was led in procession. "For the Egyptians the ideal society on Earth . . . was a fundamental reflection of a divine order," observed Barry Kemp.[24]

Sacred Science, Sacred Technology

Geometry, astronomy, and sacred records (hieroglyphics) were marshaled to assure the dependability of relationship to the environment. Geometry, necessary to reestablish field boundaries when markers had been swept away in the flood, was not a mundane skill but a hallowed occupation believed originated by the god Thoth and entrusted to trained scribes. Temples were located according to geomancy and oriented to important points in the revolutions of the Sun and stars. Papyri containing these arcane branches of knowledge were kept by scribes in the House of Life, the temple library.

Irrigation was a form of sacred technology shown in art as an activity of the pharaoh and the gods themselves. Canal building was believed to be a major occupation of those in the blessed world beyond death. Some scholars maintain that the absolute monarchy of the pharaoh grew out of the need to marshal labor and to direct hydroengineering on a national scale.[25] This theory is supported by the King Scorpion Macehead from the First Dynasty, which shows the king digging a canal, and the fact that "Canal-digger" was an important title. It is true that all Egyptian males, except those in the nobility and priesthood, were obliged to perform compulsory labor, ostensibly for the pharaoh, during the agricultural fallow season, from two to four months a year. This labor force was expended on great public works, both monuments and structures for water control and distribution. But recent research has discovered that local officials supervised most irrigation work, and Butzer states that the small provinces called nomes developed as local irrigation units.[26] Irrigation increased the cropland area beyond that originally flooded by the Nile. The two types of land were kept distinct. Local laborers dredged channels, dug ditches, built earthen dams, constructed dikes and basins, and raised water with buckets, activities that were considered parts of a holy occupation. Major projects sponsored by the pharaoh were commemorated as good works; inscriptions boast, "I brought the Nile to the upland in your fields so that plots were watered that had never known water before" and "I caused the water of the Nile to flood over the ancient landmarks."[27]

Environmental Problems in Egypt

Even though Egypt's agriculture was for the most part sustainable, environmental problems appeared. One was ironically a result of the success in producing the ancient world's most reliable food supply, as even the most dependable system of subsistence will fail with overpopulation. When population increased to a level that required a year of good harvest, an abnormally low harvest would bring famine. Works of art such as the Causeway of Unas at Sakkara show people starving, their ribs prominently visible. Egypt suffered because fat years were interspersed with lean ones, and the population had peaks and valleys as a result. Governmental officials tried to even out fluctuations of supply and demand by storing surplus in good years and distributing it when harvests failed. The biblical story of Joseph's interpretation of the pharaoh's dream, and his advice to build granaries to prepare for hard times, reflects the actual situation in Egypt.[28] The store-chambers of the Ramesseum, built at the order of Ramses II, could have held $16,520$ m^3 ($590,000$ feet^3) of grain, enough to support $3,400$ families for a year.[29] In difficult periods, prices fluctuated. In the fifty-five years between the reigns of Ramses III and Ramses VII, for example, emmer wheat rose from eight to twenty-four times base price.[30] At times, famine relief had to be distributed over large districts. Even so, Egypt remained a breadbasket of the ancient world, exporting wheat and barley with few interruptions. The Egyptians' joy in their environment can be sensed in pictures of activities such as plowing and hunting. But there was little realization that nature was being damaged in the process. For them, the Earth was unchanging: time ran in cycles, not along an inexorable line. Changes, some destructive, nonetheless occurred, including salinization, deforestation, overdevelopment, and habitat destruction.

Egypt suffered less than Mesopotamia from salinization because the Nile flood leached salt from the soil. But it occurred in irrigated areas and was serious in the Fayum, an oasis below sea level where Nile water seeped and evaporated.

Deforestation was a major problem, which may seem surprising because most of Egypt was not forested. But although more than 90 percent of the country is desert, the watered land had sections full of trees. Before clearing, the Nile Valley supported an evergreen forest of fig, jujube, acacia, and other species. Pollen analyses in the Nile Delta show that there were many wetland plants, including trees.[31] This changed as cultivation extended. Tomb paintings show trees being cut to clear land. Egypt had supplies of firewood and fine woods for carving and cabinet making but few tall, straight trees, and had to import timber from Phoenicia and other lands to the north. Egyptian ships reached Byblos as early as 2650 BCE to obtain cedar, juniper, fir, pine, and other timber for construction. Cedar wood from Mount Lebanon was called "a wood which [the God] (Amun-Re) loves," so that journeys to secure it were believed to be commanded by the god.[32] In the Middle Kingdom, as excavated tombs in Lebanon show, Egyptian influence dominated the Phoenician coast through political and cultural forces that followed the timber trade. In the New Kingdom, the same area was conquered outright.

In Egypt itself, in addition to cutting trees for fuel and other purposes, pasturing domestic animals depleted the vegetation. The reverence of Egyptians for sacred trees acted against total deforestation. Trees were worshipped, and deities were shown in tree form. Isis, for example, was symbolized by a tree with breasts from which Pharaoh received milk. The Tree of Life portrayed in mortuary paintings with the deceased bowing low before it or drinking from a spring of water at its base was not just imaginary. Trees such as ished and palm were planted in temple gardens beside sacred lakes and tended by priests and their servants. The planting of a tree was considered to be a good work that aided the soul. Great trouble was taken to plant and water trees near tombs and mortuary temples such as the terraced monument of Hatshepsut.[33] Officials and affluent citizens planted gardens and groves, and pharaohs had plantations of valuable species for royal use. Sycamore trees were exempted from taxation. The king rewarded his subjects for planting trees along roads, canals, field boundaries, and other places, and tree farming became an art.

The need for wetlands, plants, and wildlife in sustaining the ecology of this land threatened by desert is evident. But the habitats of wild animals, birds, and aquatic creatures shrank, perhaps so slowly that few people noticed. As Butzer observes, eventually "the almost total disappearance of large game from the [Nile] valley, with increasing importation of captured animals for symbolic hunts by the nobility, argues for eradication of the natural vegetation."[34] Even the ubiquitous papyrus became less prevalent, though it did not totally disappear from Egypt before the end of antiquity.

Animals were sacred to the Egyptians. They were regarded as visible manifestations of deities: the jackal of Anubis, the lioness of Sekhmet, and many others. Groups of animals were kept in temple precincts, and when they died were mummified and accorded honorable burials. Tens of thousands of animal mummies have been found in special vaults: Horus hawks, Thoth ibises, Bastet cats, and so on. Worship did not prevent wild animals from being hunted, however; still less did it save them from the effects of habitat destruction. In predynastic times, as petroglyphs attest, Egypt possessed a variety of species as rich as now found in East Africa. But by the end of the Old Kingdom, elephant, rhinoceros, wild camel, and giraffe were missing or rare. Barbary sheep, lion, and leopard were still present, but in reduced numbers. Some of this depletion was due to climate change, since the Sahara did not dry to its present aridity until well into the Old Kingdom. But some of the reduction of animal numbers was also due to deliberate destruction. Amenhotep III boasted of killing 102 lions—the prey of kings—by his own hand.[35] By the Middle Kingdom, the ranges of antelope species had been limited and their numbers decimated.[36]

The abundance of birds, particularly waterfowl, once astonishing in Egypt, a "land of whirring wings,"[37] was gradually reduced. Nobles enjoyed bird hunting in marshes, but there were fewer marshes as drainage proceeded. Inscriptions say Ramses III gave over 426,000 waterfowl to temples, including 9,350 per year to the Temple of Amun at Thebes alone. Some of these became part of temple flocks, while others were offerings; sacrifice in Egypt did not consist of the ritual killing of animals and birds, but the presentation to the gods of prepared food dishes that were consumed by priests after the ceremony. Bird life, diminished but not destroyed by the ancients, is today at a low ebb. The ibis is scarcely seen, and of fourteen species of duck in ancient Egyptian art, only one now breeds there.[38]

A similar fate awaited the fish. Some were protected; it was forbidden even for pharaohs to fish in sacred temple lakes. A stele from Abydos reports the words of Ramses IV: "I ate nothing I should not eat, I did not fish in the sacred lake, I did not hunt with the bird-net, I did not shoot a lion at the festival of Bastet."[39]

Egypt at the end of the ancient period was much changed environmentally, but still productive and full of life. The Nile continued to bring annual floods, with sufficient water and sediment in most years to guarantee good crops. Grain, other foodstuffs, and crops such as flax for linen and papyrus for paper were usually abundant enough to meet Egypt's needs and to be exported, as well. Egypt was not lacking in environmental problems such as gradual loss of natural vegetation and wildlife, but in every case where Egyptians realized the sacredness of the Earth and living creatures, that awareness helped to mitigate damage and to preserve life and the environment.

Egypt was in most respects self-sufficient, so that the Egyptians were content with their land. Some modern writers interpret this contentment as an attitude that was "insular and self-satisfied."[40] That this was not the case is clear from the vigor with which they pursued the timber trade abroad to obtain a necessary resource in which they were not well supplied. At home, too, they understood their relationship to the land to be governed by the gods and by sacred principles derived from Ma'at, the universal order that controlled the pharaoh and even the gods themselves, and harmonized the people with their natural environment.

Conclusion

The environmental history of earlier human societies in the Mediterranean basin or peripheral to it serves as background to Greece and Rome, which followed and were in many important ways influenced by those societies. Paleolithic and Neolithic lore and lifeways formed traditional patterns that persisted at least in part into the classical period and helped to determine Greek and Roman treatment of the natural environment. The civilizations of Egypt and Mesopotamia were in contact with the Greeks and Romans throughout their formative period, and the latter tended to regard the former as foreign but wise and learned civilizations. In turn, they reflected their influence in terms of environmental attitudes and practices, as in other aspects of their culture. There were differences too important to ignore, however. Egypt and Mesopotamia were river valley civilizations that grew up in regions of large deserts; the Greek and Roman homelands lacked large rivers and were located in the Mediterranean climatic zone. Their environmental setting and their responses to it were therefore distinct.

Four

Concepts of the Natural World

Classical Greek and Roman civilization marked a long and creative period during which an immensely varied number of ideas developed and flourished. Some of these concepts were supportive of a balanced human relationship to nature, and others were not.[1] In order to learn how environmental problems developed in the ancient world, it is important to understand the prevailing attitudes of people about the natural world they inhabited, and therefore how they were likely to treat it. The Greeks and Romans traditionally regarded the world as a sacred place where the gods of nature, who shared some human qualities, were present. Thus they were expected to treat the environment with awe and care, and this was practiced to a considerable extent. With the appearance of philosophers who questioned or denied the activity of the gods, the older attitudes weakened.[2] The new thinkers rejected traditional mythological explanations of the world and insisted that the human mind could discover the truth about nature through reason. The varying views of the world offered by reason included some beautiful images of the Earth as a living organism, and others in which chance and materialism produced what is seen. Differing ethical systems either provided strong motives for conservation, or left humans free to exploit the environment.

A few of the best minds were keen observers of nature who insisted on making their explanations consistent with what could be seen, which began the process of scientific inquiry. Virtually all of these thinkers assumed too easily that the inner workings of the human mind are congruent with the outer workings

43

of the universe, and many of them shared an antipathy to experiment, which limited their discoveries and sometimes led them into fallacious speculation. Still, ancient philosophers and scientists made many impressive discoveries, and they made a tentative start in the ecological field of inquiry.

To what extent do the attitudes of people toward their environment, and their knowledge of it, determine the kinds of environmental problems they will have, or the ways in which they will approach them? Ideas, however unrelated to reality they may sometimes be, are not entirely irrelevant to the way people act in the world and toward natural objects. It is instructive to observe the history of attitudes among these people that may have affected their practices in adaptive or maladaptive ways.

Nature as the Sphere of the Gods

The people of the ancient Mediterranean felt that nature manifested the activities of the gods, whether they perceived them as personifications of natural forces, as the Greeks characteristically did, or as numina, mysterious presences in the natural world, as the Romans tended to do before they adopted Greek ideas on these matters. Any natural phenomenon could be seen as the result of a god's operation. Therefore any human activity that affected the environment could be seen as attracting the interest of or provoking a reaction from some god or goddess, and ought to be undertaken with caution.

Gods of Nature

All the major gods had associations with nature, and many of the minor ones were divinized natural features like winds and rivers. The Greek god of the sky was Zeus (a cognate of the Roman Jupiter), who "sometimes shines brightly, sometimes rains."[3] When a mighty thunderhead advanced across the Mediterranean landscape, it was perceived as the presence of Zeus, king of the gods, who made the wind blow, hurled the lightning, and spoke in the thunder. Of a particularly foul spell, Homer said, "Zeus rained the whole night through."[4] Myth said that Zeus had divided the natural world between himself and his two brothers: Poseidon took the waters as his portion, and Pluto reigned in the regions underground. Demeter was the personification of growing grain; the Delphic oracle spoke in literal fashion of "scattering Demeter forth, or gathering her in."[5] Even the gods associated most closely with aspects of human life had deep connections with nature; the religious tradition did not distinguish sharply between human beings and the rest of nature. Athena's early concerns were the olive tree, owl, and serpent. Aphrodite stirred passions not only in human beings,

A Boeotian vase, circa 680 BCE, depicts the Mistress of Animals (Potnia Therôn) protecting creatures of the land (wolves, bull), sea (fish), and air (birds). The swastika, common in ancient art, here represents the cycle of the seasons and life. Now in the National Archaeological Museum, Athens. (2011)

but also in "birds that fly in air and all the many creatures" of land and sea.[6] The music of Apollo (called the "mouse-god" by Homer) charmed a "tawny troop of lions" along with "dappled lynxes" and fawns in the mountain forest, causing them all to dance with delight.[7] Asclepius healed through snakes and dogs.

Certain gods had preeminent roles in nature and deserve special mention. First was Earth herself, Gê or Gaia, Mêtêr Pantôn, Terra Mater, "oldest of gods," mother of gods, humans, and every living thing.[8] Her worship was immensely ancient, and can be traced far back into the Stone Age. Her creative womb bore all that exists, including first of all the sky, according to Hesiod, and all it contains. Many of her offspring were monsters; her fecundity had a dark side. The ancients believed they were born from her, nourished by her, and returned to her at death. "Mistress, from you come our fine children and bountiful harvests; yours is the power to give mortals life and to take it away."[9] She was honored as having her own law, a natural law deeper than human enactments and beyond repeal. It is not the justice of human morality; it is simply the way things are. "Earth is a goddess and teaches justice to those who can learn, for the better she is served, the more good things she gives in return."[10] Who treat her well receive blessings; who treat her ill suffer privation, for she gives with evenhanded measure. Earth forgives, but only to a certain point, when the balance tips and it is too late: famine, disease, disaster, and death ensue. A fragment preserved in a late source surmises that Themis, the goddess of law, Gaia's daughter and alter ego, planned the Trojan War with Zeus in order to thin out the overpopulated tribes that were oppressing the surface of Mother Earth.[11]

Another important Greek nature deity was Artemis, *potnia therōn* (lady of wild things), adopted into the Roman pantheon by assimilating Diana to her. She was paradoxically both huntress and protectress of wild animals. Her worship involved conservation practices by hunters and others, and initiation rituals that introduced children to such practices, giving them the sense of close identification with animals and their tutelary goddess. Though myth called her a virgin, in Ephesus she was shown as the fertile, multiple-breasted mother of animals, her body covered with images of such creatures as lions, deer, cattle, and bees.[12]

As Greco-Roman religion developed, Pan was recognized as universal god of nature. Etymologically, *pan* means "all" in Greek, so that a primal god of herd animals, "soft streams," "close thickets," "snowy mountains and rocky peaks,"[13] became Great Pan, the "all-god," nature personified, who ruled "all things" (*ta panta* was the closest word in ancient Greek to what is today termed the "natural environment"). An Orphic Hymn calls him "green power in all that grows, procreator of all."[14] Pan's travail represents the depletion of the natural environment through everything it suffered at the hands of the Greeks and Romans.[15]

Divination

Since nature was full of gods, natural events could serve as the medium for discerning their intents. To a skilled augur, birds of many kinds, singly or in groups, on the left or on the right, bearing prey or flying free, displayed the plans of gods from the world of nature. In the sound of thunder or the rustling of leaves, the gods' words could be heard by those who knew how to listen. There were skeptics even in Homer's time, but they were regarded as improvident fools. In the *Odyssey*, Eurymachus remarked that "many birds there are that fare to and fro under the rays of the sun, and not all are fateful"[16] when a seer had predicted from the encounter of two eagles that Odysseus would soon return. The result of this untimely rationalism was that the doubter failed to take warning and was killed by the angry husband upon his return. Not only did the gods send birds, but they could also take their forms: "Athena and Apollo of the silver bow in the likeness of vultures sat upon the lofty oak of father Zeus."[17]

Diana (Artemis), the Greco-Roman goddess of the hunt and protector of animals holds a quiver of arrows and leads a deer. This is a Roman copy (first or second century) of a lost Greek original attributed to Leochares (ca. 325 BCE). Now in the Louvre, Paris. (1998)

Statue of Pan (fifth century BCE), god of nature. Now in the National Archaeological Museum, Athens. (2011)

Sacred Places

Both Greek and Roman religion had a strong sense of locality. The presence of gods was felt in places of natural beauty and through traditional associations. Socrates knew a spot on the banks of the Ilissos stream where the North Wind had carried off Orithyia, princess of Athens; there was an altar to Boreas there.[18] Both great gods and lesser spirits haunted wild, beautiful locations such as springs, caves, groves, and places with wide, inspiring views. Specific features of the landscape had their particular deities: rivers had gods, springs had nymphs called naiads, and lakes had others called limniads. There were oreads for mountains, napaeae for valleys, and leimoniads for meadows.

The love of the ancients for their native lands is well known; they thought of their own territories as central and particularly blessed by the gods.[19] Virgil addressed his country, Italy, with images of the old agricultural religion: "Hail, great mother of harvests! O land / Of Saturn, hail! Mother of men!"[20] The sacred places where gods were manifest turned the map of a local territory into a holy text that could be read by those who knew the alphabet of landforms and watercourses.

Each sanctuary had a location and orientation dictated by the natural setting, especially features that could be perceived as bodily forms, including feminine breasts and hollows and masculine promontories. The oracular temple of Delphi was located in a spot commanding one of the most spectacular scenes on Earth, looking up at the "shining cliffs" of Mount Parnassus and down a deep gorge to a distant blue gulf. The healing shrine of Asclepius and its great theater are set within a comforting natural amphitheater at Epidaurus. The mountain view from Zeus's oracle at Dodona is majestic. Vincent Scully showed that ancient sacred architecture was always erected with full awareness of, and adaptation to, its natural context.[21] The sacredness of the place existed before it was dedicated or a temple constructed there, and anything built or done there had to recognize the powers present in earth and sky.

Ancients knew the wilderness as a place with few human inhabitants or none at all, *erēmia* in Greek or *solitudo* in Latin. But the gods were present there, and when they invaded the human world, it was often out of wilderness that they seemed to come. High mountains were revered as sacred spots; sometimes a throne, and often an altar, was erected on a summit for Zeus or another deity. Olympus, the highest mountain in Greece, was home to the gods of the upper world, but many other mountains had their own patrons. Apollo haunted Parnassus, and "mountain-born" Dionysus roamed the forest on its flanks. Poseidon held forth with Athena on the high cape of Sunium. There is a Hill of Ares (Areopagus) in Athens, though it was no longer a wild place in classical times. Mount Helicon sheltered the Muses, goddesses of the creative arts. Pan had a sanctuary on Mount Parthenion. But Artemis outdid all the others; when her father Zeus allowed her as a girl to choose her own presents, among the gifts he gave were all the mountains in the world.[22]

Roman Religion

Roman religion followed its own course even though it shared some sources with Greek religion, and in later times exhibited great openness to Greek myths and religious practices. Romans were not without reverence for wild places, and they went so far as to personify mountains like Father Apennine as gods in their own right. But Roman religion had a strongly agricultural flavor, reflecting the early observances of farm families close to the land who depended on the orderly cycles of nature for subsistence. The numerous Roman religious festivals followed a calendar based on the round of activities of the ancestral farm, from hanging a plow on the boundary marker in the Compitalia in January to the festivals of Saturn and Bona Dea, deities of the soil, in December. Roman gods were associated with the natural environment, and they were extremely numerous. Their hierarchy ran from great deities like Mercury, god of flocks, to local spirits of springs like Juturna. The Romans possessed gods of the farmhouse and storehouse (*penates*) and of the fields (*lares*). A god or goddess was the growing spirit of every major crop: Ceres of grain, Liber of wine, and so on. Beyond that, every major and minor activity of the farm had a deity that could be invoked for its success, such as Vervactor for first plowing, Repacator for the second, Imporcitor for harrowing, Insitor for sowing, and even Sterquilinius for manuring. On the margins lurked Silvanus and other wild gods of the forests.

Nature, Justice, and Pollution

Both Greeks and Romans perceived order and balance in nature. They felt that the gods, or a principle of justice that even the gods had to obey, kept everything in its correct place, spatially and temporally. "The immortals have appointed a proper time for each thing upon Earth, the giver of grain."[23] When everything holds its proper time and place, then all is right on Earth and in heaven, and justice reigns. To overstep the bounds and to attempt to change the natural arrangement of things is to do injustice and to upset the gods. The Greeks in particular thought that rearranging land and sea was a prideful challenge to Zeus, who had ratified their limits when he divided the world with his brothers. When the people of Cnidus tried to dig a canal through the neck of land that connected them to Asia Minor, the workmen suffered many injuries from flying rock splinters. Seeking the reason, they sent an inquiry to the Oracle of Delphi and received an uncharacteristically clear reply: "Do not fence off the isthmus; do not dig. Zeus would have made an island, had he willed it."[24] They stopped work immediately. When the Persian king Xerxes invaded Greece, building a bridge of boats across the Hellespont, turning sea into land, cutting a canal through the Athos peninsula, his army drinking rivers dry and setting forests on fire, the Greeks regarded it all as evidence of the pride that goes before a fall. When the Colossus of Rhodes fell in an earthquake, it was believed the gods were angry at human presumption, and an oracle forbade its reerection.[25]

Pollution was a most egregious violation that was believed to bring divine punishment on the polluter. Traditional texts describe an impressive list of taboos against pollution of various kinds.[26] Pollution was for the Greeks and Romans a qualitative concept, not a measurable phenomenon. The Greek verb *miaino*, the noun *miasma*, and the adjective *miaros* all have the connotation of "bloodstain" and imply ritual impurity. Similarly, the Latin *polluere* and *pollutus* carry a moral and ceremonial sense along with the meaning of sullying with filth. The early Greek poet Hesiod cautioned his audience against urinating or defecating in springs or rivers, a prohibition that occurs as part of a long list of magical injunctions. Such rules embody the astute response of the ancestral Greeks to experiences with disease and poisoning. These taboos contain fossilized wisdom, the result of sound precautions in the past that were given the authority of religious sanctions such as avoiding affronts to river gods. Deliberate pollution aroused public wrath, as when Emperor Nero bathed ostentatiously at the intake of the Aqua Marcia, one of Rome's aqueducts.[27]

For the ancients, the natural environment was endowed with living, divine beings who maintained its order and resisted the ill-considered actions of human beings. Because of their presence, ancients felt that acts of social injustice could bring environmental punishments, and that the gods could manifest their wrath in natural disasters:

> And even as beneath a tempest the whole black earth is oppressed, on a day in harvest-time, when Zeus pours forth rain most violently, when in anger he grows wrathful against men that by violence give crooked judgments in the place of gathering, and drive justice out, reckoning not on the vengeance of the gods; and all their rivers flow in flood, and many a hillside do the torrents furrow deeply, and down to the dark sea they rush headlong from the mountains with a mighty roar, and the tilled fields of men are wasted.[28]

Justice was seen not only as fairness among people, but also as keeping proper relationships between people, the natural environment, and the gods, so that the whole universe might stay in balance. The balance was maintained not only by punishments but also by rewards. Though sometimes capricious, the gods responded with good gifts when people acted in ways pleasing to them and cared for the environment wisely. The way in which nature, under the aegis of the gods, responds to care, good leadership, and justice is told beautifully in a simile from the *Odyssey* that is a companion piece to the one from the *Iliad* quoted above:

> Lady, no one of mortals upon the boundless Earth could find fault with you, for your fame goes up to the broad heaven, as does the fame of some blameless king, who with the fear of the gods in his heart is lord over many mighty men, upholding justice; and the black Earth bears wheat and barley, and the trees are laden with fruit, the flocks bring forth young unceasingly, and the sea yields fish, all from his good leading; and the people prosper under him.[29]

Sacrifice was made to the gods, usually in the form of slaughtering, cooking, and eating domestic animals, although wild animals were sometimes offered. Bloodless sacrifices, such as pouring wine, oil, milk, or grain or presenting fruit, cakes, or cheese, were also made. Many of the ancients believed that sacrifice was a gift to the gods in expectation of benefits, or in thanksgiving for them. The Latin phrase was *do ut des* "I give [to you] so that you will give [to me]." Comparative ethnography also suggests that sacrifice was a form of common meal shared with the god, since the worshippers consumed most of what was offered. The sacrificed substance often represented the god. Because the number of victims was sometimes in the hundreds, the effect on the environment through killing animals, consuming fuel, and releasing smoke into the atmosphere must have been considerable. Sometimes sacrifice was used as a way to avoid the environmental protections that religion otherwise afforded to sacred places and their inhabitants, as in the prayer which Cato advised landowners to make "to the god whom it may concern" in order to gain permission to cut down trees in a temple grove.[30]

Oneness with Nature

Ancient religion recognized the essential oneness of mankind with nature. This relationship can be seen notably in mystery cults such as the initiation ceremony at Eleusis, in which thousands saw and heard the enactment of the myth of Demeter and her daughter Persephone, whom Pluto seized and carried off to his underworld kingdom. In an agonized search for her beloved child, Demeter stopped all crops from growing, threatening the destruction of human life and the end of sacrifices to the gods. Zeus finally decreed that Persephone should be restored to her mother if she had not eaten anything in the underworld. Since she had tasted only four pomegranate seeds, a compromise was reached: Persephone would spend four months each year underground, during which the crops would not grow, but for the other eight months she would live with her mother, who would prompt seeds to sprout and clothe the Earth in living green.[31] The myth signified the origin of the seasons, the four months underground being the dry season between the grain harvest and planting. But the mysteries of Eleusis also identified the life and death of humankind with the dying and rising of vegetation and its goddesses in the never-ending cycle of being: people die and, like seeds, are buried in the earth. But as seeds send forth shoots in response to healing moisture, the initiates of the mysteries would flourish again and live a happy life in the other world.

Orphism and Pythagoreanism: The Living Earth

The Orphic mysteries and their refinement by philosophers and religious teachers such as Pherecydes, Pythagoras, Philolaus, and Empedocles offered a more intellectually developed recognition of oneness with nature. Orphic cosmology envisioned the organic unity of the world and the cyclical interplay and balance of the elements and creatures within it: a strikingly ecological conception. Orpheus is shown in art and literature as expressing the harmony of nature; when he played the lyre and sang, he was quickly surrounded by animals and even trees, in which his song awakened sympathetic attraction. Pherecydes, reputed teacher of Pythagoras and the first philosopher to write about nature and the gods, says that the three first principles were Time (Chronos), Life (Zas), and Earth (Chthoniê);[32] the latter two through their union created the world as the great winged Tree of Life of which all creatures were parts.[33] Like some modern environmental philosophers, he considered the whole Earth to be a single living organism.

The Pythagoreans, who adopted the Orphic worldview, were pantheists who held that the universe is spherical, animate, ensouled, and intelligent.[34] All things share the same elements, so that no creature comes out of nothing nor is completely destroyed, but a constant process of recycling takes place. This natural cycle was balanced and harmonious, not chaotic. Philolaus defined harmony as "a unity of mixed elements that are various, and an agreement of elements that disagree."[35] The Pythagoreans believed that harmonies can be expressed as mathematical proportions. Since all living things, including humans, have a common origin and natural ties, and are formed of the same components—including the soul—they are all related and should be treated with respect. They forbade killing animals or plants, as well as eating food "that has had life"; that is, food that required killing an organism.[36] They were more than vegetarians, banning beans and many other plant foods along with meat. Many foods could be consumed without killing, so far as the ancients knew, such as milk, cheese, honey, wine, oil, fruits (so long as one did not eat the seeds), and leafy vegetables. The strongest reason they adduced for not killing was that all living things had the same kind of souls, and that after death those souls passed into other bodies. Some of them "become lions, such as make their lairs on the hills . . . or they become laurel trees with goodly foliage," said Empedocles, who added, "in the past I have been a boy and a girl, a bush, a bird, and a silent water-dwelling fish."[37] Plato, who followed the Pythagoreans in many respects, used this doctrine of metempsychosis as the basis of his famous Myth of Er.[38] He gave a systematic account of the theory that the cosmos is "a living creature, one and visible, containing within itself all living creatures which are by nature akin to itself." This great living creature is "endowed with soul and reason."[39] The Stoics also held that the cosmos is sentient, rational, and pervaded by harmony in which all living things partake. It is self-sufficient because it nourishes and is nourished from itself.

The idea of Earth as a living organism has been revived in modern times as the result of rational scientific inquiry into atmospheric chemistry and other phenomena by James Lovelock, who chose the name of the ancient Greek Earth-goddess, Gaia, for his hypothesis: "Any living organism a quarter as old as the Universe itself and still full of vigor is as near immortal as we ever need to know. She is of this Universe and, conceivably, a part of God. On Earth she is the source of life everlasting and is alive now; she gave birth to humankind and we are a part of her."[40]

Esthetics and the Enjoyment of Natural Beauty

There can be no doubt that the Greeks and Romans delighted in many aspects of nature. They were encouraged in this regard by the wild and cultivated beauty of Mediterranean landscapes. Flashing sea, rocky islands, and waving forests, all seen in the clear Mediterranean light, made patterns that were reflected in art and celebrated in literature.

The subjects of painting included landscapes and animals in motion. Though the nonceramic painting of the Greeks is almost completely lost, it can be deduced from literature and Etruscan and Roman adaptations that included portrayals of nature. The walls and floors of Pompeii and other Roman cities were covered with renditions of trees, mountains, seascapes, lifelike birds, mammals, and creatures of the sea. Architecture and sculpture also adapted motifs from nature. Leaves, flowers, and heads of animals were repeated in roof ornaments and column capitals. Sculptors have been justly praised for their portrayals of the human body, but they also exercised their skill on other aspects of the natural world. Bulls, wild boars, lions, elegant horses of the Parthenon, vaulting deer of Artemis, olive trees, and fountains were carved in stone that seemed to gain a life of its own.

Poetry and prose also voiced a love of nature. Homer constantly used epithets such as "Chalcis with its beautiful streams," "Pelion of the waving leaves," "Antheia with deep meadows," and countless others that are possible only for a writer who admires natural beauty and knows the reader does, too.[41] Many Homeric similes depend on nature's power to move the human mind: "Even as in heaven about the gleaming moon the stars shine clear, when the air is windless, and forth to view appear all mountain peaks and high headlands and glades, and from heaven breaks open the infinite air, and the shepherd joys in his heart."[42] It is certain that the poet had often joyed in his own heart at a fine wild scene.

Lyric and dramatic poets also sang praises of the land and sea. Sappho depicted a meadow pasture with spring flowers and breezes.[43] Euripides is credited with this fragment: "Dear is this light of the sun, and lovely to the eye is the placid ocean-flood, and the Earth in the bloom of spring, and wide-spreading waters, and of many lovely sights might I sing the praises."[44] A school of pastoral writers in Hellenistic Alexandria, of whom Theocritus is best known, adopted a romantic style of describing nature that emphasized the bucolic delights of the countryside. As for philosophers, Plato often voiced his admiration of nature, notably near the beginning of the Phaedrus, where Socrates remarks: "Upon my word, a delightful resting place, with this tall spreading plane-tree, and a lovely shade from the high branches of the willow. Now that it's in full flower, it makes the place ever so fragrant. And what a lovely stream under the plane tree, and how cool to the feet!"[45] In the section of the *Critias* concerning Atlantis, Plato described mountains as both beautiful and useful.[46]

Roman writers often followed this Greek tradition, but the Romans had their own more pragmatic tradition of agricultural writing in Cato the Elder, Varro, and Columella. Direct statements about enjoying the natural world were common among the Romans. Cicero observed: "If we have dwelt some time amid mountains and forests we take delight in them."[47] Pliny the Younger added: "There is nothing that gives either you or me as much pleasure as the works of nature."[48] Many authors had moved to Rome from country towns, which helps explain the depth of their feeling for rural settings. Two lines from Virgil typify his landscape description: "For now the farmhouse gables are smoking in the distance, / And larger shadows fall on the lofty mountains."[49] Roman writers also sung the glories of a nature wilder than farmland. "How fair the sight of . . . fir-trees, mountain-born, / And beauteous lands that owe no debt or wage / To implement of man!"[50] Virgil added, "May I love the streams and the forests!"[51] Elsewhere he described streams tumbling down rocky canyons, and loved to name mountain peaks.

Appreciation of natural beauty is one reason the Greeks and Romans made many ascents of high mountains. Rome's most famous mountaineer was Emperor Hadrian, who "climbed Mount Etna to see the sunrise, which is many-colored, it is said, like a rainbow."[52] Hadrian also ascended Mount Casius in Syria by night, again "for the sake of seeing the sunrise," and narrowly escaped being struck by lightning.[53] A mountain in Pontus was the scene of his third known climb. Hadrian was far from alone in climbing Etna; he had been preceded by the philosopher Empedocles, Seneca's friend Lucilius the Younger, and an unknown number of less famous tourists.[54] Climbing Etna was a common goal of the able-bodied visitor to Sicily. As Strabo remarked, "near Centoripa is the town of Aetna . . . whose people entertain and conduct those who ascend the mountain; for the mountain-summit begins here."[55] Etna was not the only mountaintop destination; a guidebook gave advice to travelers on various routes to the summit of Mount Parnassus.[56] Besides the aesthetic motive, there were two other reasons for climbing mountains: they were high places where the gods could be worshipped, and they were observatories of interesting phenomena —places where knowledge could be gained.

Nature as the Theater of Reason

Greek philosophers invented the idea of nature (*physis*) as everything that exists in the world outside human culture (*nomos*), and regarded it as a proper object of rational investigation. Beyond simply admiring nature, they tried to understand it. This was first done by the natural philosophers, who wondered what the basic building blocks of the universe were and how they were put together. Thales made two cryptic statements: "All things are water" and "All things are full of gods."[57] As an illustration of the latter assertion, he pointed to the lodestone and its mysterious attraction for iron. In doing so he may have attempted to distinguish matter and energy as the primal entities.

Others advanced air, fire, and earth as basic elements, alone or in combination. Some postulated that various kinds of motion produced the changes seen in nature, while others denied the reality of motion and change. These philosophers shared a common assumption about the natural world, that it can be understood by the human mind because it possesses a rational order of its own. As Aristotle was to put it, "nature does nothing in vain."[58] Some early thinkers made rationality a creative force in their views of the universe; Heraclitus called it *logos* (reason) and Anaxagoras called it *nous* (mind). But the result of the excursion of the Greeks into natural philosophy was to develop a series of mutually exclusive systems of explanation, all of which seemed rational, but none of which could defeat the others. It is impossible to speak of consensus among the Greeks on the natural environment.

Plato developed a beautiful view of cosmological unity, but for the most part made human society, not the natural environment, the object of inquiry. A few lines after the lyrical description of nature quoted above, Plato made Socrates add that trees and open country would not teach him anything, since he was interested only in what he could learn from men in the city.[59] His ethics was

concerned with establishing an absolute standard of justice between human beings. Even so, Plato's writings are full of insight about the relationship between
human beings and nature, the environmental problems that arise in that relationship, and possible solutions.

Aristotle investigated questions about the natural world, using a more systematic and inductive method than the natural philosophers before him had
discovered. He gathered from his research that the living and the nonliving
merged with one another in gradual stages, thus preserving the dominant Greek
view of the universe as a living, harmonious system.[60] But Aristotle's scheme was
hierarchical. Although he thought making sharp distinctions between classes of
beings was difficult, so that "in most of the other animals can be discerned traces
of the psychical modes which attain their clearest differentiation in man,"[61] as
Anthony Preus explained, "there is one ultimate ruler, and each level is subordi-
nate to the next higher level, as in an army."[62] Aristotle asserted that plants exist
for the sake of animals, animals for the sake of man, and that inferior men are
natural slaves of the superior.[63] This doctrine supports human use of nature in
any way that is conducive to human good, and it has been extremely influential
in the history of Western environmental philosophy. Aristotle himself would
not have justified the misuse of animals or their senseless slaughter, but others
later derived from his teaching that animals and plants of lower orders have no
purpose of their own and no inherent right to existence.

Aristotle's student Theophrastus did not accept the idea that other creatures
exist to serve mankind. He did not deny that there is purpose in nature; for
example, he found the purpose of an annual plant to be the production of seed
to provide for a new generation. But the purpose of things in nature, Theophrastus maintained, is not always evident. He asked for an "effort to determine the
conditions on which real things depend and the relations in which they stand
to one another"[64] through careful observation rather than the facile assigning of
final causes. His philosophy might have given birth to an ethics of consideration
for other forms of life, had it been more influential, but he had few followers.

Quite a different concept came from Leucippus and Democritus, who maintained that the world is purely physical, composed of indivisible particles (at-
oms) whose movements are purely mechanical and governed by accident. This
view denied the idea of design in the universe but had the rational consistency
characteristic of Greek thought. According to Epicurus, whose cosmology followed Democritus, there is no creator, and nature works through blind physical
cause. His ethics, based on anthropocentric rational hedonism, held little promise as a caution against environmental damage. Still, some Epicureans supposed
that animals and plants could not have been created for human use because so
many people are fools, and anyway there is not enough human intelligence in

the world to make creation with this purpose worthwhile. Through the poet Lucretius and others, Epicureanism became influential among the Romans.

But the Romans were more profoundly influenced by the Stoic school, founded by a Cypriot named Zeno and taught in Roman times by the slave Epictetus, his student Arrian, and the philosopher-emperor Marcus Aurelius. Like the Epicureans, the Stoics were materialists. They nonetheless held that the cosmos has unity, order, and cyclical development, and is animated by a fiery soul, of which all individual souls are fragments. Nature is designed by divine reason, as Cicero explained:

> Unless obstructed by some force, nature progresses on a certain path of her own to her goal of full development . . . In the world of nature as a whole there must be a process towards completeness and perfection . . . There can be nothing that can frustrate nature as a whole, since she embraces and contains within herself all modes of being . . . Since she is of such a character as to be superior to all things and incapable of frustration by any, it follows of necessity that the world is an intelligent being, and indeed also a wise being.[65]

Within this world, humans are bound to act with justice, which is a compact between humans. The Stoics accepted Hesiod's dictum that "human beings have no compact of justice with irrational animals," and Aristotle's hierarchy of plants, animals, and man.[66] All decisions regarding the environment should therefore be made with respect to the possible effects on other humans.

The argument of the Stoics on this point with the Neoplatonists, who were even more Pythagorean than Plato had been, was whether beasts are rational or not; the Neoplatonists claimed they were. Neoplatonism's exponents were Philostratus, the eclectic Plutarch, and most importantly Plotinus. In some respects they followed Pythagoras more closely than Plato. Plotinus held that the universe is the expression of The One, the ground of being. The cosmos is informed by a World-Mind and animated by a World-Soul. As nature unfolds from The One, there is less unity and more individuation, but every being still contains every other being. So far, so good. But bare matter, the Neoplatonists taught, is the source of evil. Since the body is matter, the body is evil (*sôma sêma*, "the body is a tomb," was a common saying of theirs). The proper course for a human soul was to purify itself of matter and rise toward spiritual union with The One. The natural environment, as material, tied the soul to the lower world, and so the body and should be rejected as a delusion. Injunctions of the Neopythagoreans that may sound environmentalistic are really intended to help the soul escape from attachment to the physical world. Early Pythagorean rules about diet and against sacrifice were relaxed among the Neoplatonists as concern for pure spirit and the next world replaced reverence for life.

The Roots of Ecological Science

Although ancient thinkers never used the word "ecology," they originated inquiries that would today be called ecological. They were forerunners of the science of ecology, even if their ideas reached fruition only in modern times.

The Presocratics

The philosophical grounding for ecology is the notion of the world as a biological system within which cycles of interaction and change occur. This idea appears in the surviving fragments of Empedocles, who held that all things share the same elements, so that there is a constant process of interchange in which no creature comes out of nothing nor is finally destroyed.[67] This might today be compared to the flow of energy and matter in an ecosystem. Empedocles conceived the universe as an endless recycling: "There is no birth in mortal things, and no end in ruinous death. There is only mingling and interchange of parts, and it is this we call 'nature' . . . When these elements are mingled into the shape of a man living under the bright sky, or into the shape of wild beasts or plants or birds, men call it birth; and when these things are separated into their parts men speak of hapless death."[68] Anaxagoras enunciated a similar idea: "Nothing exists apart; everything has a share of everything else."[69]

Anaximander seems to have intuited a relationship between evolution and predation. He wondered how human beings, who are weaker than many other animals and who spend a long childhood in a defenseless state, could have survived in earliest times. He decided they had originally grown as embryos in a fishlike form that protected them from predators.[70] Empedocles added the idea of natural selection. Believing that all creatures arose from a mixture of the elements, he stated that only those whose structure fitted their purpose had survived, while those with an odd assortment of parts had perished.[71] He speculated as to why various animals and plants prefer different environments, though his answer is unclear: one source says he thought that animals whose nature was fiery "flew up into the air," another that they became aquatic to cool off their inner flames.[72] He puzzled over the roles of climate, moisture, and soil in plant growth, attempting to work out a concept of harmony between organisms and environment.

Herodotus, who had a wide-ranging interest in natural history and often repeated fantastic stories about animals and plants without necessarily believing them, pondered the relationship between predators and prey. He noted that timid animals that are eaten by others produce young in abundance, while predators bring forth only a few offspring, thus achieving a balance of numbers.[73] Plato repeated this idea, crediting it to Protagoras.[74]

The Peripatetics

Aristotle, whose "philosophical emphasis is clearly the natural world" and whose "starting point . . . was biology and the notion of organismic development and function,"[75] was interested in the relationships among living things and between them and the physical environment. He observed that "all things are ordered together somehow, but not all alike—including fishes and fowls and plants; and the world is not such that one thing has nothing to do with another, but they are connected."[76] It is this principle that makes the study of ecology possible, and Aristotle's own observations on ecological relationships, contained in his biological writings, were so intelligent that he has been given credit for introducing "ecologic considerations into scientific literature."[77]

Aristotle noted the food preferences of various species, and the competition "between such animals as dwell in the same localities and subsist on the same food,"[78] particularly when supplies run short. The lion and civet will compete for meat, and the kite will steal food from the raven. "Thus we see . . . their mutual friendship or enmity is due to the food they feed on and the life they lead."[79] Modern ecologists explain fluctuations of animal populations as resulting from reproduction, predation, availability of food, and climate. Aristotle gave a description of a spectacular population increase and subsequent population crash among mice, in which he noted all the important factors. To help explain the population fluctuation, he reported what might be called an experiment in population ecology. A female mouse "in a state of pregnancy was shut up by accident in a vessel containing millet seed, and after a little while the lid of the vessel was removed and upwards of 120 mice were found inside it." He went on to recount a plague of mice that appeared suddenly, devouring all the crops. The predators—including foxes, ferrets, and pigs—were active but ineffective in thinning the numbers until heavy rains fell and the mice disappeared at once.[80] Theophrastus made similar observations, but he attributed the population drop to disease.[81] Other ecological relationships described by Aristotle include territoriality among mammals and birds and animal behavior such as competition and dominance within species, migration, and hibernation. He discussed symbiosis, including parasitism and commensalism, through examples including the pinna (a mussel) and a pinna-guard (a small crab). "If the pinna be deprived of this pinna-guard," he said, "it soon dies."[82]

Theophrastus, whose most important surviving scientific treatises deal with plants, was the most consistently ecological ancient writer.[83] He observed that a plant flourishes best in an "appropriate place" (*oikeios topos*), which now might be termed its "habitat" or "site."[84] He distinguished plants adapted to environments that were arid (xerophytes), moist (hydrophytes), and saline (halophytes), and to various soil types. He discussed the effects of slope, exposure to wind and sun, and elevation on conditions in small areas (microclimates) and the plants that grow in them, and noted that mountains provide an unusual variety of such conditions.[85] He saw that plants of limited distribution (narrow endemics) may be associated with particular mountains or isolated marshes. He did not consider plants only as individuals, but investigated the effects that they exercise on one another when growing in groups, thus taking a step toward the concept of the ecosystem. Theophrastus classified plants into four groups by habits of growth: trees (*dendra*), shrubs (*thamnoi*), sub-shrubs (*phrygana*), and herbs (*poai*). It is possible to see in these a workable classification for Mediterranean plant associations: forest, maquis, garigue, and steppe (grassland). He also described how plants compete or cooperate with, and parasitize, one another, and their interactions with animals. He was particularly interested in the process of cultivation and human effects on plants in general, including extinctions and the impact of removing vegetation on climate. More than half of Theophrastus's botanical writings deal with ecological observations. In many cases, he anticipated terms that would become part of the lexicon of scientific ecology. In others, his ideas have to be corrected in light of more recent work, but it is hard to fault a writer of such rationality and good sense.

Strato of Lampsacus and Demetrius of Phalerum, students of Aristotle and Theophrastus, were instrumental in founding the Museum of Alexandria in Egypt, a research institution sponsored by the Ptolemies. Not only was the Museum of Alexandria connected with the greatest library in the ancient world, but it possessed a botanical garden with plants from many parts of the world, including India. It also had a zoo with a diverse study collection of animals and birds.[86] There is unfortunately no surviving evidence of ecological research at the Museum of Alexandria or similar institutions of the Hellenistic Age.

The Romans

The Romans were fascinated by Greek science, although they added little to it. Pliny the Elder's *Natural History* is an amazing collection of unusual facts and fictions, some from his own observations but most from earlier writers such as Theophrastus. Roman agricultural writers made a number of useful comments that bear on ecological subjects, but they can hardly be called students of ecology.

Theories of Environmental Influence

The idea that the natural environment has a formative influence on peoples and civilizations is an important theme in intellectual history. Its earliest extensive consideration came from the school of Hippocrates. *Airs, Waters, Places* investigated the effects of different environments on human health, both physical and mental. The writer believed that one must understand nature as a whole to understand the human body and soul. The climate, seasons, prevailing winds, drinking water, topography, and exposure of a place, he maintained, determine to a great extent the physique, temperament, intelligence, and culture of the people who live there, along with the diseases that characteristically afflict them. The same environmental factors affected the growth of domestic and wild animals and plants in each region. Hippocrates observed, "In general you will find assimilated to the nature of the land both the physique and characteristics of the inhabitants."[87] His pioneering environmental studies were based on careful observation of the regions discussed.

Thucydides noted that environment had important effects on history, including warfare. The thin, dry, unrewarding soil of Attica, he thought, had made that land unattractive to potential invaders and thus saved it from conquest and depopulation. Its relative safety made it a refuge for victims of war, but the numbers of people exceeded the land's capacity to feed them, and Athens was forced to send out colonies to relieve population pressure.[88] Democritus saw the environment as a teacher, believing that many advances in human civilization resulted from observing habits of other animals. People learned weaving from spiders and singing from birds, and built houses of clay because they had watched swallows at work on their nests.[89]

Environmental Determinism

An extreme form of the idea of influence is environmental determinism—that environmental forces alone shape human life and culture. In ancient times, the most popular variety of this doctrine was astrology, which taught that the changing positions of stars and planets controlled human life. The climatic zones of the Earth were considered to be under the influence of diverse zodiacal constellations and planets, accounting for the differences in peoples and animals found there.

Another type of environmental determinism held that the Earth is growing old and decaying, with dire results for humankind. Hesiod presented this idea in his myth of the Five Ages, in which the earth became less fertile and human life shorter as the Golden Age gave way to the Silver, Bronze, and Iron

Ages.[90] Lucretius also gave currency to the doctrine of nature's senescence. Earth is eroding, and if she is a mother, like human mothers she will become barren, while mankind's monuments will fall into ruin. No permanent improvement can be expected, because history is a process of decline.[91]

Environmental determinism had an optimistic side, too. Some Romans explained their rule over other peoples by appealing to Rome's superior environmental situation. If environments shape nations, then the nation with the best environment must inevitably prevail, possessing a natural right to rule. People have a tendency to see their own lands as central and pleasant, so it is not surprising that Aristotle had made a similar claim on behalf of the Greeks.

Nature as Ennobling Influence

Another positive application of the idea of environmental influence is the notion that people who live close to nature are morally superior to those in urban centers. This is the theme of the *Euboean Discourse* of Dio Chrysostom, who described the visit of a shipwrecked traveler to a hunter's family in the wilds of a large island.[92] The hunters were self-sufficient, living on what they obtained directly from nature. After describing their idyllic home, where they lived in natural honesty, hospitality, and unspoiled nobility, the author brought them to a city and into contrast with the corruption of "civilized" society.[93] Roman poets who liked to escape to the countryside expressed similar sentiments. Horace, Martial, Juvenal, and others did so with the firm conviction that they were not simply shunning human society but were exposing themselves to the good influences of nature, choosing their company more wisely, and finding living space enough to recover their essential humanity. "There's no place in the city for a poor man to get a little peace and a chance to talk."[94]

Human Effects on Nature

Counterpoised to the idea that the natural environment determines the expression of human nature is the idea that mankind can change the environment. The second idea is as old as the first in the works of classical authors; Homer's poems resound with the sound of axes and falling trees. It was the opinion of Anaxagoras that human beings were cleverer than beasts in manipulating the world because they had hands rather than hoofs or paws.[95]

The Positive View

Most often the impacts on the natural world are shown in a positive light; Sophocles gave the chorus in *Antigone* a hymn to sing in praise of mankind's ability to control other creatures and to change the Earth, although it ends with an ironic twist: man crosses the sea and plows the soil, he snares birds and beasts, and tames the horse and mountain bull. He knows speech and thought, and how to avoid frost and rain, but not how to escape death, or to prefer justice to evil.[96]

From Hesiod on, writers lauded agriculture, believing that through it mankind was improving the Earth by creating ordered patterns of beauty as well as producing food. Like Anaxagoras, Cicero praised the cleverness of human hands and the many things they could do—including agriculture, domestication of animals, building, mining, forestry, navigation, and hydrology—and concluded with this insight: "Finally, by means of our hands we endeavor to create as it were a second world within the world of nature."[97] Strabo believed that people worked in partnership with nature to rectify the deficiencies of the environment, as in Egypt, where the hydraulic technology of the Egyptians assured that the land could be irrigated even when the Nile flood failed to reach its usual height.[98]

Stoic philosophy saw human ability to change the environment as resulting from mankind's participation in the rational, creative life of the natural world itself. The design of the world, Seneca noted, included provision for human activities; metals, for example, are hidden in the earth, but mankind possesses the ability to discover them.[99] Human beings were the natural caretakers of the Earth, and its creatures were placed in their custody. Well-planned efforts make the world more beautiful and serviceable for human purposes; in this view, beauty and utility are synonymous. Mankind improves plants and animals through domestication. In the same way, the extension of civilization was seen as making up a defect of the wilderness, which was a "haunt of beasts" or "barren waste."

The Negative View

Some human impacts were viewed as environmental damage. Herodotus felt that mighty works like bridges and canals demonstrated hubris and infringed on the natural order. In one of the most perceptive analyses in ancient times of human impact on the Earth, Plato described the deforestation of Attica and the resultant soil erosion and drying of springs, so that "what now remains compared with what then existed is like the skeleton of a sick man, all the fat and soft soil having wasted away, and only the bare framework of the land being left."[100] The Greeks did not regard change as an automatic good; many of them reached the conclusion that under mankind's hand the Earth was undergoing degeneracy, not progress.

Some Romans made similar observations. Cicero maintained, "the products of nature are better than those of art."[101] Others were aware that human activities often produced results that were neither beautiful nor useful. Pliny the Elder complained that people abuse their mother, the Earth.[102] The idea that meager crops could be blamed on an aging Earth was attacked by the wise agriculturist Columella, who placed the blame for nature's infertility not on some supposed senescence or changing climate, but on poor husbandry.[103] A good farmer knows how to restore soil to fertility, but those who misuse the land should not be surprised when the result is diminishing crops and sterility. Horace scorned "the owner contemptuous of the land."[104] Pragmatic Roman attitudes could encourage wise use of resources, with an eye to sustained returns in the future.

Conclusion

To what degree did the ideas held by the Greeks and Romans about nature affect their practical treatment of the Earth and its living inhabitants? There is no simple answer. Some protection was undoubtedly afforded to the environment by religious beliefs and rituals. Hunters spared some animals, particularly the young of wild creatures, because gods and goddesses like Artemis and Pan were thought to punish their killers. Sacred groves of trees were saved by prohibitions against cutting them. Major changes of the landscape were avoided because they were believed to challenge the gods and bring on their vengeance. Animism in general provided an enchantment of nature that made people think twice before harming it. Philosophy encouraged the rational use of the mineral, vegetable, and animal realms. Scientific thinkers not only pointed out problems, but sometimes also suggested solutions.

There remains the undeniable fact that the natural environment suffered considerable damage at the hands of the Greeks and Romans. This damage was not as serious or widespread as has occurred in modern times, and some areas of the Mediterranean survived with relatively little impairment. But it was greater than one would expect from people who held positive views of the natural environment. Why?

The pattern of Greek and Roman attitudes toward, and ideas about, the natural environment is extremely complex. In this chapter it has been possible only to touch on a few of the major themes in religion, philosophy, science, and literature. The information that survives from the ancient world inevitably has a social bias. The people who left evidence of thought on these subjects were the upper-class intellectuals of their respective societies, and even though they were also often landowners and farmers with intimate knowledge of the Mediterranean land, they do not necessarily reflect the characteristic mind-set of peasants, woodcutters, hunters, fisherfolk, and laborers. Obviously the latter group outnumbered the former, and their actions had an immeasurable impact on the environment.

Religion permeated all levels of society, and it can be assumed that the common folk were more traditionalistic and therefore more likely to preserve the practices of the deep past than questioning philosophers were. The overwhelming environmental orientation of ancient religion was toward preserving the natural order. Still, it is characteristic of human beings to evade religious prescriptions when it is in their self-interest to do so. It is possible that tree worshippers might have preserved a few sacred trees while cutting down whole forests, if they needed wood for fuel. Custom provided sacrifices and prayers that could be used to atone for invasion even of a sacred grove. Some of the mystery religions taught the oneness of human beings with the universe and nonviolence toward other forms of life, but they also stressed purity of soul and escape from the physical world. Religious agnosticism and doubt trickled downward in later classical times, and the spread of Christianity weakened the older nature religion.

Philosophers were a tiny minority in any century, and they disagreed with one another intensely. Facing a period of time that spans 1,200 years, it is hard to make meaningful generalizations about them. Of course they had influence far beyond their numbers, and doctrinal schools of philosophy such as the Pythagoreans, Stoics, Epicureans, and Neoplatonists had a multitude of followers. Many Roman emperors were Stoics, and in a position to apply their philosophy in a way that would affect widespread areas of the Mediterranean basin and beyond. Stoic ethics taught that human beings should remain in the jobs that fate assigned them, and perform them well with responsibility to all. There were occasional attempts to carry philosophical systems into consistent practice in a few short-lived utopian communities. But it is almost impossible to identify a general pattern of environmental effects deriving from the competitive philosophies of the ancient world.

Ancient religion, or some forms of philosophy, could well have provided constructive environmental attitudes. But these would not have been effective in environmental conservation without knowledge of the workings of nature and the effects of human actions. There were places where a body of traditional knowledge, the result of centuries of trial and error, survived. One such body of knowledge was among subsistence farmers, whose practices often reflected successful adaptations to the ecosystems in which they had to live or perish. They took fairly good care of the land as long as their own lives were not disrupted by war, which was unfortunately often. Science in general, and ecology in particular, had only a small beginning among the Greeks and barely survived among the Romans. It would have been difficult to decide which practices were likely to bring the best results when an environmental problem appeared for the first time, or was exacerbated in the course of time from a tolerable level to an intolerable one.

It must be assumed that the course of environmental problems in antiquity was not chiefly the result of Greek and Roman concepts of the natural world. It was also, and probably more importantly, the result of the technology they inherited and developed; the population levels they reached at various times; the agricultural and other economic measures they took to feed, clothe, and shelter themselves; and the common patterns of their rural and urban lives. Only through studying the interaction of all these factors will it be possible to understand the ecological failure that underlies the decline of ancient Mediterranean civilization.

Five

Deforestation, Overgrazing, and Erosion

No environmental problem that the Greeks and Romans faced was as widespread and prominent as the removal of forests and resulting erosion. In a passage of the *Critias* that has been quoted often, and deservedly so,[1] Plato observed that the mountains of his homeland, Attica, were heavily forested not long before his own time, but had been laid bare by the cutting of timber and by grazing. The result was serious erosion that had washed away the rich, deep soil and consequently dried up the springs and streams that formerly existed there. Strabo complained that the forests near Pisa, once fine, had been exhausted for shipbuilding and, at the time he was writing, for the construction of buildings in Rome and villas of "Persian magnificence" in the surrounding country.[2] Other authors record that wood of good quality, especially large trees useful for ships' masts and temple roof beams, had disappeared from many areas and had to be sought in less accessible mountains.[3]

The reason for concern about the disappearance of trees was wood's predominance as a basic material for buildings, tools, machines, means of transportation, and fuel. Today, substances obtained from mining—metals, coal, oil—are used in many of these applications. But in ancient times, bronze and iron were less utilized, and fossil fuels were rare enough to be curiosities. So important was wood that its name (*hylê* in Greek, *materia* in Latin) was a synonym for "substance" or "material."

Coniferous forest near Pertouli, Macedonia, Greece. This represents the appearance of many Mediterranean forests at relatively high altitude before deforestation. Courtesy of the Goulandris Natural History Museum, Kifissia, Greece. (1988)

Consumption of Wood

Wood and its carbonized product, charcoal, were the most important fuels in ancient households, public facilities such as baths, and industries, producing both heat and light. Fuel consumption constituted the most extensive use of wood by far, accounting for perhaps 90 percent. Metal refineries and pottery kilns used prodigious amounts, placing great pressures on the forests. While some forestland was doubtless managed as coppice, where stems and branches were taken out selectively and the forest allowed to regenerate and provide a sustained yield, it is hardly a coincidence that the areas around ancient mining centers became among the most deforested. Towns and cities also constantly demanded the services of woodcutters, charcoal burners, and haulers who brought fuels to marketplaces on the backs of mules or donkeys. Phaenippus made twelve drachmas a day, quite a large sum, by keeping six donkeys busy carrying firewood into Athens.[4]

Lumber was a fundamental article of the trade in building materials in the ancient Mediterranean. Much of this commerce traveled by water, allowing the users of timber to tap supplies along coastlands and rivers. Often logs were floated down natural watercourses or canals to ports, and there loaded on merchant ships. A typical lumber port would be located near the mouth of a river with a mountainous, forested watershed, like Thessalonica in Greece, Luna or Ravenna in Italy, or Colchis at the eastern end of the Black Sea. Ports without major rivers had the mountains at their backs, like Antandros and Genoa. Rome imported much timber from outside Italy, but a large proportion of the city's supply came down the Tiber River from the highlands, its entry point located at the Porta Trigemina.[5] The wood market was in the Porticus inter Lignarios, near the docks.[6] From this place, lines of carts carrying long logs of pine or fir made the streets shake, according to Seneca, and Juvenal added that the innocent stroller in the streets at night ran the risk of being maimed by a wide-swinging tree trunk.[7]

Governments encouraged the timber trade through privileges, tax incentives, and advantageous leases and conditions of sale.[8] The use of wood most often mentioned in ancient literature is shipbuilding. From keel to mast, almost everything in a ship came from trees, as did pitch to caulk the vessel. This was true of merchant vessels and warships alike, although ancient authors give more attention to warships. Attempts to secure supplies of timber for the latter played a major role in ancient diplomacy and warfare. When Histiaeus of Miletus founded a colony in Thrace, the Persian Megabazus warned King Darius that the area was valuable because it had "abundance of timber for building ships and making oars" and therefore made Histiaeus too powerful. In the Peloponnesian War, one of Athens's main purposes in launching the Sicilian Campaign was to conquer a source of shipbuilding timber.[9] Later in the same war, the Persian governor of Asia Minor helped the Spartans win by giving them access to the forests of Phrygian Mount Ida and advising them "not to be discouraged over a lack of ship's timber, for there is plenty of that in the King's land."[10] Timber was also used for war machinery such as siege engines, as well as for other military purposes. Detachments of soldiers were sent to cut wood for fortifications and fuel.[11] Deliberate destruction of forests, usually by fire, was a common tactic in warfare. The Persians under Xerxes burned the woods during their invasion of Greece. It is clear that warfare was continually affected by timber supply, and in turn was a major force in the process of deforestation.

Methods and Technology of the Timber Industry

Literature and inscriptions give considerable information, if limited in quantitative data, on the process of forest exploitation among the Greeks and Romans. Loggers took great pride in their work; a grave inscription on Mount Parnes announces, "I never saw a better woodcutter (*hylotomon*) than myself."[12] Such men knew the forests well; Theophrastus often takes advantage of the expertise of lumbermen from areas that supplied the Greek timber trade, including Macedonia, Mount Ida, and Arcadia. Columella advised a landowner who wanted beneficial use from his forests to have his overseer instructed by "a good forester" who would not "refuse to impart to one desirous of learning them the principles of his art."[13]

Trees were cut with double- or single-bitted axes, long metal saws with set teeth, and wedges, tools similar to those used as late as the mid-twentieth century. Shovels uprooted smaller trees. The branches were then lopped off, and the logs pulled out by oxen or other draft animals. Large logs might have pairs of wheels attached to them to make hauling easier. After they arrived at a place where they could be at least partly prepared, logs were cut into sections of transportable length and perhaps split into thick beams and planks. Theophrastus, guided by the experience of woodcutters he knew, gave directions for splitting pine and fir logs in the best way so as to take advantage of the grain.[14] Logs to be used as masts were kept whole. Emperor Tiberius ordered larches brought from the Alps, one of which measured 36.5 m (120 feet).[15] Finally, boards of the desired length and thickness could be sawn, with one man standing below, either in a pit or under a supported log. In the later Roman Empire, sawmills powered by water might have been used; there is no direct evidence, but a poet describes a watermill driving a saw to cut marble in fourth-century Gaul, and such a machine could easily have been adapted to timber.[16]

Other Causes of Forest Removal
Clearing for Agriculture

The removal of forests to make room for farming was a prominent feature of the ancient world. New farms were established in forested regions without necessarily cutting all of the trees, at least not at once. Older farms often reserved sections as woodlots. Agricultural writers commend several ways of "reducing a wooded area to an arable state."[17] The axe and saw were regular pieces of farm equipment. Trees were uprooted or cut down, the useful parts removed and the rest burned and the ashes plowed under as fertilizer. Trees that grew naturally on a plot were used as indicators of crops that would do well if planted there, although wise farmers knew that good forest sites were not always suited for other crops. Pliny remarked: "A soil in which lofty trees do brilliantly is not invariably favorable except for those trees: for what grows taller than a silver fir? Yet what other trees could have lived in the same place?"[18]

Archaeologists who have made exhaustive regional surveys provide evidence of forest removal for agricultural purposes. One is Curtis Runnels, whose work in Greece uses archaeology and geological stratigraphy to examine the relation between human settlement and landscape through time. He says, "Recent archaeological work is changing a long-standing view of the impact of agriculture on the land in Greece. The evidence mounts for episodes of deforestation and catastrophic soil erosion over the past 8,000 years. Many scholars believe they resulted from a long history of human land use and abuse."[19]

Other researchers have examined a variety of lines of scientific evidence in reconstructing regional ecology. A study by Bruno Pinto and colleagues of northern Portugal over the long term during the Holocene (postglacial period) concluded that in a district where the highlands had already suffered from tree removal, Roman agricultural technology along with economic and population relocation cleared the richer valley soils with "a major impact on the forests."[20]

Overgrazing

One of the most consistent and widespread forces of environmental degradation in the ancient Mediterranean basin was the grazing of domestic animals. The largest portion of the land area, unsuited to cultivation, was used as pasture. Even some areas that would have been arable were devoted to grazing by owners of large tracts, especially in Italy. But perhaps the worst effects of grazing were in making deforestation permanent and exacerbating erosion. As Varro complained, "grazing cattle do not produce what grows on the land, but tear it off with their teeth."[21] Such a statement ignores the positive function of animals in manuring the land. Grazing animals by themselves will not destroy a mature high forest, although they can make a disturbed situation worse, and shepherds often deliberately disturbed the forests. Goats are particularly destructive. In Morocco, they climb trees to get at the argan fruit, whose seeds pass through their digestive tracts and then are pressed for oil. But goats also climb trees to eat the foliage, not only in Morocco but also in Spain, Greece, and elsewhere, including the island of Montserrat and even Texas. Goats are extremely destructive of saplings and small trees. V. P. Papanastasis, an expert with the Food and Agriculture Organization of the United Nations, avers: "Domestic goats are blamed for much of the destruction of the Mediterranean forests . . . It is not goats per se that are the real culprit but the continuous, uncontrolled overgrazing for which humans are responsible."[22]

The four major grazing species in Greco-Roman times were cattle, sheep, goats, and swine. Each has its own dietary preferences, and together they form a synergistic partnership that is destructive to most vegetation within reach. Cattle prefer grass and leaves, so the herders will cut tree branches or whole trees to let them graze. Pigs especially like acorns, chestnuts, and beechnuts, so

Goats and sheep grazing on a rocky hillside. Courtesy of the Goulandris Natural History Museum, Kifissia, Greece. (1988)

the swineherds drive them into the forest, where they destroy the seeds that are the means of reproduction of the trees. Sheep eat grass right down to the soil and also pull up the roots of all but the hardiest plants. Shepherds will set fires to burn other vegetation and encourage the growth of grass. Goats are most destructive of all, and their ability to eat almost anything is proverbial, but given the choice they prefer woody plants such as bushes and young trees. In areas where the forest has been cut down, grazing animals, goats in particular, will prevent forest regeneration. Numerous herds of goats browsed almost everywhere in the Mediterranean, and they were adaptable, prolific, and easy to care for—the "poor man's cow." Goats and sheep together can strip a hillside bare, open it to erosion, and drive away competing wildlife, forcing the whole ecosystem to regress down the scale of succession and energy. Limiting the number of grazing animals could have prevented this slide, but such limitation was almost never practiced. If one herder left any vegetation untouched by his flocks, other herders would no doubt have used it the same season.

The ancients observed that goats could damage plant cover. Plato knew how controversial the goat was, proposing an argument between a man who thought it a valuable animal and another who regarded it as a destructive nuisance.[23] The comic poet Eupolis wrote a play with a chorus of goats, and had them bleat a list of their favorite foods:

> We feed on all manner of shrubs, browsing on the tender shoots
> Of pine, ilex, and arbutus, and on spurge, clover, and fragrant
> Sage, and many-leaved bindweed as well, wild olive, and lentisk,
> And ash, fir, sea oak, ivy, and heather, willow, thorn, mullein,
> And asphodel, cistus, oak, thyme, and savory.[24]

This could well serve as a botanical list of the most typical plants of the maquis, the Mediterranean scrub forest ecosystem, and it should be noted that a number of timber trees are included on the goats' bill of fare. They were usually consumed while young and small. The significance of pastoralism is not that it destroys high forests but that it makes permanent what destruction went before. The effect of goats may be judged from a statement by J. R. A. Grieg and J. Turner in the early 1970s: "In a place not far from Kopais we saw woody plants regenerating vigorously in a goat-proof enclosure, effectively demonstrating that the present sparse vegetation is due to grazing."[25]

Grazing sheep, goats, and to an extent cattle involved transhumance, the annual shift to cooler, moister pastures with a later growing season in the mountains during the dry summer. As a result, livestock consumed mountain vegetation at the time it was growing, and with the prevalent overgrazing, erosion was always a danger. In addition, manure was lost to the farms during the summer months. Animals could still graze at lower elevations in the summer, but only if pastures were irrigated, and the scarce water was often needed for other purposes.

Fire

Ancient writers knew that the destruction attendant upon pastoralism included fire to clear brush and forests. Virgil said as much in a simile of the *Aeneid*:

> Just as, in summer, when the winds he wished for
> Awake at last, a shepherd scatters fires
> Across the forests; suddenly the space
> Between the kindled woods takes fire, too.[26]

These fires, as well as wildfires started by lightning or volcanic eruptions, usually burned until they reached a barrier or were put out by rains; they would not be fought unless they threatened a settlement. Fires during the long, dry Mediterranean summer are often catastrophic and bare the slopes to erosion, though the plants are adapted to fire and show remarkable powers of recovery if not prevented by grazing.

Urbanization

Ancient writers were aware that cities stood where forests had once flourished. Speaking of the disappearance of *thyon* (sandarac) trees from Cyrene, Theophrastus remarked that "there was an abundance of those trees where now the city stands, and people can still recall that some of the roofs in ancient times were made of it."[27] And in the words of Ovid: "Here where now is Rome, the world's capital, were once trees . . . men lived in huts of which there were few to be seen."[28]

Place names often preserved the memory of forests that had been encompassed by the growth of cities and towns. An Athenian fortress was designated Peuke (Pine). The Caelian Hill, one of the seven on which Rome was built, was originally called Querquetulanus (Oak Hill), and the Viminal (Willow Hill) was named for willows (*vimina*). A place on the Campus Martius was called Oak Grove after the Italian or winter oak. The Aventine Hill was once "covered with trees of every kind . . . but the whole place is now covered with buildings including, among others, the Temple of Diana."[29] Of course the effects of urbanization were more far-reaching than the simple clearing of sites for cities; through the ever-extending tentacles of the timber trade, the needs of the city for wood grasped and denuded forests many miles away.

The Process of Deforestation

It would be interesting to know exactly which areas of the Mediterranean basin were deforested, and at what times. Ancient forests are unfortunately no longer directly observable, so scholars must depend on proxy evidence, including ancient writings, archaeology, anthracology, pollen studies, edaphology, sedimentology, ice cores, and climatic studies including computer modeling. What Fredric Cheyette says of Dark Age studies is generally true of ancient environmental history: "For further progress in refining and correcting the story of this important and still obscure period of European history will demand the communication and cooperation of specialists in all these fields [archaeology, palynology, climatology]. Historians with their traditional tools can no longer go it alone."[30] Classical writers give the impression that the devastation was extensive, as they describe places as wooded which were not so in later times, or mention forests that had disappeared in their own day. J. R. McNeill judges, "without a doubt a substantial measure of Mediterranean deforestation and consequent erosion happened in classical times, say between 500 BC and AD 500." He adds, "By the time the Roman Empire began to totter [third century AD] it is likely that no extensive forest remained in the plains or low hills surrounding the Mediterranean."[31] Most of the land surface was covered at one time, perhaps far in the past, by forests of various types. Pliny said there once was a forest of giant trees in Egypt, and Diodorus chronicled the passing of the rich forests of Spain and his homeland, Sicily.[32] "In those days," asserted Livy of fourth-century BCE Italy, "the Ciminian Forest was more impassable and appalling than were lately the wooded defiles of Germany."[33] Livy himself would have found precious little forest where Fabius's army had marched with such difficulty against Hannibal two centuries earlier. Traces of vanished forests persist in names of places that once played a part in the lumber trade, such as Elatea (Firtown), Pityoussa (Pineville), Castanea (Chestnutburg), and Xylopolis (Timber City).[34]

Exploitation of forests began near centers of demand, such as cities and mining districts, and expanded into more isolated places as time went on. The environs of Athens were mostly bare by the end of the fifth century BCE, and the nearby island of Euboea, where the relict forests suggest abundant original growth, produced only inferior timber once the requirements of the silver mines at Laurion had stripped it of accessible wood. Forestlands that were more easily reached were cleared first. Lowlands lost their trees before the mountains, and forests near rivers were exploited rather than those farther away. The areas most praised as sources of good timber in classical times tend to be mountainous regions with heavier-than-average rainfall; Macedonia, the Alps, Illyria, the Atlas Range, the southern coast of the Black Sea, and Corsica are examples. But it would be misleading to suggest that the progress of forest removal was steady and cumulative. Some forests were leveled, grew again, and were reharvested more than once. Although forests were seriously depleted in ancient times, not all of them were destroyed, and the area remaining in forest was undoubtedly larger than that existing in the late twentieth century.

Literary sources are not the only evidence for forest history. In recent years, much interesting information has come from palynology, the study of pollen grains contained in deposits of dust, soil, and mud. Quantitative pollen analysis began with Lennart von Post in Sweden in 1916,[35] and spread through the rest of Europe and North America in the 1920s. The number of pollen studies has increased exponentially, so keeping abreast of the information on a regional scale is daunting. Brian Huntley and John Birks published pollen maps for Europe over the past 13,000 years.[36] Valérie Andrieu and associates developed a computerized database covering the Mediterranean Basin, emphasizing palynological evidence for human activity.[37]

Pollen is well preserved under certain conditions, and the grains from various plant species differ markedly in shape, so that scientists can recover from a column of accumulated material such as lake sediments or cave-floor deposits a record of the relative abundance of pine trees or grain, to give two examples, over a long period of time. The deposits can be dated by the radiocarbon method, although there is often a significant margin of error, making it difficult to relate changes in vegetation to specific historical events. Even so, general observations can be made, and recent studies have given us more exact knowledge. Pollen diagrams make it clear that forest history is far from simple. In a single region, forests may have become established and then been removed many times. In northern Greece, for example, paleobotanists have discovered a pattern indicating that forests survived best in settled times, but when invasions occurred, peasants moved into refuge areas in the mountains, cleared forests, and planted fields of wheat and barley. When conditions became more stable, they abandoned these retreats and moved down to the richer plains, allowing forests at higher elevations to recover.[38] Because movements of peoples occurred often over centuries in Macedonia, this cycle was repeated several times there. But palynology also shows that forests persisted in parts of the northern Mediterranean basin through medieval times, whereas they were gone in some populated areas of southern Greece as early as the Middle Bronze Age. Pollen cores from Messenia show that pinewoods had disappeared from coastal areas near Pylos by the Middle Bronze Age or early in the Late Bronze Age.[39]

Textual evidence such as treaties between Athens and the Macedonian kings indicates that in classical and Hellenistic times the city had to depend on the forested north for timber.[40] Not all Mediterranean forests were exploited in ancient times; the most remote mountains, particularly those located on strategic borderlands, escaped ruin. One such forest in Greece, which has apparently remained untouched since time immemorial, was discovered in the Rhodope Mountains north of Drama near the Bulgarian frontier. A national park of 585 hectares (1,450 acres) was set aside by Greece in 1975 to protect a portion of this unique forest of beech, fir, Norway spruce, and other trees, with its rich population of birds and mammals.[41] Among the birds found there are the capercaillie, golden eagle, and black and griffon vulture, while the mammals include bear, wolf, lynx, red and roe deer, and chamois. The scenery is exquisite, with mountains, gorges, streams, and waterfalls.

Effects of Deforestation

The most common results of deforestation in the Mediterranean basin are erosion of the hillsides, flood as the waters are no longer retarded and absorbed, interference with the water supply, and siltation of lowlands and coastlands. George Perkins Marsh, who served in Constantinople and in Rome for a period longer than any other American ambassador, understood this form of environmental deterioration well: "Vast forests have disappeared from mountain spurs and ridges; the vegetable earth accumulated beneath the trees . . . the soil of alpine pastures . . . are washed away . . . rivers famous in history and song have shrunk to humble brooklets . . . harbors . . . are shoaled by the deposits of rivers at whose mouths they lie."[42] As Helen Rendell notes, "a vegetation cover is the most effective protection against erosion."[43] Once the land was bare of trees, torrential rains washed away the unprotected earth. Erosion destroyed uplands that might have grown trees again, and the silt, sand, and gravel that reddened the rivers was deposited at their mouths along the shores of the virtually tideless Mediterranean Sea. This greatly altered coastlines, in some cases pushing them many miles farther out to sea, as is the case around the mouth of the Peneios River.

Changes in Forest Ecology

Useful information is found through anthracology,[44] the analysis of charcoal evidence found in archaeological contexts. Charcoal is often used for radiocarbon dating, but anthracology also uses microscopic study of charcoal fragments to determine the species of trees or shrubs that were carbonized, and to detect changes in the presence and proportion of various species over time. Explicitly ecological interpretations of carbon analysis appeared around 1940.[45] The methodology has been applied in Mediterranean countries since the 1960s.[46]

Lucie Chabal and Fanette Laubenheimer excavated at Sallèles d'Aude, near Narbonne, where a Gallo-Roman potters' workshop with fourteen kilns was active from the first to the fourth century.[47] This covers the period from Augustus to Constantine, including the Golden and Silver Ages of the Roman Empire and the third-century economic crisis. The kilns burnt thousands of cubic meters of wood, at a rate rising to 360 m³ (152,600 board feet) per year, then declining to 132 m³ (55,900 board feet) per year.

The industrial complex was located above a floodplain at the confluence of the Cesse and Aude Rivers, close to the resources essential to ceramic manufacture: clay, water, and wood. A sequence of exploitation displayed three periods of species preference. In the first phase, after the kilns began operation, from about 10 BCE to the mid-first century, the most commonly burnt species included moisture-loving trees such as deciduous white oak, with alder, ash, and elm. Relatively soon, the proportion of these trees declined and disappeared, indicating the destruction of the forest on the floodplain. In the second phase, from 50 to 150 CE, the potters exploited a deciduous oak forest beyond the plains, where the removal of that species favored its replacement by holm or holly oak, an evergreen species more tolerant of arid conditions. This process was commonly noted in Mediterranean France.[48] As Jean-Louis Vernet notes,

Boulders and other material deposited by torrents near Laphistos, Greece. Courtesy of the Goulandris Natural History Museum, Kifissia, Greece. (1988)

"cutting and repeated fires favor the holm oak more than the white oak, as it is better able to sprout from its stump. The holm oak was able in this way to fill in some of the gaps left by the white oak; deciduous oak practically never reappears."[49] In the third phase, from around 150 to 310, evergreen holm oak was the dominant species consumed. Where evidence shows replacement of deciduous oaks by evergreen oaks, it is reasonable to suspect anthropogenic disturbance of the local forest ecosystem, which created a dryer microclimate. Charcoal analysis at the eastern end of the Mediterranean in southern Syria, for example, shows that evergreen oak appeared in the Roman period and gradually supplanted deciduous oak, which now grows only in a restricted area.[50] This line of evidence shows that it in evaluating deforestation, it is important not to simply establish whether there were still trees in an area, but to note the disappearance of species and the replacement of some species by others.

The evidence of palynology corroborates this conclusion. Analysis of a pollen core, with assistance from radiocarbon dating, can show the changing abundance of pollen rain and the relative frequency of kinds of pollen over a period of time, often centuries or millennia.

A good example is the Marsillargues diagram from a core taken from a lagoon site near the French Mediterranean coast.[51] Here the "Juglans line" marks the appearance of walnut pollen associated with the founding of Roman colonies in this area. Afterward, there was an episode of deforestation with the felling of beech and oak to clear agricultural land, leading to increased pollen of culti-vated plants. The main sign of the episode of deforestation, a sharp reduction of forest tree pollen, is clear. Henry Lamb and associates analyzed cores taken from Tigalmamine Lakes in the Atlas Mountains of Morocco.[52] Lamb's pollen diagram shows a decline in tree pollen from the time of the Roman Republic to a low in the fifth century. There was a decline of oaks, with a disappearance of deciduous oaks, and a sharp rise in grass pollen. Lamb states that this was a severe period of forest degradation, since pollen data show that all tree species declined in various degrees.

The Roman writer Lucan tells us that the Romans exploited the forests of Mauretania (within the same area as modern Morocco): "This was a very fertile area which had never been disturbed in the search for metals . . . The timber of Mauretania was the people's only wealth. They were innocent of its value, it was the leafy shade of the citrus [sandarac[53]] that they enjoyed, and they lived happily. Into the forest hitherto unknown our axes came: we search out tables for our banquets from the end of the earth."[54] Lamb believes that anthropogenic forest degradation began about 250 BCE and has continued ever since. Clear-ance, shredding of trees for animal feed, and grazing of sheep and goats con-tinue to the present day.

Disruption of the Water Supply and Flooding

Forests regulate runoff from the precipitation they receive. Like a sponge, the plants and soil hold water, preventing floods and releasing a year-round supply to springs and streams. Ancient writers were aware of this function, as Vitruvius explains:

> Water . . . is to be most sought in mountains and northern regions, because in these parts it is found of sweeter quality, more wholesome and abundant. For such places are turned away from the sun's course, and in these especially are many forest trees . . . nor do the sun's rays reach the earth directly and cause the moisture to evaporate. Valleys between mountains are subject to much rain, and because of the dense forest, snow stands there much longer under the shadow of the trees and the hills. Then it melts and percolates through the interstices of the earth and so reaches to the lowest spurs of the mountains, from which the product of the springs flows and bursts forth.[55]

Other authors similarly noted the connection between forests and water sup-ply. Pausanias visited a place "clothed with oak woods" and remarked of it, "no town in Greece is more abundantly supplied with flowing water than Phellae."[56] Ancients also noted the effects of deforestation in light of this relationship. Pliny commented, "devastating torrents unite when from hills has been cut away the wood that used to hold the rains and absorb them."[57] As Plato observed, the water that rushed unimpeded down mountainsides was no longer available to feed the springs. Perhaps for this reason, he portrayed his ideal Atlantis as having springs surrounded by plantations of appropriate trees. Without forests, streams that formerly flowed clear all year long became intermittent and muddy, existing only as dry courses during the summer, while hundreds of springs dried up. Due to the denudation of the Tiber watershed, Rome suffered floods that covered the lower parts of the city and backed up the sewers. The first recorded flood was in 241 BCE, and records indicate increased flooding of the river from that time onward.[58]

Erosion and Siltation

Once the land was bare of trees, the torrential rains of the wet half of the year washed away the unprotected earth. Unimpeded erosion destroyed uplands that might have grown new trees, and the silt, sand, and gravel that reddened the rivers were deposited at their mouths along the shores of the virtually tideless Mediterranean Sea. Coastlines shifted drastically, sometimes moving miles out to sea, as happened around the mouth of the Po River. The new wetlands were unhealthy to humans because they served as a breeding ground for malarial mosquitos, but the wetlands were useful as homes for water birds and other animals, and as spawning places for some species of fish.

Erosion and siltation around the Mediterranean in ancient times were large in scale, and the amount of soil removed from the highlands was significant. Deposits along the coasts and in valleys and lowlands can be measured, as well as dated from artifacts found in them or by radiocarbon analysis of organic materials. Such studies indicate that erosion was a complicated and highly localized process.[59] Thermopylae, the famous pass between cliffs and sea near the mouth of the Spercheios River, was narrow enough in 480 BCE that a small Greek army could hold it against a vastly superior Persian force. Today, accretion of river deposits has widened the land at least 8 km (5 miles) seaward from the battle site.

Plato recorded that soil erosion following the deforestation of Attica left the mountains wasted like rocky skeletons.[60] He complained of the sediments that had been deposited in lower places, obscuring the Earth's natural beauty.[61] Pausanias compared the silt deposits laid down at the mouths of two rivers: the Achelous, whose watershed was uninhabited and therefore forested, "does not wash down so much mud on the Echinadian islands as it would otherwise do," but the Maeander, whose valley had been cleared, "had turned the sea between Priene and Miletus into dry land."[62] Siltation clogged harbors at river mouths, as was true of Miletus in the case just mentioned, and Herculean labors were needed in many places to retain them. Repeated efforts to keep open Ostia, Rome's major port at the mouth of the Tiber, are described in ancient sources, apparent in archaeological studies and evident in modern aerial photographs showing successively constructed and abandoned harbor basins.[63] Paestum declined when her anchorage filled, and much later Ravenna, the chief Roman naval port on the Adriatic coast, lost access to the sea through a similar process.

Climate

Local climates, also called microclimates, change when forests are removed. Deforested tracts in upper ranges of elevation became windier and more arid. How far beyond the immediate area such effects might be felt is a matter for conjecture, but it seems certain that the aridification of some lands of the Mediterranean is at least in part due to human interference with regional environments. Malaria and other debilitating illnesses that contributed to depopulation were a secondary result of deforestation and erosion, since mosquitoes bred in the new marshes created by the soil and water that accumulated in lowlands. The fact that mosquitoes were disease carriers was unknown to the ancients, but they certainly knew that low, damp country had to be avoided at the peril of life and health.

Effects on the Economy

Deforestation had an economic impact, too, inflating the price of wood. As abundant sources near the centers of consumption disappeared, it became more rare and had to be imported over longer distances. Increased prices were particularly noticeable for fine woods, but timber and fuel prices increased, as well. Detailed price lists survive from a few periods and places, and these seem to show a pattern of rising prices.[64] Pay in kind for Athenian jurors included fuel-wood, the third necessity along with bread and *opson* (fish, fruit, etc.). The shortage and high cost of building timber due to deforestation contributed to a shift from wood to stone construction in both Greece and Rome, and even from brick to marble, in early imperial Rome, since bricks required firing and therefore wood fuels. Deforestation also increased costs of transportation, not only because of the greater distances merchants had to go to find wood, but also because of the scarcity of timber adjacent to shipbuilding centers, which drove up the price of ships. Warships had priority over merchant vessels in competition

Erosion after deforestation on Mount Parnes, near Athens, reminiscent of Plato's description of the landscape's "bare bones." (1966)

for materials. Strategies of warfare and diplomacy were often aimed at obtaining supplies of timber and other forest products such as pitch, and guarding the sea-lanes and roads over which they were transported.[65]

Forest Management and Conservation

The importance of timber supply and the effects of deforestation and erosion were evident to ancient observers, who often lamented them. Therefore it is not surprising that governments as well as private landowners exercised care in assuring a continued supply of wood from the forests under their control. Unfortunately, such efforts were far from universal, not always effective, and were diminished by other policies that encouraged exploitation and destruction of forests.

Private Efforts

Agriculture included some forestry; Greek and Roman farmers often did not clear all their land. Cato included a woodlot as the seventh in a list of nine requirements for a good farm.[66] Large estates contained forests that supplied timber, food (nuts, berries, and honey), and foliage for fodder. Planting trees for timber was common, and they were also planted to line roads, to shelter fields, and to mark boundaries. Landowners propagated trees from their own nurseries. Pliny the Younger remarked that the mountain slopes around his villa were "covered with plantations of timber."[67] Cultivated trees added so much to property value that when Crassus would not include some large trees in the sale of his estate, Domitius refused to buy it, even though he had previously offered a princely sum.[68] Columella condemned neighbors who cut down trees near property lines, thus reducing the value of adjoining property as well as their own.[69]

Public Efforts

Because timber was of great economic and military importance, governments considered forests a proper area of their concern. The sovereign power, whether city or empire, usually asserted ownership of all unoccupied forestland within its territory. Government supervision of forests and watersheds included regulation of the forest products trade, the timber harvest, and the construction of works to provide or control water supply, drainage, and erosion. Responsibility for these matters was regularly delegated to designated officials; in some cities the timber trade was under *agoranomoi* (overseers of commerce), while forestland in the countryside was supervised by *hyloroi* (custodians of forests) who, says Aristotle, had "guard-posts and mess-rooms for patrol duty."[70]

It was a recurrent policy of governments to encourage private exploitation of forests by leasing the right to cut trees on public land as a means of revenue, or by sale or grant of public forestland to private entrepreneurs or consortiums. During the Greek settlement of Cyprus, rulers "permitted anyone who wished, or was able, to cut the timber and keep the land thus cleared as his own property, and exempt from taxes."[71] Rome also granted title to cleared land. Forestland owned by the city of Rome was turned into a residential subdivision by the tribune Icilius.[72] It was Roman practice to rent tracts of woodland for development to syndicates of *equites*, citizens of second-highest rank who were usually businessmen. In the late Roman Empire, forestland belonging to the emperor was regularly sold to private owners who would pay taxes on it and provide services, either as regular obligations or as "liturgies," supposedly free gifts. These included payments in kind of lumber, charcoal, and burnt lime for mortar and fertilizer, and wood for weapons. Government policy was fortunately not always directed to the encouragement of deforestation. Conscious of the danger of a diminishing supply of wood, the state sometimes regulated private land so as to encourage conservation. Plato's recommendation that landowners be fined if fire spread from their property to timber on a neighbor's land doubtless represented actual Greek law.[73] Decrees of Ptolemy Euergetes, Macedonian ruler of Egypt, prohibited unauthorized cutting of wood by private individuals on their own land and required planting trees.[74] Land leases elsewhere also contained restrictions on timber cutting and stipulations for replanting.

There were public forestlands, as well. Although some were granted to individuals or communities, large tracts remained in government hands, and measures were taken, albeit sporadically, to prevent encroachment and assure their use for the good of the state. When Scipio Africanus needed fir trees to make masts for the fleet he used against Carthage in 205 BCE, he found them in "forests belonging to the state."[75] Wise administrators limited timber harvest; Theophrastus said that in Cyprus "the kings used not to cut the trees . . . because they took great care of them and managed them."[76] He added that later rulers of that island reaped the benefit of their predecessors' restraint; there Demetrius Poliorcetes cut timber of prodigious length for his ships. Some magistrates were foresighted enough to protect public lands against greed-motivated exploitation and found political support for their efforts. When the Roman tribune Servilius Rullus proposed that Rome sell some state forestland to raise money for other programs, Cicero was able to appeal to popular sentiment to keep the forests in the ownership of the republic. Knowing that there were profiteers in high positions behind Rullus's proposal, Cicero attacked them:

> What they need now is money, money that cannot be questioned, money that can be counted. I wonder what this watchful and shrewd tribune has in mind? "The Scantian Forest is to be sold," he says. Did you discover the forest in the list of abandoned land holdings? . . . Would you dare to sell the Scantian Forest in my consulship? . . . Would you rob the Roman people of what gives them strength in war, and in peace a more easy life?[77]

Governments such as that of Ptolemaic Egypt, where the need for local wood was acute, encouraged tree plantations. There a nationwide tree-planting project covered wasteland, private land, royal estates, and the banks of rivers and canals.[78] Trees were started in government nurseries. Laws protected plantations by regulating the felling of older trees, the lopping of branches, and the removal of fallen trees. Sheep and goats were excluded from areas where young trees had been planted. In addition, governments created and protected parks and sacred groves of trees.

Conclusion

One can hardly imagine ancient Greek and Roman civilization without wood and other forest products. As the major source of fuels, building materials, transportation, and both military and commercial supplies, trees were of criti-

Braided channels of the Peneios River below Meteora, Thessaly, Greece, the effect of deposits from erosion evident in the steeper slopes upstream. (1959)

cal importance to ancient peoples. It is as yet impossible to say with complete certainty just how far deforestation had proceeded by the eclipse of the Roman Empire in the West in the fifth century. The historian's ability to quantify many crucial developments is limited by inadequate sources, although new studies based on paleobotany and archaeology are promising. Scholars have differing views on the matter, and it is likely that the overall pattern was complicated, including periods of forest recovery alternating with periods of destruction. But the general impression is that the extent of forest removal and consequent erosion was widespread and severe, especially in the south and east, and particularly near urban centers, though certainly not limited to those places. In mountains distant from rivers and ports, thick forests, and even a few virgin forests, managed to survive.

The extent of deforestation and erosion in ancient times was certainly not as great as in the twentieth century. Even so, these environmental conditions were serious enough to produce profound social and economic effects. Shortages of wood and rising prices were among these effects, but not the direst. Much more permanent and damaging was the devegetation of steep slopes by logging and grazing and their resultant vulnerability to rains, which are often torrential in the Mediterranean winter and in summer thunderstorms. Erosion swept away fertile soil, leaving rocky slopes where trees could hardly have grown even if they had been protected. Silt, sand, and gravel from the mountains were deposited in lowlands and along the coasts, choking ports and creating poorly drained, silt-clogged marshlands. Deforestation, overgrazing, and erosion produced the most visible, far-reaching, and relatively permanent changes in the Mediterranean landscape of all those caused by human activities in ancient times.

Six

Wildlife Depletion and Loss of Habitat

An awareness of the possibility that wildlife might be totally extirpated appears in a Greek myth. According to the story, the mighty hunter Orion offended Artemis, goddess of the wild (or, as some versions have it, Gaia or Gê, Mother Earth) by boasting that he would kill every wild beast in the world. In retaliation, the goddess sent a giant scorpion to sting him. But Zeus intervened by setting both the hunter and his arachnid enemy in the sky as constellations opposite one another: Orion and Scorpio.[1] Mythological evidence reveals important aspects of ancient attitudes. That wildlife might be eliminated, at least from certain areas, was recognized by many emperors, kings, and affluent landowners who set aside animal preserves where only they could hunt or provision their tables. Likewise, sanctuaries were set up where wildlife was sacred to the gods and could not be killed except under carefully prescribed conditions. Poets sang about the disappearance of wild animals: "Oh distant Nasamonian lands of the Libyans, your barren plains are no longer visited by flocks of beasts of prey, you no longer tremble at the lion's roaring in the desert; for Caesar has caught a vast number of them in nets . . . and the former lofty lairs of wild beasts are now pasturages."[2]

The relationship between humans and animals did not begin with the Greeks, of course. Hunting, fishing, and gathering were the major occupations of ancestral people for the majority of their existence on Earth. Long before the classical period, the ancestors of the Greeks and Romans were hunters and fishers who lived in precarious balance with the species on which they depended, and the attitudes of these preagricultural people survived as relics in religion and folk practices, and in doctrines such as Orphism and Pythagoreanism. In spite of these facts, wildlife was depleted in ancient times. Although hunting in moderation need not reduce wildlife populations, attitudes changed, moderation was not always practiced, and other factors such as the modification of habitats led to the depletion of some species.[3]

Hunting and the Gods

Greco-Roman writers thought that hunting might be a purer way of life that had survived from a better time. Dio Chrysostom described a family of hunters as living close to nature on Euboea, where the greed and injustice of city-dwellers had not as yet corrupted them.[4] Even later hunters whose ways were not so primitive believed that hunting was controlled and practiced by the gods and goddesses, Artemis in particular. The gods were protectors of game species, allowing them to be taken solely when need existed, and when permission had been asked and granted. Thus it was believed that a wise hunter would not heedlessly slaughter his prey but take the gods into account. When a huge stag wandered across the path of the hungry Odysseus, he concluded that it had been sent by one of the gods, so he killed it in gratitude, but when his men slaughtered the sacred wild cattle of the Sun-god Helios, he knew that evil would overwhelm them.[5] As an example of the survival of earlier, reverential attitudes toward animals, an Athenian law provided that anyone who killed a wolf must pay for its public burial.[6] Phintias, tyrant of Acragas, had a dream warning that Artemis would send a wild sow to kill him because he had omitted her sacrifices. He immediately promised to issue coins with the goddess's head on one side and a wild boar's head on the other.[7] Arrian, who wrote a hunters' handbook, advised his readers never to ignore the gods: "Men interested in hunting should not neglect Artemis of the wild, or Pan, or the Nymphs, or Hermes, god of the ways and pathfinder, or any other god of the mountains. If they do neglect them, needs must that their endeavors fall short of completion. Their hounds will be injured, their horses lamed, their men come to grief . . . One must . . . dedicate first-fruits of the chase no less than one must offer the spoils of war after a victory."[8]

Gods and goddesses inspired respect for animal life and enjoined practices that would make hunting less destructive, but they did not forbid hunting as long as hunters killed only to obtain nourishment and recognized the sacrifice of animal life. Before taking an animal, the prudent hunter would consider whether the act would offend a deity such as Artemis, and would avoid killing pregnant females and young animals, thus encouraging the reproduction of

Mosaic of a hunter making an offering to the goddess Artemis in a sacred grove after a successful wild boar hunt. In the Hall of the Great Hunt, Villa del Casale, Piazza Armerina, Sicily, Italy. (1992)

game species. Xenophon says that the good hunter will spare young hares for Artemis's sake.[9] He also dedicated the first share of his kill or catch to the goddess, and provided her with an altar on his hunting grounds.[10]

Not only did the gods protect some animals, but they also appeared in their forms. Dionysus changed his shape to that of a lion or bull to frighten his enemies or to drive them insane, and Zeus became a swan, an eagle, a bull, and countless other creatures including an ant, usually when it suited his amorous purposes. The appearance and movements of birds in particular could reveal the intentions of the gods, and there were augurs skilled in interpreting them.[11] But the protection that birds and animals might receive from their close association with the gods is problematic; concerning birds whose appearances were taken as omens, John Pollard remarks: "They revered them but ate them just the same."[12]

Sacred Groves as Wildlife Refuges

The *hiera temene* (sacred enclosures), lands set aside as sacred precincts of the gods, offered protection to the animals that lived there, which was enforced by laws of the local communities to which the shrines belonged. Hunters were forbidden to enter these lands with their dogs and weapons. On Mount Lycaeus, if a hunter saw his quarry go into the precinct of Zeus, he had to wait outside, believing that if he entered he would die within the year.[13] One tale cautioned that the huntress Atalanta had been turned into a lioness for violating a sanctuary of Zeus.[14] In some sanctuaries lived deer or wild goats sacred to Persephone or Artemis, none of which could be hunted, although special permission might be given to capture a victim for sacrifice to the pertinent goddess. Sacrifices of wild animals were rare in Greek but not in Roman times; however, most sacrifices in both periods consisted of domestic animals.[15]

As a rule, wild animals in sanctuaries were sacred to the gods, and to kill them incurred punishment. Mythology, literature, and art are full of examples, such as Artemis's destruction of the hunter Actaeon by the horribly appropriate method of having his own hounds tear him to bits.[16] Although the usual story says he was killed because he saw her naked, that version is not found until late in Greek history.[17] If, as seems likely, there was an earlier version of the myth that attributed his demise to hunting a deer in the goddess's sacred demesne, then the punishment truly fit the crime. He had, in any case, boasted to Artemis of his hunting prowess.[18] Bragging was also a fault of Agamemnon, the best-known literary figure to be punished for hunting in a holy place. As Sophocles says, "when taking pleasure in [Artemis's] sacred grove, he startled an antlered stag with dappled hide, shot it, and shooting made some careless boast."[19] In vengeance, Artemis caused winds that prevented the sailing of the fleet against Troy until Agamemnon sacrificed his daughter "in quittance for the wild creature's life."[20] The evidence of inscriptions shows that it was not only in literature that penalties were exacted for hunting in the groves.

To provide another example of a site where animals were given the protection of a *temenos*, tortoises were preserved on a peak in Arcadia where "the men of the mountain fear to catch them, and will not allow strangers to do so either, for they hold that they are sacred to Pan."[21] Similarly, the Athenians would not let anyone harm the little owls of Athena that nested on the Acropolis, or the snake that had a den there and that received offerings of honey cakes.[22] No fishing was allowed in the waters of sacred groves, under penalty of death. In some, it was lawful for priests, but the priest of Poseidon at Lepcis abstained from fish, probably because they were sacred to the sea-god.[23] Artemis's eels were taboo in the spring of Arethusa, and at Pharae fish sacred to Hermes could not be caught.[24]

The *Arktoi* of Brauron

An initiation into the mysteries of humankind's relationship with animals was celebrated every four years for the children of Athens. This was the *Arkteia*, a festival dedicated to Artemis at the rural sanctuary of Brauron. Little girls, and

Tortoise (*Testudo marginata*) at Delphi, Greece. (1992)

perhaps little boys, too, were covered with symbolic bearskin robes and called "bears" (*arktoi*). Although there were a few bears in Attica at least as late as the first century, they were already rare by the Golden Age of Athens, and saffron-dyed robes were substituted for the bearskins.[25] The festival was appropriate for Artemis, as she was believed to care for the young of both humans and animals, and myths said she sent wild animals as foster mothers to suckle orphaned infants.[26] Sculptures and vase paintings show children holding small animals such as hares and doves in poses of affection, even kissing them. These were not animals to be killed, since the sacrifice at Brauron was only a symbolic drop of blood from a small cut. Little girls performed a dance with slow, solemn steps imitating the movements of bears. Children sometimes wore bear masks.[27] The dominant idea of this initiation was the inculcation of respect and even love for wild creatures. A renewal of the festival was held in the city for young women near the age of marriage. The *Arkteia* shows that the worship of the gods had a positive side; Artemis might be seen as an early patron of environmental education.[28]

Kinds of Hunting

The exalted view of hunting as the pastime of the gods, under their eyes as protectors of animals, is not the only or even the most prevalent concept of hunting found in the surviving evidence from the Greeks and Romans. Hunting was also regarded as a means of obtaining food and other resources, as a form of commercial gain, as a way to prepare for and to support military activities, as a safeguard for agriculture and herding, and as a sport or entertainment.

Subsistence Hunting

Although ancient civilization was founded on an agrarian base, and cultivated plants and domestic animals provided the bulk of the diet and materials for clothing, wildlife still served as a source of food, leather, furs, feathers, and the like. For many families, hunting was a means of supporting or supplementing the diet, especially in rural areas and during earlier periods before many species had become rare or disappeared. Deer, boars, hares, and goats were among the mammalian species hunted for food in Homeric times and after. Turtles, frogs, and a wide variety of birds also graced the rustic table. Fishing is known from art as old as the Minoan frescoes, and seafood, including shellfish, was a major source of protein for common people.

Commercial Hunting and Fishing

Those who did not hunt for themselves could purchase animal products from a widespread trade supplied by professional hunters, who organized game drives like those seen in North African mosaics.[29] Small-scale commercial hunters also supplied the marketplaces. There one could buy wild meats such as venison and many kinds of birds, from peacocks and flamingos to small songbirds.[30] The furs of beavers and other animals from distant mountains could be had, as well as ostrich feathers and various kinds of leather. Greek and Roman demand brought wild animal products even from beyond the Mediterranean basin. Ivory from African and Indian elephants was used in works of art from huge chryselephantine statues to delicate miniatures and was inlaid in furniture of every kind, including writing tablets, desks, spoons, and other objects. Ivory in incredible quantities went into statues such as Phidias's 13-m (40-foot) Parthenon sculpture of Athena and that of Zeus at Olympia, so large that it was one of the Seven Wonders of the World. In one day's exhibit in Ptolemaic Alexandria, 600 elephant tusks were shown, indicating that at the least 300 of the mighty beasts had died.[31] Wild animal skins were worked into clothes and furnishings, and fur and feathers served as decorations for fine ladies' costumes and men's military uniforms.

Urban tastes supported a large fishing industry and provided work for entire villages. Fresh fish came daily to market from local fleets, and importers brought salt fish from Egypt, the Black Sea, and the Atlantic coast of Spain. Among the favorite species were red mullet, parrot wrasse, sturgeon, turbot, brill, common bass, hake, sole, and eel.[32] The Romans loved fermented fish sauces with names such as *alec, garum, liquamen,* and *putrilago.*[33] Commercial interests met these demands not only by operating fishing fleets, but also by culturing fish in fresh and salt ponds. C. Sergius Orata ran a business on Lake Lucrina that raised fish for the elegant table.[34] Beds of shellfish like oysters were carefully tended and protected against competitors. Products of the sea were collected for purposes other than food, sponges for example, or the murex mollusk that produced the famous purple dye for the robes of kings and Roman senators.

Defense of Agriculture and Herding

A reason ancient writers often gave for the destruction of wildlife was that it served as a safeguard for agriculture and herding, which was doubtless a major motive both for governments and the common people. Predators were killed to protect animals on farms or herds in the countryside, while birds and herbivorous mammals were persecuted because they competed for the same vegetation as domestic animals or invaded croplands. Homer often uses the simile of lions pursued by herders in describing battle.[35] Other writers describe relentless attempts to extirpate wolves, jackals, foxes, and bears. These efforts promoted hunting, but the desire to protect cropland also may have had the opposite effect; laws in some places forbade hunting on horseback because it trampled the crops.[36]

Hunting and Fishing as Sport

Hunting for its own sake as a sport, or in order to collect trophies and to boast of one's proficiency and success, is a pastime that probably developed soon after mankind began to live in urban conditions. In classical Athens, an older male lover (*erastes*) is often portrayed presenting the prey he has killed as hunter to his young beloved (*eromenos*).[37] Plato approved of sport hunting to develop skill and courage in young men, but he would have forbidden netting, trapping, and night hunting, as well as all forms of fishing, in his perfect state.[38]

In art and history, the hunting of various animals was portrayed as a sport of kings and heroes such as Alexander the Great.[39] As such, he was following a tradition of hunting as a mark of excellence among the Macedonian nobility.[40] The Sidon sarcophagus shows Alexander and Persian nobles hunting stag, lion, and panther.[41] Emperor Hadrian loved hunting; he killed a bear at Hadrianoutherae (a name meaning "Hadrian's beasts") in Asia Minor, a lion in Egypt, and a boar elsewhere.[42] Both Hadrian and later Marcus Aurelius portrayed themselves as engaged in the hunt on their coinage, a valuable propaganda image. The lion was considered royal prey, and laws often forbade anyone other than the monarch to hunt them. Julius Alexander, a Syrian of ordinary rank, was condemned to death in 189 for usurping the emperor's privilege by slaying a lion from horseback.[43] It was not until 414 that an imperial law permitted commoners to kill lions.[44] Kings also engaged in boar hunts, just as epic heroes had done.[45] Kings sometimes fished for sport: Anthony and Cleopatra did so, and the Egyptian queen tricked her lover by having one of her slaves attach a salted fish to his hook. Their conqueror, Augustus Caesar, also enjoyed angling.[46] Not everyone thought fishing was a royal sport, however. A character of Plutarch's, Aristotimus, disparaged it as an ignoble activity.[47]

Kings and emperors often reserved hunting lands for themselves; in the case of Greek and Roman potentates, setting aside such sanctuaries was partly an imitation of the Persian King of Kings and his satraps, whose parks called *paradises* were as a rule "full of wild beasts" to hunt.[48] Xenophon, and later Alexander, saw many of these. Since many sport hunters were affluent landowners, they also created preserves for their favored activity, as Xenophon did. There were game parks, aviaries, and large fishponds in Rome. Varro had a place near Tusculum where he fed wild boars and roe deer, but was far outdone by Quintus Hortensius, whose Laurentum estate had a game preserve of 50 *jugera* (86.5 hectares or 35 acres) surrounded by a wall. At feeding time, Hortensius blew a horn to attract the animals, and an actor dressed as Orpheus played a lyre as if his song were enchanting the wild beasts.[49] He gave his preserve the Greek name *therotropheion*, but there were others called in Latin *roboraria*, *vivaria*, and *leporaria*. These were places that preserved many animals to show off to guests, and because common hunters were excluded, there were defenses against poachers.

A series of ancient handbooks, some of which have survived, purported to give advice to sport hunters. These are usually entitled *Cynegetica*, from Greek words meaning "to lead dogs," as hunters often used packs of dogs in pursuing game. The Linear B tablets of Pylos in Mycenaean times identify hunters with the proto-Greek word *ku-na-ke-ta-i* (the equivalent of classical Greek *cynegetai*).[50] Authors of the classical treatises include three Greeks: Socrates's friend Xenophon and Epictetus's disciple Arrian, both avid hunters, and Oppian, who probably was not. The Latin writer Nemesianus of Carthage is represented by fragmentary works on hunting and bird catching. The sport of fishing also has its literature, the *Halieutica* of the Latin poet Ovid, which actually contains little about fishing, and a similarly titled work by Oppian. Ausonius, writing in Gaul, devoted much of one of his poems to fishes and fishing.[51] All these works portray hunting or fishing as sports of the well-bred gentleman, and sometimes advise him to limit his catch, to spare certain animals, and to avoid unworthy methods for sportsmanlike reasons.

Wildlife Used as Entertainment: The Arena

Wildlife also provided entertainment for large numbers of people. If an animal or bird were rare and either odd or beautiful, it might simply be exhibited. Often animals were tamed and taught to do tricks, as bears and lions commonly were. Small, popular shows where one animal fought another, such as cockfights or dogfights, usually involved domestic species, although at times wild birds or beasts were baited to combat or devour each other. Fights were staged between partridges or quails. In a strange game called "quail-tapping," popular in Athens, a quail was put in a ring and the owner took bets on whether it would stay, even if knocked on the head.[52] But for sheer spectacle, exploitation of animals and spectators, and waste of life, nothing could exceed the Roman arena.

The shows put on first in Roman circuses, and later in amphitheaters, for popular amusement exhausted the ingenuity of their producers. Sometimes these were pageants or plays in which animals played a part, often involving violence or sexual perversion in addition to acrobatics. Even rare animals, at first exhibited as curiosities, were afterward mutilated and killed. From the middle years of the Roman Republic, criminals were executed by being faced with wild beasts that had been starved or were goaded into attacking them. *Venationes*, or mock hunts, in which armed men on foot or horseback chased and killed animals, constituted a major part of the shows. The arena, so called because it had a floor covered with sand, became soaked in blood. These contests were subjects of many mosaics and paintings.

The first *venatio* in Rome apparently took place in 186 BCE by Marcus Fulvius Nobilior, conqueror of Aetolia.[53] For whatever reason, a law forbade the use of African beasts for this purpose, but Cnaeus Aufidius allowed exemptions in 170 BCE.[54] The following year, the *aediles* (the magistrates responsible for the shows) exhibited sixty-three leopards, forty bears, and some elephants. Elephants had been seen for the first time in Rome in 275 BCE, when Manius Curius displayed at his triumph a number he had captured from Pyrrhus of Epirus, who had brought them to Italy for his military campaign. Romans jokingly called them "Lucanian cows" after the province where they had fought Pyrrhus. Elephants were first "hunted" in the circus in 99 BCE, and were pitted against bulls twenty years later. In the late Roman Republic, the variety of wild animals and the number killed increased dramatically. Scaurus, in 58 BCE, brought crocodiles and hippopotami from the Nile. Soon afterward, Pompey had twenty elephants

Interior of the Colosseum, Rome. It featured a floor covered by sand (arena) at the level of the walk. Underneath were facilities for gladiators and animals, including elevators. (1992)

and 600 lions killed by armed Gaetulians. Caesar at various times showed a lynx from Gaul, forty elephants, and a giraffe he had received as a present from Cleopatra. Numbers continued to rise as the early emperors attempted to gain popularity by entertaining the people. Augustus held twenty-six *venationes* in which 3,500 animals were killed, including tigers from India.[55] Claudius was not the only emperor who enjoyed watching the beast fights. Nero, in addition to his more infamous shows including live reenactments of the fall of Icarus and the coupling of Pasiphae inside a hollow cow with a bull, also flooded an arena and displayed polar bears catching seals. At the dedication of the Colosseum under Titus, 9,000 animals were destroyed in one hundred days, and Trajan's conquest over Dacia in 107 was celebrated by the slaughter of 11,000 wild animals. To these hecatombs in the city of Rome must be added the numerous *venationes* held in other towns throughout the empire.[56]

The "hunters" in these sadistic spectacles were called *bestiarii*, trained in schools like that of Domitian on the Caelian Hill.[57] Sometimes they used dogs or horses in the arena. Many of them were proud of their skill, and there were families who followed the occupation through generations. A technology of death supported them; cages were constructed under amphitheaters, complete with elevators and ramps to bring the beasts up to the arena without endangering the attendants too much.

There was enormous demand for a constant supply of animals, supported by an organized business that captured and transported them. Many citizens found employment in this enterprise. It was far from easy, since the beasts had to be kept in good condition in pits, nets, cages, or boxes, and carried or led from place to place until they were delivered. For the most part it was a private enterprise on which the government levied an import tax of 2.5 percent.[58] Roman officials and the military amply assisted the trade, however, and soldiers were dispatched to round up the animals. Individuals transporting animals destined for the emperor's shows could requisition food and accommodations from the towns through which they passed. This was no small expense for towns on the usual routes, considering the size and number of the animals, and late imperial edicts limited the time they could stay in one city to seven days.[59] Those destined for Rome landed at wharves in the Campus Martius and were held temporarily in the enclosure for wild animals outside the Praenestine Gate.[60] There were extensive imperial menageries, including one for the elephant herd at Ardea under the care of an officer titled the *procurator ad elephantos*. A large proportion of the creatures collected for this trade must have died along the way.

Protests against the Show Hunts

Romans of every social level from emperor to common people attended the games, and most Romans who wrote about them approved. There were few protests against the bloody "sport" of the *venationes*, which is perhaps not surprising in light of the fact that objections to the killing of humans in the gladiatorial exhibitions were also rare. In 55 BCE, the elephants in Pompey's show at the dedication of his theater gained the crowd's sympathy when, wounded by javelins, they defended themselves by snatching the shields of their attackers, attempted to break out of their enclosure, and trumpeted piteously. Cicero protested, "what pleasure can it possibly be to a man of culture, when . . . a splendid beast is transfixed with a hunting-spear . . . the result was a certain compassion and a kind of feeling that the huge beast has a fellowship with the human race."[61] When he governed Cilicia, Cicero refused to make his provincials collect leopards for the games, noting an extraordinary scarcity of the animals.[62] Cicero's edict proves the existence of the species in Asia Minor as late as the first century BCE.

King Juba II of Mauretania objected to the destruction of African wildlife by the Romans, and his son Ptolemy, grandson of Antony and Cleopatra, closed the arenas in Mauretania, shut down the animal port of Hippo, and enacted a conservation law to preserve animals.[63] These measures were ineffective; several species of animals became extinct in North Africa, and others declined. Marcus Aurelius, the Roman "philosopher-king," also disliked the cruelty of the games. In earlier times, a few writers voiced opposition to hunting of any kind, a teaching of the Pythagoreans, who refused to have anything to do with hunters, butchers, or priests who sacrificed animals. Varro also was anti-hunting: "There you go, chasing wild boars on the mountains with your spears, or stags, which never did any harm to you, with your javelin. What a 'splendid' art!"[64] The historian Sallust called hunting a "slavish occupation."[65] Even a confirmed hunter such as Arrian said one should not take pleasure in the sight of the kill.[66]

The Technology of Hunting and Fishing

Achilles outran deer, said Pindar, and caught them with his bare hands.[67] This simplest form of hunting is not unknown among primal people, but Greeks and Romans generally used assistance. Sometimes other animals were pressed into service, such as the hunting dogs known from Mycenaean times and whose domestication for this purpose probably goes back to the Paleolithic Era.[68] Various breeds were trained for the work; a fresco from Tiryns shows hunters with a huge hound. Hunting from horseback is not as ancient as hunting with dogs but certainly dates from pre-Homeric times. It was widespread in classical days, and is described by Xenophon and Perses.[69] Falconry, regarded as a sport of Persians and other barbarians, was practiced among the Greeks, according to Aristotle, and became popular with the last of Roman aristocrats.[70] The use of prey animals as bait, such as tethering goats to catch lions in a pitfall, was a common technique.[71] But sporting hunters like Xenophon denounced the use of a female animal's own young to trap her, such as tying up a fawn to draw a doe.[72]

A repertoire of hunting implements developed. The idea that hunting and warfare are similar, and can use the same weapons, is much older than the classical period; a dagger from Bronze Age Mycenae shows shield-bearing warriors attacking lions with their spears, and a ring of the same period bears the design of an archer shooting a stag from a chariot.[73] The literature of hunting often mentions spears and javelins, which were redesigned for use against specific prey such as boars. Nets have been used since time immemorial; a wild bull caught in a net can be seen on one of the Vapheio cups dated to Mycenaean times. In Greece and Rome, nets of strong linen ropes were preferred. Deer and boars, as well as many other animals, were taken in nets of various designs.[74] Xenophon lists three types: purse, road, and long nets, but there were doubtless others. A purse net was a large bag with a mouth that could be closed by a noose, a road net was a rectangular one used to block game trails, and a long net was crescent shaped with a belly and was usually set up in a forest where it could be hidden. Foot snares, devices that combined hidden nooses with wooden or iron spikes set in plaited circles of twigs, often over small pits, were also common.[75]

Birds were caught in nets, snares, cages, and on rods or branches smeared with sticky birdlime. They were decoyed, called by clever imitators, attracted by mirrors, or lured with food as bait. As an instance of the latter, a small pit was dug, filled with berries, and two potsherds were balanced over it by a peg; when the bird dislodged the peg, the potsherds covered the hole and trapped the bird.[76] Birds were brought down with small arrows. A huge bird like the ostrich was a considerable exception; Arabian ostriches were chased on horseback.[77]

Fishing technology is a subject unto itself. Nets and spears were utilized; as Homer says of the Laestrygonians, "like folk spearing fishes they bore home their hideous meal."[78] Hand lines and poles of cane or light elastic woods, often 2–3 m (6–8 feet) long, were used.[79] Fixed lines were made of horsehair, flax, or a fiber called *sparton* taken from the stems of the *genista* shrub, a plant common on Mediterranean hills. Floats were carved of cork. Hooks were fashioned of iron or bronze, and baited with real insects or with feathers and other materials to make an artificial fly.[80] Poisonous vegetable substances such as cyclamen root were used to kill fish in small bodies of water, a practice condemned by Plato.[81] Commercial fishermen erected towers to sight schools of tunny and other large fishes. At night, torches were carried on fishing boats to attract the catch.[82] Finally, skates and other fish were attracted by music and dancing.[83]

Ownership of Wildlife

The ownership of game and fish in enclosures or ponds was vested in those with title to the land; outside private places, it rested with sovereign authorities, or with those to whom they delegated it, as was the case also with unoccupied, virgin, or abandoned land.[84] Rivers, and the fish in them, were considered public property in Roman law.[85] But poaching by common people happened constantly, whether on public, private, or sacred land. The prevailing attitude was that wild animals belonged to "no one" until they were caught, and then they belonged to those who caught them. The state asserted its interest only in exceptional cases, as in protecting the animals inside a sacred *temenos*, but generally its policy was to encourage agriculture, grazing, and the reduction of the number of wild animals.

Introduction of Exotic Species

Did human activities that brought living animals from distant places establish viable populations of invasive species?[86] Animals frequently escaped from captivity, becoming a source of fear and sometimes merriment.[87] A law made keepers liable to fines for injury or damage caused by beasts in their charge. An escaped wild animal could be killed by anyone and its body kept and used.[88] But certainly Europe did not again become home to roaming herds of elephants and rhinoceroses as during the waning centuries of the Ice Age. The Greeks and Romans knew of numerous fossil remains of these extinct animals; although some were mistaken for the bones of earlier gigantic heroes or the remains of fantastic creatures like griffins, others were recognized for the genera they actually represent.[89] But smaller exotic species became established. The cat came to Greece from Egypt, where it had been domesticated and worshipped for more than 1,000 years, by the fifth century BCE. The Greeks brought cats to southern Italy, and cats were known to be in Rome in the first century; there is a mosaic in Pompeii showing a cat with its paw on a hen, another introduced species.[90] Chickens reached Greece via Persia in the seventh century BCE. Dogs have been companions of humans almost everywhere for millennia, but new breeds were imported from Egypt, Persia, India, and the far north. Undoubtedly, some dogs ran wild in Europe. Other domesticated animals such as sheep, goats, cattle, donkeys, horses, and mules were introduced in early times that are beyond the compass of this study, but breeds of these animals continued to be found in and brought from lands as distant as India.

New species of birds, in addition to the chickens already mentioned, continued to be introduced in classical Greek and Roman times. Sophocles first mentioned in fifth-century BCE Athens the guinea fowl from Africa, which were kept around a temple in Leros, but it is not noted in Rome before Varro in the first century BCE.[91] Pheasants, which take their name from the River Phasis in the Transcaucasus, are mentioned in Aristophanes's play *The Birds*.[92] Falconry, an art known earlier in Asia, is described by Aristotle as practiced by the Thracians; it is likely that local birds of prey were tamed, but exotic ones might have come with the knowledge of the skills of the sport.[93] Parrots and other birds kept as pets undoubtedly escaped or were released, and may have started wild populations where the climate permitted. Pigeons probably introduced themselves. There were likely more inadvertent introductions than deliberate ones, and this was true not only of birds, but of small creatures like snakes and rodents, as well.

An example of intentionally introducing a fish species for commercial exploitation comes from Roman times. Pliny reports that Optatus Elipertius, prefect of the fleet under the emperor Tiberius, collected fish, the brilliantly colored scarus or parrot wrasse, from the seas between Rhodes and Crete, and planted them along the Ostian and Campanian shores of Italy. Pliny adds, "careful protection by land and sea rendered poaching almost impossible. For the period of five years any scarus caught in the nets had, under heavy penalties, to be returned straightway to the water. The enforcement of these wise regulations effected [a] mighty thriving of the fish."[94] He gives another example, saying that Sergius Orata planted oysters in the Lucrine Lake. Others attempted to establish oyster beds on the island of Chios and near Bordeaux.[95] Wealthy Romans kept many fishponds both fresh and salt, and we can be sure that they sought out and paid well for exotic fish distinguished by their beauty or tasty flesh.

Introduced invertebrates must have been numerous, but few are mentioned in the sources. African snails, including very large ones, were brought in as a delicacy and raised in gardens.[96] Their tendency to "run away" was noticed. The invasion of some species of mosquitoes may be deduced from the spread of malaria in Greece and Italy.[97] It is often the case that one species cannot be introduced by itself because it is dependent on another species. Thus the arrival of bubonic plague and infected fleas was undoubtedly contemporaneous. The silkworm was cleverly smuggled from Sogdiana to the eastern Roman Empire by monastic agents of Justinian in the sixth century.[98] Fortunately, the white mulberry tree had also been introduced, so the caterpillar had its source of food readily available.

Depletion and Extinction

The surviving evidence gives the impression of declining wildlife populations, and the gradual extinction of certain species in one area after another. Writers often note that animals are no longer found where they were once abundant. Lion bones have been unearthed in archaeological sites such as the Mycenaean palace of Tiryns.[99] Herodotus reports that when the Persians invaded Greece, lions came down from the mountains to attack the camels in their baggage trains.[100] Aristotle also notes their presence in his homeland, but they were gone by the first century BCE.[101] Leopards and hyenas also disappeared from Greece, and lynxes, wolves, and jackals were limited to the mountains, where today they hold out in small numbers. Bears could be found in the Peloponnesus up to 100 CE, and probably much later; a few still exist in mountainous northern Greece.[102] Hunting reduced wild cattle, sheep, and goats to remnant herds, and eliminated them from some islands in Classical times. This was only one of a series of extinctions of island fauna, following the earlier disappearance between 6000 and 2000 BCE of dwarf forms of elephants, hippopotami, antelopes, and deer; giant forms of shrews, hedgehogs, and dormice; and still other endemics.[103]

Procuring animals for the Roman arena cleared larger mammals, reptiles, and birds from the areas most accessible to professional hunters and trappers. They exhausted the hunting grounds of North Africa, where elephant, rhinoceros, and zebra became extinct. The hippopotamus and crocodile were banished from the lower Nile to upper Nubia. By the fourth century, a writer could lament that there were no elephants left in Libya, no lions in Thessaly, and no hippopotami in the Nile. Lions had been extirpated from western Asia Minor, although the king of beasts persisted in Syria, where Emperor Julian hunted them, and in the Taurus Mountains; in both these areas a few could be found as late as the nineteenth century. In the Atlas Mountains there were reduced numbers, and a few lions may remain there today.[104] Distant areas felt the Roman demands; ti-

Relief of a lion attacking a giant warrior, from the frieze of the Treasury of the Siphnians. There is textual, archaeological, and artistic evidence for the existence of lions in classical Greece, and of their extinction there. Now in the Archaeological Museum of Delphi, Greece. (2011)

gers disappeared from Armenia and from Hyrcania in northern Iran, the closest sources to Rome.[105]

Collecting animals for the games was not the only cause of disappearance; all these creatures were hunted and killed for other reasons, too. Among the causes of the North African elephant's extinction, for example, were the use of the animal in warfare and, more importantly, the ivory trade. The Romans were persistent, efficient, could pay well, and came to dominate the commerce in animals and animal products throughout the Mediterranean basin, so the major responsibility for extinctions was theirs. Bird populations also diminished. The former richness of Mediterranean bird life can be sensed today in such relatively undisturbed areas as the French Camargue near the mouth of the Rhone River with its flocks of flamingos or Coto Doñana in Las Marismas on the lower Guadalquivir River in Spain. But these are the precious exceptions. The birds in Aristophanes's play berate humans for persecuting them, setting snares and lime twigs for them even on temples.[106] Ancient people devoured species that seem to have had too little meat to make the effort worthwhile, but so do some modern Greeks and Italians.

There were also complaints of the depletion of fisheries. It has been suggested that the disappearance of mosquito-eating fish from Italian marshes aided the spread of malaria in the second century BCE and thereafter.[107] Increasing prices for fish on the Roman market may indicate that there were fewer left to catch than before. The finest rare fish might have sold for their weight in gold; three mullets once brought 30,000 sesterces at Rome, and Pliny says this species rarely exceeded two pounds in weight.[108] As seas go, the Mediterranean was not particularly rich in fish, so its parts most accessible to fishing fleets could have been impoverished. Introduction of domestic species that competed with wild ones must have happened countless times, particularly on islands. The devastating effects of goats, rats, and opportunistic birds like pigeons have been observed in newly discovered lands since the fifteenth century; there can be no doubt that foreign species were introduced in isolated places as they were visited by ships or settled by new groups of people in Greek and Roman times.

The process with the most damaging effect on all forms of wildlife was, as it still is, habitat destruction. The clearing of forests, the spread of agriculture, the introduction of weeds and other exotic plant species, the overgrazing of grasslands, and the draining of lakes and wetlands all affected wildlife even more seriously than hunting. Two areas that were the objects of persistent attempts at drainage throughout antiquity may serve as examples: Lake Copais in Boeotia and the Pontine Marshes near Rome. Although neither of these large wetlands was completely drained in antiquity, many thousands of acres of irrigable tillage land were recovered by the construction of canals and tunnels, with conse-

Dolphins and fish decorate a mural in the Palace of Knossos (ca. 1400 to 1200 BCE), Crete, Greece. (1992)

quent effects on birds, fish, and other wildlife.[109] Many lakes and marshes in the Mediterranean basin were drained; in the prevailing limestone country, natural underground channels often existed that could be cleared or widened.

Study of Animals

Observation of animals in the wild or in captivity helped philosophers gain knowledge of the natural world. Aristotle, the greatest ancient commentator on animal anatomy and behavior, believed in the importance of direct observation, and some of his comments have been vindicated in modern times. He recorded that the male catfish guards the eggs he has fertilized, as well as the young up to forty or fifty days old. Early nineteenth-century European biologists did not believe his findings, since the catfish they knew did not behave in this way, but it was subsequently noticed that Greece has a catfish species (*Parasilurus aristotelis*) that does, which was undoubtedly known to Aristotle or his informants. Aristotle also reports facts that could have been discovered only by means of dissection.[110] Unfortunately, many of his other statements are simply wrong, and could have been corrected by observation.

The Peripatetic school of philosophy strongly shaped the Museum of Alexandria, a research institute founded by Ptolemy I Soter and Ptolemy II Philadelphus with the aid of Demetrius of Phalerum and Strato of Lampsacus, both followers of Aristotle and Theophrastus. This unique institution continued Aristotle's interest in observation of animals by maintaining a botanical garden and large zoo. Among the many animals and birds exhibited were elephants, Saiga antelopes from north of the Black Sea, oryxes, hartebeests, ostriches, camels, parrots, cheetahs, and a chimpanzee. In addition, during the reign of Ptolemy II alone, there were "twenty-four great lions, leopards, lynxes and other cats, Indian and African buffaloes, wild asses from Moab, a python forty-five feet long, a giraffe, a rhinoceros, and a polar bear (whose journey south must have been exciting), together with parrots, peacocks, guinea-fowl, pheasants, and many African birds."[111] To collect such animals for study, the Greco-Macedonian rulers of Egypt sent out far-ranging expeditions, some of which penetrated into Ethiopia by way of the Red Sea. Indian or Greek merchants and ambassadors brought numerous animals from India to Mediterranean cities. An Indian delegation, with wild animals including tigers, tortoises, and a python, was welcomed by Emperor Augustus on Samos in 21 BCE.[112] Augustus Caesar "took especial delight in 'untold numbers and unknown shapes of beasts.'"[113] One can imagine his delight in capturing the Ptolemaic menagerie when he conquered Egypt; doubtless many of the animals killed in the excessive *venationes* at his celebrations came from that source. Thus did scientific curiosity yield to bloodthirsty prurience, but the two kept company in Rome. The medical writer Galen says that physicians assembled at dissections of elephants and presumably other animals killed in the games to gain anatomical knowledge.[114]

Pets and the Love of Animals

The bond between humans and domestic animals is well known in classical literature from Homer onward; Achilles's horses wept for Patroclus, their driver, and Odysseus could not suppress a tear when his old hound Argos recognized him after so many years.[115] Cats had been domestic pets in Egypt for more than a millennium before making their way to Greece. But wild animals were sometimes loved and respected, too. Arion was not the only character to be rescued from drowning by a dolphin. Pythagoras is said to have had a bear that kept him company, and an eagle that would fly down and perch on his shoulder. These stories may or may not have been true, but it is certain that the Greeks and Romans captured and tamed an amazing variety of wild animals and kept them on their land or in their homes. Only emperors could own elephants or lions, but in republican times at least one private citizen had impressed his friends by riding an elephant when he came to dinner at their homes.[116] Among those attested in private households or collections are mammals and reptiles such as Barbary apes, monkeys, ferrets, hedgehogs, deer, giraffes, gazelles, captive wild goats, and harmless "house" snakes. Many birds including peacocks, various pheasants, parrots, cranes, storks, flamingos, rails, crows, starlings, magpies, thrushes, and nightingales were kept individually or in aviaries; some were valued for their song, others for their ability to learn to talk.[117] Captive animals, especially smaller ones, could have escaped and established wild populations in areas where they had not existed before, but there seems to be no record of it happening.

Something of an ancient animal rights movement existed among writers, mostly of Pythagorean bent, who honored the sanctity of all forms of life and maintained that animals possess rational souls. Ovid made Pythagoras a character in *Metamorphoses* and had him advise King Numa against using animals for food, since it was through eating the flesh of living creatures that the Golden Age came to an end, and against animal sacrifice as making the gods into partners of mortals in wickedness.[118]

Plutarch also spoke on behalf of animals. In the dialogue *Whether Land or Sea Animals Are Cleverer*, set as a learned debate among cultured huntsmen, he argues that animals possess a degree of reason. Human beings, he adds, also have reason only to an extent; if what we wish to demonstrate is "true reason and wisdom, not even man may be said to exercise it."[119] But since animals are rational,

The sculpture of a faithful dog lies on the tomb of his owner in the cemetery of Keramikos outside the Dipylon Gate of Athens. (1967)

we are unjust if we kill them when they have not injured us. Plutarch does not go as far as the Pythagoreans, however; he would permit killing animals "in pity and sorrow," as well as eating meat as an unfortunate necessity.[120] But Plutarch's most entertaining comments on this subject are contained in a brief conversation between Odysseus, Gryllus, and Circe. With her magic arts, Circe had changed many men into various species of animals. Odysseus won the right to have his sailors retransformed and furthermore asked Circe to do the same for the other Greeks. Circe agreed on the condition that Odysseus would convince a spokesman for the beasts that it was better to be a human than an animal. Chosen to speak for the beasts was Gryllus, a hog granted the power of speech by Circe. He refused the chance to return to human form because animals, he maintained, are superior to mankind in every virtue: courage, temperance, and intelligence. Besides, animal virtues are natural; humans must cultivate theirs. Odysseus, in spite of his fame as a persuasive speaker, lost the contest. Driven to use the argument that beasts cannot be rational because they have no inborn knowledge of God, he left himself open to Gryllus's riposte that Odysseus's father was Sisyphus, a notorious atheist.[121] That the dialogue was not a mere set piece is clear from Plutarch's serious objections elsewhere to hunting, animal slaughter, and the excesses of the arena. Rejecting the proposition of Hesiod and the Stoics that "human beings have no compact of justice with irrational animals," Plutarch exhibited admiration and sympathy for the myriad forms of living things and was an early defender of animal rights.[122] Unfortunately, neither in his case nor in any other known from ancient times does it seem that such ideas resulted in practical programs to help wildlife.

Conclusion

In many areas throughout the ancient world, wildlife was depleted and even disappeared. The combined evidence of literature, archaeology, and distribution in more recent times indicates that some species became extinct, while others had their ranges restricted owing to habitat alteration and killing for various purposes. The process of wildlife depletion was not uniform, however. Primarily because of the lower human population in antiquity as compared to modern times, refuges existed where habitats had not been altered and hunting pressure was low. Also, as the palynological evidence indicates that deforestation occurred in cycles with periods of recovery, wild species must also have rebuilt their numbers during intervals when human demands and environmental impacts relented.[123] Fluctuations in numbers of animal species occur even without human intervention, as ecological interactions occur among species and with environmental changes. Still, some of the effects of Greek and Roman exploitation of wildlife were irreversible, as when species were made totally extinct or extirpated from islands or other areas where their natural reintroduction was impossible. But the introduction of domestic and feral species such as goats and cats to formerly isolated places initiated predation and competition with native species and the destruction of the vegetation on which they depended. The result of all these factors was depletion and extinction of wildlife and an impoverishment of ecosystems.

Seven

Agricultural Decline

The ancients knew well that agriculture has an impact on the environment. In the play *Antigone*, Sophocles's chorus sang that Man does many things,

> And she, the greatest of gods, Earth—
> Ageless she is, and unwearied—he wears her away
> As the ploughs go up and down from year to year
> And his mules turn up the soil.[1]

The results of all this labor were neither predictable nor always rewarding. Many writers voiced the complaint that Earth was not producing as well as she once did. Hesiod sketched a history of the world as a series of steps declining from the Golden Age, when mortals found that "the fruitful field unforced bare them fruit abundantly and without stint," to the Age of Iron, his own time, when to get their daily bread humans could "never rest from labor and sorrow by day."[2] Lucretius also complained of lessening harvests, comparing the people among whom he lived to their happier ancestors:

> But the same Earth who nourishes them now
> Once brought them forth, and gave them, to their joy,
> Vineyards and shining harvests, pastures, arbors,
> And all this now our very utmost toil
> Can hardly care for, we wear down our strength
> Whether in oxen or in men, we dull

The edges of our ploughshares, and in return
Our fields turn mean and stingy, underfed,
And so today the farmer shakes his head,
More and more often sighing that his work,
The labor of his hands, has come to naught.
When he compares the present to the past,
The past was better, infinitely so.[3]

Both Hesiod and Lucretius subscribed to the antithesis of the idea of history as progress, which is not to say that the infertility of which they complained was a mere rhetorical device. Agricultural writers, too, spoke of a decline in productivity, resulting either from the senescence of Earth or from the failure of mankind to care for her. There is evidence of lower yields, farmers leaving land that could no longer support them, and deserted fields, not only in literature but also in laws enacted to counter these trends. Failure of the soil to support the people, whether through declining productivity or local increases in population, led to land hunger that was expressed in emigration and conquest of new territories. Large cities found it necessary to import grain from distant shores to feed their people.[4]

Agricultural decline was not constant—there were periods of improvement— and it did not follow the same course everywhere. Egypt, with the annual gift of fertile silt deposited by the Nile flood, was exceptional. Still, it is hard to avoid the impression that agriculture in major parts of the ancient world faltered, and that the situation was particularly bad during the late Roman Empire. Because agriculture was the basic and most widespread economic activity, agricultural decline was a problem of the greatest seriousness, with major effects on the natural environment. All ancient civilizations were agrarian. Other industries were less developed, making up a much smaller segment of the total economy than in modern times. Agriculture was by far the most important sphere of employment and investment. The fortunes of agriculture affected all other activities, and would therefore constitute an indicator of the degree to which the Greeks and Romans maintained or failed to maintain a healthy relationship to the natural environment. While agriculture was a way of life for those living at the subsistence level, for many of the affluent it was also a business engaged in for profit. It is necessary to review the nature of Mediterranean agriculture before considering the environmental problems connected with that way of life and business.

Mediterranean Agriculture

Greco-Roman agriculture was adapted to soils and climate that presented the farmer with challenges.[5] Rich soils well suited to cultivation do not cover the majority of Mediterranean lands; less than one-fifth of Greece's land is arable due to prevalent mountain ranges, and although Italy is better favored, the Apennine chain, often steep and formidable, runs the length of the peninsula. Pliny the Elder says the predominant soil, *terra rossa*, is difficult to work and weighs down hoes and plowshares with enormous clods.[6] When it dries, it forms a crust. All this augurs hard work for the farmer.

The Mediterranean climate, so deceptively pleasant, presents a dilemma to the native cultivator. As Hesiod said of the climate of his home Ascra, it was "bad in winter, sultry in summer, and good at no time"; in other words, not good for farming.[7] The rains, not overly abundant in most of the basin, come mainly in the colder months between October and April, when heat and light energy for growth is least available. Fortunately, temperatures rarely drop below freezing, except in the mountains, so growing winter crops is possible. The summer is hot and dry, making irrigation necessary for almost anything that matures in that season. There are important tasks for the farmer in virtually every month.

This farm on the south shore of Lake Lugano, Italy, strongly suggests the appearance of an ancient Roman farm. (1959)

Crops

Grains, grapes, and olives comprise the "Mediterranean triad" of agriculture. Grain, the source of bread, was the most important dietary staple. The crops were mainly barley and wheat, with some millet and panic grass; oats and rye do not do well in the dry conditions of Greece and Italy. Barley was commoner than wheat, cheaper, and not preferred, although the fact that sacrificial cakes for religious rites were made of barley indicates its traditional predominance. Winter wheat was planted in early fall and harvested in May or June, its success depending on winter rains. Spring wheat, harvested in fall and requiring irrigation, was grown less often. All grains preferred relatively flat, rich lowland soil.[8]

Legumes consisted in part of pulse crops such as lupines, vetch, kidney beans, peas, broad beans, lentils, and chickpeas, sown annually in spring and watered when in bloom. They provided food for animals as well as humans. Farmers also planted fodder crops such as alfalfa and clovers, which thrive best if irrigated.[9] Sesame, rape, turnips, and hemp were other common crops.

Vineyards

"Wine does of a truth moisten the soul and lulls our griefs to sleep," said Socrates.[10] It was the drink most often served in Greece and Rome, and vineyards occupied a major portion of the agricultural landscape. The grapevine is a perennial; it can be pruned so as to support itself, or trained on stakes, trellises, or trees. Trees were popular props, so that all three major food plants could grow in the same field: vines climbing up olive trees, with grain sown between the rows.[11] The vine prefers well-drained, rocky soil and can be planted on fairly steep hills, often terraced. Grapevines had to be protected against such pests as caterpillars and mice;[12] traps were set for foxes, which have a fabled love for grapes.[13] Cato the Elder says a vineyard of one hundred *jugera* (25 hectares or 63 acres) required two oxen, three donkeys, an overseer, his wife, and sixteen slaves.[14] The vintage came in September in Italy and Greece, when bunches of grapes were cut and placed in baskets, and then trodden by workers who had carefully washed their feet and wore clothes that absorbed sweat.[15] The must (juice) was put in pottery vats to ferment. Most wine was consumed within three or four years, and mixed with water before drinking. Drinking water was often flavored, and purified to some extent, with sour wine.

Slaves or donkeys operated these revolving double-cone grain mills in Pompeii, Italy (79 CE). (1994)

A vineyard near Pisa, Italy. (1994)

Kistoi, large vases used for oil, wine, or grains, in the archaeological site of Akrotiri (ca. 1625 BCE) on the island of Thera (Santorini), Greece. Study of dregs in the vessels establishes that the painted designs identified their contents. (1992)

Orchards

Varro once asked: "Is not Italy so covered with trees that it looks like one great orchard?"[16] Of the many fruit trees that grew there, and in other Mediterranean lands, the most prevalent was the olive. The fruit was sometimes treated and eaten, but more usually pressed for oil, a staple in cooking and the most important source of fat in the diets of Greeks. As the major export, olive oil was the economic mainstay of Athens. The trees require well-drained sites but can thrive in a variety of soils, so that many groves are sited on hillsides. Since trees had to be spaced between 8 and 18 m (25 and 60 feet) apart, and it took about fifteen years for a new plantation to produce well, they were more likely to be planted by landowners with capital and large holdings. So valuable were olive-producing trees that Athens enacted a law against uprooting more than two per year by any landholder.[17] Irrigation was often necessary, and pruning was essential. The fruit ripened in October, when harvesters spread cloths under the trees and beat the branches with long, slender poles.[18]

Among fruit trees, figs were favored. Ancient farmers practiced caprification, the fertilization of the fruit by attaching male branches of wild figs containing gall wasps to domestic trees.[19] Similarly, the role of pollen in getting date palms to set fruit was known. Other orchard trees included apple, pear, plum, apricot, pomegranate, carob, lemon, and citron. Some varieties were introduced from abroad: in 73 BCE, Lucullus introduced the cherry from Cerasus in Pontus.[20] The peach reached Asia Minor from China in the second century BCE by way of Persia, hence its Latin name, *malum Persicum*.[21] Nuts such as almonds, walnuts, and pistachios were also planted.

Agricultural Specialties

Market gardens, whose fresh produce was intended for timely sale, grew up close to large cities. Among their products were cabbage, asparagus, artichokes, cucumbers, garlic, onions, and leeks. Flax, the source of linen, was a prevalent winter crop in Egypt, where the Greeks encountered it. Much of Greece was too dry for flax, but it was sown as a spring crop in the Po Valley, moist parts of Spain, and the Black Sea coast.[22]

Animals in Agriculture

Almost every Mediterranean farm had domestic animals. Cattle were important for plowing and pulling carts, but their milk was not much used. Adapted to meadows and forests, cows ate not only grass, but also the leaves of low tree

A large, old olive tree in Agrigento, Sicily, Italy. Olive trees live and bear for centuries. (1994)

branches, giving pastures a parklike appearance. Horses were more useful in the military, chariot races, and transportation than in agriculture. To be able to afford horses conferred social dignity; one of the upper classes in Athens was called *hippeis* and a similar one at Rome the *equites*, both meaning "horse owners." At home on moist plains, horses did not do well in mountainous areas like most of Greece. The iron horseshoe was invented in the second century BCE; before that, horses went unshod or fitted with leather shoes.[23] More often seen carrying loads on the farm were donkeys or their vigorous hybrid offspring, mules. Sheep and goats were sources of milk, cheese, wool, hair, skins, and meat. They might be allowed to graze on crops before the plants flowered in order to keep them from going too much to leaf and to encourage seed development. Also, farmers sometimes grazed sheep in orchards to keep down surface growth and to manure the ground, but goats were kept out of orchards due to their penchant for eating tree leaves and bark.[24] Sheep were sheared twice a year, in spring and fall.[25] Pigs completed the mammalian component of the farm menagerie. Pork was the favorite meat of the Romans; there are fifty recipes for it in Pliny's cookbook. As forest animals, pigs enjoyed roaming in the woods to consume beechnuts, acorns, and chestnuts. There were many breeds of each farm species; especially prized varieties were widely imported.

Farmers often cultured eels and other fish in lakes or ponds. Beekeeping was much practiced (the art was regulated by Solon in 594 BCE) because honey was virtually the only sweetener known and beeswax was useful. Rough silk was made from native worms; Chinese silkworms were not introduced to the Mediterranean until the sixth century. Among farm birds, geese, ducks, and pigeons were common from early times. Peacocks, guinea fowl, and pheasants were sometimes kept.[26] Chickens are first mentioned in the sixth century BCE, having made a long journey from South Asia as domesticated birds.[27] Cockfighting soon became popular, and Themistocles included it in a festival at Athens after the Persian War.[28]

Agricultural Technology

Greek and Roman agricultural implements and machines were relatively simple, and many of them, or ones much like them, had been used for thousands of years. Technological innovation was not unknown but came slowly and met with resistance grounded in tradition. Typical of tools used in agriculture were the spade, hoe, mattock, and pick.[29] The plow never entirely replaced them because crops were often interplanted with trees and vines, and cultivation had to take care of the roots. Vines were pruned, and bunches of grapes cut, with special knives and billhooks. The simple wooden plow, even with an iron share, broke the soil without turning it over, so a field had to be plowed at least twice. This served to make cultivation labor-intensive. Horses were small, and the horse collar, which enabled a horse or mule to pull more efficiently, was introduced only in late antiquity, so plowing was usually done with oxen under a yoke. Seed was sown by broadcasting and plowed under. Harvesting was done with iron sickles. Grain was loosened from chaff by having animals tread on it, or by a threshing sledge, a heavy board with flints embedded in the underside. Later, small wheels sometimes replaced flints on the sledge (a Carthaginian innovation). After threshing, the grains were separated by winnowing, either throwing it into the wind with a pronged shovel, allowing the chaff to blow away, or by tossing it in a fan (*vanna*) or basket.

Mills for crushing grain and grinding it into flour showed technological advance.[30] The earliest devices were the mortar and pestle and the saddle quern (a stationary stone over which another is pushed forth by hand). The rotary quern, with a round upper stone revolving on a lower one, appeared around 600 BCE. The donkey-driven mill, used to crush silver ore at Laurion, was adapted to grind grain by 300 BCE. It had a hollow, waisted stone looking like two cones joined at a common, open vertex, which revolved on a lower conical stone. Grain thrown into the top would emerge as flour at the bottom.[31] The first Greek watermill had a vertical axle with the millstone mounted directly on it, so that the wheel had to turn horizontally. Later the undershot waterwheel (where the water flows beneath the wheel) was connected to a millstone by gears. The great mill at Barbegal, Provence, in the following century, had sixteen overshot wheels (with the water falling on the wheels from above) in two parallel sets of eight each, and could meet the needs of 80,000 people.[32] Presses operated by wedge, beam, or screw were used for grapes and olives.

While ancient agricultural techniques persisted for centuries with some degree of success, technology failed to sufficiently advance production. Varro advised "a degree of experimentation" in agricultural methods, but innovation was rare.[33] The *vallus*, an animal-drawn reaping machine from northern Gaul, is mentioned by Roman writers from the first century onward, but it was not adopted to any major extent on Mediterranean croplands.[34] Other technical improvements of the northern barbarians, like the wheeled plow, did not catch on because they were not suited to light southern soils.[35]

Environmental Problems of Agriculture

There were several possible reasons for the declining yields about which so many ancient authors complained. Plant growth, on which animal and human subsistence depends, is governed by a number of ecological factors. These in-

119

clude such variables as solar energy; air supply and temperature; water supply; availability of mineral and organic plant foods; the action of other organisms that consume, compete, or cooperate; the presence or absence of toxic substances; depth and other physical properties of the soil; and the genetic qualities of the seed. Unfavorability in any one of these variables may produce temporary or permanent agricultural decline, and some of them presented problems to the Greeks and Romans.

Climate

The Mediterranean climate has abundant sunshine and generally equable temperatures. The most limiting factor is the light rainfall, coupled with a high rate of evaporation that prevails over much of the basin in summer. Precipitation is extremely variable from year to year, which makes dry farming a chancy enterprise. Climate is a factor over which human beings had almost no control, other than choosing to plant at times and in places that were likely to be favorable. Some of the desertification along the margins of the Sahara in North Africa toward the end of the Roman period may have been exacerbated by climate change, although human disturbance of the natural environment, particularly deforestation, seems the primary cause.

Soil Exhaustion

Plants absorb nutrients from the soil; if these nutrients are not replaced, yields will diminish from year to year. Apparently this happened in large parts of the Mediterranean area, and nutrient depletion increased through the centuries. Many Latin writers connected the deteriorating situation in their own days with exhaustion of the soil.[36] Columella remarked that no one alive in his day could recall when the grain harvest produced as much as four times the seed that had been sown.[37] Why? Were farmers unaware of methods to restore depleted soil? On the contrary, Greek and Roman books on agriculture show that authors had a thorough understanding of intensive agriculture and knew how to keep soil productive. And theirs was not just theoretical knowledge, but represented the accumulated experience of peasants and landowners. When they were not hindered by economic or environmental crises, Greek and Roman farmers were probably as productive as any before the nineteenth century.

Columella attacked the idea, held by Lucretius and others, that Earth produces less and less because she is growing old. Unlike that of an aging woman, the fertility of Earth, he holds, can be restored by proper agricultural practices that any farmer should know.[38] The use of fertilizers was one of these methods. "Sowing must not take place except on ground that has been manured," maintained Pliny the Elder.[39] Farmers knew the value of animal manure, and compared that of different species. Sheep and goats, it was said, produced richer dung than cattle or horses. Pigeon droppings were especially prized, and keepers of the temple on Delos made a tidy income by selling droppings of the sacred birds in their dovecote.[40] Human waste was also used; Athens piped city sewage out through the Dipylon Gate to a reservoir and then by brick-lined canals to fields on the nearby plain. Workers under the supervision of a town official, the *coprologos*, removed and then spread human waste on local fields.[41] The best writers recommended composting.[42] Such soil-enriching crops as lupine, bean, and vetch could be plowed under as green manure. Broken or powdered limestone or chalk was applied as mineral fertilizer. Marble was burnt to make fertilizer, a process that consumed excessive amounts of wood and charcoal and sometimes destroyed works of art. Marl (a loamy mixture of clay, shells, and lime) was mined and applied to the land. On Aegina, burrows excavated to remove marl were adapted for underground homes by people called Myrmidons (ants).[43]

One of the oldest methods of restoring soil fertility was fallowing, combined with repeated plowing to bury weeds. Hesiod said that fallowing is "the guardian against death and ruin."[44] More economical is crop rotation, where soil-restoring legumes are planted in alternate years with other crops. The ancients observed that legumes enrich the soil, although the reason was unknown.[45] Ancient authors gave various rotational schemes, but their use in the Mediterranean was limited by the small size of farms and the necessity of planting each species only where soil and exposure would favor it.[46]

Seed selection was another way to improve yields. Planters favored the best varieties and saved seed from plants in their prime.[47] Hybridization occurred, although it was not understood. Theophrastus's observation that changes that "take away from the nature of the plant" are noticed in the third year after the seed of annuals is planted in a new environment may reflect the fact that, in hybrid crosses, it is the third generation that exhibits variation.[48]

Land Ethics

It is clear from this sampling of the vast store of Greco-Roman agricultural knowledge that ancient farmers knew how to treat the soil. Xenophon enunciated a basis for agricultural land ethics when he commented, "Earth willingly teaches righteousness to those who can learn; for the better she is treated, the more good things she gives in return."[49] Only because he possessed the agricultural competence to restore exhausted land did he offer this advice to those who wanted to gain honestly in land speculation: buy mistreated land, improve it through proper methods, and sell it at a profit.[50] Cicero voiced a similar idea, saying "the farmer keeps an open account with the Earth."[51]

When the ancient farmer was able to carry out the principles he understood, he could usually maintain the fertility of the soil. Farms were generally small. In Athens, for example, they varied from 2.5 to 50 hectares (6 to 125 acres), and Alcibiades's 28 hectares (70 acres) was considered large.[52] The share of each colonist at Metapontum was 6 hectares (15 acres). Allotments for Romans in the Gracchan land reforms were 7.5 hectares (19 acres), and Julius Caesar's veterans received just over 16 hectares (40 acres). It may well be that on smaller subsistence farms where traditional peasant wisdom was applied, productivity held up better than it did on the huge Roman ranches (*latifundia*) under the stresses of monoculture and overgrazing. That in spite of a wealth of agricultural knowledge there was decline, particularly in the late Roman Empire, indicates that other factors—economic, political, or military—prevented maintenance or regeneration of the land base.[53]

Erosion Control

The intervention of nonagricultural factors may be seen clearly in the case of erosion control. Certainly erosion, the physical removal of the soil by water or wind, is the most radical form of soil exhaustion and the least amenable to restoration. Erosion was well known to Greek and Roman landowners, and they took measures such as ditching and terracing to control it in hilly terrain. Terracing was commonly used in the Greek islands and mountains; parts of Italy such as the slopes of Vesuvius, Etna, and the Apennines; and in Roman provinces.[54] It survives today with its original purpose. I recall arriving in terraced vineyard country just east of Delphi in central Greece on the morning after a violent thunderstorm. I spent some time watching a farmer recovering soil that had washed down off a terrace by shoveling it into baskets, loading them two at a time onto the pack saddle of a single donkey, leading the animal back up to the top of the terrace, and emptying the baskets there. The same scene, including replacing stones in terrace walls, must have been repeated countless times by that farmer's predecessors. Such antierosional measures are labor-intensive.[55] If anything interrupts the labor, walls collapse, ditches are choked, and erosion accelerates. Erosion due to lack of maintenance was surely sometimes the fault of absentee landlords who failed to keep watch over what was happening on their land. Warfare especially could prevent maintenance by making a territory unsafe, by conscripting farmers, or by killing them. Rural populations were the manpower resource of ancient armies, and as men were recruited to battle, the land often suffered. Study of underwater siltation at the mouths of Mediterranean rivers indicates that erosion was more rapid during periods when a particular drainage basin was the locale of warfare.[56]

Water Supply: Problems Related to Irrigation

As mentioned above, irrigation was a necessary supplement to rainfall. Water was taken from springs, streams, and rivers and diverted into fields, pastures, orchards, vineyards, and market gardens. It was time-honored practice; Homer mentions it,[57] and there is a germ of truth in the myth that Danaus first brought irrigation to Argos from Egypt.[58] Plato provided for its regulation in his ideal state.[59] History records that governments were active in overseeing water use. Themistocles, as water commissioner in Athens, dedicated a statue of a water-bearing maiden from the fines paid by people who had stolen from the public supply to irrigate their own farms.[60] The laws of Justinian defined irrigation rights, allowing for the use of all the water in a stream.[61]

Cisterns, dams, and reservoirs were constructed to save winter flow for use in the dry season. Water was conducted through aqueducts and canals to the farms. Channels were of varying diameter; inscriptions survive that tell how long

Terraces, originally for vines, on the island of Samos, Greece. (1990)

owners could let water run into their holdings.[62] An aqueduct near Rome used for irrigation was the Aqua Crabra. Roman irrigation works in North Africa were impressive in size and extent, including aqueducts and masonry dams to control and divert the waters of rivers that today almost never carry a usable flow, owing to deforestation and desertification.[63] Several devices could raise water from channels. The shaduf, a pivoted, counterbalanced pole with a bucket, was known in early Egypt and continues to be used today. Pumps such as the spiral Archimedean screw and the two-cylinder Ctesibian force pump were employed from Hellenistic times into the Roman Empire. A number of waterwheels like those described for mining and milling were also adapted for irrigation.[64]

A troublesome problem of irrigation is salinization. It can be avoided by good drainage, but in poorly drained basins, salt can concentrate in the soil to the point where plant growth suffers. Coastal marshes and river deltas where the flushing action of fresh water is impeded suffered salinization from encroaching seawater.

Agricultural Policy

Governments in ancient times were concerned with agricultural production, often undertaking major works of irrigation and drainage. The state's motivation was not only the need to feed the people, but also to secure resources for its activities.

Taxation

Taxes bore heavily on the agricultural sector because it was by far the predominant source of production. The administration and the army depended on these taxes for salaries, equipment, and supplies. As long as agriculture was productive and flourishing, the state was strong, but when productivity was low, the tax base would shrink, and then even a relatively light tax would seem oppressive to farmers.[65] From the early third century onward, the Roman government collected an annual tax, the *annona militaris*, which did not vary with the yield of the harvest. Such a tax encouraged the depletion of the land while depriving farmers of the means to restore it; much marginal land must have gone out of production as a result. Contributing to the decline of the Roman Empire was the fact that primary producers were unable to uphold their essential part in the economy because of repeated increases in taxation, which they could not pay due to low productivity. The dwindling of population in the late Roman Empire resulted from the inability of rural families, after paying rent, taxes, and other exactions, to rear enough children to offset the high death rate.[66]

The Impact of the Military

Greek and Roman governments expected agriculture to provide resources for the military, and they placed unsupportable pressure on the agrarian segment of society. The result was that agriculture failed even where, with proper care, the soil could have produced adequate harvests. To this must be added the devastation of warfare itself. Ancient armies lived off the land. Deliberate environmental warfare like that waged by the Spartans in Attica during the Peloponnesian War, when they burnt farms and chopped down olive orchards, was not rare in Greece.[67] The destruction caused by war in the Roman Empire was particularly acute during the third century, when almost-constant military campaigns of rival claimants for the imperial throne devastated the countryside.

Expansion of Agriculture into New Territories

One effort of ancient governments was to encourage farmers to open new land. If the total production acreage could be enlarged, the tax base would increase, and the effects of declining productivity might be countered, at least in part. Removing forests or draining marshes opened new, undepleted soil for planting, although crops would visibly decline after a few years, as Columella noted. A study of lowland deposits near Rome showed that in the second century BCE, a period when urban settlers opened new lands to cultivation, the rate of erosion was ten times that before the disturbance.[68] That there would be further bad results of removing the wetlands, with the disappearance of fish and wildfowl that depended on lakes and marshes, hardly came to the notice of ancient writers. Lucretius saw one aspect of what was going on:

> The opulence of the Earth
> Led folk to clear its wealth, convert the woods
> To open harvest-fields, kill the wild beasts . . .
> [Woodcutters] made the woods climb higher up the mountains,
> Yielding the foothills to be tilled and tended.[69]

On disturbed land, introduced cultigens and weeds replaced native species, while many plants disappeared. Sometimes these had been valuable, as in the case of wild silphium, a gum-producing plant used as a spice and a medicine that had been the mainstay of the trade economy of Cyrene, where it was endemic until excessive collection and grazing extirpated it.[70]

Governments and speculators drained lakes and marshes through tunnels and ditches to open acreage to agriculture.[71] The Spartans drained marshes in the Eurotas valley, but the greatest achievement of the kind was the draining of Lake Copais in the Hellenistic period.[72] Theophrastus noted that the draining of country in Thessaly and Thrace produced marked changes in local weather.[73] Roman projects of the middle to late republic and early empire are too numerous to list. Many were successful, but some failed despite repeated attempts. For example, the Pontine Marshes in Italy are said to have been drained by Appius Claudius (312 BCE), Cornelius Cethegus (182 BCE), Julius Caesar, Augustus, Nerva, Trajan, and finally by Theodoric the Ostrogoth in the sixth century. Any lack of success of this and other projects has been attributed to inadequate technical knowledge, incompetent or fraudulent workmanship, and failure to appreciate the magnitude of the problems.[74]

Abandonment of the Land

A major problem faced by the ancients, the Romans in particular, was that of abandoned fields (*agri deserti*). Livy observed that deserted areas in Italy had been formerly thickly populated.[75] In Campania alone under Theodosius, there were 528,000 *jugera* (135,000 hectares or 330,000 acres) that had lapsed from cultivation.[76] Parts of North Africa, later desert, once had extensive groves of olives, as olive presses found in archaeological sites there testify. It may seem strange to discuss this problem when the expansion of agriculture into new lands was just mentioned above. But the two processes often went on at the same time. Farmers abandoned land that had become unproductive because of erosion and other forms of soil exhaustion, and moved to lands recently cleared or drained whose fertility had not yet been sapped. As noted above, deforested land will produce good crops for a few years before it becomes exhausted. Vladimir Simkhovitch remarked, "What happens when the fields fail to reward labor and are abandoned? If the highlands are not capable of covering themselves readily with vegetation, the topsoil is washed away and a desert is left, while the deserted lowlands with clogged-up drainage are bound to turn swampy and unhealthful."[77]

Governments tried their best to keep land under cultivation. Ownership of unclaimed or abandoned land was offered at times to anyone who would occupy and cultivate it.[78] If the land in question was deeply eroded, such incentives would have been ineffective because no one could have made it productive without expending large amounts of capital. But in cases where damage to the land was not severe, a number of years of fallow, even without plowing, may have helped restore fertility.

Replacement of Cultivation by Stock Raising

A process similar to abandonment in some of its effects was the conversion of large areas from cropland to pasture. In many cases it may be difficult to distinguish one from the other, since owners of extensive *latifundia* devoted to ranching often acquired abandoned cropland for their holdings, and forced smallholders off the land in order to take control of it. Latin writers comment on this change in land use, which began when rich Romans appropriated public land. Pliny complained, "the large estates are ruining Rome as well as its provinces."[79] Seneca asked the owner of a *latifundium*, "How far will you extend the boundaries of your possessions? An estate which formerly held a whole nation is now too narrow for a single lord."[80] The trend had been viewed as a problem ever since the end of the war with Hannibal, which had depopulated much of rural Italy. The preference of large landowners for livestock over cultivation is epitomized in a comment attributed by Cicero to the first Roman agricultural writer: "Cato, when asked what is the most profitable thing in the management of one's estate, answered: 'Good pasturage.' 'What is the next best?' 'Fairly good pasturage.' 'What is the third best?' 'Bad pasturage.' 'What is the fourth best?' 'Tilling the soil.' "[81]

Livestock ranches could be run profitably with a few trained slaves, much less labor than required for crops. But Varro differed, holding that huge estates given over to raising stock were harmful because they deprived arable land of the services of animals in controlling vegetation and providing manure. The conversion of arable land into pasturage was punishable by Roman law, but the law proved ineffective; the wealthiest Roman citizens opposed it. Declining Italian grain production was made up by imports from the provinces. From the late republic on, Rome brought in countless shiploads of grain to feed the urban population, and it is estimated that these imports supplied three-fourths of the city's food.[82] The distribution of cheap grain in Rome helped to ruin grain production in central Italy and reinforced the tendency to convert from crop production to grazing.

Declining Population

The inevitable results of chronic agricultural decline were food shortages, famines, and depopulation. During many periods, and certainly after the second century, most of the Roman Empire had a declining population and agricultural work force, resulting in lowered food production. Falling population aroused concern, particularly in regard to Roman citizens, and laws encouraging marriage and childbearing were enacted. Augustus provided an award of 1,000 sesterces to every head of family who produced a child.[83] The legal rights of childless citizens were curtailed. Conscientious emperors from Nerva to Constantine established charitable institutions such as alimentary foundations to feed orphans and other needy children.[84] Diocletian tried to counter the effect of a declining number of children raised to maturity by means of the Edict of Occupations, which required bureaucrats and military men to provide sons who would fill their official positions when they retired or died. But this measure did not touch the root of the problem, which lay in the inability of the land, as the Romans treated it, to support an increasing population.

Conclusion

The environmental sustainability of agriculture in the Mediterranean basin can scarcely be doubted, so long as the limitations of the Mediterranean ecosystem are recognized. Measures must be taken to prevent erosion; to maintain the biotic community that comprises fertile soil; to preserve and restore the forests, wetlands, and water resources whose interaction with agricultural areas is necessary to sustain them; and to limit population growth. It might appear that ancient societies never reached the capacity of the Mediterranean basin to sustain agriculture because today the area supports a higher population than existed there in ancient times. But one may ask whether the present energy budget of Mediterranean agriculture, with high inputs of chemical fertilizers and insecticides, and high outputs of air, water, and soil pollution, is sustainable.

The small farm typical of ancient agriculture described by such writers as Xenophon, Varro, and Columella may offer a model of sustainability. That farm was a complex ecological unit. A wide variety of annual and perennial plants, shrubs, and trees were grown, each in the portion of the land best suited for it by soil, topography, and exposure. Sections of forest, whether original or replanted, were used as woodlots, and trees were planted to shelter fields and buildings from wind and sun. Animals grazed on fallow land, or among the trees to control vegetative growth, and enriched the soil with their manure. The topography of the zone is generally more congenial to small farms of the kind that native peasantry developed than to vast stretches given over to one crop in monoculture that is vulnerable to insects and diseases. Agriculture balanced with nature is a state of affairs that can be upset by a tax structure that makes unreasonable economic demands. It requires peace and is disordered by war. It also requires a willingness to try new methods carefully, to recognize error, and to listen to Earth and to be taught by her. As an ancient writer said, "It is thus that the Earth conceives and yields her harvest so that food is provided for all the creatures, if winds and rains are neither unseasonable nor excessive; but if anything goes amiss in the matter, it is not deity we should charge with the fault, but humanity, who have not ordered their life aright."[85]

Eight

Industrial Technology and Environmental Damage

That human technology can damage the Earth is not just a modern idea. The elder Pliny remarked, "Mountains were made by nature herself to serve as a kind of framework for holding together the inner parts of the earth . . . We quarry them and haul them away for a mere whim."[1] He also noted the human failure to restore and reclaim: "But least of all do we search for means of healing [the wounds caused by mines in Mother Earth], for how few in their digging are inspired by the desire to cure!"[2] Ancient technology was capable of creating works of remarkable size, but it also inflicted scars on the landscape that can still be seen, from the quarries of Pentelicus in Greece to the mining pits of Spain to more widespread erosion resulting from the removal of vegetation to supply charcoal burners. There was other damage that is difficult to assess today but noticed by ancient writers: the pollution of air and water by poisons released in extractive activities and industrial processes. In addition to its ritual and moral meaning, pollution was also given something like its modern sense of contaminating water, air, and earth with the waste products of human activities, including industrial processes.[3]

Technological Capacity

According to Greek myth, Prometheus originated technology by bringing fire from the Sun and instructing mortals in its use. That the stolen gift was a dangerous one may be symbolized by the wrath of Zeus, who punished Prometheus by chaining him to a crag in the Caucasus Mountains and causing him to be tortured daily.[4] Greek and Roman thought remained ambivalent about technology, both proud of the great works of humankind and sure that these works marred the Earth, challenged the gods, and called forth divine retribution. The extent of damage done by technology to the environment depends in large part on the efficiency of machines and the nature and magnitude of available energy sources. In general, more powerful technologies produce effects that are deeper and more widespread, effects produced directly and indirectly through demand for resources such as fuel. In the ancient world, the sources of energy available to industry consisted of human and animal labor, wood and charcoal fires, waterpower, and (for transportation) wind power. Of these, human labor either directly or by means of machines undoubtedly accomplished the most. Oxen were used for pulling; horses, mules, and donkeys for carrying and pulling. Small size and the lack of an efficient harness reduced the efficiency of equines, particularly horses. Wood and its partially oxidized product, charcoal, was by far the most common fuel, although other vegetable substances were also burnt. Coal was known, but rarely used, and petroleum was regarded as a curiosity. Waterpower was harnessed by wheels, and wind power by sails. The steam engine and windmill, both known to the Greeks of Alexandria, received no common practical use.

The mechanical engineering devices invented by the Greeks and Romans or adopted by them from older civilizations or from the so-called barbarian peoples beyond their frontiers increased in number and sophistication as the centuries passed. Technological improvement was not rapid or steady, however, and there were retreats as well as advances. The simplest machines, known from much earlier times, were the lever, the wedge, and the wheel and axle. The engineering scientist Archimedes of Syracuse, who boasted concerning the lever, "give me a place to stand and I will move the earth," was not the only one to develop applications of simple machines.[5] Winches (horizontal drums around which ropes or chains wound) were used to move cranes and hoists and to drag heavy objects such as blocks of stone or ships. From 515 BCE onward, cranes lifted column sections and other architectural members; before that, levers and rocking cradles had sufficed.[6] A crane used to lower an actor onto the stage in the Greek theater, the "machine" of the (Latin) *deus ex machina*, was powered by a man using his weight to revolve a *carchesion*, or cage wheel. The pulley, which provides mechanical advantage in lifting, was known in Assyria in the eighth century BCE and was adopted in Greece not long afterward. Multiple pulleys appeared by the fifth century BCE. The screw principle, an innovation of the third century BCE, was used in Archimedes's pump, a device used widely in irrigation and mining that raised water by revolving a broad-threaded screw inside an inclined tube. At the same time, Ctesibius of Alexandria described the two-cylinder piston pump; it was cast by the lost wax technique in Roman times, and archaeologists have uncovered more than twenty examples.[7] Gears were developed with sophisticated ratios and arrangements; the most noteworthy example is the Anticythera Machine, an astronomical and calendrical computer of the first century BCE that was probably made in Alexandria.[8] In the same century Vitruvius described the waterwheel in its undershot form: that is, one in which the water revolves the wheel by passing underneath it. The overshot wheel appeared a century or two later. Both forms were widely used to power grinding wheels and saws, and a wheel turned by animal, human, or waterpower raised water in mines and in irrigation.

Technological innovation occurred at various times during this period. Not all of the machines invented were widely adopted. An intriguing example of an unproductive invention was the prototype steam engine described by Hero of Alexandria.[9] Hero mounted a free-spinning, hollow sphere on a pipe and bracket on the lid of a vessel in which water was boiled. Steam rose through the pipe into the sphere and escaped through open pipes, bent at right angles, on the surface of the sphere, causing it to rotate. While this engine was adapted to no practical use, Hero does describe other elements of machinery such as pistons and valves that conceivably could have been combined with the steam principle he had discovered to produce a useful steam engine. It is interesting to speculate why the steam engine was not developed further, and also why Hero's windmill, which he used to work the water pump of a musical organ, was not adapted in ancient times to the more prevalent uses it received during the medieval period.[10]

Technological innovation depends on a body of knowledge and experience leading up to a new application, a need for the new device, its efficiency and therefore economic viability, and social receptivity to it.[11] The first two certainly existed for the steam engine and windmill. The windmill, but possibly not the steam engine, could have been made efficient at the time. Why the Romans were not receptive is a puzzle. It has often been said that their use of slaves inhibited technological advance, and there are stories about their rejection of specific inventions. Emperor Tiberius is said to have heard that an unbreakable, flexible glass had been invented, and promptly to have ordered the invention suppressed and the inventor's workshop destroyed because he feared the substance would be more valuable than gold and would depress the monetary system. Pliny the Elder, who doubted its truth, recorded the story. Vespasian, a later emperor, is reported to have rejected a new column-moving machine on the grounds that it would do the work of many men and produce unemployment.[12] Yet efficient cranes were in common use in Roman construction, and the existence of slavery did not prevent the acceptance of many new machines and industrial processes, some of which were operated by slave labor. Of course the adoption of these machines would have increased the impact on—and exacerbated the problems of—the environment.

The sheer magnitude of the ability of ancient technology to alter the landscape may be illustrated by the dimensions of Roman roads, which were constructed as not only as straight as possible, but permanently and deeply, almost like buried walls, as Plutarch aptly described them: "The roads were driven through the countryside, exactly in a straight line, partly paved with hewn stone, and partly laid with impacted gravel. Gullies were filled in, intersecting torrents and ravines were bridged, so that the layout of the road on both sides was the same, and the whole work looked level and beautiful."[13] The labor and materials expended on road construction and the extent of changes made to the countryside were greater than might have been required for an adequate system. In order to lessen a grade south of Rome, a road was cut 35 m (117 feet) deep through solid rock, and another, the Via Cassia, has one road cut 1,486 m (4,875 feet) long, 20 m (66 feet) deep, and 6 m (20 feet) wide. The total length of the Roman road network at the end of the second century has been estimated at 90,000 km (56,000 miles) of major highways, more than enough to circle the world twice, and 320,000 km (200,000 miles) of smaller roads, in all almost long enough to reach the Moon.[14]

Extractive Industries

The industries that involve direct removal of materials from the earth include mining, quarrying, and digging of various substances that are the raw materials for pottery, glass, brick, concrete, mortar, fertilizer, and the like. These human activities impact the earth, producing pits, tunnels, and underground cave-like chambers. Such scars in turn expose the landscape to erosion and allow chemicals to leach into water at a faster rate than would occur under natural conditions. In addition, these industries and their associated processing industries such as metallurgy and ceramics place demands on forests for wood for construction, and wood and charcoal for fuel.

Mining

The Greek playwright Aeschylus put into Prometheus's mouth the claim to have given to mortals the knowledge of metals and mining:

Next the treasures of the earth,

The bronze, iron, silver, gold hidden deep down—who else

But I can claim to have found them first?[15]

According to Lucretius, however, humans discovered metals when they set forest fires and found them melted, oozing out of veins in the earth. They experimented with the stuff and found they could fashion it into tools and weapons.[16] The Greeks and Romans inherited from earlier civilizations the knowledge of a variety of metals and continued to exploit them, developing new methods along the way.

The most important metals and the ores from which they extracted them were gold, from auriferous quartz; silver, from argentiferous galena; copper, from chalcopyrite and chalcocite; tin, from cassiterite; lead, from galena; iron, from pyrites and hematite; zinc, from calamine; and mercury, from cinnabar.[17] Ore extraction methods included placer mining (washing the material from alluvial sand and gravel), open-pit mining, and tunneling into veins deep below the earth. To these, the Romans added hydraulic mining, in which forceful flows of water were directed on ores to wash them down to places where they could be recovered.

Mining extended to virtually every area of the ancient Mediterranean basin. The Athenians inherited the works of their Mycenaean ancestors, who had mined silver at Laurion since before 1500 BCE. Silver mines on the island of Thasos had been worked by the Phoenicians before the Greeks.[18] The Spartans had an iron mine, the source of fine weapons, in southern Laconia. Deceleia, a foothill suburb of Athens whose capture by the Spartans helped them win the Peloponnesian War, was particularly valuable because of its mines. Philip of Macedon conquered Chalcidice chiefly so he could exploit the placer gold of Mount Pangaeus. Alexander the Great took a *metalleutes* (mining engineer and prospector) named Gorgus with him to India, where he found salt, silver, and gold.[19] Like the Greeks, the Romans looked down on mining as degrading labor, though they were willing to profit by it. Italy was dotted with mines that had been worked by the skilled Etruscans and other pre-Roman peoples. They found iron on Elba, tin in Gaul, and copper at Tres Minas and elsewhere in Spain, a province whose exploitation for metals by the Romans became famous. The First Book of Maccabees, for example, remarks: "Now Judas had heard what the Romans had done in the country of Spain for the winning of the silver and the gold which is there."[20] Tin, used in bronze manufacture, was taken from mine tunnels in Cornwall.[21] The conqueror of Dacia, Trajan, enriched his imperial treasury with gold from mines there. Roman mines were scattered from northern Britain to the eastern desert ranges of Egypt. The mines mentioned here are by no means all that existed, but they indicate the number and variety of those worked in ancient times.

Many of these mines were of respectable size, even by modern standards. At Laurion, more than 2,000 vertical shafts gave access to over 140 km (87 miles) of tunnels.[22] Some Roman silver mines in Spain were about 245 m (800 feet) deep. The Rio Tinto mines had eight levels of galleries about 7.6 m (25 feet) apart. Spanish silver mines produced nine million denarii per year at the height of their productivity, and those near Carthago Nova alone employed 40,000 men in 179 BCE.[23] Six mines in southern England during the second century produced 550 metric tons of iron per year.[24]

Since in theory natural resources such as metallic ores belonged to the sovereign power, the state supervised their exploitation. When a new ore body of gold or silver came to light, a gold rush may have ensued as miners flocked to enrich themselves, but the officials were not far behind with their rules and contracts. One such a scene occurred at Ivrea (Eporedia) in the foothills of the Pennine Alps around 150 BCE. Because coinage was predominantly gold and silver, the mines of precious metals increasingly became property of state treasuries. Laurion belonged to the city government of Athens and was administered by a democratically chosen board. The Roman Emperor Tiberius began the practice of acquiring all gold and silver mines for the imperial treasury, and by the time of Vespasian the process was complete.[25] Hadrian and his successors controlled the mines, leasing them to contractors. Sometimes public officials directed the operation of mines, but more commonly state-owned mines were leased to syndicates of private entrepreneurs who often employed slave labor. Slaves were hired from contractors at an agreed wage that was paid to the contractor, not the slave.[26] Condemned criminals often suffered sentencing to labor in the mines.

Greek and Roman miners accomplished work on an amazing scale considering the level of their technology. Their tools are similar to those still in use until recently. Picks of horn, antler, and stone were employed in early times. Copper and bronze are softer and more brittle than many kinds of stone, so iron was later used extensively for mining tools. Iron picks dating to around 500 BCE were found in a mine on the island of Siphnos.[27] A pick with a curved blade, about 21.5 cm (8.5 in) long, was typical at Laurion. Stone hammers persisted in some places until the fourth century, when they were replaced by iron hammers. A hammer was used to drive the gad, called *xois* in Greek, a spike used to break rock or ore. Roman gads often had an eyelet fitted with a wooden handle to reduce the chances of the miner hitting his hand with the hammer. Where there was room and a vein rich enough to justify the effort, battering rams of up to 68 kg (150 lb) were used to break the matrix. To move broken ore, there were rakes with wooden handles and flat or spoon-shaped, short-handled wooden spades. Archaeology has revealed many other types of tools, including wedges, crowbars, hoes, and metal saws. To carry ore along the tunnels there were baskets, or leather bags with shoulder straps like backpacks. These could be attached to ropes and wound to the surface by cranes, capstans (vertical cylinders rotated manually, used for hoisting weights by winding in a cable), winches, or animal power. Otherwise miners could climb ladders, sometimes made of notched tree trunks.

Another method of breaking rocks, safer in an open-cut mine than in a tunnel but used in both, was to heat the rock with fire to a high temperature and then pour vinegar on it; the sudden cooling would contract and crack it. Wine or vinegar was considered superior to water for this purpose because the acidity helped break down limestone. Hannibal used this method to open a road for his elephants through the Alps.[28] As shafts and tunnels lengthened, dangerous sections might be lined or supported with timbers. Bodies of ore were often undermined and deliberately collapsed by removing stone or wooden supports.[29]

Working in shafts and tunnels requires artificial light, and in ancient times this meant burning wood or using a torch made of splinters of softwood or skin soaked in fat or a lamp consisting of a shallow stone or ceramic dish filled with oil and supplied with a wick. Such illumination devices, combined with the use of fire in quarrying, created a need for ventilation. Shafts were opened and air encouraged to move through them by waving fans or linen flaps.[30] The air leaving the mine was inevitably polluted.

Another constant problem in mines was drainage; along with the need for air supply, it limited the depth to which shafts and tunnels could be sunk. Where topography permitted, tunnels could be dug at a downward incline to the surface to divert underground rivers. One such drainage tunnel 2 km (1.25 miles) long exists in a mine at Coto Fortuna in Spain. Elsewhere, water had to be bailed with buckets or baskets, or by some more sophisticated means such as the Archimedean screw (Greek *cochlias*; Latin *cochlea*) described above, piston pumps, or waterwheels. Fragments of a large wooden waterwheel that was used to drain the deep workings of a gold mine were discovered at a Roman mine in Dolaucothi in southwest Wales.[31] A "nest" of eight waterwheels in series was found in a Spanish Roman mine at Rio Tinto, showing a further development of technology.[32] In hydraulic mining, favored by the Romans, the initial problem was to bring a sufficient flow of rapidly moving water to the ore, then to provide for the recovery of valuable material, and, finally, drainage. Using a strong current of water brought from high altitudes and conducted through canals or aqueducts that often consisted of troughs of timber, they brought the river to the ore and then to settling tanks for separation. This meant the redirection of streams from their natural channels, as well as their pollution with many sub-stances, some poisonous. Not all impurities could be precipitated in settling tanks, as some of them were soluble.

THE SILVER MINES AT LAURION

As Pericles told his fellow citizens at a time of crisis, "You must realize the power of Athens, and feed your eyes upon her from day to day, till love of her fills your hearts."[33] The economic and military power of Athens hinged on silver. It came from mines near Laurion, in Athenian territory, and was struck into coins called "owls" because they bore on one side an owl, sacred bird of Athena, goddess of war and wisdom, whose head appeared on the obverse. So dependable was the purity (99%) and quality of the coin that it became standard in Greece and beyond. How much silver was produced during the period of greatest activity? The mines yielded silver, lead, and other metals from the second millennium BCE, but prodigious silver production began with the discovery of a rich ore vein in 483 BCE. The figure reported by the Aristotelian *Constitution of Athens*[34] is 100 talents, equal to 2.6 metric tons, enough to make 600,000 drachmas worth of coins. It happened between two Persian invasions that threatened Athens's exis-tence, when Themistocles got the assembly to appropriate the windfall to build 200 warships.[35]

Themistocles's navy defeated the Persians at Salamis, securing Greek survival. Aeschylus, who fought at Salamis, refers to Laurion in his plays as "rich new god-given treasure . . . sudden gifts not hoped before!"[36] In the years that fol-lowed, ore was accessible, the need was great, the supply of slaves was plentiful, and output rose to 200 talents or more, continuing high during the fifth century. Laurion silver undergirded Athenian naval supremacy, enabling Athens to free Greek cities from Persian rule. The power of Athens reached its zenith under Pericles, who began the works whose remains still crown the Acropolis. The Parthenon required 469 talents of silver over fifteen years, most of which came from Laurion. During the Peloponnesian War, Spartan incursions attacked the mines, but production revived during the months the Spartans were absent. Nicias, the biggest supplier of slaves to Laurion, arranged a truce, but silver making was interrupted again when the Spartans, at the advice of Nicias's trai-torous rival Alcibiades, built a year-round fort in Attica and encouraged the ill-treated mine slaves to desert. Twenty thousand escaped and production ceased, recovering when the war ended.[37]

In the fourth century BCE, Athens revived and upgraded the mines, recover-ing part of her empire. Athens went on to flourish under Lycurgus (338 to 326 BCE), again with an annual production of 200 talents. But by 323 BCE, ores were exhausted and production negligible. Average annual production from 483 to 326 BCE can be estimated at 100 talents. The human cost during this period was horrendous. Thousands of slaves—men, women, and children owned by affluent citizens with contracts granted by city magistrates—did heavy work under hellish conditions including tight spaces, a lack of oxygen, danger of collapse, oppressive heat, poisons, long hours underground, and poor food. The silver produced annually was about 2.6 tons, but silver represented a tiny percentage of the ores, averaging one part silver to 429 parts lead. Humans were exposed to lead by breathing dust or the volatile lead vapor released by the smelting process. Lead poisoning helps explain the short lifespans of mine slaves—they typically died after working four to nine years.

The environmental costs incurred by the mine were also great. Effects on surrounding ecosystems included suppression of vegetation, lead ingestion by herbivores, and its concentration in the food chain by predators. Huge piles of waste accumulated, including slag from smelting. Many kilometers of underground tunnels altered the landscape and changed patterns of drainage. Pollution of streams and wells resulted. It is clear that these operations resulted in deforestation; in ancient Greece, heat energy for metallurgy derived from combustion of wood or charcoal, and metallurgy constituted the largest consumer of fuel wood. Fossil fuels were not used. The loss of forests in quantitative terms needs to be addressed. Statistics are scarce in ancient records, but not absent, and comparisons can be made, so it is possible to estimate within limits. Wood and charcoal were required at each stage of the process from mining ore to striking the owl coins. The ore found in 483 BCE was in a limestone-shale contact 50–119 m (165–390 feet) below the surface, reached through pits and tunnels.[38] Tunnel props, often of olive wood, were used but not much needed because gallery tunnels were only 60–100 cm (2.3–3.3 feet) high and 60–90 cm (2.3–3 feet) wide, and water seepage was rare.

Workers sorted rocks, putting promising pieces into leather buckets that other slaves, often women and children, dragged out. The rocks went into a workshop where men hammered big ones into little ones. The next step was the washery, where a stream of water carried off lighter waste material, about 60 percent of the mass. The scarce water was recycled, becoming polluted with toxic chemicals.

Smelting consumed the greatest quantity of wood in the form of charcoal, which is more efficient in generating heat. A furnace was filled with alternating layers of ore and charcoal, the weight of charcoal being about 66–100 percent of that of ore. When the temperature reached 750°C, smelting began. Silver melts at 960°C, lead at 327°C, so lead vapor entered the air. Laurion lacked

Entrance to a mine tunnel in the Laurion mining district, Attica, Greece. (2011)

high chimneys to disperse the effluents,[39] and a liquid lead-silver mix flowed out of the furnace, reacting with oxygen to form lead oxide, which blew away, polluting the environment. Slag was skimmed off, containing about half the remaining lead. Charcoal is made by burning wood in an oxygen-poor chamber, in a pit or above ground in a pile covered with earth. The charcoal used at this stage in the process implies that a huge amount of wood was used—seven tons of wood yield one ton of charcoal.[40] Refining brought about the final separation of silver from lead. The lead-silver mix was placed in a cone-shaped cupel lined with wood ash or bone ash, the bone ash having been produced in a wood fire. Cupellation required a temperature between 810 and 950°C; anything higher caused the silver to "spirt off." The lead oxidized and was absorbed into the lining, the silver remaining as a virtually pure button. Again, heat was provided by wood. Silver from cupellation went to the mint, where blanks were heated to avoid cracking, using more charcoal.

What was the extent of deforestation caused by mining and metallurgy at Laurion? Looking at an average year, 2.6 tons of silver would have required cupellating 156 tons of lead-silver after smelting, because the ratio of silver to lead at that stage was 1:60. That amount of lead-silver entailed smelting 1,115 tons of ore, which in turn required 743–1,000 tons of charcoal. Even with the lower figure, other uses of charcoal raised the amount to at least 817 tons. Because one

Excavated remains of an ancient site for silver ore treatment and smelting at Laurion, Attica, Greece. (2011)

ton of charcoal was obtained from seven tons of wood, the total amount of wood required was 5,203 tons.

Greek forest on average contains 1.166 tons of wood per hectare, according to a Greek Forest Research Institute study. Not all of this would be available for charcoal production or fuelwood, however. At most, one ton could be used, assuming the forest was clear-cut, so the wood required for smelting 100 talents of silver could be supplied by deforesting about 52 km² (20 miles²) of land. Cumulative deforestation over 160 years would bring the total deforested area to 8,476 km² (3,273 miles²).

Some wood was provided by coppice; that is, plantations of trees that sprout from stumps after cutting. Pines, which do not regrow after cutting, made up two-thirds of Greek forests. Trees suitable for coppice, mainly oak and beech, were the other third available for the industry. If half of the wood used for smelting came from coppice, on a cycle of twenty to thirty years, the land required would be 216 km² (83 miles²), equal to 5.7 percent of the area of Attica. This would reduce divestiture to 6,933 km² (2,677 miles²). But the near-ideal conditions for coppice in northwestern Europe do not occur in Greece. Cattle, goats, and other herbivores commonly entered these woods, devouring small trees. Goats found small trees and shrubs delectable, and climbed to get what they otherwise could not reach.

Regrowth of cutover land must also be allowed for. Timber species can grow from seed or be replanted. The theoretical cutting cycle (the period required to reach harvestable size) is eighty years for pine and 120–180 years for oak and beech; over 160 years there might be two crops of pine and up to 1.5 of broadleaved species. This figure assumes full regeneration, however, and is unrealistic. The same species may not come back; evergreen oak regularly replaces deciduous oak. After forest removal, the vegetative cover often reverts to *maquis*, a brushland ecosystem, and under less favorable conditions to low-growing *garigue*. The ubiquitous grazing of goats, which ate young trees and prevented forest regeneration, exacerbated the situation.

Attica is semiarid, but brief, heavy rainstorms are common. When trees are cleared from a mountainside, the limestone-based soil erodes at a rate fifty times greater than on forested slopes. A study of sediments in Greece by Curtis Runnels gives evidence of episodes of deforestation and erosion. "In each period the soil that forms above the [erosional] deposits is thinner, less developed and less able to support vegetation" than in the earlier periods.[41] At higher elevations, the soil was stripped away, and only the rocky substrate remained. His evidence suggests a period of deforestation and erosion in the fifth and fourth centuries BCE. Plato, writing in the *Critias* in the fourth century BCE, described the scenario exactly:

> What now remains compared with what then existed is like the skeleton of a sick man,
> all the fat and soft earth wasted away,
> and only the bare framework of the land being left.

> But at that time the country was undamaged,
> and had much forest-land in its mountains,
> of which there is evidence even to this day;

> For there are some mountains which now have nothing but food for bees,
> but they had trees no long time ago,
> and rafters from those felled there to roof the largest buildings are still sound.
> Cultivated trees grew tall and strong,
> and the soil produced plentiful pasturage for flocks.

> It was enriched by yearly rains from Zeus,
> and did not lose it, as now, by flowing from the bare ground into the sea;
> but the soil it had was deep, and it received the water,
> storing it up in the retentive loamy soil;

and let water flow down from high ground to the low ground of every district,
providing abundant springs to feed streams and rivers.

Even now there are still shrines,
left over from the old days at sites of former springs,
as evidence of the truth of this account of the land.[42]

Mount Hymettos is an example of what Plato saw. A long mountain on the eastern side of Athens more than 1,000 m (3,000 feet) high, 22 km (14 miles) long, and 6 km (2 miles) wide, it is visible from everywhere in the city. Forested in early classical times, it was bare by the mid-twentieth century, the prevailing vegetation being low-growing spiny plants. A reforestation program succeeded on lower slopes, but rocky parts above 500 m (1,500 feet), denuded of soil, presented problems. Replanting involved blasting pits in the rock, filling them with soil, and planting conifer seedlings. The young trees reached only 2.5 m (8 feet) before dying or exhibiting desiccation due to lack of soil and water. Thus regrowth of forest was not possible over much of the territory. The proportion treated in a sustainable way with replanting and care of natural regrowth cannot have been over 50 percent, a generous estimate. If so, the cumulative deforestation would be reduced to 3,466 km² (1,338 miles²), which is close to the total land area of Attica, 3,808 km² (1,470 miles²). Attica was not fully forested, however, having been subjected to felling over preceding centuries; it is reasonable to assume that 25 percent cover remained. Attica, even if every tree was cut, could provide only 952 km² (368 miles²) of needed forest. In fact not all of Attica was deforested, since relict forests survived and sacred groves remained in addition to whatever coppice groves and sustainable plantations may have existed. The remaining wood, at least 80 percent, had to come from somewhere else.

Silver mining did not cause all the deforestation, however. Athens had a major pottery industry, exporting vases around the Mediterranean, and olive oil, the most important export, was sold in large amphorae. So was Attic wine. These vessels had to be fired in kilns. Athenians heated their homes with charcoal. Wood was needed for cooking fires. Demands for fuel gave woodcutters profitable work; Phainippos made twelve drachmas a day by selling six donkey loads of wood.[43] Wood was needed for construction; marble temples had wooden roofs requiring good-sized beams. The navy and merchant fleets required timber to build hundreds of ships. Ships' masts had to be tall and strong; appropriate trees were rare in Attica, so they were imported from the north. Treaties with Macedonia gave Athens preference in the timber trade. Ancient writers were well aware of wood shortage and the search for supply. Thucydides has Brasidas, the Spartan commander, urge his ship crews not to hold back "for the sake of saving timber."[44] He notes that the Athenians regarded the loss of Antandros, with "every facility for shipbuilding and nearby Mount Ida with an abundance of timber," as important enough to gather a force and retake it in weeks.[45] He says Alcibiades told the Spartans that obtaining timber was a reason the Athenians mounted the armada to invade Sicily.[46]

Where did the wood come from? Overland transportation was slow and expensive, so inland forests, especially in high mountains, were spared the worst exploitation. Some would have come from islands and coastlands in the Athenian-dominated Aegean. The furnaces of Laurion were relocated near the coast, and a port for barges was constructed. As J. E. Jones noted, "the coastal position of these furnaces reflect the deforestation of Laurion by then and dependence on foreign fuel."[47] Theophrastus cites sources for timber in Macedonia, Thrace, Asia Minor, and the south shore of the Black Sea. Wood came from Cyprus, Sicily, and southern Italy. These places were accessible through ports and by rivers that could float rafts of logs. The ripple of deforestation that began at Laurion spread out like a tsunami to the Mediterranean coasts, resulting in a timber shortage reflected in rising prices and a decline in Athens's power. As Paul Gilding put it, "if you cut down more trees than you grow, you run out of trees."[48]

David Mattingly starkly portrays the environmental impact of a mining operation in Roman times based on his archaeological work at Wadi Faynan, Jordan, the Roman copper mines in the desert north of Petra.[49] Peter Thonemann gives a summary in his review:

> This was one of the largest mining and smelting operations in the Roman world, infamous for the horrific treatment of Christians condemned to hard labor. The smelting process demanded huge quantities of charcoal, and the vast human and animal workforce needed food and fodder. As a result, the surrounding landscape was farmed and grazed far beyond its normal carrying capacity, resulting in the permanent desertification of the region. Simultaneously, the smelting process generated such intense heavy-metal pollution that the landscape is still today dangerously toxic, with alarming consequences for the local Bedouin population. "What we have here," Mattingly concludes, "is an operation that defies normal rules of economic rationality in the service of a superstate. The ecological and human consequences of the rape of this landscape were profound in antiquity and are still with us to the present day."[50]

Quarrying

Quarrying presents many of the same problems and uses technology similar to that of mining. Its aim is to remove large, potentially useful blocks of various kinds of stone. Most ancient quarries were of open-pit type, but in certain places where strata of useful stone led underground, tunnels and galleries were excavated. This was the case in the quarry of fine crystalline marble on the Greek island of Paros, and also in part of the infamous limestone quarry at Syracuse, where Athenian soldiers were interned after their defeat in the Sicilian Campaign. In the latter quarry, there is one quarry face 27 m (88 feet) high and 2,000 m (6,560 feet) long. Over 112 million tons of stone was removed from this single quarry during its period of use.[51]

Evidence of ancient quarrying methods can still be seen on Mount Pentelicus, the source of the white marble used in the Parthenon and other public buildings. Blocks of stone were freed from the matrix by vertical cuts made with bronze saws; the softness of bronze was compensated for by the use of abrasives such as powdered quartz. The horizontal break below the block was made by cutting notches with picks into the rock along a line, driving wooden wedges into the notches, and then soaking the wedges with water so as to swell them until the block split loose along the line. The rough blocks had wooden sledges built around them and slid down the mountainside along tracks on their runners or on rollers, the speed of descent controlled by ropes looped around posts set in holes cut in the rock. When it was necessary to go uphill, they were pulled up inclined planes by capstans. At the base of the mountain, the blocks were loaded onto carts and pulled into the city by oxen. Further shaping of the block happened at the building site, with final details of carving done after it was put in place.

Quarrying in the Roman Empire was similar.[52] Tools found in archaeological sites include pickaxes with broad edges, iron wedges, and saws.[53] During the fourth century, saws in quarries were sometimes driven by watermills, such as the one found near Trier.[54] The Romans stockpiled ready-cut blocks, often near rivers so they could be shipped as needed to Rome, where the Marble Wharf was ready to receive them.[55] The finest marble quarry was located at Carrara, near Luna by the sea, which began production as early as 100 BCE.[56] The massive amount of fine stone incorporated in the growing city is indicated by Seneca's famous dictum that Augustus Caesar found Rome a city of brick and left it a city of marble.[57] Fine stone was shipped widely beyond Rome; the palace of Fishbourne in southern Britain, for example, used marbles from Gaul, Italy, and Asia Minor.[58] Roman taste in stone buildings favored huge size; the eighty-ton blocks of Carrara marble that comprise Trajan's Column are dwarfed by one block cut in the reign of Antoninus Pius for the Temple of Bacchus at Baalbek, which measures 28 m × 4.25 m × 4.25 m (68 feet × 14 feet × 14 feet) and weighs 1,500 tons.[59]

There were special types of quarries, too. Good lava millstones were highly valued, and the Romans shipped them by the Rhine from a quarry at Niedermendig. Emery, a fine abrasive, took its name from a quarry at Cape Emeri on the island of Naxos; Pliny the Elder calls the substance *Naxium*. There were salt mines, but most salt was evaporated from the water of the Mediterranean, which is saltier than the larger oceans, or from salt springs or lakes like the Dead Sea and Lake Tatta in Asia Minor.[60] Clays for ceramics are relatively common in the Mediterranean basin, but potters sought out particularly fine ones high in calcium.[61] Glass is manufactured from sand, a common material, but certain sands of especial purity and color were particularly prized. The soft, white sand of the river Volturnus was much used because it produced colorless glass.[62] Substance of great weight and volume removed from the earth was required for the production of concrete and mortar. Mortar was known as early as Minoan times in Greece.[63] The Romans invented concrete construction, called *opus caementicum*, before the early second century BCE. Concrete consisted of aggregate—that is, pebbles or broken stone (*caementa*) from quarries, mixed together and bonded with mortar made from lime and pozzuolana, a volcanic ash found in central Italy, especially around Vesuvius. The mix was blended with water and poured into forms made of wood, brick, or hewn stones. Water caused the mixture to harden, and it was discovered that mortar hardened well under water, so that concrete could be used in bridges and harbor construction.[64] Such works were immense and required shipping vast amounts of the volcanic material all over the Mediterranean basin and beyond.

Environmental Effects of Mining and Quarrying

The impacts of mining and quarrying on the ancient landscape were widespread and noticeable. A mine called *Scaptê Hylê*, or "excavated forest," on the island of Thasos is mentioned by Herodotus, who says "a whole mountain there has been turned upside down in the search for gold."[65] As the name indicates, a forest was removed by the digging, and undoubtedly more trees were cut for timber and fuel. The mines at Laurion inflicted "a great scar upon the Attic landscape," and "by the time of Strabo the wooded surface of the region had been completely bared to provide timber for the mines and charcoal for the smelting of the ore."[66] Pliny the Elder provides a description of the effect of the deliberate caving-in of a gallery in a Roman mine: "The fractured mountain falls asunder in a wide gap, with a crash which it is impossible for human imagination to conceive, and likewise with an incredibly violent blast of air. The miners gaze as conquerors upon the collapse of nature."[67] Scars left by ancient quarries such as those at Pentelicus and Syracuse are visible today, although some are being obliterated, along with the archaeological information they contain, by modern projects much larger than the ancient ones. In addition to the direct effects of the excavations, erosion of the hillsides was triggered by the removal of protective cover. Some people were aware of these processes and wished that something could be done to repair the damage, as the quotations from Pliny at the beginning of this chapter indicate. But land restoration or replanting after mining was not a Greek or Roman practice.

Another effect of mining was the diversion of large amounts of water, much of it near the headwaters in the mountains, which had "portentous consequences for the face of the earth."[68] A gold-mining project of an Alpine tribe called Salassi in the second century BCE diverted most of the flow of the Durias River and deprived the farmers in the lower valley of water that they had used for irrigation. When the Romans conquered the Salassi, this diversion continued under the publicans who held the mining contracts.[69]

Not only were streams redirected and their channels dried, but the ground and surface waters also became polluted. Poisons such as lead, mercury, and arsenic got into the water used in hydraulic mining or leached out of mines through drainage. Even long after a mine was abandoned, pollution continued, and metallic salts traveled down from higher elevations to places where the contaminated water was used for drinking or irrigation.

Ancient authors also noted the problem of air pollution. Mine workers suffered its worst effects. Lucretius gives a description:

> What stenches [the mine at] Scaptensula breathes out underground! And what poison gold mines may exhale! How strange they make men's faces, how they change their color! Have you not seen or heard how they are wont to die in a short time and how the powers of life fail those whom the strong force of necessity imprisons in such work? All these effluences, then, earth sends steaming forth, and breathes them out into the open and the clear spaces of heaven.[70]

Vitruvius recommended testing air in mines with lighted lamps.[71] This practice may sound dangerous, but methane, the most common explosive gas in coalmines, seldom occurs in metalliferous ores. Impure air came not only from gases trapped below ground, but also from the poisonous fumes of fires used for lighting the tunnels and breaking rocks. "The miners meet with flinty rocks which they break up by heating them and pouring vinegar on them . . . steam and smoke make the air in the galleries unbearable."[72]

The working conditions in mines were truly horrid. Workers often lived underground, coming up to the open air once a week.[73] Excavated skeletons have provided evidence of cave-ins and suffocation. Miners were often slaves or condemned criminals, but there is occasional evidence of concern for safety and health; a bronze miner's helmet similar to the modern style was found in a

Spanish lead mine.[74] The "good emperors" of the second century provided baths near mines and other benefactions.

Technology permitted ancient miners to utilize only rich ores lying relatively near the surface, and accessible deposits were eventually exhausted. Gold mines were often worked out and then abandoned. Copper mining ceased on the Greek mainland before classical times, so ores on Euboea and Cyprus were more heavily exploited. On Euboea, they gave out in the first century BCE. During the late republic, the Senate forbade mining in Italy, but it is unknown whether the prohibition was intended to preserve local supplies for emergencies, to aid contractors in Spain, or to prevent concentrations of mine slaves who were prone to revolt.[75] In any case, there was an ever-widening search for raw materials.[76] Trajan conquered Dacia partly in order to exploit its mines. The tin mines of Spain gave out in the middle of the third century, and the Romans had to exploit reserves in distant Britain. At the same time, a shortage of precious metals created a crisis that threatened the monetary system. In the following century, the imperial government created officials with titles such as *Comes metallorum per Illyricum* to oversee the location of new mines and the supply of metals. Eventually, the Romans worked out most rich surface deposits in the empire.

Metallurgy, Ceramics, and Allied Industries

After they were mined, ores were processed to separate the useful metals: gold, silver, copper, iron, tin, zinc, and mercury. Furnaces were temporary structures of clay and stone. They are portrayed on ceramic objects as tall and narrow; sometimes they were provided with chimneys. Others were excavated in the earth in the form of bowls or shafts. Most smelting techniques required high temperatures and therefore large amounts of fuel. Some of them also employed salts or other metals such as lead or mercury; the utility of acids was little known. That some Roman processes were more efficient than Greek approaches may be gathered from comments such as Strabo's on the refineries at Laurion: "The silver mines in Attica were originally valuable, but now they have failed. Moreover, those who worked them, when the mining yielded only meager returns, melted again the old refuse, or dross, and were still able to extract from it pure silver, since the workmen of earlier times had been unskillful in heating the ore in furnaces."[77] Modern technology allowed resmelting of ancient slags to begin at Laurion in 1864.

Once the metal was isolated, the smith, "Athena's servant," worked it into jewelry, utensils, tools, weapons, or armor.[78] This process required more fuel and produced additional pollution. Coinage generated pressure for precious metals. During the first century BCE, the Roman mint consumed fifty metric tons of silver a year; many coins were then 94 percent pure. Each ton of silver required removing about 100,000 tons of rock from the mines. The demand for gold and silver increased in subsequent centuries, as large amounts were spent for luxuries from beyond the eastern frontiers, for which there were few exports to offer in exchange. Caches of Roman coins have been excavated in India and Southeast Asia.[79]

The importance of the ceramics industry in Greece and Rome may be judged by the vast number of *ostraca* (shards of pottery) found in archaeological sites. The factories required tremendous amounts of fuel that was burnt in cupola-shaped kilns. Shortage of fuel in Italy during the Roman Empire may be a reason for the shift of the "Samian" pottery industry to manufacturers in Gaul and other provinces. Bricks and tiles were produced in huge kilns. One tile kiln near the Temple of Heracles at Nemea measured 5 m (16 feet) in each direction, and yet it made only 140 of the huge tiles required for that structure.[80] Bricks were staples of Roman construction. It is said that Domitia Lucilla, mother of Marcus Aurelius, made a fortune fabricating them for the great villa of Hadrian at Tivoli. Anyone who has seen the immense brick ruins there can well believe in the profitability of that concession. Glass blowers and glaziers had busy establishments in Roman times, with additional fuel needs. A major industry throughout ancient times was limestone kilning for fertilizer, plaster, and mortar, which used not only limestone from quarries but, especially in times of war and social upheaval, buildings and statues, as well. To provision one limekiln for one burn in the highlands of Greece required 1,000 donkey loads of juniper wood, and fifty kilns required 6,000 metric tons of wood yearly.[81] Roman kilns for this purpose have been found at Tretau in Gaul, at Iversheim on the Rhine, and elsewhere.[82]

Environmental Effects of Metallurgy and Related Industries

The major fuel required for industrial processes was charcoal, produced by the partial combustion of wood in an oxygen-poor atmosphere, although wood itself was utilized, too. In Greece, the import and sale of charcoal and wood were controlled by *agoranomoi* (superintendents of the market).[83] Charcoal made from various woods was valued for different purposes.[84] Combined with use in cooking and heating, industry produced a demand for wood that contributed to widespread deforestation. In the Mediterranean basin, at least seventy to ninety million tons of slag from the Greco-Roman period are known, representing the divestiture of fifty to seventy million acres (twenty to twenty-eight million hectares) of trees. Faced with demands like these on sylvan resources, Rome increasingly turned to forest-rich northern Europe for metals and glass, areas such as the Vosges, the Forest of Dean, and even beyond the frontiers in Slupia Nova, Poland. "A widening ripple of cut forests" spread outward.[85] There were complaints of wood shortage even in Gaul. Coal was used only where no wood was available. Pliny reports that coal was burnt in Campania to make bronze because of the wood shortage there; in Britain it was shipped by canal to the treeless fenland.[86] Iron used less fuel than copper in smelting, which helps to account for the preference for the black metal over bronze.[87] The Romans found other fuel-saving strategies. The depletion of forests on the iron-rich island of Elba explains why only the first stage of smelting was done there; the bloom was shipped to the nearby mainland port of Populonia, where wood and charcoal from the Ligurian Mountains was available.[88]

Air pollution resulted not only from wood and charcoal smoke, but also from the fumes of various noxious substances that were heated or burnt. Speaking of metallurgists in Spain, Strabo observes that "they build their silver-smelting furnaces with high chimneys, so that the gas from the ore may be carried high into the air, for it is heavy and deadly."[89] The poison there was lead, often a major component of silver ore. Vitruvius noticed its effect on those whose jobs kept them in contact with it: "We can take example by the workers in lead who have complexions affected by pallor. For when, in casting, the lead receives the current of air, the fumes from it occupy the members of the body, and burning them thereupon, rob the limbs of the virtues of the blood."[90] That air pollution from smelting was not minor or merely local may be indicated by the fact that measurements of the lead content of arctic snow preserved in glaciers in Greenland show a marked increase in concentration at the time when the Romans began more efficient smelting in the second century BCE.[91]

Vitruvius also worried about lead in the water supply; some industrial activities were known to pollute streams.[92] Lead in pipes and the joints of aqueducts could have contaminated water that was acidic, although much of the water in the Mediterranean area flows through limestone and is charged with calcium carbonate, a material that can be deposited as travertine inside aqueduct channels and pipes and consequently can isolate the water from lead. The Greeks and Romans were in greater danger of lead in their food, particularly acidic food prepared and served in lead and silver vessels. Some have speculated about the effect of lead poisoning on segments of the ancient population, as its effects include infertility and impaired nerve activity in the brain and elsewhere. Tests of bones from burials have shown elevated levels of lead.[93] Mercury poisoning may also have presented a problem, at least for workers who smelted the metal from cinnabar, or who worked in gold, where mercury was used to make amalgam in a process that vaporized some of the mercury.

Conclusion

Industrial technology was by no means as important a segment of the total economy in Greek and Roman times as it is in the modern world, but it advanced in size and techniques and made many changes in the ancient landscape. Among its greatest environmental impacts were exhaustion of accessible ores, scarring of the land and deforestation with consequent erosion, diversion and pollution of water, air pollution, and exposure of workers to injurious materials. Ancient writers noted all of these effects, and a few were countered by measures to protect the health of workers; for example, chimneys were constructed to disperse air pollution from smelters. Because of the relatively small size of ancient industries as compared with modern ones, the total effect of most of these problems was not as great, but there were exceptions. Perhaps most important was deforestation. Wood and charcoal were the usual fuels, and fossil fuels were almost unknown, so forests suffered proportionately more from ancient industry than during the Industrial Revolution, when the world turned to coal as fuel. It has been estimated that the Roman iron smelting center at Populonia used as much wood annually as is produced by 400,000 hectares (one million acres) of Mediterranean coppice forest.[94] Of course, forests are renewable resources, but their yield was not usually sustained. The impairments inflicted by ancient industry on the natural environment, although scattered, seldom entirely healed over with a mantle of soil and vegetation, and many of the scars are still visible today.

Nine

War and the Environment

Historians present ancient warfare as a story of arms and armor, of tactics and strategy, of sieges of cities and the fortunes of empires. But they seldom consider the effects of warfare and militarization on the environment, and the reciprocal impacts of environmental damage done by wars in the ancient societies that waged them. Nevertheless, a damaging aspect of ancient social organization as it affected the environment in ancient Greece and Rome was its inclination toward war. Ancient evidence is not silent on the subject. Sometimes environmental damage was an attendant result of military activities, but it was also used as an instrument of warfare.

Epics chronicle heroic exploits against nature. In Homer's *Iliad*, the greatest warrior of the Achaeans, Achilles, fought a battle against the river Scamander.[1] The river, angry because Achilles was polluting his waters with the dead bodies of Trojans, called on his brother, the river Simoeis, and attacked Achilles with a flood that would have killed him without the intervention of other gods. To help him, the god Hephaestus started a forest fire, and the conflict did not end without a brouhaha among virtually all the gods. The battle, according to Homer, caused serious damage to the riverbank and the elms, willows, tamarisks, clovers, rushes, and galingales, and "all those plants that grew in abundance by the lovely stream of the river,"[2] as well as the eels and other fish.

Hunting as Preparation for Warfare

Hunting was often regarded as a form of warfare, and art often portrayed humans in battle with animals. The idea that hunting and warfare are similar, and can use the same weapons, is much older than the classical period; a dagger from Bronze Age Mycenae shows shield-bearing warriors attacking lions with their spears, and a ring of the same period bears the design of an archer shooting a stag from a chariot.[3] The literature of hunting often mentions spears and javelins, which were redesigned for use against specific prey such as boars. Xenophon called hunting "excellent training in the art of war."[4] His friends the Spartans deliberately used it in this way, perhaps explaining the oft-told Spartan story of the boy who was carrying a stolen fox under his cloak. It was said he met his military trainer and stopped to talk to him, but the fox got loose under the cloak and gnawed at the boy's abdomen. Even so, the boy continued to stand without showing any sign of pain until he fell over dead.[5] The story was intended to illustrate the young Spartan's tolerance for pain, and his willingness to die rather than admit he had stolen, but why he should have taken a fox can perhaps be explained best in the context of hunting as preparation for war. The Roman Army employed military methods in hunting to provision troops with meat; soldiers or paid professional hunters scoured the countryside in hostile or uninhabited regions. Hunting for large animals such as lions and boars involved organization and tactics like those of war, and many species were reduced in number and extirpated from sections of the Mediterranean basin.[6]

Society and Economy

Ancient cities and empires were warrior-dominated societies. Our impression that they were never at peace for long is partly because ancient historians mostly took war as their subject, but the impression is nonetheless accurate. The ancients may never have regarded war as the normal state of life, since in the words placed by Herodotus in the mouth of Croesus, "no one is stupid enough to prefer war to peace; in peace sons bury their fathers and in war fathers bury their sons."[7] Still, war was a prevalent tribulation for ancient societies and for the natural environment. Athens in its Golden Age had many more years of war than of peace, and in Rome, the gates of the temple of Janus, which were closed during peacetime, were usually open. Even the *Pax Romana* that began with Augustus and lasted, with few breaks, for 200 years, did not end warfare along the frontiers, including the conquest of Britain, and the size of the army and its consumption of finances and natural resources increased sharply. Fifty years of war in the third century left no major province untouched by battle, during which commanders in the provinces sought to seize power, plunging the empire into sporadic warfare. The battlefields were predominantly in the settled regions of the central empire, and destruction befell houses, barns, orchards, and the rural population. The average period of rule of the emperors between 235 and 284 was two years, hardly enough time to establish policy, and all of the emperors were military men, few of whom had any understanding of economic principles. Prices rose astronomically; the price of wheat in Egypt, for example, was 8 drachmas per *artaba*[8] in the second century, 24 drachmas in the mid-third century, and 220–300 drachmas in the late third century.[9] Emperors facing financial emergency increased the minting of coinage, thus exposing it to debasement. Due to the inflation of the value of precious metals, the cost of the metal in coins rose above their face value, forcing the issuing of coins in less valuable materials such as bronze or lead (perhaps with an easily eroded wash of silver). Silver could be used for coins of higher denominations in a never-ending inflationary process. The tax base of the empire, which depended on agricultural productivity, was shrinking. There were onslaughts of plague in 251–66 and afterward, and emperors made up a deficit of manpower by allowing groups of barbarians to settle within the empire.

Environmental Warfare

Armies typically targeted cities, but war also exacted toll from agriculture, as campaigns devastated the countryside, slaughtered farmers and their families, and requisitioned or destroyed crops and buildings. Armed conflict had direct effects on the environment. Theophrastus remarked that when an army had marched over a field of growing plants, hardly anything remained visible, and due to the compaction of the earth, crops growing there the next year might be stunted. The land in the actual battlefield, however, was another story. The blood of the slain and wounded, and the corpses if they were buried in situ, could fertilize the fields. After the battle of Massalia, in which the Roman general Marius defeated the Teutoni, Plutarch reports: "It is said that the people of Massalia built fences around their vineyards with the bones of the fallen, and that the soil, after the bodies had wasted away in it and the rains had fallen all winter upon it, grew so rich and became so full to its depths of the putrefied matter that sank into it, that it produced an exceedingly great harvest in later years, and confirmed the saying of Archilochus that "fields are fattened" by such a process."[10] Such damage, or enrichment, was incidental to military operations, but deliberate destruction of the ecological base of the enemy was a customary part of ancient warfare.

Armies lived off the land, of course; the conditions of transport did not always permit supply from home, and plunder of stored grain, growing crops, and animals in invaded countries was unavoidable. As Neil J. Goldberg and Frank J. Findlow maintained, "because of the restricted method of land transport available to the Romans, or any military force before World War II, an army was forced literally to live off the land on which it stood."[11] But calculated environmental warfare, in which an enemy's natural resources and food supplies were demolished, was also not a rare event. A Biblical commandment forbids Jewish soldiers to cut down fruit trees while besieging a city.[12] This exceptional regulation suggests that such destruction was otherwise a common practice of armies. As the agricultural historian Victor Davis Hanson notes, "Ravaging of cropland was central to warfare of most societies of the past."[13] Hanson quotes a comment attributed to Socrates: "Men cut the grain that others have planted, and chop down their trees, and in all ways harass the weaker if they refuse to submit, until they are forced to choose slavery rather than war with the stronger."[14] Tacitus has the Caledonian chief Calgacus tell his men that the Romans "make a desert and call it peace."[15] In spite of the abundant references to this type of environmental warfare in ancient sources, however, most modern military historians of the ancient world have paid scant attention to it.

We have the most information about a case actually witnessed by Socrates—the invasion of the lands of Athens by the Spartans in the Peloponnesian War, in which they devastated farms and fields and chopped down olive orchards and vineyards, hoping to cause shortages in the besieged city. The attack took place in two phases. In the first, King Archidamus of Sparta waged annual campaigns to wreak havoc on Attica in an unsuccessful attempt to goad the Athenians into venturing outside their impregnable city walls to fight an infantry battle that he was sure he would have won. In part, the tactic of devastating the landscape may have been forced on the Spartans because at that time siege warfare had not developed to the point where an assault on the walls could promise success, and the Athenians were well supplied by sea. In the second phase, the Spartans built a fort at Decelea in Athenian territory from which they could continuously ravage and plunder the countryside. Many historians believe that the damage done to Athenian agriculture by these invasions was major but not the main cause of Athens's defeat. The Athenian Navy controlled the sea, and provisions came in through the port of Piraeus, which was protected and connected to the city by the Long Walls. Donald Kagan sees the destruction of vines, olive trees, and houses as a serious blow to Athens's major export crops (olive oil and wine)—and therefore the balance of trade—and he incidentally says that the second phase deprived Athenians of the revenues of the silver mines at Laurion.[16] But

Hanson emphasizes the difficulty of destroying the major Mediterranean crop plants.[17] Olive trees are big, with trunks that reach 6 m (20 feet) in diameter. They are deeply rooted and have hard wood that resists the axe, survives fire, and readily resprouts from a stump. Moreover, they were numerous; Sophocles describes the olive as a tree no man could "destroy or bring to nothing."[18] Grapevines are also deep rooted, regrow from the roots, and were even more numerous. Growing grain is impossible to set on fire until it matures and dries out, after which it is immediately harvested. Sophocles concludes that serious damage to Athenian crops would have required the labor of more troops than Sparta could have made available, and that agriculture would have recovered quickly after the war. "The damage that did occur to farmland during war was more often a result of dislocation—the evacuation of farmers, the driving off of slaves and livestock, the death in battle of farmer-hoplites themselves—than of the physical destruction of trees, vines, and cereals."[19] Hanson's opinion must be respected because he has a lifetime of experience as a farmer of Mediterranean crops in California. But he must explain references such as that of Lysias to devastation in Attica: "Many plots at that time were thick with private and sacred olive trees, which now have for the most part been cut down, so that the land has now become bare."[20] And if ravaging crops did little damage, it is hard to explain why Athenian seaborne troops faced obvious dangers to raid Spartan agriculture and to ravage the lands of Megara, an ally of Sparta near Athens. Along with this fact are many other examples of "laying waste to the land" in ancient history, such as happened to Corcyra, Acanthus, Mende, Melos, and others. Hannibal devastated the land during his invasion of Italy, although not completely, since he wanted the aid of other Italian cities against the Romans. Studies have shown that during periods of military incursion, farmers often escaped from dangerous, low-lying lands subject to ravaging and looting and found refuge in more isolated, forested, mountainous regions where they could clear trees and plant crops. The effects on the two environments are major: the lowlands become a landscape of abandoned fields, while the mountains suffer deforestation. Probably both conditions contributed to deforestation.[21]

Damage to Agriculture

Roman farmers experienced economic and other disasters due to the organization of Roman Imperial society for war and the military.[22] They knew agricultural remedies for problems like siltation, salinization, and soil exhaustion through the leaching of essential minerals but could not always apply them because of political and military pressures. The tax system bore most heavily on the agricultural sector of the economy, whether the levies were collected in coin or in kind. Taxes such as the Roman *annona militaris* (an annual tax to support the army) was assessed upon the farmers, depriving them of resources they could otherwise have used to improve the land. Citizen farmers were conscripted for military service, forcing them to abandon their land, and too often were killed in battle, so that manpower left available to care for the land declined. Then the theater of war was often the countryside; farm families were killed, their property requisitioned by the troops, their crops, buildings, and terraces destroyed. The reliefs of Trajan's Column show soldiers setting fire to villages and rounding up peasants as prisoners and slaves. Sometimes damage could be repaired, but more often agricultural ecosystems were not given time to recover, leaving them vulnerable to insects and diseases. It is no wonder that ancient writers complained of abandoned fields (*agri deserti* in Latin). Furthermore, when terraced hillsides were abandoned, the terrace walls were no longer maintained, and when they collapsed, the amount of erosive material that washed down into lowlands and coasts increased greatly. This is one of the reasons why harbors silted up in the war-ravaged decades of the later Roman Empire. More general studies of deposited material along the Mediterranean coasts have shown that erosion increased significantly in watersheds during and after periods when they were theaters of warfare.[23]

If warfare damaged settled agriculture, did it also destroy other lands such as pastures, brushlands, and forests? Wars were fought for the possession of such land, especially when located near territorial boundaries, as Timothy Howe explained in a study for the Association of Ancient Historians.[24] Conquering productive enemy land was more advantageous in the long run than devastating it, and in that case it would be better to gain territory in an undamaged state. When the Romans lost some of their most valuable agricultural land in North Africa, the economic costs meant that they had difficulty supporting their army.[25]

Fire and Water as Weapons

The Mediterranean climate has a long, dry summer season, during which vegetation is easily ignited, often by lightning but also by shepherds and soldiers. The resulting fires can engulf thousands of hectares. Setting such fires is used in contemporary times as a means of political expression; records of wildfires in Greece during the twentieth century show unmistakable upswings in election years. Mediterranean vegetation, especially the prevalent brushland called maquis, is adapted to fire and will almost always regenerate in the course of a few years. Setting fire in pastures, forests, and wildlands—unlike farmlands— seldom seems to have been done in order to damage enemy territory, but it was often done to gain a military advantage or to kill enemy troops. During the Battle of Pylos, Spartan warriors were isolated on a brush-covered island in the bay, and Athenian soldiers landed without knowing the exact location or number of the Spartans. A fire started in the Athenian camp and burned off the vegetative cover, enabling the Athenians to find and capture 120 of the Spartiates, the first time Spartans had been known to surrender.[26] Thucydides says that the fire was an accident, although if so it was a lucky one, and there is the possibility that the Athenians started it deliberately. Commanders even ordered sacred groves to be burned if foes had taken refuge in them; in 494 BCE, King Cleomenes I of Sparta burned the grove of Argus, and thousands of Argive soldiers were incinerated.[27]

Interference with the water supply of enemies is a method of environmental warfare often mentioned in ancient sources. Rivers were dammed or redirected to deprive cities of water, or they were deliberately contaminated. Cases of surreptitiously polluting rivers and wells are numerous. Xenophon described a plan used by King Cyrus of Persia, who gained entrance to the city of Babylon by diverting the Euphrates and sending his army through the walls on the riverbed.[28] Frontinus included examples of these schemes in his *Stratagems*.[29] Lucius Metellus flooded out his Spanish enemies, and Julius Caesar cut the water supply of the town of the Cadurci to force its surrender.

Forests and Warfare

Damage to forests resulted from the military's constant need for wood to build fortifications, war machines, and shelters; to burn as torches; as signal fires; and simply to cook food and to keep warm. Shipbuilding was a major use of wood in war and peace, one mentioned often by ancient writers. It required great amounts of wood, including tall, straight tree trunks for masts. Strategies of warfare and diplomacy were often aimed at obtaining supplies of timber and other forest products such as pitch, and guarding the sea-lanes and roads over which they were transported.[30] Historians in Greece and Rome saw timber supply as a major factor determining naval strategy in particular. In the Punic Wars, Rome rushed ships to completion, from tree to sea, in as little as forty to sixty days.[31] Supplies dwindled; Dionysius of Syracuse, for instance, found all the shipbuilding material he needed in the rich forests he controlled in Magna Graecia (southern Italy) around 400 BCE, but Hiero, another tyrant of the same city a century and a half later, had to search far and wide for a mast suitable for a large warship.[32] Theophrastus notes that good timber was found mostly far away from major cities, implying that nearer forest resources had been exhausted. International diplomacy often hinged on obtaining shipbuilding supplies. A treaty between Amyntas, king of Macedonia, and the Chalcidians required the latter to obtain the king's permission and to pay duties to export fir timber for ships' masts but allowed them to trade less strategic lumber freely. Pharnabazus, the Persian Satrap of Phrygia (in Asia Minor), helped sway the course of the Peloponnesian War by giving the Spartans access to the forests of Mount Ida and counseling them "not to be discouraged over a lack of ship's timber, for there is plenty of that in the King's land."[33] Athens made treaties with kingdoms in northern Greece to obtain wood for shipbuilding; a fourth-century treaty between Athens and Perdiccas pledged the Macedonian regent to export wood suitable for oars only to Athens. But another way to get forests was to conquer them; Alcibiades told the Spartans that forest conquest was one of the Athenians' major purposes in launching the Sicilian Campaign in 415 BCE.[34]

Areas both strategically located and rich in forests, like Cilicia and Cyprus, were often objects of conquest by powers needing to build up their navies. Colonies were established as timber ports; the Athenians founded Amphipolis on the river Strymon below heavily forested mountains in Thrace, so their consternation when the Spartans took that city is understandable.[35] General Brasidas of Sparta had launched his northern campaign with the object of cutting off Athens's timber supply from that region and redirecting it to Sparta and her allies, including Corinth. In the second century, the Roman Empire faced a declining supply of large timber for purposes such as shipbuilding, so the prudent Emperor Hadrian established a forest reserve in the mountains of Lebanon, where trees of the most important species were declared property of the emperor, and could not be cut without his permission. More than a hundred stone boundary markers inscribed with warnings against timber thieves remained in place until the twenty-first century:

Boundary of the forests of the emperor Hadrian Augustus:

Four species of trees reserved under the imperial privilege.[36]

Scholars disagree about which species were included in the four that the emperor protected, but it is certain that the famous cedar of Lebanon (*Cedrus libani*) was one of them. The other three are probably the fir (*Abies cilicica*), the black pine (*Pinus nigra*), and the Juniper (*Juniperus excelsa*). Some suggest cypress and box, but the size and shape of these two tree species argue against their use for timber, which was the point of Hadrian's edict.[37]

The damage done to forests during Roman warfare is prominently portrayed in the great spiral relief of Trajan's Column. That monument in Rome celebrates Trajan's conquest of Dacia, a territory in modern Romania, and is regarded by experts as a principal source of information about Roman military equipment and operations.[38] More than 200 trees are represented in the relief. Many are shown being chopped down vigorously by axe-wielding Romans or Dacians. Sometimes the military axmen clear roads through thick woodland to allow passage for the legions. More often, they can be seen carrying away logs and using them to make siege terraces, catapults, battering rams, and beacon fires. One such beacon, not yet ablaze, is made of 144 logs.[39] There are many structures that demanded timber in their construction: camps, forts, palisades, other defense works, warships, boats, and barges loaded with barrels. Then there are the bridges of boats, huge assemblages of wood. Two of them, shown near the beginning of the relief, cross the Danube: "Each boat carries, amidships, a stout pier of logs firmly held together by horizontal slats. In between every pair of boats there is a pontoon of closely fitted planks; and the piers and pontoons carry the timber roadway structure of the bridge, with railings at the sides."[40] Each of the soldiers crossing the river carries a wooden stake. The emperor offers sacrifice on a fire altar. The work to supply the huge amounts of wood necessary for military operations was done by *classiarii*, technical support units for the army, directed by "axe masters." If necessary these men could fight with their axes, as the column relief shows. The transformation of the landscape by these operations was massive. Toward the end of the relief, a scene in northern Dacia where a forest god contemplates a little lake among the woods, rich in game such as deer and boars, is followed by a landscape where a single tree bears only two meager tufts of leaves above a trunk, almost all of whose branches have been lopped.[41]

Use of Animals in Warfare

Ancient armies used animals, both wild and domestic, in warfare. Xenophon wrote *The Art of Horsemanship* around 400 BCE. Horses were used in cavalry warfare and to pull chariots, and they aided in military communication. They were also used as pack animals and to pull supply wagons; donkeys and mules performed a similar function. Ancient Sumerian art shows donkeys pulling carts containing warriors into battle. By 1700 BCE, invaders from Asia had introduced horses and chariots to Egypt; the Scythians and other peoples of the Eurasian grasslands north of the Black Sea, an environment particularly suited to horses, were among the earliest to develop cavalry. The first horses used in cavalry were relatively small, but increasingly large horses were preferred as cavalry soldiers adopted armor. Ferghana (now in Uzbekistan) was a noted source of fine, large cavalry horses for China, Persia, and the Mediterranean. According to J. Edward Chamberlin, Alexander the Great's legendary horse Bucephalus was possibly of the Ferghana breed.[42] The Persian emperor required several of the provinces to send an annual tribute of horses. The Persians, and Romans in the period of the

The emperor Trajan's Column, in his Forum in Rome, bore a spiral relief celebrating the conquest of Dacia. It provides much information about the Roman army and its use of natural resources. (1959)

late empire, developed *cataphracti* or *clibanarii*, fully armored cavalry, and the horses themselves might be armored, so that these animals had to be powerfully built. Providing horses with grain, grazing, and water had important environmental effects. Increasingly larger horses would have made greater demands on resources, as well as impact on the land. Alexander allocated each of his cavalry horses (he had as many as 7,000) 5 kg (10 lb) each of grain and hay, as well as 38 L (10 gallons) of water daily, and tried to give them one day a week for grazing. He preferred to time his expeditions into specific regions when harvests were available to feed his horses.[43]

Camels were used in battle and to pack supplies, owing to their advantage as animals adapted to an arid environment. The Arabs were apparently first to create a camel cavalry, and they used camels in battle against the Assyrians in the seventh century BCE. Herodotus says that Cyrus of Persia used camels to frighten the horses in the army of Croesus of Lydia (547 BCE) and that, when Xerxes brought camels into Greece, lions came down from the mountains to attack them.[44] The city of Palmyra in Syria had a camel corps in the third century, and when the Romans defeated them in 272, Queen Zenobia attempted to flee on a camel.[45] The camel was inferior to the horse in warfare, but Diocletian's edict on prices indicates that transport by camel was less expensive than transport by wagon.

Elephants were captured, trained, and used on the battlefield, resulting in a constant drain on the wild population. This happened first in India around 1100 BCE, judging from Vedic hymns in which war elephants are mentioned. Indian battles sometimes involved thousands of elephants. The Persian Empire used Indian war elephants, which Alexander the Great initially met in battle in 331 BCE, and later famously in the encounter with the Indian King Porus on the Indus River. His successors used both Indian and African elephants. Pyrrhus and Hannibal took the great beasts into Italy to use against the Romans, both ultimately unsuccessfully. At the battle of Raphia in 217 BCE, 102 Indian elephants under Antiochus III of Syria defeated seventy-three African elephants of Ptolemy IV, collapsing the left wing of Ptolemy's battle formation, although Ptolemy managed to win the battle. Even though today African elephants are considerably larger than Indian elephants, every ancient author who commented on their comparative sizes stated the reverse,[46] perhaps because the African elephant of antiquity was a smaller North African race that is now extinct. The Carthaginian elephants that invaded Italy with Hannibal in the third century BCE came from the north slope of the Atlas Mountains, but there are none there now.[47] Romans used elephants, too, if briefly: the senatorial army under Scipio and Cato that faced Julius Caesar in North Africa sent elephants into the Battle of Thapsus, which they nonetheless lost.

War dogs had an advantage over elephants. Elephants often trampled soldiers on their own side, but dogs could tell friends from enemies. Almost every ancient Mediterranean civilization used dogs in battle. Mastiffs are shown in reliefs with Assyrian soldiers. Molossian hounds from Epirus, the homeland of Olympias, mother of Alexander the Great, were the preferred breed of Greeks and Romans until the discovery of British fighting dogs, which were integrated into the Roman army. Every legion employed a dog company. Dogs were trained

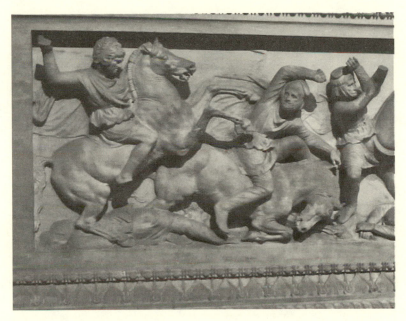

The Alexander Sarcophagus (fourth century BCE), unearthed near Sidon, Lebanon, in 1887, depicts Alexander the Great on horseback at the Battle of Issus and shows the use of animals in warfare. Now in the Istanbul Archaeological Museum, Turkey. (2007)

to attack, and often fitted with spiked collars and armor. They were also used to guard camps and to warn against the approach of enemies.

Adrienne Mayor has assembled evidence for use of weaponized animals of many species in ancient warfare, including birds, pigs, bears, rodents, snakes, bees, wasps, scorpions, beetles, assassin bugs, and jellyfish.[48] Beehives or ceramic pots filled with various noxious creatures were catapulted at the enemy. Hannibal lobbed jars full of serpents onto the ships of Eumenes of Pergamum. The defenders of Hatra, a site in present-day Iraq, facing a Roman invasion led by Septimius Severus, filled clay pots with "poisonous flying insects" and hurled them at the legionaries.[49] During sieges, the defenders were known to release stinging insects into tunnels being excavated by the attackers, as Aeneas Tacticus advised in his book *How to Survive under Siege*.

Disease and War

Even microorganisms spread through armies, as soldiers were weakened by the conditions of march, encampment in hostile territory, and exposure to foreign populations and organisms. Sometimes plagues were spread deliberately among the enemy, although the danger of unintended results, including reinfection of one's own personnel, is obvious. Famine and disease were companions of war among the four horsemen, and not uncommonly the number of deaths in armies from pestilence was greater than those in battle. Athens suffered from plague near the beginning of the Peloponnesian War, when Pericles as a war measure ordered the rural population to take shelter in the limited space inside the city walls. The Spartans postponed their annual invasion of Attica in order to avoid the danger that their soldiers might catch the plague. Conversely, when soldiers from the Athenian armada tried to besiege Syracuse in 413 BCE, the Syracusans turned the tables and confined the invaders to a low-lying part of the coast that they knew to be malarial,[50] which contributed to the eventual disastrous defeat of the Athenians. Another siege of Syracuse, this time by the Carthaginians in 396 BCE, ended when a plague decimated the attacking army. Had they succeeded, Rome might have come closer to losing the First Punic War. Pandemics seem to have increased in frequency when Alexander's expedition, followed by Roman trade, made contact with south Asian populations, bringing microbes home to add to pathogens already present in the Mediterranean basin. After Augustus, Rome experienced plagues of increasing severity. Especially disastrous was the plague in the reign of Marcus Aurelius, the symptoms of which were described by the medical writer Galen. Soldiers returning from Mesopotamia brought the plague to Rome in 164, and it killed as much as one-third of the population; 2,000 deaths per day in the city of Rome were reported at its height. Plagues were disasters for Rome's enemies, too; they blunted the incursions of Huns and Vandals. The effects of epidemics on the Mediterranean peoples were significant. Human populations usually rebound after attacks of pathogens because survivors tend to be resistant, and birth rates rise as if to replace lost numbers. But if wars interfere, losses may be repaired more slowly. Plague is associated with famine and declining agricultural production, as farmers may die from the disease or flee from the districts it attacks.

Conclusion

Ancient warfare in the Mediterranean area had demonstrable environmental dimensions, many of which were understood and intended by the participants. But others were the unfortunate side effects of conflict. In particular, a balance with nature is a condition of peace and is upset by war as a matter of course. Ancient historians noted the direct impacts of battle, but just as important were the effects of the military-oriented organization of societies on the natural environment and resources.

Ten

Urban Problems

The impact of ancient cities on the natural environment—the land and its resources, air and water, and animal and plant populations—produced problems prefiguring many of those familiar in modern settings, such as air and water pollution, traffic and noise, and difficult decisions regarding land use and urban planning. The urban environment received graphic criticism in ancient times. The most vocal complaints were directed against the defects of Rome, then the world's largest city, by its own poets. "The smoke, the wealth, the noise of Rome"[1] repelled Horace, who also objected to suburban encroachment on fertile farmlands. Martial inveighed against the noise pollution that disturbed his sleep, cataloguing its many sources, including predawn traffic, busy bakers, metalworkers' incessant hammers, and loud schoolteachers.[2] Juvenal expanded the list of urban ills, decrying traffic congestion, fires, public works projects that destroyed natural beauty, chamber pots emptied out upper-story windows, and ever-increasing crime and vandalism. "Where have we ever seen a place so dismal and lonely," he groaned. "We'd not be better off there than afraid, as we are here, of fires, / Roofs caving in, and the thousand risks of this terrible city?"[3] Though complained about most by Romans, urban environmental ills also existed elsewhere. Athens, Alexandria, and scores of others suffered from crowding, noise, air and water pollution, accumulation of wastes, plagues, and additional dangers to life and limb. Impacts of cities on the natural environment were not limited to their immediate neighborhood because each city made demands upon the resources of a hinterland of considerable extent, even in many cases overseas.

City Planning

Ancient cities have two major forms: those that grew organically but planlessly, usually around a defensible height, and those that reflect the imposition of a rational structure on a natural site. Earlier Greek *poleis* exemplified the former image; streets in Athens were a jumble of narrow passageways beneath the fortified Acropolis, giving way only to the Sacred Way, a large ceremonial road, or to the open space of the Agora, where there were facilities for trade and city government. Rome was also an unplanned city and remained so in spite of many attempts by consuls and emperors to provide order to a situation that was not so much chaotic as an adjustment of human habitation and movement to the shape of the natural site, with its topography and drainage, and to the structures that had been established in the historical past.

City planning found its sphere in the establishment of new colonies, the expansion of ports, and the restoration of centers damaged by war. In the case of a new town, a site had to be selected, traditionally by divination.[4] The founder of a city, called *oikistēs* (Greek) or *conditor* (Latin) was usually credited with having received a sign of divine favor that would direct him to the proper site. Alexander the Great was directed by a figure in a dream to the place where his greatest foundation, Alexandria in Egypt, would be built.[5] The god Apollo, through his Oracle of Delphi, took a particular interest in the location of Greek colonies. Doubtless his priests had some knowledge of environmental conditions at likely sites. They sent people from Thera to found a city in Libya, for example, and would not accept the attempt to colonize an island off the Libyan coast as a fulfillment of the oracle.[6]

Philosophers were more "scientific" about choosing locations for new cities. But Plato retained some of the old belief in divination, teaching that, in addition to the physical characteristics of a site, a city founder should take account of the spirit of the place. "Some localities have a more marked tendency than others to produce better or worse people, and we are not to legislate in the face of the facts," he remarked, implying that *nomos*, human culture, must be altered to accord with the natural environment in a particular *topos*, or locale.

Some places, I conceive, owe their propitious or ill-omened character to variations in wind and sunshine, others to the waters, and yet others to the products of the soil, which not only provide the body with better or worse sustenance, but equally affect the mind for good or ill. Most markedly conspicuous of all, again, will be localities which are the homes of some su-

The Parthenon (fifth century BCE) and other sacred and public buildings crown the Acropolis on a limestone hill in the center of Athens. The locations of many ancient cities were determined by topography, which included a high place like this. (1992)

pernatural influences, or the haunts of spirits who give a gracious or ungracious reception to successive bodies of settlers. A sagacious legislator will give these facts all the considerations a person can, and do the best to adapt legislation to them.[7]

The Hippocratic work *Airs, Waters, Places* maintained that a city's position in relationship to solar exposure, prevailing winds, and the quality of its climate and water supply determined the health of the people living there.[8] This doctrine was applied to the siting of new towns; Hippocrates believed that an eastward aspect is healthiest for a city, and Aristotle agreed.[9] Vitruvius advised taking the direction of prevailing winds into account when planning the orientation of streets and placement of buildings.[10]

Rectilinear Plans

City planning, the conscious creation of an artificial living environment, is of great antiquity and began with the rise of city-states in Mesopotamia. Many

Greek cities were deliberately planned; for instance, an inscription from Colophon shows that citizens appointed a planning committee of ten who hired an architect.[11] The first name of a city planner that has been preserved is Hippodamus of Miletus, a "metrologist" who "discovered the method of dividing cities"[12] by applying principles he observed in celestial phenomena to urban design.[13] He believed 10,000 citizens to be the ideal size for a city.[14] He is chiefly associated with the "Hippodamian" plan, in which regularly spaced, straight streets cross one another at right angles to make rectangular blocks, some of which are designated as locations of public buildings and the marketplace. He observed, and perhaps participated in, the rebuilding of his home city after the Persian Wars (479 BCE). He created a new plan for Athens's port Piraeus (451 BCE) and another for Thurii, Pericles's Panhellenic colony in Italy, in 443 BCE. It is not impossible that he planned a new Rhodes in 408 BCE, though he would have been an elder statesman by that time.[15] The Hippodamian rectilinear plan was much copied, as at Olynthus in 432 BCE and Priene in 350 BCE, and in colonies in Magna Graecia, such as Agrigentum and Metapontum; but it was too rigid for many sites, and some new towns—such as Elis (471 BCE), Megalopolis (371 BCE), and Mantinea (371 BCE)—had irregular plans.[16]

Radial Plans

Meton, another Greek urban planner, also based his designs on celestial phenomena.[17] Aristophanes in *Birds* caricatured him as the would-be architect of Cloudcuckooland, and the plan suggested there is radial: "In its center will be the market-place, into which all the straight streets will lead, converging to this center like a star."[18] Plato described Atlantis as a perfectly radial city with alternating circles of land and water, and the geometrically regular model city in his *Laws* had twelve equal precincts centered on the acropolis.[19] He advised against a city wall: "No, if men must have a wall of sorts, they should construct their dwellings from the outset in such a fashion that the whole town forms one unbroken wall, every dwelling house being readily defensible by the uniformity and regularity with which all face the streets. Such a town, with its resemblance to one great house, would be no unpleasing spectacle."[20] Vitruvius designed an ideal city with eight sides and radial symmetry, a rigid and rational conception that was never built. Wheel-like cities were almost nonexistent in practice. Rhodes and Halicarnassus were compared to theaters in reference to the shape of their sites, not a circular arrangement of streets.[21] The modern Greek architect Constantine Doxiadis detected a radial arrangement in ancient monumental centers such as acropolises, sacred enclosures, and agoras, when viewed from their ceremonial entrances.[22]

Hellenistic and Roman Plans

Alexander and his successors, busy founders of cities, used variations of the Hippodamian plan. Their standard arrangement consisted of lines of uniform rectangular blocks, each approximately twice as long as broad.[23] Dura-Europos in Syria was founded in rectilinear style by Nicanor about 300 BCE.[24] Many Hellenistic cities, especially great capitals like Alexandria and Antioch, were planned with long boulevards lined with colonnades, statuary, and trees. Public buildings were placed at the ends of fine vistas. Deinocrates designed Alexandria with wide avenues and canals, dominant positions for major structures, and walls integrated into the total plan. Pergamum, whose steep site prevented straight streets, was reconstructed as a magnificent terraced crescent intended to impress the beholder with the might of the Attalid kings who commissioned it. Such lavish constructions increased the demand for stone, metal, and timber.

When the Romans founded towns on open sites, they revealed a conception of standardized environmental order. Everywhere from the Sahara margins to the British Isles, one finds a plan based on that of the military camp. Nearly square in outline, its fortified walls were pierced by four gates, one on each of the sides. Two main roads connected the gates on opposite sides and met each other at right angles in the enclosed space. These roads were termed by land surveyors (*agrimensores*) the *cardo*, from a word for "hinge" or "axis," and the *decumanus*.[25] Examples of such city plans include Aosta, founded 2 BCE in an Alpine valley, and Thamugadi, Algeria, around 100 CE.

The city of Rome, home of the orderly Romans, shows a lack of the neat planning visible in the colonies, and a violation of principles set forth by Vitruvius. Crooked streets wandered among and over the famous seven hills and extended out past the irregular courses of successive walls. Rome lay beside the Tiber in a "pestilential region," as Roman writers admitted.[26] The Forum was originally a marsh. Projects for drainage and sanitation were undertaken, but the dampness of the site remained a problem. Sections of the city were sometimes realigned after fires, as Nero did, and other emperors built supplementary forums alongside the old one, but because of the city's size, a thorough replanning was impossible.

Urban-Centered Organization of Land

A city is more than just the built-up area. It is an ecosystem, including the surrounding lands upon which it depends for food and other resources. In the Mediterranean city-state, town and country were a unit, or so writers thought;[27] Aristotle says that Hippodamus "divided the land into three parts: one sacred, one public, the third private: the first was set apart to maintain the customary worship of the gods, the second was to support the warriors, the third was the property of the husbandmen."[28] In describing his model city, Plato turned as a necessary preliminary to an examination of natural features such as the sea, mountains, and forests.[29] An ideal for the philosophers was that a city should be self-sufficient, finding all the natural resources it needed in its own territory. In fact, this never occurred.

The Greeks and Romans distinguished landscapes according to the ways in which they were used, or not used, by human beings. First was the area within the wall, if there was one, and also the suburbs. These environs comprised the city proper (*polis, urbs*), the land occupied by and most altered by human inhabitants. Within this area were the fortress (acropolis or *asty, arx*), with temples, treasuries, and other official buildings; the marketplace (*agora, forum*), with governmental and commercial structures; and residential quarters.

The productive rural area was divided into three distinct categories, mixed as they might be in the actual countryside.[30] Cultivated land (*aroura, ager*) consisted of cropland, gardens, and orchards. Next was grazing land (*nomos, saltus*) and its herds of animals, which was separate from the preceding category; the farmer and cowherd may not be friends. The third category was woodland (*hylê, silva*), forests used as sources of fuel, timber, fodder, and other products.[31]

Beyond these lands lay the uninhabited landscape—wilderness (*erêmos* or *erêmia; deserta, solitudo,* or *vastitas*). These words all refer to the emptiness of the land: its lack of people. One might be tempted to exclude this category from consideration as part of the urban ecosystem, were it not that the city government universally asserted sovereign ownership of wilderness within its own territory. Wilderness contained resources such as wildlife that could be hunted or ores that could be mined, and its living and nonliving components interacted with other parts of the urban ecosystem. The final category of land was sacred space (*temenos, templum*), areas set aside for worship and dedicated to gods and goddesses. *Temenê* could be located physically within any of the other categories, but theoretically sacred space is even more untouched than wilderness because economic activities including hunting and wood gathering were nominally forbidden.

Population

A small, independent, self-sufficient city was the classical Greek ideal. Most *poleis* were of modest size and, in spite of the development of manufacturing and commerce, basically agrarian. There must have been hundreds like Priene, with only 4,000 inhabitants, and few like Athens and Syracuse, with populations in the hundreds of thousands. Plato designed the republic for a citizen body numbering 8,000, but later in *Laws* provided space for just 5,040.[32] Of course the total population of these utopias would have been larger, allowing for wives, children, and slaves, although Plato did not envision a large number of resident foreigners such as lived in Athens.

The Hellenistic Age was a period of rapid urbanization in which large, splendid capitals arose with heterogeneous populations. The artificial environments of these great centers were pervasive enough to imbue the literature of the age with nostalgia for country life and rural scenes as major themes. Theocritus, born on the rustic island of Cos, created the genre of pastoral poetry in urbane Alexandria. An estimate from 60 BCE gives the size of the free population of Alexandria as 300,000 and states that it was then the largest city in the world, which suggests a total size of about a million, including slaves and foreign residents.[33]

Rome grew to become the most urban of Mediterranean cities. In the fourth century BCE, a wall 11 km (7 miles) long served as a defense of the central city. The city claimed a peak of perhaps 1.2 million residents by the middle of the second century.[34] Long before that, in the first century BCE, Vitruvius spoke of an immense number of citizens needing countless places to live.[35] Over the centuries the city expanded, including a large area outside the walls. Roman writers commented on the suburban sprawl, with villas of the rich occupying the nearby hills; as Horace said, "rich men's luxurious buildings leave few acres for the plow."[36] Although the residential area spread far across the surrounding land, the success of Roman armies in controlling the Mediterranean made new walls unnecessary until the third century, when uprisings of Roman armies in the empire made the capital vulnerable. Emperor Aurelian began a wall 19 km (12 miles) long, enclosing a larger section of the city. Still, Rome was not huge by modern measures; the area inside the new walls covered just under 14 km^2 (5.3 miles^2). Suburbs extended outside these new walls.[37]

Environmental Problems of the City
Crowding, Traffic, and Noise Pollution

While ancient cities did not approach the size of modern ones, and none had the population of several millions common in many of today's cities around the world, they did crowd their people into small areas with narrow, usually unpaved, streets. This was true of Athens, where perhaps 100,000 inhabitants occupied a city whose walls were nowhere farther than a mile from the Acropolis. Except for those who could afford villas on the hills outside the walls, Athenians had little space.[38] No wonder Socrates sought the tree-shaded banks of a small river outside the city for his conversation with Phaedrus.[39] Some of the planned

Hellenistic cities with their wide avenues may have been less congested; Strabo makes Alexandria sound so, although he says the ancient buildings had been neglected in his time, the first century.[40] Even there, one imagines much of the city had a bustling ambience.

The figures available for Rome indicate a high density of occupation, particularly when one allows spaces for parks, public buildings, and the ample dwellings of the rich. "The main population of the city . . . lived in cramped, noisy, airless, foul-smelling, infected quarters, paying extortionate rents to merciless landlords, undergoing daily indignities and terrors that coarsened and brutalized them," said Lewis Mumford.[41] Cicero and Martial complained of poor streets that were narrow, muddy, dusty, slippery, and unlighted.[42] Some cities, such as Pompeii, provided stepping-stones for pedestrians to keep their feet out of the mud and ordure. In Rome, only major streets were paved, and all were filled with crowds. Subura, the most densely inhabited quarter, seethed with people.[43] Traffic crawled slowly but nonetheless dangerously, and getting through the streets was a struggle.[44] Pedestrians, wagons, and the well-to-do in sedan chairs disputed the right of way with tipsy, overloaded marble carts.[45] To alleviate the congestion that threatened to strangle the city, Julius Caesar's law, the *Lex Iulia Municipalis*, prohibited wheeled traffic in the city between sunrise and two hours before sunset, except for sacred chariots and vehicles performing essential public services such as rubbish collection and construction.[46] No doubt there was a rush hour between roughly 4:00 and 6:00 p.m., especially since the streets were not lighted at night. Thus modern efforts to close parts of Rome to cars have an ancient precedent. The law was strictly enforced at first, and extended to other cities by later emperors, but fell into disuse in the chaotic third century.[47] Caesar's law did little to lessen noise pollution but shifted much of it to night hours, when it would disturb the sleep of urban dwellers whose walls were thin or whose windows were open. Noise came not only from traffic but also other sources such as industry, trade, building and demolition, and the numerous baths. Writers often complained of the din.[48]

Housing

The characteristic Mediterranean house was built of brick or stone, with a wooden roof covered with tiles. Whenever space and resources permitted, it surrounded an inner courtyard, and rooms opened inward rather than outward, an arrangement well suited to the climate. This plan was found inside towns as well as outside; in Pompeii (a resort town), houses were comfortable, only one or two stories high, facing inward and insulated from the street, with pools and gardens in open peristyles. But demands on space limited this plan's use in more

A paved street in the city of Pompeii, Italy, had sidewalks and stepping-stones that enabled pedestrians to cross without stepping in mud and ordure while leaving spaces for the wheels of carts to pass. The city, covered by ash from the eruption of Vesuvius in 79 CE, was excavated beginning in the eighteenth century. (1959)

congested cities. There, as in Ostia, the port of Rome, buildings rose several stories, and families lived in small apartments.

In Rome the houses of the wealthy were spacious, but the majority of people lived in uncomfortable apartments in *insulae*, structures whose heights must sometimes have exceeded seven stories, since Augustus Caesar set a limit of 21 m (70 feet), which Trajan later lowered to 18 m (60 feet).[49] The reason for these restrictions was the danger of collapse; *insulae* were often too tall for their foundations and supports.[50] There was no running water in these tenements; the tenants had to use a public fountain down the street, as well as public latrines, or a commode. Some of the latrines had a stream of water underneath the seats to carry waste into the sewers or elsewhere. No glass or screens kept insects out, and dust, dirt, and rubbish tended to accumulate. Since the tenements had no fireplaces or chimneys, charcoal braziers had to be used for heating, cooking, and oil-burning lamps for light; the smoke was supposed to blow out through the windows. In spite of danger and discomfort, more and more apartment buildings were constructed; by 350, there were 46,602 of them in Rome.[51]

This Roman latrine in Corinth, Greece, was unusual for its construction over running water on its way out of the city. (1992)

Fire

Since floors and roofs were made of wood, and lamps and charcoal fires common, there was an ever-present peril of fire. Building fires happened often and were not easy to extinguish once they took hold in the crowded city. A vivid picture is given by a second-century resident of Rome: "We catch sight of a certain apartment house, many stories in height, enveloped in flames and the whole neighborhood burning in a huge conflagration."[52] Because of the danger of fire and the absence of fire escapes, the uppermost floors in *insulae* had the least expensive apartments. Crassus profiteered by buying collapsed or damaged buildings at bargain prices, some of them while they were still burning.[53] Augustus formed a brigade of 7,000 freedmen firefighters, but it was only partly effective.[54] He also built a wall around the forum as a firebreak.[55] The famous fire of Nero (64 CE) was only one in a series of conflagrations that destroyed sections of the city. One of Nero's edicts was a fire safety building code promulgated after that disaster.[56]

Water Supply

Water was at first provided from nearby rivers, or from springs and wells within the city, such as the fountain of Peirene at Corinth.[57] As cities grew, local water supplies were exhausted. Solon encouraged digging wells in Athens, and dozens have been discovered in the Agora excavations.[58] Wells were circular, dug by hand, and lined with wood, stone, or brick. Vitruvius describes methods of locating underground water and likely sites for wells, such as observing water evaporation, burying a bronze or lead vessel or lamp and looking for condensation, and judging the soil, topography, and types of plants.[59] But wells became inadequate.

Rivers often carried pollutants and varied greatly in volume, while local sources of water proved inadequate or dried up as cities grew, so governments reached out to distant supplies through aqueducts. Aqueducts ran at ground level as covered canals or were raised or buried to maintain a working grade. About 530 BCE, the people of Samos excavated a tunnel through a mountain to bring water to the city.[60] Designed by Eupalinus of Megara, this remarkable work, which still exists, was about 1,036 m (3,400 feet) long and six feet square in cross section. At intervals, vertical shafts connected the tunnel to the surface. It was bored from both sides of a mountain at once, and the two sections would have come close to an exact join at the halfway point, but before reaching that point, each bore swerved as if the engineers were trying to guarantee an intersection, which they achieved. To contain the ceramic aqueduct pipe, a channel about 0.9 m (3 feet) wide and 6–9 m (20–30 feet) deep was cut into the floor of the tunnel on one side. Also, because the slope of the tunnel was not sufficiently steep to let water flow rapidly, the channel has a steeper gradient than the main tunnel. The engineer Theagenes devised an underground aqueduct from Mount Pentelicus to Athens that again had a vertical airshaft every 15 m (50 feet).[61] Meton built another aqueduct to Piraeus. "At Olynthus a very fine specimen has been found, designed to bring water to a city fountain from hills several miles to the north, and showing a knowledge of engineering which few would have attributed to the Greeks before Hellenistic times," remarks Wycherley.[62] The inverted siphon presents an example of Hellenistic engineering. In his *Pneumatics*, circa 65 CE, Hero of Alexandria described the principle, but it had been used for centuries.[63] Eumenes II of Pergamum had commissioned in 180 BCE a closed-pipe inverted siphon system with a pressure of 183 kg/cm^2 (260 lb/in^2) at the lowest point.[64]

Roman aqueducts are surviving wonders of the ancient world, and Frontinus boasted, "With such an array of indispensable structures carrying so many waters, compare, if you will, the idle Pyramids or the useless, though famous, works of the Greeks!"[65] Hydraulic engineers made a major impact on the environment by gathering water from springs, lakes, and streams over a large part of the countryside, water that was no longer available in its original location for vegetation, wildlife, and agriculture. When all the aqueducts of Rome were fully operating, they carried at least one-third more water than the average flow of the Tiber.[66] The first, the Aqua Appia built in 312 BCE by Appius Claudius, ran entirely underground for 16 km (10 miles). The Anio Vetus, 270 BCE, crossed ravines on small bridges and was 64 km (40 miles) long. Later aqueducts were even longer, and were partly raised on high arcades that give the visual impression most people today have of Roman aqueducts. The Aqua Claudia, built in 47 CE, had an arcaded section of 13 km (8 miles). Romans constructed aqueducts for cities other than Rome; Augustus ordered the Flumen Augusti for Alexandria.[67] Hadrian built aqueducts in many places throughout the empire.

The height of arches in raised sections was limited by the stonework's strength to 21 m (70 feet), so greater heights were achieved by adding additional tiers. The Pont du Gard in Provence has three tiers and reaches a height of 55 m (180 feet). The Romans made pipes of wood, ceramic with leaded joints, or lead. Lead pipe sections were made by folding rectangular sheets into triangular or circular shapes, and would take pressure only up to 50 lb/in^2 without extraordinary measures such as setting them in stone or concrete.[68] The slope of an aqueduct had to be calculated carefully to keep the flow at optimum volume and at the same time to prevent overflow, and hydraulic engineers responded well to the challenge. Vitruvius recommended that the slope be not less than 1/200, but the aqueduct of Nemausus (Nîmes), which crossed atop the Pont du Gard, actually varies between 1/1,500 and 1/14,285, slopes that appear level to the eye.[69]

On entering the city, most water from aqueducts was conducted into tanks where sediment settled out, guaranteeing cleaner water. The tanks were built in pairs so that while one was being cleaned, the other continued to operate. Then the water traveled in pipes to points of use. Distribution in Rome was recorded in three categories: public items such as fountains, cisterns, military supplies, and official buildings, 44.3 percent; baths, 17.1 percent; and private houses, 38.6 percent. In the fourth century, Rome had eleven public baths, 856 private baths, and 1,352 fountains and cisterns.[70] The public received water through fountain houses such as the Enneakrounos (Fountain of Nine Spouts) in Athens, or the lavish Nymphaeum at Miletus.[71] Cisterns stored water for times of need; one of the largest was underground in Constantinople, built by Justinian in 528, which is 138 m (463 feet) by 65 m (240 feet) in size, has 336 columns supporting the roof, and could hold 80,000 m^3 (2,800,000 feet^3) of water. A nearby cistern, called the "Hall of 1001 Columns," actually has only 224 of them.[72]

The Pont du Gard carried the water of the Roman aqueduct of Nemausus (Nîmes) 48.8 m (160 feet) above the Gard River. Completed in 60 CE, it is the highest of all Roman aqueduct bridges. It supplied water to fountains, baths, and homes in the city. (1984)

City governments carefully supervised water supply, and the office of water commissioner was an important one. In Athens, the superintendent of the fountains was elected by show of hands.[73] This places the office in the category of those who, like the generals, needed special skills and therefore could not be selected by lot. Water theft, a fairly common offense, was punishable by fines.[74] Rome had officers called Aquarii in charge of supply and maintenance. Augustus appointed a board of *curatores* controlled by the Imperial Procurator Aquarum, which was given sole responsibility by Claudius.[75] Sextus Julius Frontinus, the author of a valuable book on aqueducts, filled this office from 97 to 104 CE. Measures to obtain and safeguard water supply were characteristic of the Romans wherever they went, and were one of the keys to the success of their legions. Without clean water, soldiers and colonists would have been decimated.

Water Pollution

Ancient physicians and hydrologists stressed the need for pure water.[76] Vitruvius noted that sunlight causes the purest particles of water to evaporate, concentrating the pollutants—the "heavy, coarse, and unhealthy parts"—in what is left. He advised testing water for purity by methods such as evaporation, sedimentation, boiling, and the addition of wine, a powerful antiseptic, in small quantities.[77] To purify water, authors say, one can expose it to sun and air; filter it through tufa, lamp-wicks, or wool; allow it to percolate through clean sand; or boil it.[78] Athenaeus of Attaleia wrote *On the Purification of Water*, discussing filtration and percolation, but it survives only in short citations in Oribasius. Sources of water varied greatly in purity. The quality of water from the Roman Aqua Virgo and Aqua Marcia was so fine that even settling was not needed. But water from the Aqua Alsietina was undrinkable, and used only for mills, ornamental fountains, and sewer flushing.[79] The channels of aqueducts were generally covered with stone slabs to prevent pollution.

Vitruvius knew that lead pipes could be dangerous. "Water . . . is made injurious by lead, because white lead is produced by it; and this is said to be harmful to the human body." He then described symptoms of lead poisoning in workers exposed to it, and concluded that "water should not be brought in lead pipes if we desire to have it wholesome."[80] Lead pipes will contaminate acidic water, and certain bacteria found in water systems may provide the acidity necessary to put the lead into solution. But fresh water in the Mediterranean area is often charged with calcium carbonate from limestone, which buffers acidity and can deposit travertine in pipes and channels. These deposits are sometimes many centimeters thick in aqueducts, and would have kept the lead in channel joints from leaching into the water.[81] The insides of aqueducts were waterproofed with maltha concrete, a pinkish mixture including lime, pork fat, and the milk of unripe figs.[82]

Waste Disposal

Garbage and sewage presented a challenging problem for ancient cities. Inhabitants tended to deposit refuse in any opportune spot, or simply to throw it out a window, although care was advisable since one could be sued for damages. Laws in Athens and elsewhere directed that waste be carried outside the walls for a certain distance before it was dumped.[83] Street cleaning is mentioned in many

Roman laws, as well as in inscriptions at Pergamum and other places in the eastern Mediterranean. Caesar required every citizen to keep the street in front of his residence swept clean.[84] Drainage sewers were often covered, and excess water in the city supply was used to keep them flushed out. Athens had a sewer that provided fertilizer for her own fields.[85] But not every Athenian house was connected to the sewer; many had their own cesspools.

As a result of its huge size, Rome generated more waste and had the potential to do more damage to the environment than other ancient cities. But Rome also took additional measures to protect public health. The Cloaca Maxima was Rome's main drain. About 4.5 × 3.3 m (15 × 11 feet) in cross section in some places, it could be maintained by workmen from within.[86] Under ordinary conditions, much of Rome's waste matter was flushed out through sewers and into the Tiber, which, it was hoped, would carry it past Ostia into the sea. There was no sewage treatment. Often during floods, the Tiber backed up through the sewers and inundated lower sections of the city. It was reported that the drain in the floor of the Pantheon looked like a fountain at such times.[87] During the empire, Rome had spacious public latrines richly decorated with marble and mosaics and seemingly designed for conversation as well as their primary purpose. Vespasian met with criticism when he taxed public conveniences, creating history's first pay toilets.[88] The sewers drained the latrines, and some large private houses, but not usually the *insulae*. People dumped every imaginable form of refuse into the river, including stale grain and bodies that had been denied burial.[89] The level of odor pollution can be imagined. It is no wonder that there is only one mention of drinking from the Tiber in all Roman history.[90] Swimming in it, which is mentioned, must have taken place upstream off the Campus Martius.[91] To deal with the accumulated mess, conscientious emperors dredged the river; Augustus "widened the bed of the Tiber and cleaned it out, filled as it had been for some time with rubbish and narrowed with projecting buildings," and much later Aurelian followed his example.[92] Augustus appointed *curatores alvei et riparum Tiberis* (supervisors of the river bed and banks of the Tiber), and Trajan added the sewers to their jurisdiction.[93]

Air Pollution

Countless cooking and baking fires; smoky lamps; charcoal fires to heat rooms; smoke pouring from furnaces in the baths, from metal working, and from kilns for firing of pottery; and ubiquitous dust meant that a city's polluted air could be seen a long way off. To Homer, smoke was the first sign of human habitation.[94] Horace remarked on the thousands of wood-burning fires in Rome.[95] Many people are surprised to discover ancient references to air pollution, but

The Mausoleum of Hadrian (now the Castel Sant'Angelo) stands above the Tiber River and the Pons Aelius, later known as the Bridge of the Angels, in Rome. The river, with its several bridges, is an integral influence on the plan of Rome, but it also suffered from water pollution. (1959)

even in the nineteenth and twentieth centuries, in large nonindustrial cities with few cars, fires and the dust of human activities produced a heavy pall. Temperature inversions, which were natural occurrences as common in ancient times as they are in the Mediterranean basin today, suspended smoke and dust over cities. Air pollution was familiar to the Romans, who termed it *gravioris caeli* (heavy heaven) or *infamis aer* (infamous air).[96] A trip out to the country, in the right direction, offered welcome relief. But Martial commented that the Sun was so obscured by the smoke and dust in the city that people coming back from the countryside would lose their tan after a few days.[97] There was a "brown cloud" in ancient Rome as in many modern metropolises. The difference lies in the chemical constitution of some of the pollutants and their amounts.

Vermin and Disease

Mankind has always been accompanied by a number of opportunistic organisms that share human habitations, flourishing in the conditions created by humans and threatening human health. The laws of ecology are not repealed when a city is founded, and they do not always operate to the benefit of its human inhabitants. A number of these organisms are vectors of disease: rats, mice, lice, bedbugs, fleas, flies, gnats, and mosquitoes are among those found almost everywhere. With inefficient ancient methods of waste disposal, rats had plentiful sources of food, and sewers were accessible for movement and breeding. Domestic cats, dogs, and weasels helped to control their numbers to some extent. Large cities were especially vulnerable to contagious diseases. There were several altars to the goddess Febris (Fever) at Rome, with good reason.[98] The periodic pandemics of plague that spread across the Mediterranean basin attacked the cities with particular severity.[99]

Burial

Treatment of the dead was a concern of ancient cities, and obviously connected with the spread of disease. The Greeks and Romans often buried the deceased rather than cremating them.[100] Corpses were a potential source of disease, so a virtually universal law forbade burial within city walls. Outside every Greek and Roman city, therefore, tombs lined the roads. At Athens, the Ceramicus cemetery lies just outside the Dipylon Gate and contains interments from every century of the city's ancient history. Near Pompeii, Rome, and dozens of cities, funeral monuments can be seen strung out along the roads. Catacombs are found widely in the Mediterranean area. Outside Rome, they were excavated in tufa, a soft volcanic rock that also served as building material. During the Roman Republic, burial was not permitted inside the official city limits, but as time passed, the inhabited area spread beyond those limits. Bodies of paupers and others were thrown into charnel pits. At the time of Augustus, efforts were made to end this practice. Cremation became more common, and the worst of the charnel pits were covered and planted with gardens.[101]

Roads

Roads are a city's means of reaching outward to tap the natural resources of the countryside and to link to other cities through trade and exploitation. Understandably, cities maintained the roads. While classical Greeks often preferred to travel by sea, they sometimes constructed respectable roadways, as their Mycenaean ancestors did in the Argolid, perhaps the same "well-drained roads" of which Homer speaks.[102] The road used to bring marble from Mount Pentelicus to Athens was paved with limestone slabs. Sacred roads, such as those from Athens to Eleusis, Elis to Olympia, and the approach to Delphi, were partly paved. Some roads had artificial ruts to keep carts from slipping. Lines of trees were planted to shade roads; one near the Isthmus of Corinth was lined with pines, and another along the Alpheus River had myrtles and other trees.[103] Amyntas II and Philip II of Macedonia built many roads. But the travel writer Strabo complains that Greek roads were bad, poorly drained, and often steep.[104] In Hellenistic times, Greeks copied the admirable Persian roads, as well as the system of mounted messengers with post houses. Mail went by "camel express" in Ptolemaic and Roman Egypt as an alternative to shipping on the river.[105]

The deservedly famous Roman roads stretched beyond the city gates in every direction. They are some of the most notable marks the Romans left on the landscapes of Europe, Asia, and Africa. They had Etruscan road building as a model but improved on it, adopting lime mortar from the Greeks in southern Italy about 300 BCE, and realizing the usefulness of pozzuolana cement a century and a half later.[106] Roman highways are major works of construction; built with foundations secure enough to have supported a wall, they were paved with stone and concrete. Vitruvius describes a four-layer base, three to four times as deep as under a modern road.[107] They followed lines as straight as possible, crossing marshes on causeways of pilings and rivers on magnificent bridges, many still existing. The roads did not lie lightly on the countryside, nor were they engineered to follow contours and avoid erosion, although they did drain well. Engineers responded brilliantly to the challenges of narrow gorges and difficult mountain passes. Roads were wide; Augustus decreed a width of 12 m (40 feet). The labor of road building was performed by the army or by contractors hired by imperial or provincial authorities.[108] So extensive was the system that its maintenance was a serious drain on public budgets. In road building, as in much else, the Roman attitude toward the natural world was that of conquest of nature and confidence in human power. Roads secured the extent of Roman domination and made land transportation more rapid, economical, and competitive with sea transport. They encouraged the development of agriculture, mining, and industry farther from metropolitan centers by providing access to distant areas. Because of roads, more forests were felled. More plants and animals were transported, with the result that they were introduced to new lands or extirpated in their original ranges. Roads increased human mobility and reduced the inaccessibility of marginal territories, amplifying the impact of the Romans on the natural environment.

Rural Nostalgia

City dwellers developed a yearning for rural scenes as they considered the discomforts of urban life. The larger the city, the stronger the nostalgia. The polarity between city and country was a major theme in Greek and Latin literature, and the comparison was almost always favorable to the country. This strain first became prominent in the crowded city of Alexandria, where a school of pastoral writers centered around Theocritus adopted a romantic style of nature description, celebrating the beauties of the countryside.[109]

Horace, Martial, Juvenal, and others maintained rural retreats and extolled the virtues of the rustic life. But the length of time busy urbanites spent in their villas posed problems; some "seceded," abandoning Rome. Others found a hundred things to do in town, and even when they managed to escape to the country, friends and business associates hounded them and dragged them back.[110] They might compromise by buying mansions in the suburbs, spending vacations at seaside resorts, or creating and enjoying parks and gardens.[111]

Conclusion

Cities are in fact ecosystems, a series of ecological relationships.[112] This is not to say simply, as many urban sociologists have, that an interrelationship of various social and economic groups exists within the structure of a city, and that ecological concepts such as succession, distribution, and competition can be used to study their spatial arrangement and history.[113] Such a mode of study does not show the city as a genuine ecosystem; it adopts ecology as a metaphor, not a description, and creates an ideal structure that is hierarchical, not ecological. A city must not be studied in artificial isolation from its hinterland. A city is not a truncated phenomenon but rather exists in a natural context. Greek and Roman cities had an overwhelming effect on the environment where they were located. This is true both in the built-up city itself and in its immediate vicinity with various categories of land use.

Cities are, after all, habitats constructed by humans for human occupation. Many problems found in modern cities are not new; ancient cities knew them to a greater or lesser extent. But the impacts of urbanism were by no means limited to the area covered by dwellings and fields, or even to the greater territory over which a city exercised political authority. Each city exploited the resources of the land it could dominate along its frontiers, and tentacles of trade and economic power might reach outward beyond them to draw valued materials of many kinds from lands located at great distances overseas or across mountain and desert barriers. The deforestation of isolated places occurred in response to the demands of distant cities, so that the cedars of Lebanon were sacrificed to form the fleets of Antioch and Alexandria, or to adorn the palaces of Roman emperors and empresses.

Nowhere is the far-reaching economic impact of cities more evident than in the lengths to which they were willing to go to obtain grain for their hungry populations. Greece reached into the hinterland of the Black Sea, Rome imported from North Africa, and ships seeking grain visited Egyptian ports from the farthest Mediterranean cities. The failure of ancient cities to harmoniously adapt their economies to natural systems is a basic cause of their decline, and a reason why so many today are ruins within eroded and desiccated landscapes. They placed too great a demand on available resources, depleted them within their sphere, and then went as far as they could to gain access to additional resources, until this effort also failed. They faltered because they failed to maintain the balance with their own environment that is necessary to the long-term survival of any human community. They treated nature as an apparently inexhaustible mine rather than as a living system, as an exploitable empire rather than as part of an organic whole that included them as well.[114] Ecological failures interacted with social, political, and economic forces to assure that many Greek and Roman cities would disappear or be altered beyond recognition in a fragmentation of the ancient world that represented in most places a disastrous decline in the level of civilization. Environmental impacts were so great as to be self-destructive. The same forces are at work in analogous ways in the modern world, and societies are clearly directing them with attitudes derived from ancient antecedents that have already demonstrated their failure.

Eleven

Paradises and Parks, Gardens and Groves

etting aside special areas for trees, plants, animals, and natural features is not a new idea. Although the world's first national park was Yellowstone, established by the United States in 1872, the Greeks and Romans long before had preserved sections of the natural environment as sanctuaries sacred to gods and goddesses, or as hunting and pleasure grounds for rulers or the people. Sacred groves were traditional in many parts of the world from early times.[1] Babylonian, Assyrian, and Persian kings apparently felt both nostalgia for wild nature and the desire to dominate it, manifested in the many gardens and parks, including walled "paradises" in which useful and remarkable trees were planted, and where wild animals were kept for viewing and hunting.[2] Greek and Roman men of wealth and power became familiar with these spaces and created similar places on their own lands. Gardens or planted parks owned privately or publicly provided environmental amenities, undoubtedly saving certain areas from some of the environmental damage already noted.

Sacred Enclosures

The Greek and Roman landscape was dotted like a leopard skin, with thousands of places designated as sacred space. A sacred precinct, called *hieron temenos* in Greek and *templum* in Latin, was an area set aside and often walled to mark the boundary between holy and ordinary. These spaces usually contained groves of trees and springs of water, though often mountaintops or other prominent features were similarly treated. Within them the environment was preserved, as a rule, in its natural state. The motive for this conservation was religious reverence, the idea that the gods inhabited such places. The presence of deity was recognized in the quality of the environment itself. Seneca remarked: "If you come upon a grove of old trees that have lifted up their crowns above the common height and shut out the light of the sky by the darkness of their interlacing boughs, you feel that there is a spirit in the place, so lofty is the wood, so lone the spot, so wondrous the thick unbroken shade."[3] Or Ovid, who said, "Here stands a silent grove black with the shade of oaks; at the sight of it, anyone could say, 'there is a spirit here!'"[4] Virgil had Evander remark that when they saw the old tree-covered Capitoline Hill, the rural folk who lived around it exclaimed, "Some god has this grove for dwelling!"[5] This primal attitude long persisted in popular feeling, as Pliny the Elder indicated: "Trees were the first temples of the gods, and even now simple country people dedicate a tree of exceptional height to a god with the ritual of olden times, and we . . . worship forests and the very silences they contain."[6]

Worship took place outdoors; originally the temple was identical to the reserved natural site. The buildings later erected in the sanctuaries were at first simply protective shelters for the images of the gods, while the altars remained outside under trees and sky. The intent was to keep the area in as near a primeval state as possible. In archaic times many of these reserves were sections of virgin forest; although not all were groves, the special association of trees with sacred places is unmistakable, so that even treeless sanctuaries were called groves.[7] Virgil noted that the gods favor wild trees "unsown by mortal hand."[8] They were wilderness areas in the sense of being preserved from changes wrought by humans, but they were not wilderness in the sense of regions that lack human beings. They were used for worship, supervised by local authorities, and priests or guards sometimes lived in them. Management policies were developed, and as time went on, many took on the aspect of parks, with planted and cultivated trees. Pausanias described a *temenos* at Gryneum: "Apollo has a most beautiful grove of cultivated trees and of all trees which, without bearing fruit, are pleasant to smell or see."[9] On Lesbos grew a grove of apple trees dedicated to Aphrodite, to whom, as the recipient of Paris's golden apple, the apple was sacred. Temples never lost their connection with trees; it was felt that every one needed to have trees around it, and if there were none, they were planted. When the Athenians built the Parthenon on the barren limestone outcropping called the Acropolis, they excavated two rows of pits in the rock, filled them with soil, and planted cypresses in them. Similar holes are found beside other temples such as the Theseion above the Athenian agora.

The walled cemetery of an orthodox church in Messenia, Greece, with planted cypresses, represents the appearance of an ancient sacred precinct (*temenos*), with a temple and sacred grove surrounded by a protective wall. (1959)

The Extent of Sacred Precincts

Sacred enclosures were of various sizes. Some were small plots with a temple and a few trees that must have looked from a distance like the walled cemeteries filled with cypresses beside Orthodox churches in modern Greece. Apuleius spoke of travelers praying under the trees on "a little sacred hill fenced all around."[10] But the grove of Daphne was ten miles in circumference; the sacred land of Crisa, near Delphi, was a plain reserved from cultivation that covered many square miles; and a grove near Lerna stretched all the way down a mountainside to the sea.[11] Pausanias described the grove of Asclepius at Epidaurus as "surrounded by mountains on every side,"[12] implying that it was extensive. Alexander the Great found an entire island dedicated to a goddess identified as Artemis, covered with dense forests filled with deer.[13] Since sacred groves numbered many hundreds, the total area included in them was considerable, so that protection was extended to a significant fraction of the ancient landscape. Sacred centers of worship were whenever possible located near and oriented to impressive features of the landscape and the directions of important astronomical configurations.

Because the groves were strictly protected, the trees in them often grew to remarkable dimensions. It was believed that large, notable trees were uniquely cherished by the gods and served as dwelling places for tree spirits, or dryads. They were allowed to live until wind, fire, or rot brought them down. The plane trees at Pharae were hollow with age and big enough to sleep or picnic inside.[14] One hollow tree in Lycia, which must have been in a sacred grove, was 25 m

The Temple of Apollo at Delphi, site of a famous oracle and considered the center of the world, was built in a spectacular natural location on the slopes of Mount Parnassos below the Phaedriades (Shining Cliffs) and next to a sacred spring. (2011)

(81 feet) in circumference and provided Lucius Mucianus space for a banquet for eighteen.[15] Pausanias saw examples of arboreal gigantism at Psophis, cypress trees called the "Maidens" that "overshadowed a mountain," although he did not mention the size of the mountain. "These cypresses," he added, "they deem sacred to Alcmaeon, and will not fell them."[16]

Biodiversity in the Groves

The variety of plant and animal species known in sacred groves[17] makes clear that biodiversity flourished and was protected in these places.[18] Trees consisted of a mixture of species, although one kind might predominate in a given grove. The gods had favorite species considered to be sacred to them. The oak belonged to the king of gods, Zeus; the olive to his daughter Athena; the laurel to the archer-god Apollo; the apple to the love-goddess Aphrodite; the fir to Pan, the god of nature—the list could be extended indefinitely. Thus it might be expected that the groves sacred to a specific god would consist of trees considered to belong to that god. However, upon examination of the texts, this idea proves to be misleading. Groves usually consisted of mixed species; the expression "all sorts of trees" is often encountered in the literature.[19] Where a species is mentioned as comprising a grove, it might belong to any god, goddess, or hero, not just to the one to whom the tree was sacred. There were oak groves dedicated to Demeter, goddess of crops; to the messenger-god Hermes; to the war-god Ares and the hero Lycus; to those portentous goddesses, the Fates and Furies; as well as to Zeus himself. Olive groves were dedicated to Zeus, Apollo, Artemis, and the heroine Ino, not just to Athena. While the laurel was undoubtedly Apollo's special tree, there were also laurel groves dedicated to his twin sister Artemis; to Dionysus; to the Sun-god Helios; to the Hesperides, guardians of the golden apples; and to the Twins, or Dioscuri. Artemis was the "goddess of the wild forest" in general.

Of trees or large shrubs in groves, there were more than forty named species that grew in the wild in the ecosystems of the Mediterranean. Among the most often mentioned are three kinds of oak, two kinds of pine, cypress, elm, laurel, myrtle, wild olive, plane, and both black and white poplar. "Kinds" is probably more accurate than "species," since Greek texts give plants and animals common names that do not necessarily equate with the species recognized by modern taxonomy. Usually, but not always, it is possible to identify the genus or species, but there are frequent cases where one cannot be certain. About a dozen kinds of cultivated or fruit-bearing trees and vines are noted in the sacred groves, sometimes with the specific statement that they were planted there. Often it is impossible to say whether a tree in a grove was planted, since plants may have both wild and cultivated forms, and forest trees were sometimes planted, as well. Perhaps these plantations within the groves enhanced biological diversity, but they could have also altered the natural ecological state of the forest fragments that remained in the groves. Of cultivated plants in the groves, the olive is by far the most often mentioned in ancient documents, and the grapevine is second. This is not surprising; they were two of the most important Mediterranean food plants. Others include apple, fig, palm, and pear. Some groves must have taken on a parklike air, with planted or cultivated trees. Pausanias described a *temenos* at Gryneum as follows: "Apollo has a most beautiful grove of cultivated trees and of all trees which, without bearing fruit, are pleasant to smell or see."[20] On the island of Lesbos there was a grove of apple trees dedicated to Aphrodite, who, as the recipient of the famous golden apple awarded by Paris, was goddess of the apple tree.

Species of herbs in sacred groves are harder to identify. Although writers say that grass and many flowers were found there, they seldom mentioned the names of the understory plants. Those that can be identified are acanthus, alsine, lily, lotus, reed, rose, smilax, and thistle. There were undoubtedly many more, and the protection accorded to sacred groves must have improved their survival. Planting cultivated annuals like wheat, barley, and pulses was not permitted in sacred groves where there were trees, but it sometimes happened on a sacred field, or *chorion*, that was dedicated to a god or gods.

All kinds of animals visited sacred groves or made homes there. Greek and Latin writers mainly gave their attention to those that were large, or that were the usual game species, even though hunting or fishing was not permitted inside the groves. As with the plants, it must be noted that there were undoubtedly more kinds than can be found in the written sources. Among mammals, the most often mentioned are deer of two kinds, red deer and roe deer. Hares were there, but they usually avoided tree-covered places. Also called denizens of groves are bear, wild boar, wild goat, lion, and wolf. The lion still persisted in Greece in the fifth century BCE, but became extinct there early in the Roman period. Domesticated animals are often discussed in connection with sacred groves, usually to say that they were excluded from them, or sacrificed there. The kinds mentioned are cattle, dogs, goats, horses, pigs, sheep, and (in a late source) chickens. Domestic animals were forbidden, and therefore usually absent from sacred groves, but in a few cases some were kept in a grove and had sacred status. At Etna in Sicily, for example, there was a grove of Hephaestus with a pack of sacred dogs that "wag[ged] their tails and fawn[ed] on prudent people," but bit criminals and chased away the debauched.[21]

Birds were numerous in sacred groves. Again, many writers simply remark that there were lots of them in sacred groves without saying which kinds. The one most noted, as might be expected, is the nightingale with its beautiful song. Others are the crow, jackdaw, and sea crow, along with blackbird, eagle, falcon, kingfisher, owl, peacock, stork, and swan. The snake, without distinction of species, is the reptile most often named. The only others of interest to herpetologists are tortoise and frog. Fish were protected in the waters of several groves; the kinds specified are eel and the elusive peacock fish, although it must be assumed that there were many other species in those places. Mussels are noted in one river on sacred land. Ancient writers neglected invertebrates, even though we can be sure that there were countless species. The only ones that could be found in a survey of likely sources are ant, bee, cicada, and spider. It was said that Apollo had purified the grove of Clarus from "noxious creatures," including scorpion, spiders, and, to name a vertebrate, the viper.

Regulation of Sacred Places

The rules protecting land reserved for the gods were strict, numerous, and followed a consistent pattern, although specific laws varied from place to place and in different periods. The underlying principle was that the groves were property of the gods and must not be damaged in any way. These laws first defined the sacred area's boundary and prohibited trespassing. To step over the line, however it was marked, was to pass from ordinary ground to holy ground, and was allowed only for those who were prepared and would not pollute it. It is a sacred grove from which unworthy mortals were excluded by the sonorous words *Procul o procul este profani* "Keep out, profane ones!"[22] In Pellene was "a grove surrounded by a wall, sacred to Artemis the Savior . . . no man [was] allowed to enter it except the priests."[23] The grove at Pellene was an exception; usually ordinary persons could enter if they were ritually clean; that is, not guilty of serious nonabsolved crimes such as bloodshed. They might be excluded if they were carrying iron or weapons of any sort, or accompanied by hunting dogs. Women were excluded during menses and for a time during and after pregnancy. One had to be careful to know about unmarked boundaries wherever one went, because both religious and civil penalties applied even if the transgressors were unaware they had strayed onto consecrated ground.

A basic law found everywhere forbade felling trees or cutting branches. "Men call them the holy places of the immortals, and never mortal lops them with the axe."[24] Even removal of fallen dead timber or leaves was prohibited. In the grove of Hyrnetho, "of the olives and all the trees that grew there, no man might take home the broken boughs, or use them for any purpose whatsoever, but they leave the branches where they lie, because they are sacred."[25] If a tree was felled, it was believed that its spirit, the dryad, died, and the god might leave the sanctuary. All living denizens of the groves were protected, and hunting, fishing, and bird catching were strictly forbidden.[26]

Wild animals were granted haven in sacred groves, but domestic animals were excluded. Penalties were set for herders who allowed cattle, sheep, goats, swine, or horses to graze in the precincts, and animal-drawn vehicles were forbidden to enter.[27] Those who observed any infractions of the rules governing sacred places were required to report them under penalty of law.[28] Other common rules prevented plowing and sowing, as well as erecting unauthorized buildings.[29] The Sacred War was fought over the illegal cultivation of Apollo's sacred ground at Crisa. Setting fire to a sacred grove was the most heinous of crimes, even in wartime, although it did happen. Human beings who sought shelter in a grove—even slaves—were granted sanctuary, and punishment was visited upon those who violated that right. Cleomenes, who burned 5,000 Argives to death in a god's forest, was driven mad by the thought of divine retribution.[30]

Civil regulations governing sacred groves are recorded in many inscriptions, often carved on stones in the precincts themselves. The local magistrates with jurisdiction over sanctuaries were generally those who administered religious matters; there was no separation of church and state in ancient times. In Athens and Chios, the officer was called "king" (*basileus*)—not the head of state but the democratic appointee who retained the old royal title for religious purposes.[31] Priests who guarded the groves, as well as everyone else, were required to report acts of injury to officials who could prosecute the miscreants. Penalties were severe. Fines in amounts ranging from fifty to 1,000 drachmas were exacted for cutting down a tree or carrying away leaves. Since an average workman was paid one-third to one drachma per day, the fines were high enough to discourage attempts to profit by theft from the precincts. Expensive mandatory sacrifices could also be assessed. Slaves were whipped or imprisoned for the same offenses. To these heavy punishments, ritual curses were joined. Ancient polytheists never laughed at curses because the gods might hear them, and tradition was full of examples of divine retribution for infractions, stories that the common people took seriously. When Erysichthon ignored a dryad's protest and cut down her tree, he was stricken with hunger that could never be satisfied.[32] Hunger seems an appropriate punishment for a crime against the land. Others were driven mad or were changed into trees, fish, or other creatures.

Exceptions

Special exceptions were made to the protective regulations. Relaxed rules did not happen often enough to destroy the groves, but they did allow a kind of "multiple use." Most of these exceptions were intended to ensure religious use of the sanctuaries' resources. As much wood could be taken as was necessary for sacrifices, and worshippers might bear branches and wear crowns made from holy trees. Animals in the precincts, such as wild goats and deer, could sometimes be captured and offered to the deity. Furthermore, the trees in a grove could be used in building a temple. Although classical temples were mostly made of stone, their roofs required long timber roof poles and rafters. Since large trees survived in groves when they had been cut elsewhere, it is understandable that temple builders looked to the very resources they supervised, and beyond them to other sacred groves. The magistrates of Carpathos ordered a tall cypress to be felled in the precinct of Apollo and sent to Athens for use in rebuilding a temple of Athena.[33] The Athenians, in raising an inscription of thanks to their benefactors, recognized that such use of a consecrated tree was appropriate. Wood from sacred trees was believed to keep magical powers when fashioned into objects. It was therefore used to make statues of gods; staffs for augurs, speakers, and generals; military standards; scepters of office; heralds' wands; policemen's nightsticks; divining rods; and lot tokens for oracles.

Management

With so many uses for wood from sacred groves, foresters were needed to oversee their management. Mythology gave Aristaeus the title of "caretaker of groves" (*cultor nemorum*), but there is historical evidence, too.[34] The municipal guild of woodmen (*dendrophoroi*) in Athens was charged to locate, cut, and bring to the city each year the sacred tree of the Great Mother. At Olympia there was an official woodman on the staff of the sanctuary of Zeus: "His duty is to supply states and private persons with wood for sacrifices at a fixed price."[35] This priestly forester also superintended sacrifices. Thus experienced personnel selected the wood to be cut in the groves.

Since cutting sacred trees involved formal violation of the groves, special sacrifices had to be held to obtain forgiveness. Each year the Arval Brethren, a Roman priesthood who cared for a large forest dedicated to Dea Dia near the city, "offered two young pigs in order to expiate the unavoidable desecration of the sacred grove by the use of the axe in pruning and felling it . . . whenever iron was brought into the grove, as for . . . the lopping and felling of the trees . . . there were sacrifices *ob ferrum illatum* [for the bringing in of iron], and, when the work was done, *ob ferrum elatum* [for the taking out of iron]."[36] More openly mercenary, Cato the Elder provided an all-purpose prayer to be used with the sacrifice of a pig, addressed almost "to whom it may concern," to obtain permission from a god or goddess to cut wood or till the earth in a sacred grove.[37] If such a prayer were used too often, it would erode the protection offered by sanctuaries. The rules of the Arval Brethren, however, also illustrate the principle that every tree that was cut had to be replaced by planting another. Customarily, "when the trees fell from decay, or, worse still, were struck by lightning, and when replanting was undertaken, still more solemn sacrifices (*suovetaurilia maiora*) [the sacrifice together of a ram, an ox, and a pig] were offered on the spot."[38] Since trees were protected, and selected with care when cut, and because there was a firm obligation to replace every tree that fell for whatever reason, sacred groves tended to survive the general deforestation.

The groves were used for many purposes other than timber. In spite of the rules against grazing, art and literature abound with scenes of cattle, sheep, and goats foraging in sacred groves.[39] Virgil says that sheep graze where "a grove / Black with thick holm-oaks broods with holy shade."[40] Ovid reports that at the festival of Parilia, shepherds offered expiation to the gods for entering sacred groves, sitting in the shadows of hallowed trees, and lopping leafy branches for their animals to eat.[41] There would have been no use for such a ceremony unless herders often, deliberately or inadvertently, resorted to the groves. In addition to temples, other buildings of quasi-religious and public character were erected in consecrated precincts: baths, stadiums, gymnasiums, schools, old people's homes, and the ancient equivalents of hospitals.[42] Public meetings and elections sometimes were held there. These could hardly have enhanced the sylvan qualities of the groves.

Leasing and Reforestation

Sacred land was sometimes privately owned, and could in some circumstances be rented. Legal documents outlining such leases survive today. Xenophon mentioned as a well-known fact that people lease "enclosures and sanctuaries" (*temenê kai hiera*).[43] Much later, Juvenal complained that groves around Rome were being rented out to foreigners.[44] One purpose of leasing was for the removal and sale of wood and other forest products. On the island of Chios, a family called the Clytidae rented out a sacred grove on their land, and the terms were recorded in an inscription.[45] They required the tenants to reforest the grove by planting young trees,[46] indicating a similarity between the practice of replanting in the groves managed by priesthoods and those in private hands. Since some of the same people also managed forests outside the consecrated lands, they undoubtedly saw the advantages of replanting and assuring sustained yield of resources. Sacred groves could have served in an unintended way as experimental forests where conservation practices were demonstrated.

Limitation of Sacred Space

The practice of setting physical boundaries for sacred spaces consecrated and protected what was within, but by implication unhallowed the land outside. Beyond the bounds, the gods no longer protected the Earth, and people were free to use it as they saw fit. Inside the *temenos* there might be glimpsed a holy light, but outside shone only the ordinary light of day. Thus an enormous step had been taken toward desacralizing nature.[47] Pausanias, writing in the first century, gives the impression that over much of Greece, sacred groves were isolated islands of forest in a generally denuded landscape. Strabo provides similar descriptions for most of the Roman Empire, and further points out that even some sanctuaries had lost their trees: "But the poets embellish things, calling all sacred precincts 'sacred groves,' even if they are bare of trees."[48]

Paradises, Parks, and Gardens
Royal Preserves

Parks and gardens for secular purposes, public or private, were also established. Some were preserved as the property of rulers, used for hunting or enjoyment. The legendary King Alcinous of Scheria, visited by Odysseus, had a large garden with trees and fountains near his palace.[49] Parks with groves of trees in them, either natural or planted, were called "paradises," a word derived from the Persian *pairi-daêza* or "enclosure," because they represented a tradition perpetuated by Persian kings and satraps and adopted by other monarchs.[50] Soon after the Persian Wars, Gelon, ruler of Syracuse in Sicily, planted a superb royal park containing fruit trees and flowerbeds.[51] Theophrastus remarked that paradises in Syria protected fine, large Lebanon cedars.[52] Exotic trees imported and planted in these arboretums were more than curiosities; Apollonius advised Zeno to plant 300 fir trees in the paradise at Philadelphia (the site of modern Amman, Jordan), "for the tree has a striking appearance and will be of service to the king."[53] By service, he undoubtedly meant that they would eventually be felled for timber. Nero imitated the Persian paradises by planting many acres of landscaped gardens, meadows, and trees around his Domus Aurea (Golden House) in central Rome.[54] Hadrian's extensive gardens at Tivoli, 26 km (16 miles) outside the city, are deservedly famous.

Private Reservations

Wealthier landowners imitated royalty and limited forest clearance by enclosing tracts of woodland as private reserves. Quintus Hortensius built a wall around more than 50 *jugera* (20 hectares or 33 acres) of his land and treated it as a park.[55] Others planted trees of many species together in studied disorder to make an artificial wilderness (perhaps like the gardens of China, where art exhausted itself in an attempt to be indistinguishable from nature).[56] Still others made collections of exotic trees.

Urban Parks and Gardens

Smaller parks and gardens existed in cities, relieving the urban environment and offering open space and greenery. Private gardens, provided with flowing water and planted with trees, flowers, and shrubs, were often seen near opulent mansions and even relatively simple homes. A large house might enclose a sizable garden in a peristyle. Cimon of Athens made himself popular by throwing open his own garden to the people, turning it in effect into a public park.[57] Theophrastus planted a garden with specimens of imported plants and trees near the Lyceum and used it as a teaching arboretum for his students. Epicurus met with his disciples in a private garden, and his school of philosophy was thenceforth known as the Garden School. The greenbelt that virtually encircled the city of Rome, however, composed of villas and semiagricultural lands, was an unintended benefit of the desires of rich owners for quiet rural surroundings and the semblance of the farm life of their ancestors. The elaborate villas of the affluent in attractive settings outside urban centers had extensive gardens and tree plantings with fishponds, fountains, waterfalls, and grottos, where landscape art sought to outdo nature.

Parks developed by governments and open to the public provided amenities in every city. Many of these, like the Academy in Athens, were originally sacred groves and temple grounds, but statesmen added walks, plantings, fountains, and places for recreation and exercise. Some Hellenistic cities were graced with parks as part of their original plans, located so as to give a spacious impression to public areas. Seleucus Nicator had the boulevards of his capital city, Antioch, ornamented with flowerbeds, and Ptolemaic Alexandria had fine gardens along its avenues.[58] The Romans created an impressive series of private and public gardens to improve the quality of life in the cities of their empire. In Rome itself, Pompey provided a vast enclosed park containing trees, fountains, and statues.[59] Public gardens surrounded by colonnades eventually stretched across the Campus Martius and other sections of the city. Maecenas bought a large piece of land that had been used as a charnel pit for paupers, planted it with trees and flowers, and made it a public park, while the mausoleum of his powerful friend Augustus was surrounded by gardens containing cypresses.[60] Later, Vespasian expanded the green space in the most congested part of Rome by opening one large tree-shaded park near the Temple of Pax, and another around the Temple of the Deified Claudius.[61] Roman gardens were formal, with geometric lawns and flowerbeds, polygonal pools of water, symmetrical fountains and waterfalls, and trees and hedges clipped into fantastic topiaries.[62] They constituted a major attempt to make nature conform to the patterns of the human mind.

Conclusion

The Greeks and Romans appreciated the amenities of open space and greenery, whether they were found in carefully tended gardens or natural tracts that had been preserved in something like their original state. The motives for demarcation and protection were largely religious, as these areas were considered to be the precincts of the gods. It was not the act of setting them aside or surrounding them with walls that consecrated them; rather, the act of dedication recognized an original, sacred character of the places. The reservation of sacred groves was probably the greatest single means of conservation in the ancient world. Both Greek and Roman writers noted that plants and animals survived within them when they had disappeared from surrounding areas.

Other tracts of wild land were claimed and protected by sovereigns for hunting, pleasure, or timber. Gardens and parks, whether created by city governments or by private individuals, lessened the encroachment of buildings and urban crowding, demonstrating at the same time the love of the people for green open space. The motives responsible for these positive environmental developments were aesthetic appreciation on the one hand, and economic self-interest on the other. It is possible that some of the preserved areas served as resource pools providing natural resources on a sustainable basis, as in the case of groves managed for timber or to supply sacrifices.

Human greed made protecting these reserves difficult, because although the gods wanted to keep them inviolate, there was no doubt that humans desired to use them in many ways. While penalties exacted by governments and threatened by divine sanctions were fairly effective, religion and the state also allowed exceptions, permitting use of the resources they were intended to preserve, the construction of buildings, and even at times the alienation of land. Finally, the increasing dominance of Christianity at the end of the Roman Empire reversed the religious motive, adding a desire to destroy pagan shrines to existing economic motives urging that the reserved resources be used immediately for profit. Many sacred groves were then either adopted by churches and monasteries, which still protect a few of them, or were destroyed. Public and private parks and gardens survived where peace and stability permitted.

Twelve

Natural Disasters

The downfall of civilization, the Roman philosopher Seneca maintained, was inevitable:

> The entire human race, both present and future, is condemned to death. All the cities that have ever held dominion or have been the splendid jewels of empires belonging to others— some day men will ask where they were. And they will be swept away by various kinds of destruction: some will be ruined by wars; others will be destroyed by idleness and a peace that ends in sloth, or by luxury, the bane of those of great wealth. All these fertile plains will be blotted out of sight by a sudden overflowing of the sea, or the subsiding of the land will sweep them away suddenly into the abyss.[1]

When discussing environmental reasons for the decline of ancient civilizations, we must establish the extent to which they are anthropogenic; that is, produced by human activities. Seneca gave the causes of catastrophe, which can be divided into two categories: those caused by human failings—war, idleness, and luxury—and those visited upon humankind by external disasters like tidal waves and Earth movements. These two classes can be distinguished among the causes that operated in the natural environment. Of course, the effects of natural disasters are to a great extent determined by human actions, such as deciding to locate a city close to a volcano.

References to natural disasters are scattered through the surviving documents of the ancient Greeks and Romans, and abundant geological and archaeological evidence offers confirmation for them. The Mediterranean area is the unstable meeting place of several of the Earth's moving tectonic plates, so that earthquakes are common. Greek and Roman temples and other public buildings were built with this danger in mind. The Pantheon in Rome was constructed with heavy materials such as basalt and travertine near the base, tufa and clay brick farther up, and lighter pumice higher in the dome.[2] The Mediterranean basin is sporadically the scene of volcanic eruptions of various kinds and intensities, from the explosion of the island of Thera in the seventeenth century BCE to the relatively constant rumblings, smoking, and lava flows of Mount Etna. The eruption of Mount Vesuvius in 79 CE, which destroyed Pompeii and Herculaneum, is described below.

Thucydides[3] gives an excellent circumstantial account of a tsunami that struck the Aegean seacoasts in 426 BCE and concludes that the cause was an earthquake.[4] Pliny the Elder remarks that earthquakes cause waves at sea and inundations on land.[5] A major earthquake off the west coast of Crete in 365 created a tsunami that killed thousands of people in the Nile Delta and elsewhere around the coasts of the eastern Mediterranean.[6] Other earthquakes caused landslides and avalanches.[7] The climate, although much admired by northern Europeans, is unstable, with extreme variations in rainfall from year to year as well as heat waves and cold snaps, flood and drought. Floods are natural disasters because they result from excessive precipitation, but they are much more sudden and carry damaging material such as rocks and silt, when forests have been removed from the watersheds by fire or cutting by humans. The latter is certainly true of the floods of the Tiber River in Rome, which increased in frequency over the centuries as the land upstream was deforested.[8] The predictable annual flood of the Nile in Egypt provided a blessed gift of water and fertile soil, but either low or high floods could bring lean years and famine.[9] Winds such as the sirocco and mistral cause sand and dust storms, while thunderstorms are an annual occurrence, and cyclones and tornadoes or waterspouts are not uncommon.

Epidemics

Ancient sources reported another class of natural disasters, those caused by various organisms, including locust invasions, diseases of crops and domestic animals, and irruptions of commensal rodents and insects. Plagues killed appreciable proportions of human populations during their attacks. *Nosos* and *loimos*, the Greek words for plague, are general terms for disease; in Latin, the equivalents are *pestis* and *pestilentia*. The most noted instances in ancient Greek and Roman sources are the plague of Pericles in Athens, which began in 430 BCE, the plague of Marcus Aurelius in Rome in 165 CE, and the plague of Justinian in Constantinople in 542. These diseases, which are not easy to identify, killed as much as 20 to 40 percent of the population in the areas they affected. Malaria, which incrementally invaded the Mediterranean basin, became an undulating drain on health and population rather than a sudden disaster, and although they did not know that mosquitos carried malaria, people learned to avoid living in wetlands, building villages on hilltops where possible.[10]

Severe outbreaks of communicable disease were sometimes attributed to gods. The *Iliad* says that Apollo sent a pestilence upon Agamemnon's army in retribution for an insult to his priest. Apollo was given the epithet *hekebolos* "he who strikes from afar" because he sent plagues and significantly was also god of rats and mice. But he was called *epicurus* or "helper," too, because he could deliver countries from disease, as he saved Bassae in Arcadia. The god Pan revealed a remedy for plague to the magistrates of Troezen in dreams. Aesculapius, god of healing, was introduced at Rome to avert a pestilence.

Without methods of inoculation, ancient populations could develop immunities to communicable diseases only at great cost in human life. But immunities could not fully protect populations from new outbreaks of pestilence caused by mutated organisms. Diseases can change through time, so is not always possible to decide what modern diagnoses might be given to ancient epidemics. Hippocrates describes cases that sound like bubonic plague. Pandemics seem to have increased in frequency when Alexander's conquests and Roman trade made contact with population centers in the Orient, bringing exotic strains home, adding them to native Mediterranean pathogens.

There is no doubt that epidemics affected the course of ancient history. The Great Plague that weakened Athens in the Peloponnesian War is said to have spread to the port of Piraeus from Egypt. Ironically, the Athenian blockade of the shipping of their Spartan enemies was effective enough to prevent the spread of the contagion to them. Although Thucydides gives a clinical description of the symptoms of this plague, it is impossible to identify it convincingly. The Carthaginian siege of Syracuse in 396 BCE ended when the attackers were decimated by a plague. Had they succeeded, Rome might have been in a much more perilous situation in the First Punic War. Many epidemics occurred during the Roman Republic; Livy mentions a dozen or more, including one in 461 when cattle as well as people died, and corpses too numerous for burial were thrown into the Tiber. After Augustus there were plagues of increasing severity, not surprisingly, since Roman merchants then journeyed regularly to India, and even reached the court of the Han Emperor in China. A plague under Nero killed 30,000. Worst of all was the plague of Marcus Aurelius, the symptoms of which were described by Galen. It was brought to Rome in 164 by troops that had served on the Euphrates, and killed as much as one-third of the population; 2,000 deaths a day in Rome are reported at its height. Not all plague was bad for

Rome; invasions of the Huns and Vandals were blunted by it. Bubonic plague swept the known world in 540–65 under Justinian. It entered the Mediterranean through the port of Pelusium in Egypt, may have come there from India, and is said to have halved the population of the Roman Empire. The effects of epidemics on the decline of Greek and Roman civilization must have been significant. Human numbers tend to build up after attacks of pathogens because the survivors are resistant, and birth rates rise as if to replace lost numbers. But if wars and other diseases intervene, losses may not be repaired for decades, if at all. Further, there is a connection of plague with famine and reduced agricultural productivity, as farmers not only die from the disease but also may flee the districts it attacks.

Malaria

Malaria contributed to depopulation in some areas. Marshes and high water tables, conditions that encouraged breeding by the mosquitoes that carry malaria, often resulted from deforestation in the hills and mountains that formed the upper parts of watersheds. The ancient Greeks and Romans were unaware that mosquitoes were the vectors[11] (although some of them came tantalizingly close to the truth), but they certainly knew that low, damp country had to be avoided at the peril of disease and even death. Opinions vary on just when malaria entered Greece and Italy and how quickly it spread, but it probably came with the first human inhabitants, since skeletal evidence shows that it was present in the eastern Mediterranean basin as early as Mesolithic times.[12] Eventually thousands of acres of land, especially cultivated land at lower, moister elevations, were unfit for habitation because of it. The Romans periodically embarked on ambitious programs for the draining of marshlands, destroying wildlife habitat as they did so, but many alluvial deposits were too low-lying for efficient drainage and were never completely reclaimed. Beyond that, drainage of lakes and wetlands for agriculture may have created a local environment even friendlier to the species of mosquitoes that carry the organisms that cause malaria in humans.[13]

Malaria is different from the plagues described above; it is chronic, endemic to certain areas, produces debilitation over a long period, and can lead to death. Empedocles is said to have delivered Selinus from fever by draining a river marsh, a reasonable way to deal with malaria from his point of view, as it was believed that malaria was caused by exhalations from swamps, the "bad air" (*malaria*) that gives the disease its name. Malaria spread into lowlands near Rome, especially the Pontine Marshes, as people began to farm the rich soils there. Dea Febris (the Fever Goddess) became an important object of worship, and after the Second Punic War, Roman soldiers were more commonly drawn from mountain districts free of malaria. Varro came near the truth about its vector when he advised anyone establishing a farm that "precautions must . . . be taken in the neighborhood of swamps . . . because there are bred certain minute creatures which cannot be seen by the eyes, which float in the air and enter the body through the mouth and the nose and there cause serious diseases."[14] From this imprecise passage, it is hard to know whether to credit Varro with coming close to the germ theory or the realization that mosquitos carry malaria. But there is no doubt that the ancients associated mosquitos with swamps and disease. Columella says that marshland "breeds insects armed with annoying stings, which attack us in dense swarms," and other things, "from which are often contracted mysterious diseases."[15] The effects of malaria exacerbated many of the problems that led to the fall of ancient civilization. Farmers deserted rich alluvial soil that might otherwise have produced good crops, and many moved to cities where the numbers of the urban poor swelled, following the affluent, who had already become absentee landlords of rural districts. The result was falling productivity, not only because land was abandoned, but also because those who initially survived malaria were weak, and then discovered that exertion brought on renewed attacks, which led them to avoid additional work. There was a loss of energy and work time for the population in general.[16] Malaria is not just something that impinges on human populations from the natural environment, however. As noted above, its spread is facilitated by human interference in the landscape through actions such as deforestation and the erosion, deposition, and waterlogging that follows.

The Plague of Athens

An eyewitness described at least one disastrous epidemic. First-class commentator and historian Thucydides not only witnessed its progress but also suffered from it himself and survived. The onset of the plague of Athens occurred in 430 BCE, in the second year of the Peloponnesian War. Pericles, a general and the leading statesman in Athens, had led Athens into war against Sparta. Since the Spartans were the most feared army in Greece, while the Athenian navy ruled the waters of the adjacent seas, the Athenians had built strong walls around the city and parallel walls connecting it with the port of Piraeus providing naval and mercantile access to the sea without exposing themselves to Spartan incursions on land. When the war began, Pericles ordered the Athenians to abandon their farms and other holdings and to move inside the walls, abandoning the countryside to the Spartans, who made an annual invasion and ravaged the crops but did not attack the walls. Conditions inside the city were very crowded; during the emergency, citizens occupied every bit of ground, including sacred groves.

Estimates vary, but it is probable that the normal peacetime population in metropolitan Athens and Piraeus was around 100,000, with perhaps 200,000 additional in the rest of Attica. Recognizing that many Athenians were absent from the city with military expeditions on land and sea,[17] it still seems safe to say that the population within the walls at least doubled as a result of the Periclean decree. Ships brought food and other necessities into Piraeus, and it was through the port that the plague also arrived. Thucydides reported that the first cases appeared there.

Thucydides says that he started writing his history of the Peloponnesian War the moment the war started, which implies that his record is contemporary with the war's events.[18] He undoubtedly revised his text later, but the document is not complete; it breaks off six years before the end of the war, twenty years after the plague arrived in 430 BCE. Most historians believe that he died around 410 BCE. Thucydides was an Athenian citizen of an elite family with interests in Thrace (northern Greece), including gold mines at the place called *skapte hyle* "excavated forest" that ensured his wealth and position. He was an admirer of Pericles, the democratic leader of Athens, in an apparent break from a background that included connections with the most prominent conservative oligarchs. This is exceptional, since family and political loyalties went hand in hand in Athens. What Thucydides liked about Pericles was the ability to guide the democracy and keep it from foolhardy actions, at least most of the time. Unfortunately, from Thucydides's point of view, the Athenians did not always heed Pericles's advice, and there were always more radical demagogues ready to urge the people to overreach themselves.

Thucydides places his description of the plague immediately after his recounting of Pericles's funeral oration in honor of the Athenian military men who had died during the first year of the war against Sparta. This speech, one of the greatest in all written history, is a stirring democratic manifesto. The sudden descent into the horrific details of the plague's effects is arguably the starkest transition in ancient historical literature. In his book, Thucydides does not spare his readers harrowing descriptions of the cost of war in human lives and suffering, but his measured opinion is that the "thing that did the most damage and which destroyed the most human life was the virulent plague."[19]

Rumors reported by Thucydides said the disease had originated in Ethiopia, spread down the Nile through Egypt to the dominions of the Persian emperor, and then to the island of Lemnos and other parts of the Athenian alliance before advancing to Athens through Piraeus.[20] The nature of the illness was unknown to anyone, including physicians who frequently died of it after visiting the homes of the sick. Thucydides does not try to guess the name of the contagion but gives a detailed clinical description of the symptoms, which he knew well because he had experienced them himself and wanted his readers to recognize them should the disorder recur:

> Many who were in perfect health, all in a moment, and without any apparent reason, were seized with violent heats in the head and with redness and inflammation of the eyes. Internally the throat and the tongue were quickly suffused with blood, and the breath became unnatural and fetid. There followed sneezing and hoarseness; in a short time the disorder, accompanied by a violent cough, reached the chest; then fastening lower down, it would move the stomach and bring on all the vomits of bile to which physicians have ever given names; and they were very distressing. An ineffectual retching producing violent convulsions attacked most of the sufferers, some as soon as the previous symptoms had abated, others not until long afterwards· The body externally was not so very hot to the touch, nor yet pale; it was of a livid color inclining to red, and breaking out in pustules and ulcers. But the internal fever was intense; the sufferers could not bear to have on them even the finest linen garment; they insisted on being naked, and there was nothing that they desired more eagerly than to throw themselves into cold water. And many of those who had no one to look after them actually plunged into the rain tanks, for they were tormented by unceasing thirst, which was not in the least assuaged whether they drank little or much. They could not sleep; a restlessness that was intolerable never left them. While the disease was at its height the body, instead of wasting away, held out amid these sufferings in a marvelous manner, and either they died on the seventh or ninth day, not of weakness, for their strength was not exhausted, but of internal fever, which was the end of most; or, if they survived, then the disease descended into the bowels and there produced violent ulceration; severe diarrhea at the same time set in, and at a later stage caused exhaustion, which finally with few exceptions was fatal. For the disorder which had originally settled in the head passed gradually through the whole body, and, if a person got over the worst, would often seize the extremities and leave its mark, attacking the privy parts and the fingers and the toes; and some escaped with the loss of these, some with the loss of their eyes. Some again had no sooner recovered than they were seized with a forgetfulness of all things and knew neither themselves nor their friends.[21]

Modern medical historians are just as confused about how to diagnose the ancient disease as Thucydides and the Athenian doctors were. No present-day communicable malady matches exactly this list of symptoms, but disease organisms can mutate genetically and phenotypically, which is certainly possible over a period of 2,500 years. Nevertheless, numerous attempts, some of them very convincing, have been made to identify the outbreak as bubonic plague, typhus, measles, anthrax, smallpox, hemorrhagic fever, or even toxic shock syndrome or Ebola virus. Typhoid fever is possibly the most likely candidate; a study by Dr. Manolis Papagrigorakis and others at the University of Athens of the dental pulp of skulls found in a burial pit dating to the first years of the Peloponnesian War shows DNA sequences similar to those of the bacterium that causes typhoid.[22]

Thucydides writes that carrion-eating birds and dogs either died of the plague or escaped it by not touching the bodies of the dead. Typhoid is known to have canine and avian victims.

Typhoid epidemics are common in history. Outbreaks are usually local and caused by contamination of water and food by fecal material from infected persons or animals. A rumor reported by Thucydides said that the Spartans had poisoned the open reservoirs that supplied Piraeus. He did not believe the rumor, and it is unlikely that the Spartans were guilty because they were not suffering from the plague,[23] but the story does connect its spread with the water supply. It is more likely that the city's water was contaminated after the plague entered, given the overcrowded conditions. There were numerous wells, local springs, and cisterns that might have received sewage, and even the bodies of victims crazed with thirst, whereas the main supply came through an aqueduct that ran 7.5 km (2.3 miles), from nearby Mount Hymettos, built in the sixth century BCE by the tyrant Peisistratos and his sons, with branches added later from other mountains including Parnes and Pentelikos.[24] These were tunnels with vertical airshafts usable for maintenance access built at a distance apart of 40 to 50 m (131 to 164 feet); the diameter of these shafts is about 1.5 m (4–5 feet), and many of them still exist.[25] Outside Athens, the conduits met in a large reservoir, from which a branching system of underground channels distributed water throughout the city. The main one under the agora, which supplied the main springhouse called Enneakrounos (Fountain with Nine Spouts), is high and broad enough to allow two men to pass. Often pipes of baked clay, about 20 cm (8 in) in diameter, were laid within them.[26] This system was built to prevent enemies from interfering with it, but the Spartans, in control of everything outside the walls, could have cut the aqueducts at times, inadvertently causing the Athenians to use sources inside the city that, unknown to them, carried disease. Whether there was interference with the aqueducts or not, the crowding would have caused a water shortage and the use of many sources other than the aqueducts.[27]

The plague struck perhaps 50 percent of Athenians in the city, killing 25–30 percent. The army in the field also suffered from it, especially Hagnon's troops who were sent to northern Greece to help in the siege of Potidaea. The conditions of an army camp located in one position for a long time make the spread of disease easy, and Hagnon returned to Athens after the loss of 1,050 out of his 4,000 men, a 26 percent death rate.[28] The outbreak recurred twice, in 429 BCE and in the winter of 428–427 BCE, and the depletion of Athens's manpower undoubtedly contributed to the eventual Spartan victory in the war.

One might expect that the Athenians would ask which of the gods had smitten them with the plague, and which offerings to make to mollify the divine anger. Thucydides is skeptical of religion, noticing that those who worshipped the gods died with the same frequency as those who did not. He does say that old men remembered an ancient oracle that said "a Dorian [Spartan] war shall come and with it a pestilence."[29] Then, further showing his skepticism, he notes that the word *loimos* (pestilence) is pronounced about the same as *limos* (famine), and that the oracle could be taken in more than one way, as often happened. Another oracle, from Apollo at Delphi, promised the Spartans that he would fight on their side, and since Apollo's weapons in the *Iliad* are arrows of plague, which did not affect the Spartans, Thucydides recalls that some Athenians believed that depressing interpretation of the oracle. The Spartans, fearing they might contract the plague from the Athenians, did not invade Attica in 429 BCE, although they returned the next year. But the connection of disease with the gods remained; a temple to Asklepios, the god of healing and son of Apollo, was erected near the Theater of Dionysus below the south side of the Acropolis in 420 BCE after the plague abated.[30] Sophocles's play *Oedipus Rex*, written soon after or even during the Athenian plague, opens with a disease devastating Thebes, and although in the play the cause of the disaster is the refusal to accept an oracle of Apollo, the chorus specifically blames the plague on Ares, the god of war. Sophocles's Theban plague was undoubtedly a reference to the Athenian plague he had experienced, and the character Oedipus a likely metaphor for Pericles.

Thucydides is also a keen observer of the political and moral behavior of humans in times of crisis. He is the most astute social critic among ancient historians, analyzing the underlying reasons why individuals on different sides of a conflict make the decisions they do. He shows that in times of war and other disasters, they abandon more embracing considerations of community life for narrow personal interest, and society degenerates into partisanship and even anarchy. He portrays this situation clearly in the case of the plague. Because individuals who helped friends with the plague usually caught it themselves, others decided to leave them to suffer. The sacrosanct way in which the ancient Greeks held burial rites is illustrated by the character Antigone in Sophocles's play of the same name, who was willing to die in order to give her brother burial. But Thucydides says that facing the ongoing destruction of human life by the plague, the Athenians abandoned the most hallowed rituals for cremating the dead, even throwing corpses on the funeral pyres of strangers. Archaeological evidence confirms the neglect of traditional burial customs; skeletons among the 150 in the plague pit mentioned above were better arranged at the lower levels, but near the top, skeletons were found in a chaotic state as if they were simply thrown in.[31]

Those stricken by the disease crowded into sacred spaces and surrounded the shrines of springs. Individuals who cared for others in spite of the risk Thucydides honors with the term *aretê*, a virtue comparable with that of heroes.[32] Those who survived an attack did not catch the disease again, or if they did it was a mild case, so many of them thought their lives were charmed, and they went on to help the sick. But Thucydides notes that the majority, facing the likelihood of infection and death, abandoned any respect for the gods or the laws and decided to spend their money quickly and enjoy themselves in any way they pleased.

There were also political reactions to the plague. The Spartans and their allies continued to lay waste to the countryside of Attica and the plague returned virulently, while the Athenians remained crowded inside the city walls. At such a time, Thucydides understands, people look for someone to blame. In this case, the blame fell on Pericles. He had started the war and made the people evacuate the countryside. Thucydides offers a version of the speech of Pericles gave in order to justify his decisions, to rally the citizens and to gain support for a new war effort.

The catastrophe of the plague, he recognizes, could not have been foreseen. The exigencies of a war with Sparta had been predictable, but not this. "Before what is sudden, unexpected, and least within calculation the spirit quails; and putting all else aside, the plague has certainly been an emergency of this kind."[33] From the perspective of the eyewitness, this statement is correct; nothing was understood about the cause of the disease, the conditions conducive to its spread, or the possible means of moderating its severity. The only way to face the unknown malady was acquiescence. Pericles assigns the origin of the pestilence not to Apollo, nor to "the gods" in general, but to an undefined *ouranos* (heaven), which might be understood in various ways by his listeners: "The hand of Heaven must be borne with resignation, that of the enemy with fortitude; this was the old way at Athens, so don't be the ones who prevent it from being true today."[34] The citizens forced Pericles to pay a fine, but they still eventually reelected him as general.

Pericles offered no predictions about the future course of the plague, which was unforeseeable. But he could try to deal with the losses it had inflicted. To help restore the number of citizens, he sponsored a law to make it easier to gain citizenship: in the past, one had to prove that both parents were Athenians, but henceforth having only one Athenian parent would be sufficient.[35] We can only wonder if Pericles felt he was in danger of catching the plague. Two of his sons had died from it. His speech indicates that he intended to lead Athens through the rest of the war, but that was not to be. Within a few weeks, he contracted the plague and died. Thucydides estimates the total number of plague deaths among the Athenian military as 4,400 heavily armed infantry and 300 cavalry (who were from the upper class), along with "a number of the multitude."[36] The worst result of the plague according to Thucydides was that it killed Athens's best leader at the time when he was most needed. The plague returned in the two years after Pericles's death and then slowly disappeared. Athens fought the war for another quarter century, punctuated by a cold-war "peace" involving proxy wars and a hubristic but ultimately tragic campaign in Sicily. The generals who succeeded to power were hawks like Cleon, doves like Nicias, and an infamous traitor named Alcibiades, who was rehabilitated by his fellow citizens in time to lead Athens into defeat.

The Eruption of Vesuvius

An image of Mount Vesuvius painted in the quiescent years of the early first century represents a mountain robed in the green of vineyards and presided over by a benevolent Bacchus who is at the same time a bunch of ripe grapes, appropriate for the god of wine.[37] The artist, and the people who lived in the towns and farms overshadowed by the mountain, had forgotten that Vesuvius was a volcano. It was not that Romans were ignorant of volcanoes; Mount Etna on Sicily, just across the strait of Scylla and Charybdis, smoked almost all the time and coughed up lava fairly often, and small islands in the Tyrrhenian Sea such as Vulcano and Stromboli put on a good show, as well. Silius Italicus writes of a flare-up of Vesuvius in 217 BCE "with flames worthy of Etna,"[38] which is confirmed by stratigraphy in the local area and by ice core evidence from distant Greenland.[39] An earlier explosion detected by modern volcanologists is the Avellino eruption of Vesuvius around 1640 BCE, which covered the area that is Naples today.[40] Diodorus Siculus, Vitruvius, and Strabo, all writing before 79 CE, thought that the rocks and activity on Vesuvius indicated past eruptions.[41] Strabo believed they had ceased, saying, "one might infer that in earlier times this district was on fire and had craters of fire and then because the fuel gave out, was quenched."[42] Seneca leaves Vesuvius off his list of well-known volcanoes.[43] Pliny the Elder lists all the volcanoes he has heard of, and other places where fire comes out of the ground, including some near the Bay of Naples, but does not include Vesuvius.[44] He must not have recognized its volcanic character, or perhaps thought it was extinct and not worth mentioning.

It is therefore not surprising that when Pliny the Younger on one day in 79 CE[45] was called away from his books to see what he described as an awesome cloud shaped like a pine tree, with a trunk rising up in the air to a high elevation where it spread out (what might today be called a "mushroom cloud"), he had to guess which place it was coming from. Soon afterward, he learned that it was Vesuvius. He provided an eyewitness account of this eruption in his letters, which report that he had an unobstructed view of the eruption and fled from his house through the ash fall, returning later. Based on his account, volcanologists coined the term "Plinian" to refer to explosive eruptions that produce eruptive columns rising to high elevations and cover large areas with ash.

Pliny was seventeen years old at the time, son of Roman upper-class parents from the lakeside town of Como in the Alps. His mother, Plinia Marcella, was the sister of Pliny the Elder, renowned author of *Natural History*, a comprehensive encyclopedia of the Roman state of knowledge about every aspect of nature, which is extant,[46] as well as several histories that are mostly lost. Uncle Pliny was in residence as prefect (admiral) of the most important naval base in the Roman Empire at Misenum in the Bay of Naples, within sight of Vesuvius, and his sister and nephew were staying with him at his villa there. He had no children, so his will (to be read all too soon) adopted the younger Pliny and endowed him with his considerable wealth and extensive properties. Pliny the Younger's father died when he was very young, so he lived with his mother; his uncle and his guard-

This postcard image of an eruption of Mount Vesuvius in 1872 exhibits the "pine tree" shape noted by Pliny the Younger, and also pyroclastic flows pouring down the sides of the mountain. (1872)

ian Lucius Verginus Rufus were with the army on the German frontier most of the time while he was growing up. In the years after 79 CE, Pliny rose rapidly in the *cursus honorum*, the ladder of position and political power. He studied law under Quintilian, entered the Senate, was chosen as consul (the highest senatorial office), and became a member of the judicial council of the emperor Trajan. Finally he was appointed imperial legate (governor) of the province of Bithynia and Pontus (between the Sea of Marmora and the Black Sea in what is now northwestern Turkey). His trajectory was one of a man whose life was dedicated to supporting the political structure of the Roman Empire. We are lucky to have a generous sampling of his copious correspondence, including letters to emperors and literary figures such as the historian Tacitus, to whom the letters describing the eruption were written about twenty-five years after the event.[47] While we must allow for distortion of memory over the intervening time, Pliny's vivid account conveys the impression of immediacy.

The disaster had hit without any definite warning; Pliny says there had been earthquake tremors for many days before the eruption,[48] but no one had taken them seriously because they occur frequently around the area. A strong shock in 62 CE, a few months after his birth, had devastated Pompeii and other places, with damaging aftershocks as much as two years later, without an eruption. The local people responded with determination to rebuild houses and public buildings and to restore the aqueduct; the damage was still being repaired at the time of the eruption in 79 CE. In the 62 CE earthquake, according to Seneca, gases had killed thirty-five flocks of sheep near Vesuvius,[49] an indication that the quake had been stimulated by volcanic activity. Pliny the Elder connected earthquakes with some eruptions but did not identify them as warning signs of volcanic activity.[50] Even an explosive phreatic (steam) eruption that sounded like distant thunder just before the major disaster was not taken as a warning.[51]

Seismologists today continue to investigate the connection of earthquakes with subsequent eruptions of Vesuvius, and it is now possible to distinguish earthquakes that precede a volcanic eruption from other seismic phenomena.[52] Most of the epicenters of earthquakes in the region have been in the Apennines 50–60 km (30–37 miles) northeast of Vesuvius.[53] Today volcanologists also measure the rise and subsidence of the ground level as a result of the magma chamber's swelling under the volcano before an eruption, as well as its release afterward. This change in ground level affects the apparent sea level, with flooding during periods of subsidence, which is notable on the columns of temples built near the sea, due to markings left by sea creatures such as shellfish. Volcanological investigations south and east of the mountain have found a series of shallow deposits of ash, lapilli, and fine scoria indicating that relatively small eruptive incidents occurred over the years before 79 CE. The eminent Icelandic volcanologist Haraldur Sigurdsson believes that a small explosion occurred in the night or morning before the awesome event at noontime, which may have alarmed some of those closest to the caldera.[54] The family in Misenum seems not to have been aware of it, although noises like distant thunder had been heard for a few days.

Pliny says that his uncle was intensely interested in the phenomenon the moment his sister told him about it, and climbed up to where he could get the best view. His lifelong devotion to natural science asserted itself. He decided to take a small ship across the bay to observe at closer hand, and invited his nephew to join him, but the younger man decided that reading about the past was more important to him than observing the present, so he stayed behind. On leaving the house to board the boat, the elder Pliny received a letter from his friend Rectina, who was in her villa at the foot of Vesuvius and could get away only by boat. He decided to try to rescue victims of the eruption, and ordered the fleet to assist. Finding that shallow water and debris from the volcano prevented him from landing, he used the wind to cross the bay to Stabiae, where he found that another friend, Pomponianus, had loaded his boats to escape but could not because of the contrary wind and rough waves. Demonstrating unwarranted calm in the face of danger, Pliny the Elder bathed, dined, and took a nap. By then the stones and ash had piled up so deep that they threatened to trap him in his room. He and his friends realized that if they remained there they would be buried, so they went down to the shore in total darkness with pillows tied on their heads as protection against falling rocks. Pliny, an obese man who had trouble breathing, died overcome by ash, gases, and overexertion. His companions had to abandon his body. It was found two days later, his nephew learned, clothed and looking more asleep than dead. Experience studying modern volcanic disasters indicates that death under such circumstances likely results from asphyxiation due to fine ash filling and plugging the lungs and esophagus, but the reason Pliny died while the others survived was probably his corpulence, overexertion, and weak constitution.

Meanwhile, the volcanic fallout was approaching Misenum, and the younger Pliny was not only observing people's reactions to disaster, but also demonstrating them himself. First was denial. Like his uncle, he had a bath followed by dinner and then tried to sleep, but was roused when his mother, terrified, broke into his room. They sat on the terrace while Pliny resumed his reading of Livy, rejecting the warnings of his uncle's friend. Then, because the house was shaking violently and threatening to collapse, they decided to flee, along with a crowd of others. But the earthquakes threw around their carts. They paused, only to see the seawater retreating in advance of a tsunami and the ominous pyroclastic cloud approaching across the bay over Capri to the cape of Misenum itself. Pliny and his mother fled a little farther and then stopped as absolute darkness overtook them. He heard the vocal exclamations of the refugees:

> You could hear women lamenting, children crying, men shouting. Some were calling for parents, others for children or spouses; they could only recognize them by their voices. Some bemoaned their own lot, others that of their near and dear. There were some so afraid of death that they prayed for death. Many raised their hands to the gods, and even more believed that there were no gods any longer and that this was one last unending night for the world. Nor were we without people who magnified real dangers with fictitious horrors. Some announced that one or another part of Misenum had collapsed or burned; lies, but they found believers. It grew lighter, though that seemed not a return of day, but a sign that the fire was approaching. The fire itself actually stopped some distance away, but darkness and ashes came again, a great weight of them. We stood up and shook the ash off again and again; otherwise we would have been covered with it and crushed by the weight. I might boast that no groan escaped me in such perils, no cowardly word, but that I believed that I was perishing with the world, and the world with me, which was a great consolation for death.[55]

Here, as in response to the plague of Athens, people are shown either beseeching the gods for help or denying their existence. Those with a Stoic view might well have thought they had come to the cyclical, fiery end and renewal of the universe.[56] Pliny does not report anyone blaming the likeliest gods, Vulcan or the malevolent Titans, who were imprisoned under volcanoes according to mythology. And yet the gods were seen as the likely causes of such disasters. Martial, who was a contemporary of Pliny, lamented the destruction of a rich agrarian landscape:[57]

> This is Vesuvius, green yesterday with viney shades; here had the noble grape loaded the dripping vats; these ridges Bacchus loved more than the hills of Nysa [his home]; on this mount of late the Satyrs set afoot their dances; this was the haunt of Venus, more pleasant to her than Lacedaemon; this spot was made glorious by the fame of Hercules [Herculaneum]. All lies drowned in fire and melancholy ash; even the high gods could have wished this had not been permitted them.[58]

Beside the eyewitness accounts, we have striking evidence of the victims' last moments in the form of hollow impressions in the compacted ash of Pompeii that, filled with plaster and then freed from these molds, reveal the forms of humans and other animals, including their clothing, their physical positions, and even in some cases their expressions. In Herculaneum were found the bones of people who had fled to the docks in hope of escape but were killed instantaneously by the incredibly rapid arrival of heated mud and gases. Many more will undoubtedly be discovered as excavations continue.

The immediate reaction of people was to save their lives by any means pos-

This colonnade in Herculaneum, Italy, was on the shoreline in 79 CE. Many people trying to flee the eruption of Vesuvius by sea were overwhelmed and killed here by a "burning cloud" (pyroclastic flow) that roared down the mountainside at 100 km per hour (60 miles per hour). (1994)

sible. Some decided to flee, and they at least had a chance, since it seems the majority of residents who fled did survive. Others sought shelter inside their homes, temples, or other buildings; they mostly died of suffocation by ash or the hot gases accompanying pyroclastic flows.[59] In a sense, the volcano had created a trap; the lushness of the vineyards and other vegetation was the result of prior eruptions. Volcanic deposits can become some of the richest agricultural lands on the Earth because they contain a wide variety of the elements needed for plant growth. In the Mediterranean region, these rich black soils contrast with the meager red and yellow soils that develop on the prevalent limestone base,[60] attracting farmers to the very places that may be in danger of further eruptions. In addition, the pozzuolano ash deposits that were the main ingredient of Roman concrete attracted miners to the region around Vesuvius.[61] The only effective plan to avoid damage and loss of life from eruptions is to avoid settlement on volcanic soils near an active volcano. Because the length of time between eruptions can be many years, generations, or even millennia, the short-term economic needs of people lead them to bet against a new eruption in their own lifetimes or those of their children. Such decisions virtually assure future disaster.

The response of the Roman government after the eruption of Vesuvius was to offer aid, which had been considered a responsibility of the emperor since Augustus Caesar had established the precedent of giving tax relief and financial aid from the imperial treasury to cities and provinces that had suffered damage from earthquakes. He also sent a commission of seven ex-consuls to assist in rebuilding the city of Tralles in Asia Minor after an earthquake in 27 BCE.[62] Emperor Vespasian "restored to greater glory numerous towns across the Empire, which had suffered damage as a result of earthquakes and fires."[63]

The reigning emperor at the time of the Vesuvius disaster, Vespasian's son Titus, to whom the elder Pliny had dedicated his *magnum opus*, "showed not merely the concern of an emperor, but even a father's surpassing love, now offering consolation in edicts, and now lending aid so far as his means allowed. He chose commissioners by lot from among the ex-consuls for the relief of Campania; and the property of those who lost their lives by Vesuvius and had no heirs left alive he applied to the rebuilding of the buried cities."[64] So says Suetonius, who had served on the staff of Pliny the Younger and was often critical of emperors but gave qualified praise to those like Titus, whom he considered to be fair and devoted to government.[65] Titus himself went to the stricken area after the eruption, and he was there when a major fire hit Rome the next year.[66] It is probable that his reimbursement for lost property actually worked, and that well-to-do Romans were able to rebuild their villas on the shores of the bay, although they may not have been in a hurry to reoccupy them. Survivors could be helped to resettle in nearby towns. The restoration of the deeply buried cities soon appeared to be impossible, however. Repair had always taken place after earthquakes, but the sites of Pompeii and Herculaneum were not reoccupied in ancient times. Residents and looters tunneled into Pompeii, breaking through walls as they looked for treasure. In Herculaneum, the solidified pyroclastics defeated any such efforts. "When this wasteland regains its green, will men believe that cities and peoples lie beneath?" asked Statius.[67] Evidently not. Farms were opened above the phantom ruins, but the sterile volcanic ashes were transformed into soil of exceptional richness only after decades,[68] which favored speculators wealthy enough to acquire land and to wait until agricultural development was profitable, while small farmers could not afford to take the economic risk. In the meantime, Rome turned to southern Gaul and Spain to replace wine from the "vine-covered hills whose liquid produce is famous in every land and ennobles tipsiness."[69] The area the volcano had devastated was part of Campania, which was also Rome's most important nearby source of olive oil, wheat, sheep, pigs, and fish.[70] The imports of these products from Gaul to Rome rose sharply.

The land recovered its agricultural richness: as Cassius Dio observed 150 years later, "the elevated parts of [Vesuvius] are clad in many trees and vines,"[71] but the buried cities were not restored. It was not until after 1000 that a town named Resina arose, unsuspecting that Herculaneum lurked under its foundations. But cities on the northwest side of the bay had soon removed the lighter ash falls that had occurred there and revived as centers of commerce and pleasure. Emperor Hadrian had a resort on the coast of the Bay of Naples but spent little time there; he had a much more lavish one at Tivoli, and traveled constantly throughout the empire.[72]

Vesuvius was not finished. It erupted again in 172 while Marcus Aurelius was emperor, and many times afterward. It last erupted in 1944, but is still active, and another disaster is almost certainly inevitable.

Conclusion

The ancient response to the disasters examined here was for the most part uninformed, chaotic, and inadequate. Knowledge of the true causes of disease and volcanic eruptions did not exist. Assigning responsibility to the gods was only an admission of ignorance, which was tacitly understood by our learned philosophical eyewitnesses if not by the general public at the time. In spite of their

The inner crater and caldera of Mount Vesuvius viewed from above. (1959)

undeniable intelligence and inquisitiveness, Greeks and Romans of the educated classes found it challenging or impossible to explain many natural phenomena.[73]

Victims were caught unaware, although in both cases there were warnings that went unheeded because they were not comprehended: the approach of the plague from Egypt was ignored, and the earthquakes that preceded the eruption could not be distinguished from those that are commonly felt in the Mediterranean region. During both the plague and the eruption, social cohesion broke down, and most individuals tried to save themselves and perhaps also those closest to them without concern for the larger community, without knowing what was the best course of action. Thucydides believed that care for others and for society provided the cohesion necessary for the state, and that war and the plague dissolved this social glue for most people. Pliny reports that those around him when he fled from his uncle's house were disoriented, panicked, and willing to follow anyone who looked as if he knew what he was doing whether he did or not. The fact that Pliny tries to portray himself as calm in the midst of storm only protests his own disorientation. His uncle had been calm, but calmness after he had landed at Stabiae only led to his death.

In the aftermath, those in positions of leadership tried to reestablish the body politic and their own positions at its head, with success that was well intended and at least partially successful. Pericles gave a speech that rallied the people around him after some initial disgruntlement, but of course he could not stem the plague, which killed him. The pestilence ran its course but weakened the military strength and leadership of Athens. Titus shared imperial power with Vespasian for about nine years and became sole emperor only two months before Vesuvius blew its top. He organized relief efforts intended to prevent anarchy in an essential part of Italy, but full restoration proved impossible and he perished two years later, when power was seized by Domitian, a man ill suited to wield it.

These ancient case studies are worthy of careful study in the modern world, where a rapidly growing and crowded human population offers increasingly fertile ground for the mutation and spread of new diseases such as AIDS, SARS, Ebola, and bird flu. Imagining the people of modern Naples trying to cope with a new Plinian eruption offers a horrifying prospect, in which one wonders whether our increase of knowledge has improved our social wisdom and ability to cope. As the Roman poet Statius warned, "this summit does not cease its mortal threat."[74]

Thirteen

Changing Climates

That changes in the climate could be among the reasons for a civilization's decline is not a recent idea. Some Greek and Roman writers were aware of the problem of climate change, and they reflected on it. A character in one of Plato's dialogues asks rhetorically: "Can we suppose there have not been, all over the world, all manner of risings and fallings of states and all kinds of institutions, orderly and disorderly . . . and multifarious climatic revolutions which presumably lead to many modifications of living organisms?"[1]

Plato connected these changes to the rise and fall of states and other institutions. Aristotle astutely observed that climate change usually escapes human observation because it takes place by slow degrees over long periods of time.[2] Columella recalled that "many authorities now worthy of remembrance were convinced that with the long wasting of the ages, weather and climate undergo a change." One of these authorities, Saserna, supported this conclusion with the observation that in the north, less severe winters had allowed olive and grape harvests in places where these plants formerly would not grow.[3] He connected this observation with Hipparchus's statement that the Earth's poles change position in relationship to the stars, an observation identical to what is now called the precession of the equinoxes. While this fact in itself does not explain climate change, it is one of several long-term cycles of variation of the Earth's orbit and inclination, named the Milankovitch cycles,[4] that are now generally credited by climate scientists as an underlying cause of regular climatic changes.

Claudius Ptolemy kept a weather journal in Alexandria during 127–41 CE, noting that rainfall and the frequency of storms varied from year to year. He claims that the weather predictions in his book are derived from direct observation, but this assertion can be doubted because he fits such predictions into a theory of the physical influences of the planets and zodiacal signs on weather and climate.[5] For example, when Saturn, the planet of limitations, approaches the Sun, he thought cold weather could be expected. Incidentally, he mentions Roman bridges over Arabian watercourses that are now dry.

Evidence of Climate Change

Changes of climate in historical times are undeniable. The round of seasons is never exactly the same in two different years, and periods of unusual heat, cold, drought, or flood have always occurred. Though shorter fluctuations of rainfall and temperature are more easily noticed, there are long-term changes of averages over periods from decades to millennia. The climate during the centuries when Greece and Rome flourished was recognizably similar to the Mediterranean climate as it is defined during more recent times. But changes have occurred in average temperatures and rainfall amounts and patterns over large zones, and even more markedly in smaller areas where altering weather patterns may have been exacerbated by changes in the distribution of land and water, removal of vegetation, practices of herding and agriculture, and so on. There is evidence of changing sea level, glacial advances and retreats, a varying tree line in the high mountains, and the ability of farmers to raise specific crops in certain areas.

In order to understand the effects of changing climate on civilizations, and the possible reciprocal effects of the actions of human societies on climate, it would be necessary to know the timing and magnitude of changes in such factors as temperature, rainfall, and the paths of weather systems. Even though is not yet possible to give a complete account of the climatic changes that occurred in the ancient period, modern climatologists have been making progress toward that goal. Detailed weather records are extremely rare in ancient writings, so we have to depend on proxy evidence such as tree rings, pollen samples, ice cores, shells, corals, and seabed sediments. Integration of data from these various archives could in theory make sharper focus possible in what is still a general picture.

Scholars working on this problem reported in 1981: "Prior to about AD 500 the data allow only the broadest of generalisations to be made: time resolution is relatively poor and only scattered sites are represented, often in locations far from civilizations contemporary with the data."[6] Research in historical climatology continues, and the general account has improved, but much more remains to be done.

Ice cores from land in the polar regions and from glaciers at high elevations have yielded information on ancient climate.[7] Layers in such cores, one above the other, each represent the annual snowfall of a year in the past. These layers can be dated exactly using electrical conductivity, visual counting, radiocarbon dating, and stable isotope analysis, and they constitute unbroken records stretching back through centuries, millennia, and in Greenland and Antarctica hundreds of thousands of years. A fascinating aspect of these ice cores is that they do not contain just ice. Frozen within them are bubbles of air from the distant past, revealing evidence of concentrations of atmospheric gases, temperatures, dust, pollutants, and radioisotopes. Researchers can find out from them the answers to questions such as: What was the temperature in that year? How much carbon dioxide and other gases existed in the atmosphere? What kinds of pollutants were in the air? When did volcanoes erupt, spewing dust and aerosols that fell with the snow atop the glaciers?

Greenland is far from the Mediterranean and reflects global trends that may not always correspond to regional conditions, although evidence of Mediter-

Stored in the National Ice Core Laboratory at the Federal Center in Lakewood, Colorado, these tubes contain cores drilled in Greenland, Antarctica, and mountain glaciers, a vast archive of information on past atmospheric conditions. U.S. Government Photograph. (2008)

217

ranean volcanic eruptions and emissions from Roman lead and silver smelting has been found in the ice there. One would like evidence from the region itself, which is being found in ice cores from Alpine glaciers, where the records of the past are being erased by a melting trend that has recently accelerated. Sometimes the melting uncovers artifacts and human remains that also give information on climate, vegetation, and animal life in the distant past. The most noted example is the body of Ötzi, the so-called Iceman, found on a high ridge between Italy and Austria and dated around 3300 BCE, complete with his clothing, weapons, and other artifacts.[8]

A method of examining tree rings called dendroclimatology can give evidence of climate changes in ancient times.[9] Tree ring studies add to our knowledge of the ancient environment; dendrochronology can sometimes make dating possible within a single year. The wood of many species of trees shows rings indicating annual growth, rapid in the early growing season and slower toward its end. These rings are wider when environmental conditions promote growth, narrower when they are less favorable. The limiting conditions may be temperature, rainfall, and other factors, so it may be difficult to make judgments about which kinds of climatic change are involved. Trees in a geographic area develop the same ring patterns because they experience the same climatic conditions. In the Mediterranean, the most important factor in tree ring width is most often precipitation; in northern Europe, temperature is more often the critical limiting factor. Consequently, climatic judgments made from studies in central or western Europe may not apply to the Mediterranean climate zone. Cross-dating is possible between samples from living trees and older wood from archaeological sites, so that construction of sequences representing hundreds and even thousands of years has been made in the Mediterranean basin; the longest to date go back to between 9000 and 7000 BCE. An example of dendrochronology used to date an environmental event is a marked tree ring growth anomaly in the seventeenth century BCE that appears to correlate with the catastrophic eruption of a volcano on the island of Thera (Santorini) in the Aegean Sea. This eruption affected a large area, with debris fallout and tsunamis that among other effects may have helped to bring about the collapse of contemporary Minoan civilization centered on Crete.[10] After initial disturbance and evidence of volcanic pollution, a series of abnormally wide rings was observed, perhaps the result of factors such as clouds, rainfall, and a new moisture-conserving layer of volcanic ash encouraging growth during the summer, when conditions are usually hot and arid.[11]

A summer storm viewed from Assisi, Italy. (1959)

Climate Change in Prehistoric and Ancient Times

To understand the changes experienced in the Greek and Roman world, it is well to begin with the prehistoric background of the ancient Mediterranean climate. The latest climatic changes of great magnitude occurred with the end of the most recent ice age. Temperatures during the reign of ice were on the average about 7–9°C (13–16°F) colder than a mid-twentieth-century average. The northern half of Europe was covered with ice, and the higher mountain ranges of the Mediterranean bore a mantle of glaciers that descended as much as 1,500 m (5,000 feet) below the elevation of present Alpine glaciers. Since so much of the world's water was locked up in ice, the sea level was perhaps 100 m (330 feet) lower than it is now. The vegetation belts, and the animals adapted to them, were farther south. The Sahara had enough rainfall to support forests, rivers, and lakes. A warming trend interrupted by fluctuations of cold began around 15,000 BCE, and Europe emerged from the grip of the ice by 10,000 or 9,000 BCE.[12]

Further warming brought temperatures as much as 2°C (3.6°F) warmer than the mid-twentieth century in a period called the Holocene Climatic Optimum, from about 6000 to 3100 BCE. Melting ice raised the sea 2–3 m (6–10 feet) above its present level. Pollen studies indicate that trees such as wild olive, oak, birch, hazel, elm, ash, linden, and pine flourished in the Mediterranean zone.[13]

The Mediterranean climatic regime then turned drier, and the Sahara began a long, unsteady desertification that brought it closer to its modern state. Following the Holocene Climatic Optimum came a cooling period (3250 to 2800 BCE) termed the Piora Oscillation. Glaciers advanced somewhat, and pollen studies indicate that warmth-loving trees declined in Europe.[14] In the northern half of the Mediterranean area, they were replaced by cold-tolerant fir, beech, and hornbeam. Then, rather suddenly, things changed: the warming at the end of this period appears to have been extremely rapid.

The warming trend that followed was punctuated by the great eruption of the Thera (Santorini) volcano in the Aegean Sea in 1627 BCE (or slightly earlier), which put huge quantities of dust into the atmosphere, producing a cold spell. By this time the Minoan civilization was flourishing on the island of Crete and other nearby islands, and it suffered catastrophic damage from the fallout and tsunamis spawned by the eruption. The Greek-speaking Mycenaeans overcame the Minoans and conquered Crete around 1450 BCE. In Mycenaean times the warming continued, accompanied by lessening rainfall. Rhys Carpenter suggested that the end of Mycenaean civilization was caused by serious heat and drought in the Peloponnesus starting around 1200 BCE, accompanied by a serious population decrease, and encouraging evidence has been found to support his theory.[15]

Afterward, during the so-called Greek Dark Ages (1100 to 800 BCE), temperatures dropped. During the time of the Greek Renaissance (800 to 500 BCE), average temperatures were possibly 2°C cooler than during the mid-twentieth century. Of course, all such figures must be understood to be generalizations over long periods. There were many seasonal and annual variations and abnormal spells. Greek buildings had gabled roofs, and the people supplied themselves with warm mantles in winter. In Rome at the same time, authors noted snow, a Tiber that could freeze in the winter, and the presence of beeches (cold-tolerating trees) in the city.[16]

During the Hellenistic and Roman periods between 300 BCE and 1 CE, conditions were warmer than in the preceding centuries. Agriculture expanded; writers reported that vines and olives could be cultivated farther north than previously. Roman Imperial times (1 to 400 CE) experienced a moderate climate, perhaps slightly cooler than during the classical Greek period. The sea level may not have been as high, as many Roman port facilities around the Mediterranean are now under water. The earthquake-prone shores of the Mediterranean are subject to tectonic rise and fall, however, which must be taken into account.[17]

In and after the fifth century, there was a persistent descent into cooler and dryer conditions. But it would be venturing beyond the evidence to attribute the fall of Rome to this fact. Still, unfavorable climatic conditions could have driven the tribes beyond the northern frontiers to invade. Drought in Asia may have sent nomadic peoples outward in waves that eventually broke the frontiers of the Roman Empire. Movements of peoples in central Asia may have interrupted the caravan trade with China. One argument in favor of the hypothesis that drought destroyed Rome is the existence of abandoned Roman waterworks in the North African desert. But a student of that area, B. D. Shaw, argues that the environmental ruin visible there can be attributed more convincingly to effects of human occupation. Many Roman wells and cisterns are still in use, he observes; the failures of aqueducts and other large water control structures were due to neglect, damage, and disrepair.[18]

The present state of knowledge about climate change in antiquity does not permit firm conclusions about its effects, but it may have been a contributing cause in the decline of civilization and deserves further study.

Human-Caused Climate Change

That human activities may change climate might seem a modern idea, but Aristotle's discerning student Theophrastus observed it in several instances. Drainage and deforestation, he thought, affected local weather. He reported:

> In the country around Larisa in Thessaly, where formerly, when there was much standing water and the plain was a lake, the air was thicker and the country warmer; but now that the water has been drained away and prevented from collecting, the country has become colder and freezing more common. In proof the fact is cited that formerly there were fine olive trees in the city itself and elsewhere in the country, whereas now they are found nowhere, and that the vines were never frozen before but often freeze now.[19]

Both deforestation and drainage had occurred near Philippi, but in this case the effect was less freezing: "At Philippi there was formerly more freezing of trees; but at present, now that the water has for the most part disappeared underground and been dried out, and the whole country has come under cultivation, there is much less."[20] These effects possibly occurred because the land had been cleared for agriculture; previously, trees had trapped the cold air in low-lying hollows, and after they were removed, the wind carried the cold air away. Thus the effects of human agency on climatic conditions were recognized as early as the fourth century BCE.

Removing forests changes the albedo of the affected areas. Forests are relatively dark and absorb the Sun's rays, while cleared ground is relatively lighter and reflects heat energy back into the atmosphere,[21] in turn affecting atmospheric circulation and climate. Recent computer simulations indicate that environmental conditions in the Roman classical period were moister than at present, and that human modification of the land surface, including deforestation, had produced progressively drier and warmer conditions.[22] Oreste Reale and colleagues point out that before the impact of industrial emissions on global climate, there was a more ancient way in which humans interacted with the climate system: land surface usage, which changed the albedo of the surface.[23]

That emissions of "greenhouse" gases such as carbon dioxide and methane from human activities including industries and transportation are a cause of atmospheric heating is a familiar observation in modern times. William F. Ruddiman attempts to demonstrate that the same was true long ago, beginning with the spread of agriculture around 6000 BCE.[24] Cutting and burning forests for farming added carbon dioxide to the atmosphere in growing amounts, and then around 3000 BCE humans began to irrigate paddies for rice culture and to tend ever larger numbers of livestock, both of which produced methane. Together, these gases in ever-increasing quantities had a warming effect that was enough to counter what would have been a cooling period under completely natural conditions, and possibly prevented another ice age. So the greenhouse effect, which today threatens to bring about excessive global warming, existed in Greek and Roman times, and probably in early modern times as well, serving as protection against disastrous cold. Ruddiman's hypothesis could possibly explain links between land use and climate and needs further investigation.

Conclusion

From day to day, humans experience weather, not climate. A drop of rain, considered a sign from Zeus, could end a session of the Athenian Assembly and postpone an important decision to the following day. Bad weather such as a brief storm, flood, or tsunami could do immense damage to crops and structures and end many lives. It is harder to define "good weather"; in autumn it might be a sunny day that ripens fruit, while after a drought it might be a soaking rain.

Climate is weather experienced and averaged over a longer period of time, usually a year or several years, a decade or century or more. The kind of climate that is good for a civilization is one in a moderate range within which the biotic resources that support human life can flourish. The relationship between climatic variability and the rise and fall of civilizations is complex and cannot be explained simply. But climatic phases that are changeable and that contain extremes—whether of heat or cold, precipitation or aridity—present challenges that entail costs in meeting them, or may weaken a society to the point of population loss and inability to fend off invasions.

Climate constantly affected the ancient Greeks and Romans, in both positive and negative ways. The rise of classical Greece occurred during a moderately cool, moist period, but the Hellenistic age and the contemporary rise of the Roman Republic saw warmer times, sometimes called the "Roman Optimum." The great days of the Roman Empire transpired during the moderately cool, moist sub-Atlantic period, and the disintegration of the western empire happened during a deeper cooling. Again, these are all generalities and open to question. The various proxy data used to reconstruct ancient temperature and rainfall do not always agree with one another, and the margin of error that must be allowed in some of these proxies increases as research considers periods further back in time..

Aristotle warned against a logical fallacy that assumed that if event B happened after event A, then A is the cause of B. Event A may be the cause of event B, but it must be proved by some connection other than a temporal one. If the mid-first century BCE was unusually warm (as it probably was), that does not prove that climate change caused the aggressiveness of Caesar's conquest of Gaul, or the Roman civil wars and the fall of the republic. We must look for probable connections such as improved conditions for the movement of Roman troops due to dry roads and less snow in Gaul, or poorer agricultural yields on great estates causing land disputes between upper-class political leaders.

In our present state of knowledge, it is too early to apply conclusions about the effects of climate change in the ancient world to the twenty-first-century debate over global warming.[25] That may be possible in the future, although if it constitutes a warning, it may unfortunately come too late.

Fourteen

Environmental Problems as Factors in the Decline of Greek and Roman Civilization

The evidence examined in this book leads to the conclusion that environmental factors were important causes of the decay of Greco-Roman economy and society, though not the only causes, and that the most important of these factors were anthropogenic. The ancients failed to adapt their economies to the environment in harmonious ways, placed too great a demand on the available natural resources, and then depleted those resources. Thus they failed to maintain a balance with nature that is necessary to the prosperity of any human community, and the resulting environmental deterioration is still evident in the landscape. "Even to the untrained observer of the present day who views the environment of the semi-arid regions of [North Africa], there is an apparent contrast between the extensive and impressive ruins of the Roman period, both cities and large rural villas, and the desolation of the countryside about them," maintained B. D. Shaw.[1] But what were the causes of the ruination of city and countryside?

Anthropogenic Factors

The activities of *Homo sapiens* have changed the natural environment since the species arose; that fact was necessary to human survival. But some changes do not damage nature—or, if they do, nature can repair the damage over time—while other changes injure the environment and hamper its ability to sustain humankind and other living things. The ancients were sometimes aware that

224

Ruins of the Roman city of Leptis Magna, Libya. Emperor Septimius Severus was born here and built major additions circa 205. It declined and was abandoned to the desert around 600. (1970)

humans can harm the natural world. Seneca remarked, "If we evaluate the benefits of nature by the depravity of those who misuse them, there is nothing we have received that does not hurt us . . . You will find nothing, even of obvious usefulness, such that it does not change over into its opposite through man's fault."[2] Other writers portrayed a balance between humankind and nature, a kind of Golden Rule in which good or bad actions were reciprocated. Xenophon recognized that Earth has her own justice, a law deeper than human enactments, written in the nature of things.[3] If treated well, she granted prosperity. If treated ill, she would forgive, but only up to the point where the balance tipped, and by then it was too late: floods, famine, disease, and death were inevitably the result.

The evidence examined in the preceding chapters shows that the Greeks and Romans were responsible for bringing about many of the failures of nature that affected them. Most of the ecological factors that contributed to the downfall of ancient societies were the result of human activities.[4] If the people involved had seen what was happening, and had taken effort to modify its effects, they might have been able to delay or lessen the environmental disasters they were bringing about.

Deforestation and Agricultural Decline

Deforestation and its consequence, erosion, lead the list of these disasters. Loss of forests over vast tracts was evident to the Greeks and Romans, as they had in many cases disappeared within living memory.[5] The removal of a large proportion of the Mediterranean forests was the most devastating effect of human activity. Ancient economies were affected by shortages and rising prices of wood, partly owing to difficulty of transport, but the most damaging result was erosion on millions of acres of denuded slopes exposed to rains.[6] The extent of deforestation was amplified by pasturing herd animals everywhere that vegetation afforded the opportunity. They overgrazed, destroying some native plant species and preventing regeneration of trees and shrubs. After the soil was removed by torrential rain, in some places down to bare rocks, neither forests nor farms could flourish. Soil carried down from highlands was deposited on more level areas, in lakes, or in the sea at the mouths of rivers, where it often formed marshlands, breeding grounds for mosquitos carrying malaria, and forced inhabitants to relocate in drier locales. The process also added to salinization, since the saline content of both groundwater and surface water increased when erosion accelerated in the headwaters that are their source, adding dissolved salts to the runoff. It was sometimes necessary to replace food plants with low salt tolerance, such as wheat, with other crops that have a higher tolerance but are less valuable, such as barley. In severely affected areas, agriculture ceased.

Greek and Roman farmers were skilled and acquainted with methods to alleviate salinization, erosion, deposition, and leaching of essential minerals. Practices on a small Mediterranean farm tended to produce a complex and resilient ecosystem because topography often varied, and farmers planted various crops where the soil, drainage, and exposure were best. Sometimes portions of land were left forested. Such a system might be expected to persist, but Mikhail Rostovtzeff observed that if "there was exhaustion of the soil in Italy and in the provinces in the centuries after the great crisis of the third century, this must be ascribed to man, not to nature. Men failed to support nature, though they knew as well as we do, or as the Japanese and the Chinese, how it should be done. It is very probable that, in the late Roman Empire, exhaustion of the soil in some parts was a real calamity."[7]

Soil exhaustion happened as a result of economic, military, and political pressures that prevented those who owned or worked the land from applying the knowledge they possessed. Vladimir Simkhovitch maintained that farmers did not improve or rehabilitate their land because they could not afford to do so,[8] for several reasons. Taxes were collected primarily from agriculture, either as monetary payments or portions of the harvest. Such taxes weighed heaviest in the years when they could be afforded least, which encouraged depletion of the land. One typical result of pressures on agriculture was the collapse of small farmers. They often lost their land to great landowners, who preferred stock raising to growing crops and could sometimes survive local crises because they possessed other estates in distant places. But the replacement of farming by grazing reduced productivity, because animals consume plants and produce less food per unit of land, and large herds were subject to epizootics, with the result that less food became available for the general population. Where the big landowners raised grain, they planted it in wide swaths, a practice called monoculture, which creates a simplified ecosystem that is vulnerable to insects and diseases of plants.

Everywhere in the Greco-Roman world, agriculture was the base of the economic structure. The inescapable outcome of humankind's failure to support nature was that nature failed to support a large human population. Governments took measures to encourage population growth, such as making marriage and childbearing mandatory for citizens, but these enactments did nothing to remedy the underlying problems. Decreasing population and declining productivity interacted so as to make each other worse, since fewer agricultural workers meant less production, and less production could mean starvation. Diocletian's Edict of Prices reflects the serious level to which these factors had deteriorated by the late third century. It was an attempt to counter monetary inflation resulting from the scarcity of foodstuffs and other commodities by setting price ceilings. The emperor was well intentioned, but his administration's understanding of economic forces was rudimentary, and the edict was ineffective. Rising prices, food shortages, and a severe labor shortage continued to threaten the Roman Empire. The agricultural crisis was responsible for these economic challenges, and it arose from environmental situations that were, for the most part, anthropogenic. The removal of many species of animals and plants from localities or major geographical areas, and the extinction of some forms of life, affected agriculture and other human activities in ways that were not suspected. Depletion and extinction did not happen just because animals were killed. B. D. Shaw notes an even more important cause: "the tens of thousands of such animals purposefully hunted down for the arena were, of course, a small proportion of the total that must have yielded to more mundane processes such as the systematic destruction of their habitat by the expansion of agricultural settlements."[9] Removing a species results in the simplification of the ecosystem and its increased vulnerability to damage, as an ecosystem with many species possesses more ways of restoring its balance under stress than a simpler one does. The more species lost, the closer the living community is to catastrophe, so by eliminating species, the Greeks and Romans were weakening their economies.

They were unaware of this connection because it seemed to them that in killing predatory animals that sometimes attacked their herds, they were doing a good thing. But predators ate a far greater number of rodents and other animals that devour crops. Aristotle reported plagues of mice that the few remaining predators, including domestic cats and dogs, could not control, and such population explosions did far more damage to agriculture than the predators could by forays into the flocks.[10]

Industry

Compared with the modern world, industry in ancient times did not make up as large a segment of the total economy, but it did have significant environmental consequences. In many cases, scars of ancient mining and quarrying are still visible, as they are on Mount Pentelicus near Athens, although they are dwarfed or effaced by similar modern operations. Even more destructive were demands on forests for wood and fuel for mining, smelting, metallurgy, and firing of ceramics.

Although pollution was not produced on anything like the modern scale, neither was there effective technology to reduce effluents to the air or water, except for construction of chimneys to disperse noxious smoke high into the air, as noted about the silver smelters of Spain.[11] The poison there was lead from silver ore; other industrial processes released dangerous wastes including arsenic, mercury, and ammonia. Those whose work brought them in contact with these materials were in special danger.[12] But other people were unwittingly exposed to toxins such as lead. Because lead poisoning is cumulative and long lasting, people did not often connect its effects with the cause. It is not necessary to argue that it acted primarily on the cream of society to see it as an effective factor. Arsenic was an ingredient of paints and dyes, and mercury was often used in refining gold. If industry contaminated the population with poisons through food, water, air, and commonly handled objects, it could have been a cause contributing to the fall of the ancient world.

Cities

Numerous problems of cities had effects on the course of civilization; cities were the centers of society, and if the head is not sound, the body will not prosper. Pollution of the air by smoke, dust, and odors from countless urban activities made life uncomfortable and unhealthy. Ancient cities relied for light and heat on open fires, smoking oil lamps, and charcoal braziers. Water pollution presented a danger in cities, where sewage and garbage fouled groundwater and made wells unsafe. Not every center had aqueducts like the ones that supplied Rome. Urban wastes generated health problems even in Rome, where the main sewer discharged into the Tiber, putting at risk not only those downstream, but also the city itself when the river flooded and backed up untreated effluent. Athens used raw sewage as fertilizer for the fields, hardly an advisable practice from a public health standpoint even if it did represent recycling. Solid garbage was thrown into streets, where it attracted flies, rats, and other vermin, and rotted into the sludge that was so deep in some towns that stepping-stones were installed to help pedestrians cross the streets. Such places were breeding grounds for epidemics. Ancient cities devoured their own populations, as early modern ones did. Only constant immigration from the countryside allowed them to maintain their numbers and even to grow, like Rome during early imperial times.

Society and Nature

Environmental changes as a result of human activities must be judged to be one of the causes in the decline of ancient Greek and Roman civilization, and in producing the worsening conditions of the early medieval centuries. The evidence supporting this assertion comes from surviving documents of many kinds, the results of archaeological investigations, and the land itself, which bears the marks of its treatment at the hands of its inhabitants through the centuries. The processes described in this book had the cumulative effect of draining both natural resources and the people who depended on them, consequently weakening the human communities of that period. These effects can be seen in some of the earliest societies of the Mediterranean basin, but they were cumulative, and by late Roman Imperial times had forced themselves into the awareness of astute leaders and writers.

All these factors were not present throughout the ancient world at the same time, of course. How could any civilization survive if most of its forests had been removed; its soil washed away; its cropland salinized; its water and air polluted; its cities crowded, unsafe, and subject to disease; and its rural environs ravaged by war? The effects of each environmental problem were greater in some areas and less in others, and although one can speak with confidence about some times and places, unfortunately evidence is more often incomplete. Research into these topics is progressing, however, and questions regarding environmental and ecological processes in the ancient world cannot be ignored today as they were in the recent past.

What are the reasons for the failure of the Greeks and Romans to maintain a viable balance with the environment? Several factors determine how a society will relate to nature and how sustainable that relationship will be, and they can be considered for the ancient Greeks and Romans.

The social standing of women is one factor that affects a civilization's relationship with the natural world. Greek and Roman traditions were extremely patriarchal in the sense that a woman's status was determined by the men to whom she was related: her father before her marriage, her husband during marriage, her son during widowhood, and a related male guardian if none of the previously named relationships applied. She would be a member of the class to which the man belonged, but she could not exercise direct political or legal participation. A woman might be of citizen class, but she was not a citizen. Women were excluded from formal participation in Athenian democracy. In Rome, there were no female magistrates. There was often an empress (*Augusta*), but only in relationship to a male emperor. At the same time, upper-class women could wield considerable political and economic power through or on behalf of their husbands or other related men. They took a major role in the day-to-day administration of landed estates. Their influence in terms of environmental impact was therefore considerable.

The attitudes contained in the prevailing ethos of a society should have some effect on its actions. It would seem that the way people regard nature would influence their decisions about practices that affect the environment. The view of nature among the early Greeks and Romans was religious; they saw the environment as the realm of the gods. This belief led them to take great care in such activities as hunting and agriculture. Artemis would be invoked before a wild animal could be killed, and a fertilizing ceremony to Demeter would precede the planting of wheat. Such religious practices no doubt contained ecological wisdom (not to kill too many deer; to use fertilizer on crops), but they became mere rituals and lost their original connection to natural processes. Also, they yielded too easily to economic expediency, as the handy prayer advised by Cato and used before cutting trees or cultivating ground in a sacred grove, shows.[13]

In classical Greek times, many thinkers embraced an attitude of skeptical rationality that explained the world in natural terms and ignored the gods. "Man is the measure of all things," said Protagoras.[14] One embracing this view would use reason as the guide to actions in the world. But during this period, so little was known about how natural processes work that rationality was of little use. Economic self-interest reared its head here, too; Thales reportedly used his research into nature to corner the olive market one year. Aristotle regarded human reason as evidence of human superiority, announcing that the highest purpose of everything in nature was to serve man, the single rational animal.[15] Of course, more traditional attitudes survived among common folk, particularly in rural areas.

Attitudes in Roman times emphasized pragmatism. Whatever was practical and profitable was the rule in developing natural resources, but the rule was applied rather narrowly. The Romans had conquered the political world, and they seem to have thought they could conquer nature, too.[16] Here can be seen an important root of the modern ecologic crisis. To use nature as a slave by right of conquest, without considering her ability to meet the demands placed upon her, was shortsighted practicality. In late Roman times, Christianity became a dominant force. The Christian view held that nature was a trust placed by God in the hands of man, who was to care for it as God's steward. But monotheism often taught that God was separate from creation, denying any inherent sacredness in nature. The first book of the Bible said that God had given man "dominion" over the Earth, and many Christians took that command as permission to do what they wished to the environment, rather than as a call to responsibility. Most Romans before and during the Christian period regarded human activities as improvements in nature and as pleasing to God.

The way in which a society relates to nature is shaped by the knowledge of nature that they possess. People living close to the natural world as gatherers, hunters, herders, and agriculturalists accumulated a considerable body of knowledge through trial and error. The ancestors of the Greeks and Romans imparted this knowledge in the form of myths, traditions, and commonsense injunctions. But such lore is full of inaccuracies and misunderstandings. To demonstrate its failures as a guide for ecological decisions, one could compare the similar case of ancient pharmacology, in which fairly good remedies existed alongside awful, ineffective, often actually harmful concoctions. Agriculture could be carried on fairly well through use of tried-and-true methods so long as it was not disrupted by natural disasters, political and economic exactions, and war, but these disruptions were all too common.

The natural philosophers attempted to understand nature rationally, explaining phenomena by reference to physical reality, not the gods. They asked some questions that are now regarded as ecological. But reason was doomed to fail in this endeavor to the extent that it was unsupported by observation and unchecked by experiment. Even such keen minds as Democritus, Epicurus, and Lucretius, who advanced the atomic theory, engaged in doctrinaire speculation rather than empirical research into the phenomena of nature. The ancients barely achieved science worthy of the name. Aristotle came close, and his disciple Theophrastus nearly invented the science of ecology, but they had no followers who advanced beyond them. This was particularly true of the Romans, who admired and patronized Greek science but made few theoretical advances of their own. Pliny the Elder, typically, was a collector and compiler of information true and false, not an independent thinker. Many Christians thought that the study of physical phenomena was a waste of time because the material world is temporary. "The wisdom of this world is foolishness," wrote the apostle Paul.[17] So science in general, and ecology in particular, remained undeveloped after a brief period during which the Peripatetic School planted seeds that flourished, but bore little fruit.

A society can find a sustainable balance with nature only if it possesses the appropriate technology. One is tempted to say that ancient technology was more appropriate than modern, because it was simpler, utilizing human and animal power for the most part, and could do less damage over similar periods of time. But Greeks and Romans brought their efforts to bear cumulatively over centuries, so much damage was done. Even relatively simple technologies can be destructive, as the ancient dependence on wood and charcoal for energy and the resultant damage to forests demonstrate. Ironically, the very technological achievements of the Romans that moderns admire most are those that most clearly demonstrate their ability to alter and control nature in ways that were sometimes productive, but often destructive. Granted their proficiency, it is strange that they seem to have been on the verge of further inventions and a technological revolution that remained unachieved for unknown reasons, although a slave economy, psychological resistance, desire to preserve jobs, and failure to develop interchangeable parts have all been suggested. Yet it would be pointless to criticize the Romans for not achieving the Industrial Revolution 1,500 years before it actually occurred. If they had further developed their technology without improving their attitudes toward and knowledge of nature, their impact on the natural environment would have been swifter and more destructive.

A society can control and direct its effects on the environment only if it can encourage or compel its members to act in certain ways. Doing so is necessary because attaining goals that are desirable for the society as a whole entails sacrifices, even if only small ones, on the part of individuals. For example, the owner of a goat herd will not refrain from grazing his animals on a hillside where small trees are growing just because it would be good to have a forest there in a few years. He puts a marginal gain for himself ahead of a much larger gain for his community. So society must exercise some degree of coercion. But too much coercion, ostensibly for the public good, can be extremely harmful to the environment if it is directed to exploitation and not informed by ecological understanding, as the twentieth-century experience in socialist countries demonstrates all too well.

Greek and Roman governments established policies affecting agriculture, forestry, mining, commerce, and the like, but citizens were allowed some latitude of choice within these guidelines. Huge works like aqueducts, canals, and roads show that ancient states had ways of getting cooperation, but it can well be imagined that the common people evaded regulations if it was in their best interest. Greek citizens had carefully defined duties to the polis, and the polis concerned itself with the use of various categories of land, but many city-states were proud of the degree of freedom they allowed. The Roman Empire attempted to interfere in and control the lives of its citizens to a greater extent, particularly in the days of Diocletian and afterward. No ancient autocracy remotely approached the technological capabilities of a modern state to keep tabs on its citizens and to ensure they perform their social duties. But they were able to do a lot.

The economy of the ancient world was organized primarily to benefit the upper strata of society: the landlords rather than the peasantry, the rich rather than the poor, the masters rather than the slaves. Some landowners controlled huge estates, and large, wealthy families contracted with the government to exploit mines, forests, and other resources. There were also many smaller enterprises run by citizens of lesser rank, or by freedmen, and these often depended on funding from the more affluent. Dependent enterprises usually conducted trade, since commercial occupations were considered demeaning to those of upper class, although nothing prevented the latter from profiting through the labor of the former. The environmental impact of ancient societies can be seen in their ability to reach out and use resources located at great distances. Athens imported grain from Egypt and from north of the Black Sea. Roman roads and ships brought timber from the Alps and Lebanon. Tin came to the Mediterranean from beyond the Pillars of Hercules.

No picture of the effect of the ancient economy on the natural environment can be complete without an investigation of the role of slavery.[18] As Aldo Schiavone explained it: "The use of slaves became the ideal functional means of agricultural exploitation, slave labor the basis of all manufacturing, and the owner of land and slaves the ultimate protagonists of every organization of production . . . [I]t is impossible to separate the society of Rome—its material foundations, obviously, but also its ideas, convictions, mentality, ethics, and even its anthropology—from the context of slavery."[19]

The slave's status was equivocal; the law treated a slave as a "speaking tool" (*instrumentum vocale*). Mine slaves demonstrate that both Greeks and Romans relied on human labor to compensate for a shortage and inefficiency of machinery. But gradually through Roman history, especially during the second century, a degree of personhood was recognized. A freed slave could become a citizen, although of lower class. Slaves made up at least 35 percent of the population of Italy during the time of Augustus, and were similarly numerous elsewhere in the Roman Empire. Slave owners among the higher classes were known to possess hundreds or thousands. In 61 CE, for example, Lucius Pedanius Secundus had 400 house slaves, while field slaves and mine slaves were much more numerous. Many agricultural slaves worked on latifundia where they would watch grazing animals and take them to mountain pastures in summer, but Columella tells of specialized slaves skilled in viticulture, and there were slaves who managed business for their owners.[20] But slaves could not be expected to exhibit initiative in improving agricultural methods or assuring sustained yield of renewable resources. They were obliged to obey their owners' commands to do mechanical and repetitive work, had little time at their own disposal, and if they produced agricultural surplus or other income, it went to their masters. They lacked even the marginal incentives that tenant sharecroppers had in planning for personal and family rewards. A slave economy cannot as a rule benefit the environment: slave labor enabled exploiters to do more damage, and a slave class whose members were liable to be sold anywhere could not establish a relationship of responsibility with the land. Slaves performed most of the actual work in forestry, such as felling trees.[21] In addition, the fact that, as Pliny the Elder expressed it, "agricultural operations are performed by slaves with fettered ankles and by the hands of malefactors with branded faces"[22] increased the tendency of Roman citizens to think of farming not as care of the earth, but as degrading work. The Roman system of slave labor not only corrupted human values, but helped destroy the environment, as well.

A most damaging aspect of Greek and Roman social organization as it affected the environment was its inclination toward war. Balance with nature is a condition of peace. Ancient cities and empires were warrior-dominated societies, never at peace for very long. Even the famous *Pax Romana* that lasted, with few breaks, for 200 years did not end wars along the frontiers, and was followed by fifty years of war in the third century that left no major province untouched by campaigns and battles. War exacted a debilitating toll from agriculture, because military campaigns devastated the countryside, slaughtered farmers and their families, and requisitioned or destroyed crops and buildings. Farmers were conscripted and had to spend time fighting instead of caring for the land, so terraces and irrigation works were left neglected. The mere passage of armies living off the country and trampling the crops was a calamity, but calculated "environmental warfare," in which an enemy's natural resources and food supplies were demolished, was not uncommon.

Conclusion

Social organization and technology can be used either for positive or negative ecological purposes. The Greeks and Romans used them in both ways, but unfortunately the trend over the centuries was destructive. Nonrenewable resources were consumed, and renewable resources were exploited faster than was sustainable. As a result, the lands where Western civilization received its formative impulse were gradually drained, losing much of their living and nonliving heritage. This was the fate of the natural environment and human populations alike, and it was not something that arose irresistibly from a natural climatic change or other disaster. The decline in the environment in the Mediterranean basin was the result of unwise actions of the Greeks and Romans themselves, unaware as they may have been. The problems of the societies that followed them were in part the results of attempting to flourish in an impoverished environment.

Notes

Chapter 1. Introduction

1. Pl., *Critias* 111 B–D; *Leges* 6.761 B–C.
2. Vitr. 8.6.11; Strabo 3.2.8, C146.
3. George Perkins Marsh, *Man and Nature* (New York: Scribner 1864), 10–11.
4. Paul Bigelow Sears, *Deserts on the March* (Norman: University of Oklahoma Press, 1935), 27–30; Walter C. Lowdermilk, *Conquest of the Land through 7,000 Years*, U.S. Department of Agriculture Information Bulletin No. 99 (Washington, DC: Government Printing Office, 1953); Lowdermilk, "Lessons from the Old World to the Americas in Land Use," in *Annual Report of the Board of Regents of the Smithsonian Institution for 1943* (Washington, DC: Government Printing Office, 1944), 413–27.
5. Fairfield Osborn, *The Limits of the Earth* (Westport, CT: Greenwood Press, 1971), 11.
6. Pl., *Critias* 111B–D.
7. Thuc. 4.108.
8. Robert Sallares, *The Ecology of the Ancient Greek World* (Ithaca, NY: Cornell University Press, 1991), 4.
9. I searched the Thesaurus Linguae Graecae (TLG) database for morphemes relating to ecology, with the assistance of Dr. Theodore F. Brunner, Director of the TLG Project at the University of California, Irvine, as it was being developed in the early days of computer technology in 1980. Now available online (http://www.tlg.uci.edu/), the database contains virtually all Greek writings from Homer to the early Medieval period. I did not find the word *oikologia*, but *oikeios* was used for an appropriate relationship of animals and plants to the kinds of places where they occur, seemingly containing a kernel of the idea of the ecological "niche."
10. Ernst Haeckel, *Generelle Morphologie der Organismen* (Berlin: Verlag Georg Reimer, 1866), 1:238, 2:286.
11. William A. McDonald and George R. Rapp Jr., ed., *The Minnesota Messenia Expedition: Reconstructing a Bronze Age Regional Environment* (Minneapolis: University of Minnesota Press, 1972); Tjeerd H. Van Andel and Curtis R. Runnels, *Beyond the Acropolis: A Rural Greek Past* (Stanford: Stanford University Press, 1987); Tjeerd H. Van Andel, Curtis N. Runnels, and Kevin O. Pope,

237

"Five Thousand Years of Land Use and Abuse in the Southern Argolid, Greece," *Hesperia* 55 (1986): 103–28; Curtis N. Runnels, "Environmental Degradation in Ancient Greece," *Scientific American* 272, no. 3 (March 1995): 96–99; J. L. Davis, ed., *Sandy Pylos: An Archaeological History from Nestor to Navarino* (Austin: University of Texas Press, 1998); H. Helen Patterson, ed., *Bridging the Tiber: Approaches to Regional Archaeology in the Middle Tiber Valley*, Archaeological Monograph 13 (Rome: British School at Rome, 2004).

Chapter 2. The Environment

1. Fernand Braudel, *The Mediterranean and the Mediterranean World in the Age of Philip II* (New York: Harper and Row, 1972).
2. Ibid., 17–18.
3. J. Donald Hughes, *The Mediterranean: An Environmental History* (Santa Barbara, CA: ABC-CLIO, 2005).
4. Jacques Blondel, James Aronson, Jean-Yves Bodiou, and Gilles Boeuf, *The Mediterranean Region: Biological Diversity in Space and Time*, 2nd ed. (Oxford: Oxford University Press, 2010).
5. Homer, *Od.* 9.82–104.
6. Allen Perry, "Mediterranean Climate," in *The Mediterranean: Environment and Society*, ed. Russell King, Lindsay Proudfoot, and Bernard Smith (London: Arnold, 1997), 30–44.
7. Arist., *Mete.* 2.6, 363.a.21.
8. Arist., *Mete.* 2.6, 264.b.15.
9. Peter R. Dallman, *Plant Life in the World's Mediterranean Climates: California, Chile, South Africa, Australia, and the Mediterranean Basin* (Berkeley: University of California Press, 1998).
10. Thomas J. M. Schopf, *Palaeoceanography* (Cambridge, MA: Harvard University Press, 1980), 79.
11. J. Donald Hughes, "The Natural Environment," in *A Companion to the Classical Greek World*, ed. Konrad H. Kinzl (Oxford: Blackwell Publishing, 2006), 227–44.
12. Aesch., *PB* 371.
13. Richard Carrington, *The Mediterranean: Cradle of Western Culture* (New York: Viking Press, 1971), 31–35.
14. Verena Winiwarter, "Prolegomena to a History of Soil Knowledge in Europe," in *Soils and Societies: Perspectives from Environmental History*, ed. J. R. McNeill and Verena Winiwarter (Isle of Harris, UK: White Horse Press, 2006), 177–215.
15. Theophr., *Hist. pl.* 8.2.8.
16. Oleg Polunin and Anthony Huxley, *Flowers of the Mediterranean* (Boston: Houghton Mifflin, 1966), 5–13.
17. Strabo 2.2.3.
18. Blondel et al., *Mediterranean Region,* 18–19.
19. Hellmut Baumann, *The Greek Plant World in Myth, Art, and Literature* (Portland, OR: Timber Press, 1993).
20. Tegwyn Harris, *The Natural History of the Mediterranean* (London: Pelham Books, 1982), 12–15.
21. James Macintosh Houston, *The Western Mediterranean World: An Introduction to Its Regional Landscapes* (London: Longmans, Green, 1964), 112.
22. Harris, *Natural History of the Mediterranean,* 15–17.
23. Polunin and Huxley, *Flowers of the Mediterranean,* 12–13.
24. Russell Meiggs, *Trees and Timber in the Ancient Mediterranean World* (Oxford: Clarendon Press, 1982), 49–87.
25. Plotinus, *Enn.* 3.2.15.

26. J. Donald Hughes, "Europe as Consumer of Exotic Biodiversity: Greek and Roman Times," *Landscape Research* 28, no. 1 (January 2003): 21–31.

27. Jacques Blondel and James Aronson, *Biology and Wildlife of the Mediterranean Region* (Oxford: Oxford University Press, 1999), 225.

Chapter 3. Ecological Crises in Earlier Societies

1. Richard E. Leakey and Roger Lewin, *Origins* (New York: E. P. Dutton, 1977), 117; Donald C. Johanson and James Shreeve, *Lucy's Child: The Search for Our Beginnings* (New York: Morrow, 1989), 209.

2. Deut. 22:6.

3. Tobias Fischer-Hansen and Birte Poulson, *From Artemis to Diana: The Goddess of Man and Beast* (Copenhagen: Museum Tusculanum Press, 2009); Derek B. Counts and Bettina Arnold, *The Master of Animals in Old World Iconography* (Budapest: Archaeolingua Alapítvány, 2010).

4. Omer C. Stewart, "Fire as the First Great Force Employed by Man," in *Man's Role in Changing the Face of the Earth*, ed. Carl O. Sauer, Marston Bates, and Lewis Mumford (Chicago: University of Chicago Press, 1956), 115–33; Stephen J. Pyne, *Fire: A Brief History* (Seattle: University of Washington Press, 2003).

5. Michael A. Hoffman, *Egypt before the Pharaohs: The Prehistoric Foundations of Egyptian Civilization* (New York, Knopf, 1979), 85–90.

6. James Mellaart, Çatal Hüyük: A Neolithic Town in Anatolia (London: Thames and Hudson, 1967); Ian Hodder, *The Leopard's Tale: Revealing the Mysteries of Çatalhöyük* (London: Thames and Hudson, 2006).

7. Theophr., *Hist. pl.* 1.3.6.

8. Mark Nathan Cohen, *Health and the Rise of Civilization* (New Haven, CT: Yale University Press, 1989), 116–22.

9. Anne H. Ehrlich and Paul R. Ehrlich, *Earth* (New York: Franklin Watts, 1987), 59.

10. Purushottam Singh, *Neolithic Cultures of Western Asia* (London: Seminar Press, 1974), 208–12; Erich Isaac, *The Geography of Domestication* (Englewood Cliffs, NJ: Prentice-Hall, 1970).

11. N. K. Sandars, trans., *The Epic of Gilgamesh* (Harmondsworth, UK: Penguin, 1960), 68–82.

12. Thorkild Jacobsen and Robert M. Adams, "Salt and Silt in Ancient Mesopotamian Agriculture," *Science* 128 (1958): 1252; Michal Artzy and Daniel Hillel, "A Defense of the Theory of Progressive Soil Salinization in Ancient Southern Mesopotamia," *Geoarchaeology: An International Journal* 3, no. 3 (1988): 235–38.

13. Karl W. Butzer, *Early Hydraulic Civilization in Egypt: A Study in Cultural Ecology* (Chicago: University of Chicago Press, 1976), 2, 56.

14. J. Donald Hughes, "Sustainable Agriculture in Ancient Egypt," *Agricultural History* 66 (1992): 12–22.

15. Adolf Erman, *Life in Ancient Egypt* (New York: Dover, 1971), 425.

16. Hdt. 2.5.

17. Erman, *Life in Ancient Egypt*, 425.

18. Pliny, *HN* 18.7.167.

19. John Baines and Jaromir Malek, *Atlas of Ancient Egypt* (New York: Facts on File, 1980), 14.

20. Karl W. Butzer, "Long-Term Nile Flood Variation and Political Discontinuities in Pharaonic Egypt," in *From Hunters to Farmers: The Causes and Consequences of Food Production in Africa*, ed. J. Desmond Clark and Steven A. Brandt (Berkeley: University of California Press, 1984), 104–12.

21. John A. Wilson, *The Culture of Ancient Egypt* (Chicago: University of Chicago Press, 1951), 13.

22. John A. Wilson, "Egypt," in *Before Philosophy*, ed. Henri Frankfort (Baltimore: Penguin, 1949), 37–133.

23. "Joy over the Inundation," from *Pyramid Texts*, utterance 581, quoted in Adolf Erman, ed., *The Ancient Egyptians: A Sourcebook of Their Writings* (New York: Harper and Row, 1966), 10.

24. Barry J. Kemp, *Ancient Egypt: Anatomy of a Civilization* (London: Routledge, 1989), 20.

25. Karl Wittfogel, *Oriental Despotism: A Comparative Study of Total Power* (New Haven, CT: Yale University Press, 1957).

26. Butzer, *Early Hydraulic Civilization in Egypt*, 105; Hoffman, *Egypt before the Pharaohs*.

27. First Intermediate Period tomb inscription, Siut, quoted in Hoffman, *Egypt before the Pharaohs*, 313, from James Breasted, *Records of Ancient Egypt* (Chicago: University of Chicago Press, 1906), 1:188–89.

28. Gen. 41:1–37.

29. Kemp, *Ancient Egypt*, 239.

30. Butzer, *Early Hydraulic Civilization in Egypt*, 55–56.

31. Kemp, *Ancient Egypt*, 192.

32. Wilson, *Culture of Ancient Egypt*, 183, quoted from G. A. Reisner and M. B. Reisner, *Zeitshrift für aegyptische Sprache und Altertumskunde* 69 (1933): 34–35.

33. Hermann Kees, *Ancient Egypt: A Cultural Topography* (Chicago: University of Chicago Press, 1961), 78–79.

34. Butzer, *Early Hydraulic Civilization in Egypt*, 86–87.

35. Kees, *Ancient Egypt*, 20.

36. Butzer, *Early Hydraulic Civilization in Egypt*, 26–27.

37. Isa. 18.1.

38. Kees, *Ancient Egypt*, 93–94.

39. Ibid., 95. The lion was sacred to Bastet as cat-goddess, and also to Sekhmet, who bore a lioness's head.

40. Hoffman, *Egypt before the Pharaohs*, 24.

Chapter 4. Concepts of the Natural World

1. J. Donald Hughes, "Athens: Mind and Practice," in *An Environmental History of the World: Humankind's Changing Role in the Community of Life*, 2nd ed. (London: Routledge, 2009), 59–67.

2. J. Donald Hughes, "Environmental Philosophy: I. Ancient Philosophy," in *Encyclopedia of Environmental Ethics and Philosophy*, ed. J. Baird Callicott (New York: Macmillan, 2008), 1:355–59.

3. Theoc., *Id.* 4.43.

4. Homer, *Od.* 14.457–58.

5. Hdt. 7.141.

6. *Hom. Hymns* 5.35.

7. Homer, *Il.* 1.39; Eur., *Alc.* 578–81.

8. *Hom. Hymns* 30.1.

9. *Hom. Hymns* 14.4–5.

10. Xen., *Oec.* 5.12.

11. Proclus, *Chrestomathia* 1. This fragment must be used cautiously because it is probably pseudonymous and dates from the fifth century. But it may preserve an earlier story, and even if not, it represents the last phase of Greco-Roman thought from a Neoplatonic source.

12. J. Donald Hughes, "Artemis: Goddess of Conservation," *Forest and Conservation History* 34 (October 1990): 191–97.

13. *Hom. Hymns* 19.5–11.

14. *Orphic Hymn to Pan*, 11–12.

15. J. Donald Hughes, "Pan: Environmental Ethics in Classical Pantheism," in *Religion and Environmental Crisis*, ed. Eugene C. Hargrove (Athens: University of Georgia Press, 1986), 7–24.

16. Homer, *Od.* 2.181–82.
17. Homer, *Il.* 7.58–60.
18. Pl., *Phdr.* 229B–C.
19. An exception is Hesiod's comment on his own land at Ascra: "Bad in winter, sultry in summer, and good at no time" (Hes., *Op.* 640).
20. Vergil, *G.* 2.173–74.
21. Vincent Joseph Scully, *The Earth, the Temple, and the Gods: Greek Sacred Architecture* (New Haven, CT: Yale University Press, 1962).
22. Callim., *Hymn* 5.
23. Homer, *Od.* 19.592–93.
24. Hdt. 1.174.
25. Strabo 14.2.5.
26. Robert Parker, *Miasma: Pollution and Purification in Early Greek Religion* (Oxford: Clarendon Press, 1983).
27. Hes., *Op.* 757–59; Suet., *Nero* 27.
28. Homer, *Il.* 16.384–92.
29. Homer, *Od.* 19.109–14.
30. Cato, *Agr.* 139–40.
31. *Hom. Hymns* 13.
32. Theopompus, in Diog. Laert. 1.116.
33. Hermann S. Schibli, *Pherekydes of Syros* (Oxford: Clarendon Press, 1990), 69–77.
34. Empedocles fr. 8–9.
35. Philolaus fr. 10.
36. Strabo 7.3.5; cf. Pl., *Leges* 782.C.
37. Empedocles fr. 117, 127.
38. Pl., *Resp.* 10.614–21.
39. Pl., *Ti.* 30.D.
40. James Lovelock, *The Ages of Gaia: A Biography of Our Living Earth* (New York: W. W. Norton, 1988), 206.
41. Homer, *Od.* 15.295; *Il.* 2.757, 9.151.
42. Homer, *Il.* 8.555–59.
43. Sappho fr. 2.
44. Eur., *Danae* fr. 316.
45. Pl., *Phdr.* 230.B.
46. Pl., *Critias* 118.B.
47. Cic., *Amic.* 19.68.
48. Pliny, *Ep.* 1.9.6.
49. Vergil, *Ecl.* 1.82.
50. Vergil, *G.* 2.437–42.
51. Vergil, *G.* 2.485.
52. SHA, *Hadr.* 13.3. Henry Fanshawe Tozer, *A History of Ancient Geography*, 2nd ed. (New York: Biblo and Tannen, 1964), 314–37.
53. SHA, *Hadr.* 13.12.
54. Diog. Laert. 8.69; Sen., *Ep.* 79.2–3.
55. Strabo 6.2.8.
56. Paus. 10.32.7, 10.5.1.
57. Thales fr. 12, 22.
58. Arist., *Pol.* 1.3.7 (1256.b.20).
59. Pl., *Phdr.* 230.D.

60. Mohan Matthen, "The Organic Unity of Aristotle's World," in *The Greeks and the Environment*, ed. Laura Westra and Thomas M. Robinson (Lanham, MD: Rowan and Littlefield, 1997), 133–48.

61. Arist., *Hist. an.* 8.1 (588.a.13–b.17); *Part. an.* 4.5 (681.a.12–14).

62. Anthony Preus, *Science and Philosophy in Aristotle's Biological Works* (Hildesheim, Germany: Georg Olms Verlag, 1975), 217.

63. Arist., *Pol.* 1.5 (1254.b.18–19), 1.8 (1256.b.15–26).

64. Theophr., *Metaph.* 9 (34).

65. Cic., *Nat. D* 2.13 (35).

66. Hes., *Op.* 277–79.

67. Empedocles fr. 17.

68. Empedocles fr. 8–9.

69. Anaxagoras fr. 6.

70. Anaximander fr. 11, 30.

71. Empedocles fr. 57–61.

72. Empedocles fr. 72; Arist., *Resp.* 477.a.32; Theophr., *Caus. pl.* 1.22.2–3.

73. Hdt. 3.108.3–4.

74. Pl., *Prt.* 321.B.

75. George Sessions, "Spinoza and Jeffers: An Environmental Perspective," *Inquiry* 20 (1977): 481–528.

76. Arist., *Metaph.* 12.10.2 (107.a.17–20).

77. George Sarton, *A History of Science: Ancient Science through the Golden Age of Greece* (Cambridge, MA: Harvard University Press, 1952), 565.

78. Arist., *Hist. an.* 9.1 (609.b.19–25).

79. Arist., *Hist. an.* 9.1 (610.a.34–35).

80. Arist., *Hist. an.* 6.36 (580.b.10–29).

81. In Theophrastus's lost work, *Peri tōn athroōs phainomenōn zōiōn*, described in Phot. 527.b.11–528.a.39.

82. Phot. 5.15 (547.b.15–32). The pea crab, *Pinnotheres pisum*, is often found in the mantle cavity of bivalve molluscs.

83. J. Donald Hughes, "Theophrastus as Ecologist," in *Theophrastean Studies: Fifteen Papers on Natural Science, Physics and Metaphysics, Ethics, Religion, and Rhetoric*, ed. William W. Fortenbaugh and Robert W. Sharples (New Brunswick, NJ: Transaction, 1988), 67–75.

84. Theophr., *Caus. pl.* 1.9.3, 1.16.11, 2.3.7, 2.7.1, 3.6.6–7, etc.

85. Theophr., *Hist. pl.* 3.2.5.

86. W. W. Tarn and G. T. Griffith, *Hellenistic Civilization* (London: Arnold, 1952), 307.

87. Hippoc., *Aer.* 24.

88. Thuc. 1.2.

89. Democr. fr. 154.

90. Hes., *Op.* 106–201.

91. Lucr. 5.247–836; Clarence J. Glacken, *Traces on the Rhodian Shore* (Berkeley: University of California Press, 1967), 70–73.

92. J. Donald Hughes, "The Hunters of Euboea: Mountain Folk in the Classical Mediterranean," *Mountain Research and Development* 16, no. 2 (May 1996): 91–100.

93. Dio Chrys., *Or.* 7 (Euboean Discourse).

94. Mart. 12.57.4–6.

95. Anaxagoras fr. 102.

96. Soph. *Ant.* 332–75.

97. Cic., *Nat. D.* 2.60 (152).

98. Strabo 17.1.3.
99. Sen., *Ben.* 4.5–6.
100. Pl., *Critias* 111.B.
101. Cic., *Nat. D.* 2.34 (87).
102. Pliny, *HN* 33.1.2.
103. Columella, *Rust.* 1 (Pref. 1–3).
104. Hor., *Carm.* 3.1.36–37.

Chapter 5. Deforestation, Overgrazing, and Erosion

1. Pl., *Critias* 111B–D.
2. Strabo 5.2.5.
3. Pliny, *HN* 13.29; Varro, *Rust.* 1.6.5; Theophr., *Hist. pl.* 3.2.4, 3.2.6, 3.3.2, 4.5.5.
4. Dem. 42.7. (1040–41).
5. Livy 35.10.12.
6. Livy 35.41.10.
7. Sen., *Ep.* 90.9; Juv. 3.254–56.
8. Suet., *Claud.* 19.20; Tac., *Ann.* 13.51; Mikhail Rostovtzeff, *The Social and Economic History of the Hellenistic World* (Oxford: Clarendon Press, 1941), 3:335–36.
9. Hdt. 5.23; Thuc. 6.90.
10. Xen., *Hell.* 1.1.24–25. The king referred to was the Persian emperor.
11. Veg., *Epitoma Rei Militaris* 27–30, 49, 82–85.
12. Alfred Zimmern, *The Greek Commonwealth: Politics and Economics in Fifth Century Athens*, 5th ed. (Oxford: Oxford University Press, 1931), 278.
13. Columella, *Rust.* 11.1.12.
14. Theophr., *Hist. pl.* 5.1.5–12.
15. Pliny, *HN* 16.74, 16.76.
16. Auson., *Mos.* 362–64.
17. Columella, *Rust.* 2.2.8, 11–12.
18. Pliny, *HN* 17.3.
19. Curtis N. Runnels, "Environmental Degradation in Ancient Greece," *Scientific American* 272, no. 3 (March 1995): 96.
20. Bruno Pinto, Carlos Aguiar, and Maria Partidário, "Brief Historical Ecology of Northern Portugal during the Holocene," *Environment and History* 16, no. 1 (February 2010): 17.
21. Varro, *Rust.* 2; intro. 4.
22. Vasilios P. Papanastasis, "Integrating Goats into Mediterranean Forests," Unasylva No. 154 (Corporate Document Repository, Food and Agriculture Organization of the United Nations, Rome, 1985, http://www.fao.org/docrep/50630e/50630e06.htm).
23. Pl., *Leges* 1.639A.
24. Macrob., *Sat.* 7.5–9.
25. J. R. A. Grieg and J. Turner, "Some Pollen Diagrams from Greece and Their Archaeological Significance," *Journal of Archaeological Science* 1 (1974): 188.
26. Vergil, *Aen.* 10.405–9.
27. Theophr., *Hist. pl.* 5.3.7. These trees, called *citrus* in Pliny, *HN* 13.29, are not citrus at all, but sandarac, a member of the cypress family providing finely patterned, pleasant-smelling wood that was in great demand for fine furniture and endemic to isolated areas in North Africa and places colonized by the Carthaginians, such as Malta and the neighborhood of Cartagena in Spain. The botanical name is *Tetraclinis articulata* (formerly *Callitris quadrivalvis*).
28. Ovid, *Fasti* 5.93–94.

29. Dion. Hal., *Ant. Roman* 3.43.1.

30. Fredric L. Cheyette, "The Disappearance of the Ancient Landscape and the Climatic Anomaly of the Early Middle Ages: A Question to Be Pursued," *Early Medieval Europe* 16, no. 2 (2008): 127–65.

31. J. R. McNeill, *The Mountains of the Mediterranean World: An Environmental History* (Cambridge: Cambridge University Press, 1992), 72–73.

32. Pliny, *HN* 13.19; Diod. Sic. 8.5.2.

33. Livy 9.36.1.

34. These names can be found in Allen Chester Johnson, "Ancient Forests and Navies," *Transactions and Proceedings of the American Philological Association* 58 (1927): 199–209; Hdt. 7.183, 188; and Claudius Ptolemy, *Geography of Claudius Ptolemy*, transl. and ed. Edward Luther Stevenson (New York: New York Public Library, 1932), map of Macedonia, 87.

35. A. A. Manten, "Lennart von Post and the Foundation of Modern Palynology," *Review of Palaeobotany and Palynology* 1 (1967): 11–22.

36. Brian J. Huntley and Harry John Betteley Birks, *An Atlas of Past and Present Pollen Maps for Europe: 0–13,000 Years Ago* (Cambridge: Cambridge University Press, 1983).

37. Valérie Andrieu, "A Computerized Data Base for the Palynological Recording of Human Activity in the Mediterranean Basin," in *Environmental Reconstruction in Mediterranean Landscape Archaeology*, ed. Philippe Leveau, Frédéric Trément, Kevin Walsh, and Graeme Barker (Oxford: Oxbow Books, 1999): 17–24.

38. Nikolaos Athanasiadis, *Zur postglazialen Vegetationsentwicklung von Litochoro Katerinis und Pertouli Trikalon* (Basel: University of Basel Press, 1975), esp. 125–30; Achilleas M. Gerasimidis, *Stathmologikes Sinthikes kai Metapagetodis Exelexi tis Blastisis sta Dasi Laila Serron kai Kataphigiou Pierion* (Thessaloniki: Aristotelian University of Thessaloniki [*Didakyoriki Diatribi*], 1985), 106–24.

39. H. E. Wright Jr., "Vegetation History," in *The Minnesota Messenia Expedition: Reconstructing a Bronze Age Regional Environment*, ed. William A. McDonald and George R. Rapp Jr. (Minneapolis: University of Minnesota Press, 1971), 199.

40. Marcus Niebuhr Tod, *A Selection of Greek Historical Inscriptions* (Oxford: Clarendon Press, 1933), 2:111; Grieg and Turner, "Some Pollen Diagrams from Greece and Their Archaeological Significance," 191.

41. Katherine Patey, "Endangered Forests," *The Athenian* (November 1987): 18–22.

42. George Perkins Marsh, *Man and Nature*, ed. David Lowenthal (Cambridge, MA: Harvard University Press, 1965), 9.

43. Helen Rendell, "Earth Surface Processes in the Mediterranean," in *The Mediterranean: Environment and Society*, ed. Russell King, Lindsay Proudfoot, and Bernard Smith (London: Arnold, 1997), 52.

44. Anthracology is the study of charcoal evidence; the word "anthracology" derives from the Greek *anthrax*.

45. K. J. Salisbury and F. W. Jane, "Charcoals from Maiden Castle and Their Significance in Relation to the Vegetation and Climatic Conditions in Prehistoric Times," *Journal of Ecology* 28 (1940): 310–25; H. Godwin and A. G. Tansley, "Prehistoric Charcoals as Evidence of Former Vegetation, Soil and Climate," *Journal of Ecology* 29 (1941): 117.

46. Eleni Asouti, "Charcoal Analysis Web," 2009, http://pcwww.liv.ac.uk/~easouti/index.htm; George H. Willcox, "A History of Deforestation as Indicated by Charcoal Analysis of Four Sites in Eastern Anatolia," *Anatolian Studies* 24 (1974): 117–33; K. Neumann, "The Contribution of Anthracology to the Study of the Late Quaternary Vegetation History of the Mediterranean Region and Africa," *Bulletin de la Société Botanique de France* 139 (1992): 421–40.

47. Jean-Louis Vernet, "Reconstructing Vegetation and Landscapes in the Mediterranean: The

Contribution of Anthracology," in *Environmental Reconstruction in Mediterranean Landscape Archaeology*, ed. Philippe Leveau, Frédéric Trément, Kevin Walsh, and Graeme Barker (Oxford: Oxbow Books, 1999), 25–36; Lucie Chabal and Fanette Laubenheimer, "L'atelier gallo-romain de Sallèles d'Aude: Les potiers et le bois," in *Terre Cuite et Société, la Céramique, Document Technique, Économique et Culturel* (XIVes Recontres Internationales d'Archéologie et d'Histoire d'Antibes) (Juan-les-Pins: Centre National de la Recherche Scientifique, 1994), 99–129; Fanette Laubenheimer, *20 Ans de Recherches à Sallèles d'Aude: Le Monde des Potiers Gallo-Romans* (Besançon: Presses Universitaires de Franche-Comté, 2001).

48. H. Triat-Laval, "Contribution Pollenanalytique à l'Histoire Tardi-et Postglaciare de la Basse Vallée du Rhône" (PhD dissertation, University of Aix-Marseilles III, 1978).

49. Vernet, "Reconstructing Vegetation and Landscapes in the Mediterranean," 30.

50. George Willcox, "Charcoal Analysis and Holocene Vegetation History in Southern Syria," *Quaternary Science Reviews* 18, no. 4–5 (April 1999): 711–16.

51. N. Planchais, "Palynologie lagunaire de l'etang de Mauguio: Paléoenvironnement vegetal et evolution anthropique," *Pollen et Spores* 24, no. 1 (1982): 93–118; Andrieu, "A Computerized Data Base," 19, fig. 3.2.

52. Hubert H. Lamb, U. Eicher, and V. R. Switsur, "An 18,000 Year Record of Vegetation, Lake-Level, and Climatic Change from Tigalmamine, Middle Atlas, Morocco," *Journal of Biogeography* 16 (1989): 65–74. I am indebted to Diana K. Davis, who included a reference to Lamb's work in her *Resurrecting the Granary of Rome: Environmental History and French Colonial Expansion in North Africa* (Athens: Ohio University Press, 2007), 11.

53. See note 27 above.

54. Lucan, *Pharsalia* 9.426–30, quoted in Russell Meiggs, *Trees and Timber in the Ancient Mediterranean World* (Oxford: Clarendon Press, 1982), 288. Lucan lived from 39 to 65 CE, and was referring to the time of Caesar and Cicero.

55. Vitr., *De arch.* 8.1.6–7.

56. Paus. 7.26.4.

57. Pliny, *HN* 31.30.

58. Oros. 4.11.

59. John Kraft, "The General Picture of Erosion in the Mediterranean Area"; and Colin Renfrew, "Erosion in Melos and the Question of the Younger Fill," papers presented at the Deforestation, Erosion, and Ecology in the Ancient Mediterranean and Middle East symposium, National Museum of Natural History, Smithsonian Institution, National Museum of Natural History, Washington DC, April 19, 1978.

60. Pl., *Critias* 111B.

61. Pl., *Phdr.* 110E.

62. Paus. 8.24.5.

63. Russell Meiggs, *Roman Ostia* (Oxford: Clarendon Press, 1960).

64. Meiggs, *Trees and Timber in the Ancient Mediterranean World*, Appendix 4, 423–57.

65. Ibid., Chapter 5, 116–53.

66. Cato, *Agr.* 1.7.

67. Pliny, *Ep.* 5.67.7–13.

68. Pliny, *HN* 17.1.

69. Columella, *Rust.* 1.3.7.

70. Arist., *Pol.* 6.5.4 (1321b), 7.11.4 (1331b).

71. Strabo 14.6.5.

72. Dion. Hal., *Ant. Rom.* 10.31.2.

73. Pl., *Leges* 8.843E.

74. A. S. Hunt and C. C. Edgar, *Select Papyri* (London: Harvard-Heinemann, 1934), 2.210.

75. Livy 28.45.18 (*ex publicis silvis*).

76. Theophr., *Hist. pl.* 5.8.1.

77. Cic., *Agr.* 1.3.

78. Rostovtzeff, *Social and Economic History of the Hellenistic World*, 1:299, 1:480–81, 3:1169–70.

Chapter 6. Wildlife Depletion and Loss of Habitat

1. Ovid, *Fasti* 5.539–41.

2. *Greek Anthology* 4.202.

3. J. Donald Hughes, "Hunting in the Ancient Mediterranean World," in *A Cultural History of Animals in Antiquity*, ed. Linda Kalof (Oxford: Berg, 2007), 47–70.

4. Dio Chrys., *Or.* 7 (Euboean Discourse).

5. Homer, *Od.* 10.156–77, 12.297–396.

6. James George Frazer, *The Golden Bough: A Study in Magic and Religion* (New York: Macmillan, 1935), 8:221.

7. Diod. Sic. 22.5.

8. Arr., *Cyn.* 34.1–36.4.

9. Xen., *Cyn.* 5.14; Arr., *Cyn.* 16.1–7.

10. Xen., *An.* 5.3.7–10.

11. Homer, *Od.* 2.181–82.

12. John Richard Thornhill Pollard, *Birds in Greek Life and Myth* (London: Thames and Hudson, 1977), 15.

13. Paus. 8.38.5.

14. Apollod., *Bibl.* 3.9.2.

15. Under the Romans, perhaps owing to the influence of mock hunts (*venationes*), wildlife sacrifices became less rare.

16. Apollod., *Bibl.* 3.30.

17. Hugh Lloyd-Jones, "Artemis and Iphigenia," *Journal of Hellenic Studies* 103 (1983): 99.

18. Eur., *Bacchae* 337–40.

19. Soph., *El.* 563–72.

20. Soph., *El.* 563–72.

21. Paus. 8.54.5.

22. Hdt. 8.41.2.

23. Plut., *De soll. an.* 35.11.

24. Ael., *NA* 8.4; Plut., *Mor.* 976A; Paus. 7.22.4.

25. Paus. 1.32.1.

26. Apollod., *Bibl.* 3.104–5.

27. Lilly Kahil, "The Mythological Repertoire of Brauron," in *Ancient Greek Art and Iconography*, ed. Warren G. Moon (Madison: University of Wisconsin Press, 1983), 237.

28. J. Donald Hughes, "Artemis: Goddess of Conservation," *Forest and Conservation History* 34 (October 1990): 191–97.

29. K. M. D. Dunbabin, *The Mosaics of Roman North Africa* (Oxford: Oxford University Press, 1978), no. 32.

30. Ar., *Av.* 529–30.

31. Ath. 5.198D–201C.

32. William Radcliffe, *Fishing from the Earliest Times* (London: J. Murray, 1921), 256.

33. Hor., *Sat.* 2.4.73; Mart. 3.77.5, 5.11.94.

34. Pliny, *HN* 9.79.

35. Homer, *Il.* 11.129, 11.544–56, 18.573–86.

36. John Kinloch Anderson, *Hunting in the Ancient World* (Berkeley: University of California Press, 1985), 15, 25.
37. Ibid., 70–73.
38. Pl., *Leges* 7.822D–824B.
39. Anderson, *Hunting in the Ancient World*, 76–80.
40. Elizabeth Carney, "Hunting and the Macedonian Elite: Sharing the Rivalry of the Chase," in *The Hellenistic World: New Perspectives*, ed. Daniel Ogden (London: Gerald Duckworth, 2002), 59–80.
41. Judith M. Barringer, *The Hunt in Ancient Greece* (Baltimore: Johns Hopkins University Press, 2001), 186.
42. SHA, *Hadr.* 20.13; Anderson, *Hunting in the Ancient World*, 169n12.
43. Dio Cass. 69.10.3.
44. *Code Theod.* 15.11.1.
45. Homer, *Od.* 19.418–58.
46. Plut., *Ant.* 29.2.
47. Plut., *De soll. an.* 9.
48. Xen., *An.* 1.2.7; *Cyr.* 1.4.4–15.
49. Varro, *Rust.* 3.13.1–3.
50. Plut., *De soll. an.* 9.
51. Auson., *Mos.*
52. Ar., *Av.* 70; Pollard, *Birds in Greek Life and Myth*, 108; George Jennison, *Animals for Show and Pleasure in Ancient Rome* (Manchester: Manchester University Press, 1937), 18.
53. Livy 39.22; Ludwig Friedländer, *Roman Life and Manners under the Early Empire* (London: George Routledge and Sons, 1909–13), 2:62.
54. Howard Hayes Scullard, *Elephant in the Greek and Roman World* (Ithaca, NY: Cornell University Press, 1974), 250.
55. *Res Gestae* 22.3.
56. Friedländer, *Roman Life and Manners*, 2:66.
57. Ibid., 63; Jennison, *Animals for Show and Pleasure*, 174.
58. Symmachus, *Ep.* 5.60, 5.62.
59. Edicts of Honorius and Theodosius, *Cod. Theod.* 15.11.1–2.
60. Pliny, *HN* 36.40; Jennison, *Animals for Show and Pleasure*, 174.
61. Cic., *Fam.* 7.1.3; Dio Cass. 39.38.2–4; Pliny, *HN* 8.7 (20–21); Anderson, *Hunting in the Ancient World*, 87.
62. Cic., *Att.* 6.1.21; *Fam.* 2.11.2.
63. Dio Cass. 39.38.2–4; Pliny, *HN* 8.7 (20–21).
64. Varro, *Sat. Men.* 161, 293–96, 361; J. Aymard, *Essai sur les chasses romaines des origines à la fin du siècle des Antonins*, Fasc. 171 (Paris: Bibliothèque des Écoles Françaises d'Athenes et de Rome, 1951), 60–63; Anderson, *Hunting in the Ancient World*, 87.
65. Anderson, *Hunting in the Ancient World*, 86.
66. Arr., *Cyn.*, 16.6–8.
67. Pindar, *Nem.* 3.51–52.
68. Anderson, *Hunting in the Ancient World*, 14.
69. Xen., *De equis alendis* 8.1–10; Perses, *Anth. Pal.* 6.112.
70. Ctesias 4.26; Arist., *Hist. an.* 9.620A.32; *Mir. ausc.* 118.841B.15; Anderson, *Hunting in the Ancient World*, 87.
71. Xen., *Cyn.* 11.1–4.
72. Xen., *Cyn.* 9.1–7.
73. Anderson, *Hunting in the Ancient World*, 5, 10.

74. Ibid., 14n50, 38–39, 158.
75. Xen., *Cyn.* 2.9, 9, 11–20.
76. Pollard, *Birds in Greek Life and Myth*, 104.
77. Xen., *An.* 1.5.2; Ael., *NA* 14.7.
78. Homer, *Od.* 10.124.
79. Radcliffe, *Fishing from the Earliest Times*, 10, 74, 236.
80. Mart. 5.18.7–8; Ael., *NA* 14.22, 15.1; Radcliffe, *Fishing from the Earliest Times*, 158.
81. Pl., *Leges* 7.824C.
82. Oppian, *Halieutica* 3.29–31.
83. Radcliffe, *Fishing from the Earliest Times*, 242.
84. Ibid., 231–33; Mikhail Rostovtzeff, *The Social and Economic History of the Hellenistic World*, 2nd ed. (Oxford: Clarendon Press, 1957), 1:287.
85. Justinian, *Corpus Juris, Digest* 44.3.7.
86. J. Donald Hughes, "Europe as Consumer of Exotic Biodiversity: Greek and Roman Times," *Landscape Research* 28, no. 1 (January 2003): 21–31.
87. Jennison, *Animals for Show and Pleasure*, 174.
88. Justinian, *Digest* 21.1.40–42; Jennison, *Animals for Show and Pleasure*, 152.
89. Adrienne Mayor, *The First Fossil Hunters: Paleontology in Greek and Roman Times* (Princeton, NJ: Princeton University Press, 2000).
90. Hdt. 2.66; Sen., *Ep.* 121.19; Pliny, *HN* 10.73(94), 202.
91. Pliny, *HN* 37.11; Ath. 655C–F; Varro, *Rust.* 3.9.17.
92. Aristoph., *Av.* 69.
93. Arist., *Hist. an.* 620a32; *Mir. Ausc.* 841b15.
94. Pliny, *HN* 9.79.
95. Arist., *Gen. an.* 3.11; Friedländer, *Roman Life and Manners*, 2:165.
96. Varro, *Rust.* 3.14.
97. Mirko Drazen Grmek, *Diseases in the Ancient Greek World* (Baltimore: Johns Hopkins University Press, 1989), 265–83.
98. Robert Browning, *Justinian and Theodora* (New York: Praeger, 1971), 242–43.
99. Anderson, *Hunting in the Ancient World*, 4n10, 157.
100. Hdt. 7.125–26.
101. Arist., *Hist. An.* 6.31.579b7, 8.28, 8.606b.15.
102. Paus. 3.20.5, 8.23.6.
103. David Attenborough, *The First Eden: The Mediterranean World and Man* (Boston: Little, Brown, 1987), 28–31.
104. Amm. Marc., 18.7, 22.15.24; Themistius, *Or.* 10.140a; William Charles Brice, *Environmental History of the Near and Middle East since the Last Ice Age* (New York: Academic Press, 1978), 141.
105. Vergil, *Ecl.* 5.29.
106. Ar., *Av.* 504–75.
107. J. A. Thompson in Radcliffe, *Fishing from the Earliest Times*, 230.
108. Suet., *Tib.* 34; Pliny, *HN* 9.30.
109. Ellen Churchill Semple, *The Geography of the Mediterranean Region: Its Relation to Ancient History* (New York: Henry Holt, 1931), 446–54.
110. George Sarton, *A History of Science: Ancient Science through the Golden Age of Greece* (Cambridge, MA: Harvard University Press, 1952), 1:537–38.
111. Ath. 5.198D–201C; Diod. Sic. 3.36.2–4. For Ptolemy II, see W. W. Tarn and G. T. Griffith, *Hellenistic Civilization* (London: Arnold, 1952). Tarn and Griffith argue that the "white bear" cannot have been an ordinary albino bear. See also E. E. Rice, *The Grand Procession of Ptolemy Philadelphus* (Oxford: Oxford University Press, 1983).

112. Strabo 15.4.73; Dio Cass. 54.9.58; cf. *Res Gestae* 36; H. H. Rawlinson, *Intercourse between India and the Western World from the Earliest Times to the Fall of Rome* (Cambridge: University of Cambridge Press, 1926), 107–9.
113. Friedländer, *Roman Life and Manners*, 2:66, from Aur. Vict., *Caesares* 1.25.
114. Galen, *De sectis* 7.10.
115. Homer, *Il.* 23.288–94; *Od.* 17.290–327.
116. Friedländer, *Roman Life and Manners*, 2:67–68.
117. Jennison, *Animals for Show and Pleasure*, 10–27, 99–121, 126–36.
118. Ovid, *Met.* 15.60–143.
119. Plut., *Mor.* 962C–D.
120. Plut., *Mor.* 996F.
121. This riposte was also directed at Odysseus's questionable parentage, as some ancient commentators say that Sisyphus seduced Odysseus's mother, Anticlea daughter of Autolycus, shortly before her marriage to Laertes, Odysseus's ostensible father.
122. Plut., *Mor.* 999A, referring to Hes., *Op.* 277–79.
123. Jacques Blondel and James Aronson, *Biology and Wildlife of the Mediterranean Region* (Oxford: Oxford University Press, 1999), 202.

Chapter 7. Agricultural Decline

1. Soph., *Ant.* 338–41.
2. Hes., *Op.* 117–18, 176–77.
3. Lucr. 1157–68; Rolfe Humphries, trans., *The Way Things Are* (Bloomington: Indiana University Press, 1968), 85.
4. Ellen Churchill Semple, *The Geography of the Mediterranean Region: Its Relation to Ancient History* (New York: Henry Holt, 1931), 357.
5. J. Donald Hughes, "Land and Sea," in *Civilization of the Ancient Mediterranean: Greece and Rome*, ed. Michael Grant and Rachel Kitzinger (New York: Charles Scribner's Sons, 1988), 1:98–99, 108–13.
6. Pliny, *HN* 17.33.
7. Hes., *Op.* 640.
8. Kenneth D. White, *Roman Farming* (Ithaca, NY: Cornell University Press, 1970), 173.
9. Semple, *Geography of the Mediterranean Region*, 433.
10. Xen., *Symp.* 2.24.6.
11. Theophr., *Caus. pl.* 1.10.4, 3.10.8; *Hist. pl.* 4.14.7; Xen., *Oec.* 19.18; Columella, *Rust.* 2.2.24–25.
12. Theophr., *Hist. pl.* 4.14.9.
13. Varro, *Rust.* 1.8.5.
14. Cato, *Agr.* 11. A *jugerum* was about five-eighths of an acre, approximately the amount of land one man could plow with an ox in one day.
15. Columella, *Rust.* 4.25; Kenneth D. White, *Agricultural Implements of the Roman World* (London: Cambridge University Press, 1967), 97.
16. Varro, *Rust.* 1.2.6.
17. Dem., *Epit.* 71.
18. Palladius 12.1.
19. Theophr., *Hist. pl.* 2.8.4.
20. Pliny, *HN* 15.102.
21. Columella, *Rust.* 10.410–12.
22. Theophr., *Caus. pl.* 4.5.4; Humphrey Michell, *The Economics of Ancient Greece* (Cambridge: Cambridge University Press, 1963), 58.

23. Michell, *Economics of Ancient Greece*, 66.

24. Cato, *Agr.* 30.

25. Theoc., *Id.* 5.140.

26. Ath. 9.387.

27. Theognis 864 (ca. 540 BCE); Michell, *Economics of Ancient Greece*, 74.

28. Ael., *VH* 2.2.8.

29. Theophr., *Caus. pl.* 3.20.8; White, *Agricultural Implements of the Roman World*; Kenneth D. White, *Farm Equipment of the Roman World* (Cambridge: Cambridge University Press, 1975).

30. L. Alfred Moritz, *Grain-Mills and Flour in Classical Antiquity* (New York: Arno Press, 1979).

31. White, *Farm Equipment of the Roman World*, 15.

32. White, *Roman Farming*, 447.

33. Varro, *Rust.*, 1.19.2; White, *Roman Farming*, 36.

34. Pliny, *HN* 18.296; Palladius 7:4.

35. White, *Roman Farming*, 453.

36. Lucr. 2.1111–25; Varro, *Rust.* 1.9.2 praef.; Pliny, *HN* 18.4; Columella, *Rust.* 1 praef., 2.1.

37. Columella, *Rust.* 3.3.

38. Columella, *Rust.* 3.3 praef. 1–3.

39. Pliny, *HN* 18.192.

40. Cato, *Agr.* 36; *Greek Inscriptions* xi, 2, 161A, 43, 162A, 39, 278A, 20.

41. Michell, *Economics of Ancient Greece*, 53.

42. Theophr., *Hist. pl.* 2.7.4, 7.5.1; *Caus. pl.* 3.9.2; Columella, *Rust.* 2.14.5–6.

43. Strabo 8.16.6.

44. Hes., *Op.* 464; White, *Roman Farming*, 177.

45. Theophr., *Caus. pl.* 4.7.3, 4.8.1–3; Theophr., *Hist. Pl.*, 8.11.8.

46. Vergil, *G.* 1.73–75; Pliny, *HN* 18.91.

47. Theophr., *Hist. pl.* 7.3.3–4.

48. Theophr., *Caus. pl.* 1.9.3, 2.13.5.

49. Xen., *Ec.* 5.12.

50. Xen., *Ec.* 20.22–26; Moses I. Finley, *Studies in Land and Credit in Ancient Athens, 500–200 B.C.* (New Brunswick, NJ: Rutgers University Press, 1952), 82. Finley says there are "not a dozen references in Greek literature to increasing the value of a farm or urban holding."

51. Cic., *Sen.* 15.

52. Gustave Glotz, *Ancient Greece at Work: An Economic History of Greece from the Homeric Period to the Roman Conquest* (London: Kegan Paul, 1930), 247.

53. J. Donald Hughes, "Environmental Impacts of the Roman Economy and Social Structure: Augustus to Diocletian," in *Rethinking Environmental History: World-System History and Global Environmental Change*, ed. Alf Hornborg, J. R. McNeill, and Joan Martinez-Allier (Lanham, MD: Altamira Press, 2007), 27–40.

54. Semple, *Geography of the Mediterranean Region*, 440–41.

55. Columella, *Rust.* 2.8.3.

56. H. A. Koster, H. A. Forbes, and L. Foxhall, "Terrace Agriculture and Erosion: Environmental Effects of Population Instability in the Mediterranean" (paper presented at the Deforestation, Erosion, and Ecology in the Ancient Mediterranean and Middle East symposium, National Museum of Natural History, Smithsonian Institution, Wasington, DC, April 19, 1978).

57. Homer, *Il.* 21.257–62; *Od.* 7.129–30.

58. Strabo 8.6.7–8.

59. Pl., *Leges* 6.761B–C, 8.844A–D.

60. Plut., *Them.* 31.

61. Justinian, *Corpus Juris, Digest* 8.3.17, 8.5.15.

62. Cic., *Leg. agr.* 3.2.9; *Fam.* 15.18; Frontinus, *Aq.* 9; *Corpus of Latin Inscriptions* 15.7696, 6.1261, ILS 5793; William Emerton Heitland, *Agricola: A Study of Agriculture and Rustic Life in the Greco-Roman World from the Point of View of Labour* (Cambridge: Cambridge University Press, 1921), 293; White, *Roman Farming*, 158.

63. Claudio Vita-Finzi, *The Mediterranean Valleys: Geological Changes in Historical Times* (Cambridge: Cambridge University Press, 1969).

64. Vitr., *De arch.* 10.7.1–3.

65. Vladimir Grigorievitch Simkhovitch, "Rome's Fall Reconsidered," in *Toward the Understanding of Jesus and Other Historical Studies* (New York: Macmillan, 1921), 124.

66. White, *Roman Farming*, 12; Arnold Hugh Martin Jones, *The Later Roman Empire* (Oxford: Oxford University Press, 1964), 2:1043–44.

67. Victor Davis Hanson, *The Western Way of War* (New York: Knopf, 1989), 27–39.

68. Columella, *Rust.* 2.1.5–6; Sheldon Judson, "Erosion Rates near Rome, Italy," *Science* 160 (1968): 144.

69. Lucr. 5.1247–49, 5.1370–71.

70. Theophr., *Hist. pl.* 6.3.2.

71. White, *Roman Farming*, 147.

72. Strabo 8.5.1.

73. Theophr., *Caus. pl.* 5.14.2–6.

74. Semple, *Geography of the Mediterranean Region*, 444–53; White, *Roman Farming*, 160.

75. Livy 6.12.

76. *Cod. Theod.* 11.28.2.

77. Simkhovitch, "Rome's Fall Reconsidered," 116.

78. Reported of Hellenistic Cyprus by Eratosthenes, Strabo 14.6.5; of Rome in the second century, Herodian 2.4.6; and in the fifth century, *Cod. Theod.* 5.2.8, 5.11.12.

79. Pliny, *HN* 18.7.

80. Sen., *Ep.* 89.

81. Cic., *Off.* 2.25.

82. Peter D. A. Garnsey, "Grain for Rome," in *Trade in the Ancient Economy*, ed. Peter D. A. Garnsey, K. Hopkins, and C. R. Whittaker (Berkeley: University of California Press, 1983), 118–19.

83. Suet., *Aug.* 46.

84. Karl Joachim Marquardt and Theodor Mommsen, ed., *Handbuch der römischen Alterthumer*, vol. 5, *Römische Staatsverwaltung*, 2nd ed. (Leipzig: S. Hirzel, 1881), 5:141–47.

85. Pl., *Epin.* (pseud.) 979A–B; A. E. Taylor, trans., *The Collected Dialogues of Plato*, ed. Edith Hamilton and Huntington Cairns (Princeton, NJ: Princeton University Press, 1961), 1522.

Chapter 8. Industrial Technology and Environmental Damage

1. Pliny, *HN* 36.125.

2. Pliny, *HN* 33.1.2.

3. Hes., *Op.* 757–59; Vitr., *de Arch.* 8.6.10–11.

4. Aesch., *PV.*

5. Simpl., *Phys.* 1110.5.

6. J. J. Coulton, "Lifting in Early Greek Architecture," *Journal of Hellenic Studies* 94 (1974): 1–19.

7. Thorkild Schiöler, "Bronze Roman Piston Pumps," *History of Technology* 5 (1980): 17–38.

8. Derek John de Solla Price, "Gears from the Greeks," *Transactions of the American Philosophical Society* 64, pt. 7 (1974): 5–68; Vitr., *De arch.* 10.5.

9. Hero, *Pneum.* 2.6, 2.11.

10. Hero, *Pneum.* 1.43; John G. Landels, *Engineering in the Ancient World* (Berkeley: University of California Press, 1978), 29–30.

11. J. T. Schlebeker, "Farmers and Bureaucrats: Reflections on Technological Innovation in Agriculture," *Agricultural History* 51 (1977): 641–55.

12. Pliny, *HN* 36.195; Suet., *Vesp.* 18.

13. Plut., *G. Gracchus* 7; Keith Hopkins, "Roman Trade, Industry and Labor," in *Civilization of the Ancient Mediterranean: Greece and Rome*, ed. Michael Grant and Rachel Kitzinger (New York: Charles Scribner's Sons, 1988), 2:759–60.

14. Hopkins, "Roman Trade, Industry and Labor," 759.

15. Aesch., *PV* 498–500.

16. Lucr. 5.1242–66.

17. John F. Healy, "Mines and Quarries," in *Civilization of the Ancient Mediterranean*, 2:779.

18. Thuc. 4.105.

19. Strabo 15.1.30, C700.

20. 1 Macc. 8:3.

21. Diod. Sic. 5.38.4.

22. Robert J. Forbes, *Studies in Ancient Technology* (Leiden: E. J. Brill, 1955–64), 7:196; Healy, "Mines and Quarries," 2:781; Constantin E. Conophagos, *Le Lauriun antique et la technique grecque de la production de l'argent* (Paris: Olympe, 1980).

23. Diod. Sic. 5.38.4.

24. Hopkins, "Roman Trade, Industry and Labor," 757.

25. Tac., *Ann.* 6.19.1; Plut., *Galba* 5; Suet., *Tib.* 49; Strabo 3.2.10.

26. Forbes, *Studies in Ancient Technology*, 7:154–55.

27. Ibid., 192.

28. Livy 21.37.2–3.

29. Pliny, *HN* 33.21.70, 33.21.68–78.

30. Pliny, *HN* 31.28, 31.49.

31. Kevin Greene, *The Archaeology of the Roman Economy* (Berkeley: University of California Press, 1990), 145.

32. Robert H. J. Sellin, "The Large Roman Watermill at Barbegal (France)," *History of Technology* 8 (1983): 91–109; Robert J. Spain, "The Second-Century Romano-British Watermill at Ickham, Kent," *History of Technology* 9 (1984): 143–80.

33. Thuc. 2.43.1; Robert B. Strassler, ed., *The Landmark Thucydides: A Comprehensive Guide to the Peloponnesian War*, rev. ed., trans. Richard Crawley (New York: Free Press, 1996), 115.

34. Arist., *Ath. Pol.* 23.1.

35. Hdt. 7.144.

36. Aesch., *Eum.*, 945–47.

37. Thuc. 7.27.5; Strassler, *Landmark Thucydides*, 442.

38. Healy, "Mines and Quarries," 2:779–93.

39. Strabo 3.2.8, C146.

40. S. Douglas Olson, "Firewood and Charcoal in Classical Athens," *Hesperia* 60, no. 3 (1991): 411–20.

41. Curtis N. Runnels, "Environmental Degradation in Ancient Greece," *Scientific American* 272, no. 3 (March 1995): 96–99.

42. Pl., *Critias* 111b–d; adapted from Robin Waterfield, trans., *Plato: Timaeus and Critias* (Oxford: Oxford University Press, 2008).

43. Dem., *Phaenippus* 42.7 (1040–41); Hamish Forbes, "The Uses of the Uncultivated Landscape in Modern Greece: A Pointer to the Value of the Wilderness in Antiquity?," in *The Greek World*, ed. Anton Powell (London: Routledge, 1995), 68–97, esp. 85.

44. Thuc. 4.11.4; Strassler, *Landmark Thucydides*, 229–30.

45. Thuc. 4.52.3, 4.75.1; Strassler, *Landmark Thucydides*, 251, 263–64.

46. Thuc. 6.90.3; Strassler, *Landmark Thucydides*, 413.

47. John Ellis Jones, "The Laurion Silver Mines: A Review of Recent Researches and Results," *Greece and Rome*, 2nd ser. 29, no. 2 (1982): 169–83.

48. Paul Gilding, *The Great Disruption: Why the Climate Crisis Will Bring On the End of Shopping and the Birth of a New World* (New York: Bloomsbury Press, 2011).

49. David J. Mattingly, *Imperialism, Power and Identity* (Princeton, NJ: Princeton University Press, 2010), 167–91.

50. Peter Thonemann, "Splashing Out," *Times Literary Supplement*, June 24, 2011, 13–15.

51. Healy, "Mines and Quarries," 2:789.

52. Forbes, *Studies in Ancient Technology*, 7:174–77.

53. Ibid., 193. Pliny, *HN* 36.159 describes saws used in Gaul. Saws are also mentioned in Vitr., *De arch.* 2.7.5–7.

54. Auson., *Mos.* 362–64.

55. John B. Ward-Perkins, "Quarrying in Antiquity: Technology, Tradition, and Social Change," *Proceedings of the British Academy* 58 (1972): 97–115.

56. Strabo 5.2.5, C222.

57. Sen., *Ep.* 86.

58. Greene, *Archaeology of the Roman Economy*, 154–56.

59. Forbes, *Studies in Ancient Technology*, 7:175.

60. Ibid., 3:170.

61. Hendrik Bolkestein, *Economic Life in Greece's Golden Age* (Leiden: E. J. Brill, 1958), 48–49.

62. Pliny, *HN* 36.194.

63. Roman Malinowski, "Ancient Mortars and Concretes: Aspects of Their Durability," *History of Technology* 7 (1982): 89–100.

64. Kenneth G. Holum, Robert L. Hohlfelder, Robert J. Bull, and Avner Raban, *King Herod's Dream: Caesarea on the Sea* (New York: W. W. Norton and Company, 1988), 101.

65. Hdt. 6.46.

66. Theodore A. Wertime, "The Furnace versus the Goat: The Pyrotechnologic Industries and Mediterranean Deforestation in Antiquity," *Journal of Field Archaeology* 10 (1983): 448; Forbes, *Studies in Ancient Technology*, 7:148–49.

67. Pliny, *HN* 33.21.68–78.

68. Wertime, "The Furnace versus the Goat," 448.

69. Strabo 4.6.7.

70. Lucr. 6.810–15.

71. Vitr., *De arch.* 8.6.13.

72. Pliny, *HN* 33.21.71.

73. Forbes, *Studies in Ancient Technology*, 7:141.

74. Ibid., 193.

75. Theresa Urbainczyk, *Slave Revolts in Antiquity* (Berkeley: University of California Press, 2008).

76. Pliny, *HN* 3.20.138, 33.21.78; Forbes, *Studies in Ancient Technology*, 7:153.

77. Strabo 9.1.23, C229.

78. Hes., *Op.* 428.

79. Hopkins, "Roman Trade, Industry and Labor," 758–59; Michael Grant, *Roman History from Coins* (Cambridge: Cambridge University Press, 1968), 83–85.

80. Wertime, "The Furnace versus the Goat," 452; W. Rostocker and E. Gebhard, "The Reproduction of Roof Tiles for the Archaic Temple of Poseidon at Isthmia, Greece," *Journal of Field Archaeology* 8 (1981): 211–17.

81. Wertime, "The Furnace versus the Goat," 450, 452; H. A. Koster and H. A. Forbes, "The Commons and the Market" (paper presented at the Deforestation, Erosion, and Ecology in the

Ancient Mediterranean and Middle East symposium, National Museum of Natural History, Smithsonian Insitution, Washington, DC, April 19, 1978).

82. Anthony King, *Roman Gaul and Germany* (Berkeley: University of California Press, 1990), 125.

83. Forbes, *Studies in Ancient Technology*, 6:18.

84. Theophr., *Hist. pl.* 5.9.1–6.

85. Wertime, "The Furnace versus the Goat," 452.

86. Pliny, *HN* 34.96–97; Forbes, *Studies in Ancient Technology*, 6:26–27.

87. Wertime, "The Furnace versus the Goat," 451–52.

88. Forbes, *Studies in Ancient Technology*, 6:18; Robert J. Forbes, "Metallurgy," in *A History of Technology*, ed. Charles Singer, E. J. Holmyard, and A. R. Hall (Oxford: Oxford University Press, 1956), 2:59; Diod. Sic. 5.13; Strabo 5.2.6, C223.

89. Strabo 3.2.8, C146.

90. Vitr., *De arch.* 8.6.11.

91. Sungmin Hong, Jean-Pierre Candelone, Clair C. Patterson, and Claude F. Boutron, "Greenland Ice Evidence of Hemispheric Lead Pollution Two Millennia Ago by Greek and Roman Civilizations," *Science* 265, no. 5180 (1994): 1841–43.

92. Vitr., *De arch.* 8.6.10–11.

93. John Scarborough, "The Myth of Lead Poisoning among the Romans: An Essay Review," *Journal of the History of Medicine and Allied Sciences* 39 (1984): 469–75; S. Colum Gilfillan, "Roman Culture and Dysgenic Lead Poisoning," *Mankind Quarterly* 5 (1965): 3–20.

94. Wertime, "The Furnace versus the Goat," 445–52.

Chapter 9. War and the Environment

1. Homer, *Il.* 21.200–382.

2. Homer, *Il.* 21.242–46, 21.349–55.

3. John Kinloch Anderson, *Hunting in the Ancient World* (Berkeley: University of California Press, 1985), 14.

4. Xen., *Cyn.* 12.1.

5. Xen., *Lac.* 2.7–8; Plut., *Lyc.* 12.1–2, 12.17–18; Ath. 4.141C.

6. J. Donald Hughes, "Hunting in the Ancient Mediterranean World," in *A Cultural History of Animals in Antiquity*, ed. Linda Kalof (Oxford: Berg, 2007), 47–70.

7. Hdt. 1.87.

8. The *artaba* was a unit of volume used in ancient Egypt equal to about 36 L (8.5 gallons).

9. Richard P. Duncan-Jones, *Structure and Scale in the Roman Economy* (Cambridge: Cambridge University Press, 1990), 147.

10. Plut., *Mar.* 21.3.

11. Neil J. Goldberg and Frank J. Findlow, "A Quantitative Analysis of Roman Military Operations in Britain, circa A.D. 43 to 238," in *Warfare, Culture, and Environment*, ed. R. Brian Ferguson (Orlando, FL: Academic Press, 1984), 376.

12. Deut. 20:19–20.

13. Victor Davis Hanson, *Warfare and Agriculture in Classical Greece* (Berkeley: University of California Press, 1998), 4.

14. Xen., *Mem.* 2.1.13.

15. Tac., *Agr.* 30.5.

16. Donald Kagan, *The Peloponnesian War* (New York: Viking, 2003), 75, 106, 299.

17. Hanson, *Warfare and Agriculture in Classical Greece*, 35–62.

18. Soph., *OC* 694ff.

19. Hanson, *Warfare and Agriculture in Classical Greece*, 14–15.

20. Lys. 7.7.

21. Nikolaos Athanasiadis, *Zur postglazialen Vegetationsentwicklung von Litochoro Katerinis und Pertouli Trikalon* (Basel: University of Basel Press, 1975).

22. J. Donald Hughes, "Environmental Impacts of the Roman Economy and Social Structure: Augustus to Diocletian," in *Rethinking Environmental History: World-System History and Global Environmental Change*, ed. Alf Hornborg, J. R. McNeill, and Joan Martinez-Allier (Lanham, MD: Altamira Press, 2007), 27–40.

23. Claudio Vita-Finzi, *The Mediterranean Valleys: Geological Changes in Historical Times* (Cambridge: Cambridge University Press, 1969).

24. Timothy Howe, *Pastoral Politics: Animals, Agriculture and Society in Ancient Greece*, Publications of the Association of Ancient Historians 9 (Claremont, CA: Regina Books, 2008).

25. Doug Lee, "Military History in Late Antiquity: Changing Perspectives and Paradigms," in *Recent Directions in the Military History of the Ancient World*, Publications of the Association of Ancient Historians 10, ed. Lee L. Brice and Jennifer T. Roberts (Claremont, CA: Regina Books, 2011), 145–66.

26. Thuc. 4.29–30, 4.38.

27. Hdt. 6.78–80.

28. Xen., *Cyr.* 7.5.10–20.

29. Adrienne Mayor, *Greek Fire, Poison Arrows, and Scorpion Bombs: Biological and Chemical Warfare in the Ancient World* (Woodstock, NY: Overlook Duckworth, 2009), 108–9.

30. Russell Meiggs, *Trees and Timber in the Ancient Mediterranean World* (Oxford: Clarendon Press, 1982), 116–53, 423–57.

31. Pliny, *HN* 16.74; Livy 28.45.15–21.

32. Diod. Sic. 14.42.4; Ath. 5.206F, 5.208E–F.

33. Xen., *Hell.* 1.24–25.

34. Thuc. 6.90.

35. Thuc. 4.108.

36. Meiggs, *Trees and Timber in the Ancient Mediterranean World*, 85–86.

37. John Pairman Brown, *Israel and Hellas*, vol. 3, *The Legacy of Iranian Imperialism and the Individual* (Berlin: Walter de Gruyter, 2001), 134–36. There are many lists of Mount Lebanon tree species in the Hebrew Bible, but little agreement among translators as to the proper identifications.

38. Lino Rossi, *Trajan's Column and the Dacian Wars* (Ithaca, NY: Cornell University Press, 1971).

39. Frank Lepper and Sheppard Frere, *Trajan's Column: A New Edition of the Cichorius Plates* (Gloucester: Alan Sutton, 1988), plate IV.

40. Rossi, *Trajan's Column and the Dacian Wars*, 132–33.

41. Lepper and Frere, *Trajan's Column*, plates CIX, CXIII.

42. J. Edward Chamberlin, *Horse: How the Horse Has Shaped Civilizations* (New York: BlueBridge, 2006), 155–56.

43. Ibid., 160.

44. Hdt. 1.80, 7.125–26.

45. Richard W. Bulliet, *The Camel and the Wheel* (New York: Columbia University Press, 1990), 87, 102–3.

46. Polyb. 5.84; Pliny, *HN* 8.9.

47. Howard Hayes Scullard, *The Elephant in the Greek and Roman World* (Ithaca, NY: Cornell University Press, 1974), 24.

48. Mayor, *Greek Fire, Poison Arrows, and Scorpion Bombs*, 171–206.

49. Herodian 3.9.3–8; Mayor, *Greek Fire, Poison Arrows, and Scorpion Bombs*, 181–86.

50. Robert Sallares, *Malaria and Rome: A History of Malaria in Ancient Italy* (Oxford: Oxford University Press, 2002), 36.

Chapter 10. Urban Problems

1. Hor., *Carm.* 2.15.12, 3.29.12.
2. Mart. 12.57.
3. Juv. 3.6–8; Rolfe Humphries, trans., *The Satires of Juvenal* (Bloomington: Indiana University Press, 1958), 33.
4. Joseph Rykwert, *The Idea of a Town: The Anthropology of Urban Form in Rome, Italy and the Ancient World* (Cambridge, MA: MIT Press, 1988), 27–72.
5. Plut., *Alex.* 26.2–4.
6. Hdt. 4.150–59.
7. Pl., *Leges* 5.747D–E.
8. Hippoc., *Aer.* 3–6.
9. Arist., *Pol.* 7.120.1.
10. Vitr., *De arch.* 1–6.
11. Leicester B. Holland, "Colophon," *Hesperia* 13 (1944): 91–171; R. E. Wycherley, *How the Greeks Built Cities* (New York: Macmillan, 1962), 33, 202.
12. Arist., *Pol.* 7.10.4, 1330b.
13. Rykwert, *Idea of a Town*, 86–87.
14. Arist., *Pol.* 2.8.2, 1267b.
15. Wycherley, *How the Greeks Built Cities*, 19.
16. Ibid., 27–29; Anthony Kriesis, *Greek Town Building* (Athens: National Technical University, 1965), 70.
17. Ptol., *Alm.* 3.1.
18. Ar., *Av.* 1004–9.
19. Pl., *Critias* 112A–E, 115A–C; *Leges* 5.745B–E.
20. Pl., *Leges* 6.779A–B.
21. Diod. Sic. 19.45; Vitr., *De arch.* 2.8.42; Wycherley, *How the Greeks Built Cities*, 27; John B. Ward-Perkins, *Cities of Ancient Greece and Italy: Planning in Classical Antiquity* (New York: George Braziller, 1974), 19.
22. Konstantinos Apostolou Doxiadis, *Architectural Space in Ancient Greece*, transl. and ed. Jacqueline Tyrwhitt (Cambridge, MA: MIT Press, 1972).
23. Ward-Perkins, *Cities of Ancient Greece and Italy*, 19–21.
24. Kriesis, *Greek Town Building*, 71–72.
25. Ibid., 69–70.
26. Cic., *Rep.* 2.10–11; Livy 5.54.4, 7.38.
27. Moses I. Finley, "The Ancient City from Fustel de Coulanges to Max Weber and Beyond," *Comparative Studies in Society and History* 19 (July 1977): 305–27.
28. Arist., *Pol.* 2.5.
29. Pl., *Leges* 4.704–5.
30. Catherine Delano Smith, *Western Mediterranean Europe* (London: Academic Press, 1979), 166–76.
31. Pl., *Leges* 4.704–5.
32. Pl., *Rep.*; *Leges* 5.745C.
33. Diod. Sic. 17.52.6; P. M. Fraser, *Ptolemaic Alexandria* (Oxford: Clarendon Press, 1972), 1:90–91n358, 2:171–72.
34. Edwin S. Ramage, "Urban Problems in Ancient Rome," in *Aspects of Greco-Roman Urbanism: Essays on the Classical City*, ed. Ronald T. Marchese (Oxford: British Archaeological Reports, 1983), 64.
35. Vitr., *De arch.* 2.8.17.

36. Hor., *Carm.* 2.15.1–2.
37. The island of Manhattan is 87 km² (34 miles²) in size, but was not fully developed before the twentieth century.
38. R. E. Wycherley, *The Stones of Athens* (Princeton, NJ: Princeton University Press, 1978), 245–46.
39. Pl., *Phdr.* 229A–E.
40. Strabo 17.1.10, C795.
41. Lewis Mumford, *The City in History: Its Origins, Its Transformations, and Its Prospects* (New York: Harcourt, Brace and World, 1961), 221.
42. Cic., *Leg. agr.* 2.96; Mart. 5.22.5–8.
43. Tac. *Hist.* 1.8, 1.75; Juv. 3.5, 11.51.
44. Hor., *Sat.* 2.6.28; Juv. 3.243–48; Tib. 1.5.63–64; Mart. 3.46.5–6.
45. Juv. 3.254–91.
46. *CCSL* I2 593, 56–67.
47. Suet., *Claud.* 25.2; SHA, *Marc.* 23.8; *Hadr.* 22.6.
48. Sen., *Ep.* 56.1–2, 56.4; Mart. 4.12.57; Stat., *Silvae* 1.1.63–65.
49. Strabo 5.3.7; Aur. Vic., *Caes.* 13.13.
50. Juv. 3.7–8.
51. Ramage, "Urban Problems in Ancient Rome," 65.
52. Gell., *NA* 15.1.2.
53. Plut., *Crassus* 2.2–4.
54. Suet., *Aug.* 30.1.
55. Tac., *Ann.* 15.38.
56. Tac., *Ann.* 15.43; Suet., *Nero* 16.1.
57. American School of Classical Studies at Athens, *Ancient Corinth: A Guide to the Excavations*, 6th ed. (Athens: American School of Classical Studies, 1954), 27–33, 38–40.
58. Plut., *De soll. an.* 23.5.
59. Vitr., *De arch.* 8.1.
60. Hdt. 3.60.1.
61. Robert J. Forbes, *Studies in Ancient Technology* (Leiden: E. J. Brill, 1955), 1:159.
62. Wycherley, *How the Greeks Built Cities*, 210.
63. Robert J. Forbes, "Hydraulic Engineering and Sanitation," in *A History of Technology*, ed. Charles Singer, E. J. Holmyard, and A. R. Hall (London: Oxford University Press, 1956), 2:6679; Aage Gerhardt Drachmann, *Ktesibios, Philon, and Heron* (Copenhagen: E. Munksgaard, 1948), 84.
64. H. Gräber, *Die Wasserleitungen von Pergamon* (Berlin: Abhandlung Akademischer Wissenschaften, 1887); Forbes, *Studies in Ancient Technology*, 1:160–61.
65. Frontinus, *Aq.* 1.16.
66. Frontinus, *Aq.* 2.65–73.
67. *Greek Inscriptions Pertaining to Roman Matters*, 1.1055; Oribasius, *Coll. medicae* 1.337.
68. John G. Landels, *Engineering in the Ancient World* (Berkeley: University of California Press, 1978), 41–42.
69. George F. W. Hauck, "The Roman Aqueduct of Nimes," *Scientific American* 260 (March 1989): 98–104.
70. Forbes, *Studies in Ancient Technology*, 1:166.
71. Thuc. 2.15.4–5; Wycherley, *How the Greeks Built Cities*, 220.
72. Forbes, "Hydraulic Engineering and Sanitation," 2:664.
73. Arist., *Ath. Pol.* 43.1.
74. Plut., *Them.* 31.1.
75. Forbes, *Studies in Ancient Technology*, 1:165–66.

76. Forbes, "Hydraulic Engineering and Sanitation," 2:674.

77. Vitr., *De arch.* 8.4.1–2; Guido Majno, *The Healing Hand: Man and Wound in the Ancient World* (Cambridge, MA: Harvard University Press, 1975), 186–88.

78. Vitr., *De arch.* 8.6.15; Hdt. 1.188.

79. Forbes, "Hydraulic Engineering and Sanitation," 2:672–73; Oribasius, *Coll. medicae* 7.7.7.

80. Vitr., *De arch.* 8.6.10–11.

81. Forbes, *Studies in Ancient Technology*, 1:173; Forbes, "Hydraulic Engineering and Sanitation," 2:674.

82. Hauck, "The Roman Aqueduct of Nimes," 100.

83. Athenian laws: Arist., *Pol.* 7, *Ath. Pol.* 50.2. Roman laws: Justinian, *Corpus Juris, Digest* 9.3.1 pr.

84. *CCSL* 1.22.593.

85. Humfrey Michell, *The Economics of Ancient Greece* (Cambridge: Cambridge University Press, 1940), 33; Ellen Churchill Semple, *The Geography of the Mediterranean Region: Its Relation to Ancient History* (New York: Henry Holt, 1931), 414.

86. Samuel Ball Platner, *Topography and Monuments of Ancient Rome* (Boston: Allyn and Bacon, 1911), 106.

87. Ibid., 75; Pliny, *HN* 36.105.

88. Suet., *Vesp.* 23.

89. Tac., *Ann.* 15.18; Ramage, "Urban Problems in Ancient Rome," 72.

90. Frontinus, *Aq.* 1.4.

91. Ramage, "Urban Problems in Ancient Rome," 70.

92. Suet., *Aug.* 30.1.; SHA, *Aurel.* 27.3.

93. Suet., *Aug.* 37; Dio Cass. 57.14.8.

94. Homer, *Il.* 1.317, 8.183, 9.243, 18.207, 21.522, etc.

95. Hor., *Carm.* 3.29.11–12.

96. Frontinus, *Aq.* 2.88; Tac., *Hist.* 2.94.

97. Mart. 12.57.

98. Cic., *Leg.* 2.28; Val. Max. 2.5.6; Hor., *Ep.* 1.7.5–9.

99. Livy 40.19.3, 40.36.14, 41.21.5; Suet., *Nero* 39.1; *Titus* 8.3.4.

100. Emily Vermeule, "The Afterlife: Greece," and John A. North, "The Afterlife: Rome," in *Civilization of the Ancient Mediterranean: Greece and Rome*, ed. Michael Grant and Rachel Kitzinger (New York: Charles Scribner's Sons, 1988), 993–94, 1001–2.

101. Samuel Ball Platner and Thomas A. Ashby, *A Topographical Dictionary of Ancient Rome* (Oxford: Oxford University Press, 1929), 269.

102. Homer, *Od.* 6.390.

103. Paus. 2.1.7, 8.26.1.

104. Strabo 5.C236; Forbes, *Studies in Ancient Technology*, 2:135.

105. M. P. Charlesworth, *Trade Routes and Commerce of the Roman Empire* (Cambridge: Cambridge University Press, 1924), 18; Forbes, *Studies in Ancient Technology*, 2:139.

106. Forbes, *Studies in Ancient Technology*, 2:140–41.

107. Vitr., *De arch.* 5.9.7.

108. Forbes, *Studies in Ancient Technology*, 2:150–51.

109. A. Lang, trans., *Theocritus, Bion and Moschus* (London: Macmillan, 1901).

110. Mart. 68; Juv. 3.1–4, 3.315–22; Ramage, "Urban Problems in Ancient Rome," 85; Hor., *Ep.* 1.14.17; Pliny, *Ep.* 7.30.2.

111. Dion. Hal., *Ant. Rom.*; Pliny, *HN* 3.67; Tac., *Hist.* 3.79.

112. J. Donald Hughes, "An Ecological Paradigm of the Ancient City," in *Human Ecology: A Gathering of Perspectives*, ed. Richard J. Borden (College Park: University of Maryland and the Society

for Human Ecology, 1986), 214–20; J. Donald Hughes, "The Effect of Classical Cities on the Mediterranean Landscape," *Ekistics* 42 (1976): 332–42.

113. Robert E. Park, Ernest W. Burgess, and Roderick D. McKenzie, *The City* (Chicago: University of Chicago Press, 1925).

114. J. Donald Hughes, "Sustainability and Empire," *Hedgehog Review* 14, no. 2 (Summer 2012): 26–36.

Chapter 11. Paradises and Parks, Gardens and Groves

1. J. Donald Hughes and M. D. Subash Chandran, "Sacred Groves around the Earth: An Overview"; J. Donald Hughes, "Sacred Groves of the Ancient Mediterranean Area: Early Conservation of Biological Diversity"; M. D. Subash Chandran, Madhav Gadgil, and J. Donald Hughes, "Sacred Groves of the Western Ghats of India," in *Conserving the Sacred for Biodiversity Management*, ed. P. S. Ramakrishnan, K. G. Saxena, and U. M. Chandrashekara (Enfield, NH: Science Publishers, 1998), 69–86, 101–22, 211–32. See also M. D. Subash Chandran and J. Donald Hughes, "Sacred Groves and Conservation: The Comparative History of Traditional Reserves in the Mediterranean Area and in South India," *Environment and History* 6, no. 2 (May 2000): 169–86.

2. Karen R. Jones and John Wills, *The Invention of the Park from the Garden of Eden to Disney's Magic Kingdom* (Cambridge: Polity, 2005), 9–11.

3. Sen., *Ep.* 4.12.3.

4. "Numen inest"; Ovid, *Fasti* 3.295–96.

5. Vergil, *Aen.* 8.351–52.

6. Pliny, *HN* 12.2.

7. Strabo 9.2.33.

8. Vergil, *G.* 1.21–22.

9. Paus. 1.21.9.

10. Apul., *Flor.* 1.1.

11. Strabo 14.2.6; Paus. 2.37.1, 10.37.5–7.

12. Paus. 2.27.1.

13. Arr., *Anab.* 7.20.3–4. He named the island Icarus.

14. Paus. 7.22.1.

15. Pliny, *HN* 12.5.

16. Paus. 8.24.4.

17. J. Donald Hughes, "Ta iera temeni stin arhea Ellada ke i pikilia ton ikosistimaton tous [Sacred Groves in Ancient Greece and the Diversity of Their Ecosystems]," in *Perivallontiki Istoria: Meletes ya tin arhea ke ti sinhroni Ellada* [Environmental History: Essays on Ancient and Modern Greece], ed. Chloe Vlassopoulou and Georgia Liarakou (Athens: Pedio Press, 2011), 25–58.

18. Darice Elizabeth Birge, "Sacred Groves in the Ancient World" (PhD diss., University of California, Berkeley, 1982), offers a collection of most of the references to groves in ancient literature. It is comprehensive, but I was able to find a few more. This section is based on the resulting list of passages.

19. Darice Elizabeth Birge, "Trees in the Landscape of Pausanias' *Periegesis*," in *Placing the Gods: Sanctuaries and Sacred Space in Ancient Greece*, ed. Susan E. Alcock and Robin Osborne (Oxford: Clarendon Press, 1994), 231–45.

20. Paus. 1.21.9.

21. Ael. 11.3.

22. Vergil, *Aen.* 6.258–59.

23. Paus. 7.27.3.
24. *Hom. Hymn Aphrodite* 257–72.
25. Paus. 2.28.7.
26. Paus. 1.38.1, 3.21.5, 7.22.2, 8.10.4. 38.5, 54.5; Plut., *Mor.* 976A, 976C, 983–84.
27. Ovid, *Fasti* 3.263–66; F. Sokolowski, "On the Episode of Onchestus in the Homeric Hymn to Apollo," *Transactions and Proceedings of the American Philological Association* 91 (1960): 376–80.
28. Paus. 5.13.1–2, 15.6.
29. James George Frazer, *The Golden Bough: A Study in Magic and Religion*, 3rd ed. (New York: Macmillan, 1935), 1:45, 2:121–22.
30. Hdt. 6.75–80.
31. Frazer, *Golden Bough*.
32. Ovid, *Met.* 8.738–78.
33. Marcus Niebuhr Tod, *A Selection of Greek Historical Inscriptions* (Oxford: Clarendon Press, 1933), 2:110.
34. Vergil, *G.* 1.14–15.
35. Paus. 5.13.3.
36. Harry Thurston Peck, ed., *Harper's Dictionary of Classical Literature and Antiquities* (New York: American Book Co., 1923), 686–88, s.v. "Fratres Arvales."
37. Cato, *Agr.* 139–40.
38. Frazer, *Golden Bough*, 2:122.
39. Columella, *Rust.* 7.3.23.
40. Vergil, *G.* 3.332–34.
41. Ovid, *Fasti* 4.744–54, 4.757–60.
42. Pl., *Leges* 6.761C–D; Paus. 3.11.2, 14.8.
43. Xen., *Oec.* 4.19.
44. Juv. 3.13–16.
45. Adolf Wilhelm, "Die Pachturkunden der Klytiden," *Jahreshefte des Österreichischen Archäologischen Institutes in Wien* 28 (1933): 197–221.
46. Mikhail Ivanovich Rostovtzeff, *The Social and Economic History of the Hellenistic World* (Oxford: Clarendon Press, 1941), 3:1613n113.
47. J. Donald Hughes and Jim Swan, "How Much of the Earth Is Sacred Space?," *Environmental Review* 10 (1986): 247–59.
48. Strabo 9.2.33.
49. Homer, *Od.* 7.112–32.
50. J. Donald Hughes, "Paraísos no Mundo Antigo: Dos Bosques Sagrados às Ilhas Afortunadas [Paradises in the Ancient World: From Sacred Groves to the Isles of the Blessed]," in *História e Meio-ambiente: O Impacto da Expansão Europeia* [Environmental History: The Impact of European Expansion], Colecção Memórias 26, ed. Alberto Vieira (Funchal, Madeira, Portugal: Centro de Estudos de História do Atlántico, 1999), 125–40.
51. Diod. Sic. 3–4; Ellen Churchill Semple, *The Geography of the Mediterranean Region: Its Relation to Ancient History* (New York: Henry Holt, 1931), 490.
52. Theophr., *Hist. pl.* 5.8.1.
53. Rostovtzeff, *Social and Economic History*, 1:357.
54. John E. Stambaugh, *The Ancient Roman City* (Baltimore: Johns Hopkins University Press, 1988), 168–69.
55. Varro, *Rust.* 3.13.2–3.
56. J. Donald Hughes, "Mencius' Prescriptions for Ancient Chinese Environmental Problems," *Environmental Review* 13 (1989): 15–27.
57. Plut., *Cimon* 10.

58. Strabo 17.1.8–10.
59. Prop. 2.32.11–16; Stambaugh, *Ancient Roman City*, 41–42.
60. Hor., *Sat.* 1.8; Pierre Grimal, *Les Jardins Romains*, 2nd ed. (Paris: Presses Universitaires de France, 1969), 152–57.
61. R. B. Lloyd, "Three Monumental Gardens on the Marble Plan," *American Journal of Archaeology* 86 (1982): 91–100; Stambaugh, *Ancient Roman City*, 72, 120–21.
62. Semple, *Geography of the Mediterranean Region*, 495–96.

Chapter 12. Natural Disasters

1. Sen., *Ep.* 71.15.
2. Kent A. Harries, "Earthquake Resistant Construction in Classical Rome," Paper No. 448 (New York: Elsevier, 1996).
3. Thuc. 3.89.
4. G. A. Papadopoulos and B. J. Chalkis, "Tsunamis Observed in Greece and the Surrounding Area from Antiquity up to the Present Times," *Marine Geology* 56 (1984): 309–17.
5. Pliny, *HN* 2.82, 2.83, 2.86.
6. Stathis C. Stiros, "The AD 365 Crete Earthquake and Possible Seismic Clustering during the Fourth to Sixth Centuries AD in the Eastern Mediterranean: A Review of Historical and Archaeological Data," *Journal of Structural Geology* 23 (February 2001): 545–62.
7. E. Guidoboni, *Catalogue of Ancient Earthquakes in the Mediterranean Area up to the 10th Century* (Rome: Istituto Nazionale di Geofisica, 1994).
8. G. Aldrete, *Floods of the Tiber in Ancient Rome* (Baltimore: Johns Hopkins University Press, 2007).
9. Peter D. A. Garnsey, *Famine and Food Supply in the Greco-Roman World* (Cambridge: Cambridge University Press, 1988).
10. Robert Sallares, *Malaria and Rome: A History of Malaria in Ancient Italy* (Oxford: Oxford University Press, 2002).
11. Chinese writers, however, noted the connection of mosquitoes and malaria as early as the Warring States Period (476 to 221 BCE). See Sallares, *Malaria and Rome*, 49.
12. Mirko Drazen Grmek, *Diseases in the Ancient Greek World* (Baltimore: Johns Hopkins University Press, 1989), 265–83.
13. Sallares, *Malaria and Rome*, 89.
14. Varro, *Rust.* 1.12.2.
15. Columella, *Rust.* 1.5.6.
16. William Henry Samuel Jones, *Malaria and Greek History* (Manchester: Manchester University Press, 1909).
17. Victor Davis Hanson, *A War Like No Other: How the Athenians and Spartans Fought the Peloponnesian War* (New York: Random House, 2005), 80, estimates that the trireme warships in the navy required 40,000–60,000 sailors.
18. Thuc. 1.1.
19. Thuc. 1.23; Robert D. Luginbill, *Author of Illusions: Thucydides' Rewriting of the History of the Peloponnesian War* (Newcastle upon Tyne: Cambridge Scholars, 2011), 198.
20. Thuc. 2.47–48.
21. Thuc. 2.49.
22. Manolis J. Papagrigorakis, Christos Yapijakis, Philippos N. Synodinos, and Effie Baziotopoulou-Valavani, "DNA Examination of Ancient Dental Pulp Incriminates Typhoid Fever as a Probable Cause of the Plague of Athens," *International Journal of Infectious Diseases* 10 (2006): 206–14.

23. Thuc. 2.57. Thucydides says that few Peloponnesians caught the plague, although they had invaded Attica and were aware of the many funerals being held for its victims. They did not invade in 429 BCE, fearing the plague.

24. T. P. Tassios, "Water Supply of Ancient Greek Cities," *Water Science and Technology: Water Supply* 7, no. 1 (2007): 165–72; "Selected Topics of Water Technology in Ancient Greece," in *Proceedings of the 1st IWA International Symposium on Water and Wastewater Technologies in Ancient Civilizations*, ed. A. N. Angelakis and D. Koutsoyiannis (London: International Water Association), 3–26, 165–72.

25. Dora P. Crouch, *Water Management in Ancient Greek Cities* (Oxford: Oxford University Press, 1993).

26. D. Koutsoyiannis, N. Zarkadoulas, A. N. Angelakis, and G. Tchobanoglous, "Urban Water Management in Ancient Greece: Legacies and Lessons," *Journal of Water Resources Planning and Management* (January/February 2008): 45–54.

27. Hanson, *War Like No Other*, 65, 68.

28. Thuc. 2.58.

29. Thuc. 2.54.2.

30. Robin Mitchell-Boyask, *Plague and the Athenian Imagination: Drama, History and the Cult of Asclepius* (Cambridge: Cambridge University Press, 2008), 1.

31. Ibid., xii–xiii. See also E. Baziotopoulou-Valavani, "A Mass Burial from the Cemetery of Kerameikos," in *Excavating Classical Culture: Recent Archaeological Discoveries in Greece*, Studies in Classical Archaeology 1, ed. M. Stamatopoulou and M. Yeroulanou (Oxford: Beazley Archive and Archaeopress, 2002), 187–201.

32. June W. Allison, "Pericles' Policy and the Plague," *Historia: Zeitschrift für Alte Geschichte* 32 (1983): 14–23.

33. Thuc. 2.61.

34. Thuc. 2.64.

35. Pericles benefited from this new law, since he had a son also named Pericles, whose mother Aspasia was a non-Athenian. The younger Pericles became a citizen as a result.

36. Thuc. 3.87.

37. This painting of Vesuvius was discovered in 1879 on a wall in the Casa del Centenario, one of the largest houses in Pompeii. It is now in the National Archaeological Museum in Naples.

38. Sil., *Pun.* 8.653–55; see also 12.140–57.

39. Jelle Zeilinga de Boer and Donald Theodore Sanders, *Volcanoes in Human History: The Far-Reaching Effects of Major Eruptions* (Princeton, NJ: Princeton University Press, 2002), 80; Richard B. Stothers, "The Case for an Eruption of Vesuvius in 217 BC," *Ancient History Bulletin* 16, no. 3–4 (2002): 182–85.

40. R. Sulpizio, R. Bonasia, P. Dellino, D. Mele, M.A. Di Vito, and L. La Volpe, "The Pomici di Avellino Eruption of Somma–Vesuvius (3.9 ka BP). II: Sedimentology and Physical Volcanology of Pyroclastic Density Current Deposits," Abstract, *Bulletin of Volcanology* 72, no. 5 (2010): 559.

41. Diod. Sic. 4.21.5; Vitr., *De arch.* 2.6.2; Strabo 5.4.8, C246–47; Ernesto De Carolis and Giovanni Patricelli, *Vesuvius, A.D. 79: The Destruction of Pompeii and Herculaneum* (Los Angeles: Getty Publications, 2003), 41.

42. Strabo 4.5.8.

43. Sen., *Q Nat.* 6.1, 6.27.

44. Pliny, *HN* 2.110.

45. The date given in the manuscripts is August 24, but archaeological evidence, including wind direction and the fruit and vegetable remains found in Pompeii, suggests a date in autumn.

46. Pliny *HN.*

47. Pliny, *Ep.* 6.16, 6.20. It is not known whether Tacitus made use of Pliny's information in his *Histories* because his narrative breaks off in 70 CE, nine years before the volcanic disaster.

48. R. F. Newbold, "The Reporting of Earthquakes, Fires and Floods by Ancient Historians," *Proceedings of the African Classical Associations* 16 (1982): 28–36.

49. Sen., *Q Nat.* 6.1.1–2, 6.27.1–4, 6.28.1–2.

50. Pliny, *HN* 2.85.

51. Haraldur Sigurdsson, "Mount Vesuvius before the Disaster," in *The Natural History of Pompeii*, ed. Wilhelmina Feemster Jashemski and Frederick G. Meyer (Cambridge: Cambridge University Press, 2002), 29–36.

52. Raffaello Cioni, Lucia Gurioli, Alessandro Sbrana, and Georges Vougioukalakis, "Precursory Phenomena and Destructive Events Related to the Late Bronze Age Minoan (Thera, Greece) and AD 79 (Vesuvius, Italy) Plinian Eruptions: Inferences from the Stratigraphy in the Archaeological Areas," in *The Archaeology of Geological Catastrophes*, Special Publication 171, ed. William J. McGuire, D. R. Griffiths, P. L. Hancock, and I. S. Stewart (London: Geological Society, 2000), 123–42, esp. 138.

53. Concetta Nostro, Ross S. Stein, Massimo Cocco, Maria Elina Belardinelli, and Warner Marzocchi, "Two-Way Coupling between Vesuvius Eruptions and Southern Apennine Earthquakes, Italy, by Elastic Stress Transfer," *Journal of Geophysical Research*, 103 (1998): 24,487–524.

54. Haraldur Sigurdsson, *Melting the Earth: The History of Ideas on Volcanic Eruptions* (New York: Oxford University Press, 1999), 61, 67.

55. Pliny, *Ep.* 6.20.

56. Elizabeth A. Fisher and Robert A. Hadley, "Two Ancient Accounts of the Eruption of Vesuvius in A.D. 79," in *Pompeii and the Vesuvian Landscape: Papers of a Symposium Sponsored by The Archaeological Institute of America, Washington Society and The Smithsonian Institution* (Washington, DC: Archaeological Institute of America, 1979), 9–15, esp. 14–15.

57. Grete Stefani, *Man and the Environment in the Territory of Vesuvius: The Antiquarium of Boscoreale* (Pompeii: Flavius, 2010).

58. Mart. 4.44.

59. Pyroclastic rocks are fragmentary volcanic rocks consisting predominantly of pumice and volcanic ash. Pyroclastic flows are hot, turbulent avalanches of pumice, ash, and gases that pour down the slopes of a volcano at high speed, sometimes faster than 100 km per hour (62 miles per hour).

60. R. V. Fisher, G. Heiken, and J. B. Hulen, *Volcanoes: Crucibles of Change* (Princeton, NJ: Princeton University Press, 1997).

61. De Boer and Sanders, *Volcanoes in Human History*, chap. 4, "The Eruption of Vesuvius in 79 C.E.: Cultural Reverberations through the Ages," 74–107. See also Gillian Darley, *Vesuvius* (London: Profile Books, 2011), 18.

62. Mischa Meier, "Roman Emperors and 'Natural Disasters' in the First Century A.D.," in *Historical Disasters in Context: Science, Religion, and Politics*, ed. Andrea Janku, Gerritt J. Schenk, and Franz Mauelshagenitors (New York: Routledge, 2012), 15–30.

63. Suet., *Vesp.* 17.

64. Suet., *Titus* 3–4.

65. Judith Lynn Sebesta, "Vesuvius in Classical Literature," *New England Classical Journal* 33, no. 2 (2006): 99–111.

66. Alwyn Scarth, *Vesuvius: A Biography* (Princeton, NJ: Princeton University Press, 2009), 83.

67. Stat., *Silvae* 4.4.

68. Penelope M. Allison, "The AD 79 Eruption of Mt. Vesuvius: A Significant or Insignificant Event?," in *Eventful Archaeologies: New Approaches to Social Transformation in the Archaeological Record*, ed. D. J. Bolender (Albany: State University of New York Press, 2010), 166–78.

69. Pliny, *HN* 3.60.
70. Penelope M. Allison, "Recurring Tremors: The Continuing Impact of the AD 79 Eruption of Mount Vesuvius," in *Natural Disasters and Cultural Change*, ed. R. Torrence and John P. Grattan (London: Routledge, 2002), 110–14.
71. Dio Cass. 66.23.
72. Scarth, *Vesuvius*, 85.
73. Eutizio Vittori, Sabina Fulloni, and Luigi Piccardi, "Environment and Natural Hazards in Roman and Medieval Texts: Presentation of the Clemens Database Project," in *Myth and Geology*, Special Publication 273, ed. Luigi Piccardi and W. Bruce Masse (London: Geological Society, 2007), 51–59, esp. 52.
74. Stat., *Silvae* 4.4.

Chapter 13. Changing Climates

1. Pl., *Leges* 6.782A.
2. Arist., *Mete.* 1.14 (351b).
3. Columella, *Rust.* 1.1.4; Ptol., *Tetra.* 2.12–13.
4. They received their name in reference to Milutin Milankovi , the Serbian mathematician, astronomer, geophysicist, and climatologist who studied their combined effects. The definitive publication is Milutin Milankovitch, *Canon of Insolation and the Ice-age Problem* (Jerusalem: Program for Scientific Translations, 1969, repr. 1998).
5. Ptol., *Phaseis*. Daryn Lehoux, "Observation and Prediction in Ancient Astrology," *Studies in the History and Philosophy of Science* 35, no. 2 (2004): 227–46.
6. T. M. L. Wigley, M. J. Ingram, and G. Farmer, ed., *Climate and History: Studies in Past Climates and Their Impact on Man* (Cambridge: Cambridge University Press, 1981), 16.
7. J. Donald Hughes, *An Environmental History of the World: Humankind's Changing Role in the Community of Life*, 2nd ed. (London: Routledge, 2009), 254–68.
8. Konrad Spindler, *The Man in the Ice: The Preserved Body of a Neolithic Man Reveals the Secrets of the Stone Age* (London: Phoenix, 2001).
9. Peter I. Kuniholm, "Dendrochronology," in *Handbook of Archaeological Sciences*, ed. D. Brothwell and A. M. Pollard (London: Wiley, 2001), 35–46; Sturt W. Manning and Mary Jaye Bruce, ed., *Tree-rings, Kings, and Old World Archaeology and Environment: Papers Presented in Honor of Peter Ian Kuniholm* (Oxford: Oxbow Books, 2009).
10. William J. Burroughs, *Climate Change in Prehistory: The End of the Reign of Chaos* (Cambridge: Cambridge University Press, 2005), 177–79.
11. Charlotte L. Pearson, Darren S. Dale, Peter W. Brewer, Peter I. Kuniholm, Jeffrey Lipton, and Sturt W. Manning, "Dendrochemical Analysis of a Tree-Ring Growth Anomaly Associated with the Late Bronze Age Eruption of Thera," *Journal of Archaeological Science* 36, no. 6 (2009): 1206–14.
12. Hubert H. Lamb, "Climate at the Dawn of History," in *Climate, History, and the Modern World* (New York: Methuen, 1982), 104–16.
13. Hans-Jurgen Bolle, ed., *Mediterranean Climate: Variability and Trends* (Berlin: Springer-Verlag, 2003), 21–22.
14. Lamb, *Climate, History, and the Modern World*, 136; Stephen C. Porter, "Glaciological Evidence of Holocene Climatic Change," in *Climate and History*, 82.
15. Rhys Carpenter, *Discontinuity in Greek Civilization* (Cambridge: Cambridge University Press, 1966).
16. Lamb, *Climate, History, and the Modern World*, 148.
17. Doeke Eisma, "Stream Deposition and Erosion by the Eastern Shore of the Aegean," in *Climate and History*, 75–76.

18. Brent D. Shaw, "Climate, Environment, and History: The Case of Roman North Africa," in *Climate and History*, 379–403, esp. 388.

19. Theophr., *Caus. pl.* 5.14.2–3.

20. Theophr., *Caus. pl.* 5.14.5.

21. P. Lionello, P. Malanotte-Rizzoli, and R. Boscolo, ed., *Mediterranean Climate Variability* (Amsterdam: Elsevier, 2006).

22. Lydia Dümenil Gates and Stefan Liess, "Impacts of Deforestation and Afforestation in the Mediterranean Region as Simulated by the MPI Atmospheric GCM," *Global and Planetary Change* 30 (2001): 309–28.

23. Oreste Reale and Paul Dirmeyer, "Modeling the Effects of Vegetation on Mediterranean Climate during the Roman Classical Period. I: Climate History and Model Sensitivity," *Global and Planetary Change* 25 (2000): 163–84; Oreste Reale and Jagadish Shukla, "Modeling the Effects of Vegetation on Mediterranean Climate during the Roman Classical Period. II: Model Simulation," *Global and Planetary Change* 25 (2000): 185–214.

24. William F. Ruddiman, *Plows, Plagues and Petroleum: How Humans Took Control of Climate* (Princeton, NJ: Princeton University Press, 2005).

25. Hughes, *An Environmental History of the World*, 254–68.

Chapter 14. Environmental Problems as Factors in the Decline of Greek and Roman Civilization

1. Brent D. Shaw, "Climate, Environment and History: The Case of Roman North Africa," in *Climate and History: Studies in Past Climates and Their Impact on Man*, ed. T. M. L. Wigley, M. J. Ingram, and G. Farmer (Cambridge: Cambridge University Press, 1981), 382.

2. Sen., *Q Nat.* 5.18.15.

3. Xen., *Oec.* 5.12.

4. Jacques Blondel, "Man as 'Designer' of Mediterranean Landscapes: A Millennial Story of Humans and Ecological Systems during the Historic Period," *Human Ecology* 34 (2006): 713–29.

5. Pl., *Critias* 111B–D.

6. Russell Meiggs, *Trees and Timber in the Ancient Mediterranean World* (Oxford: Clarendon Press, 1982), 423–57.

7. Mikhail Ivanovich Rostovtzeff, *The Social and Economic History of the Roman Empire*, 2nd ed. (Oxford: Clarendon Press, 1957), 2:197.

8. Vladimir Grigorievitch Simkhovitch, "Rome's Fall Reconsidered," in *Toward the Understanding of Jesus and Other Historical Studies* (New York: Macmillan, 1921), 84–139.

9. Shaw, "Climate, Environment, and History," 387.

10. Arist., *Hist. an.* 6.36 (580).

11. Strabo 3.2.8.

12. Vitr., *De arch.* 8.6.11.

13. Cato, *Agr.* 139–40.

14. Pl., *Tht.* 152A.

15. Arist., *Pol.* 1.11.8 (1259a9), 1.3.7 (1254b).

16. J. Donald Hughes, "Sustainability and Empire," *Hedgehog Review* 14, no. 2 (Summer 2012): 26–36.

17. 1 Cor. 3:19.

18. J. Donald Hughes, "Environmental Impacts of the Roman Economy and Social Structure: Augustus to Diocletian," in *Rethinking Environmental History: World-System History and Global Environmental Change*, ed. Alf Hornborg, J. R. McNeill, and Joan Martinez-Allier (Lanham, MD: Altamira Press, 2007), 27–40.

19. Aldo Schiavone, *The End of the Past: Ancient Rome and the Modern West* (Cambridge, MA: Harvard University Press, 2002), 122–23.
20. Columella, *Rust.* 3.3.8.
21. Jean-Jacques Aubert, "The Fourth Factor: Managing Non-Agricultural Production in the Roman World," in *Economies beyond Agriculture in the Classical World*, ed. David J. Mattingly and John Salmon (London: Routledge, 2001), 90–112.
22. Pliny, *HN* 18.4.21.

Bibliography

Abel, Ernest L. *Ancient Views on the Origins of Life.* Rutherford, NJ: Fairleigh Dickinson University Press, 1973.

Abrams, Philip, and E. A. Wrigley, ed. *Towns in Societies: Essays in Economic History and Historical Sociology.* New York: Cambridge University Press, 1978.

Africa, Thomas W. *Science and the State in Greece and Rome.* Huntington, NY: R. E. Krieger, 1968.

Ager, D. V., and M. Brooks. *Europe from Crust to Core.* London: John Wiley and Sons, 1977.

Aldrete, G. *Floods of the Tiber in Ancient Rome.* Baltimore: Johns Hopkins University Press, 2007.

Allen, Katharine. *The Treatment of Nature in the Poetry of the Roman Republic.* Madison: University of Wisconsin Press, 1899.

Allison, Penelope M. "Recurring Tremors: The Continuing Impact of the AD 79 Eruption of Mount Vesuvius." In *Natural Disasters and Cultural Change*, edited by R. Torrence and John P. Grattan, 110–14. London: Routledge, 2002.

———. "The AD 79 Eruption of Mt. Vesuvius: A Significant or Insignificant Event?" In *Eventful Archaeologies: New Approaches to Social Transformation in the Archaeological Record*, edited by D. J. Bolender, 166–78. Albany: State University of New York Press, 2010.

Allison, June W. "Pericles' Policy and the Plague." *Historia: Zeitschrift für Alte Geschichte* 32 (1983): 14–23.

American School of Classical Studies at Athens. *Ancient Corinth: A Guide to the Excavations*, 6th ed. Athens: American School of Classical Studies at Athens, 1954.

———. *Garden Lore of Ancient Athens.* Athens: American School of Classical Studies at Athens, 1963.

Amouretti, Marie-Claire. *Le pain et l'huile dans la Grece antique: De l'araire au moulin* (Les Annales Litteraires de l'Universite de Besancon 328; Centre de Recherche d'Histoire Ancienne vol. 67). Paris: Belles Lettres, 1986.

Anderson, John Kinloch. *Hunting in the Ancient World.* Berkeley: University of California Press, 1985.

André, Jacques. *L'alimentation et la cuisine a Rome.* Paris: Librarie C. Klincksieck, 1961.

Andrieu, Valérie. "A Computerized Data Base for the Palynological Recording of Human Activity in the Mediterranean Basin." In *Environmental Reconstruction in Mediterranean Landscape Archaeology*, edited by Philippe Leveau, Frédéric Trément, Kevin Walsh, and Graeme Barker, 17–36. Oxford: Oxbow Books, 1999.

267

Angel, J. Lawrence. "Ecology and Population in the Eastern Mediterranean." *World Archaeology* 4 (1972): 88–105.

Artzy, Michal, and Daniel Hillel, "A Defense of the Theory of Progressive Soil Salinization in Ancient Southern Mesopotamia." *Geoarchaeology: An International Journal* 3, no. 3 (1988): 235–38.

Ashby, Thomas. *The Aqueducts of Ancient Rome.* Oxford: Oxford University Press, 1935.

———. *The Roman Campagna in Classical Times*, new ed. London: Ernest Benn, 1970.

Asouti, Eleni. "Charcoal Analysis Web." 2009. http://pcwww.liv.ac.uk/~easouti/index.htm.

Athanasiadis, Nikolaos. *Zur postglazialen Vegetationsentwicklung von Litochoro Katerinis und Pertouli Trikalon.* Basel: University of Basel Press, 1975.

Attenborough, David. *The First Eden: The Mediterranean World and Man.* Boston: Little, Brown, 1987.

Aubert, Jean-Jacques. "The Fourth Factor: Managing Non-Agricultural Production in the Roman World." In *Economies beyond Agriculture in the Classical World*, edited by David J. Mattingly and John Salmon, 90–112. London: Routledge, 2001.

Aubouin, Jean. "Alpine Tectonics and Plate Tectonics: Thoughts about the Eastern Mediterranean." In *Europe from Crust to Core*, edited by Derek. V. Ager and M. Brooks, 143–56. London: John Wiley and Sons, 1977.

Austin, Michel M. "Greek Trade, Industry, and Labor." In *Civilization of the Ancient Mediterranean: Greece and Rome*, edited by Michael Grant and Rachel Kitzinger, 2:723–52. New York: Charles Scribner's Sons, 1988.

Austin, Michel M., and Pierre Vidal-Naquet. *Economic and Social History of Ancient Greece: An Introduction.* Berkeley: University of California Press, 1977.

Aymard, J. *Essai sur les chasses romaines des origines à la fin du siècle des Antonins.* Fasc. 171. Paris: Bibliothèque des Écoles Françaises d'Athenes et de Rome, 1951.

Baines, John, and Jaromir Malek. *Atlas of Ancient Egypt.* New York: Facts on File, 1980.

Balsdon, John Percy Vyvian Dacre. *Life and Leisure in Ancient Rome.* New York: McGraw-Hill, 1969.

Barringer, Judith M. *The Hunt in Ancient Greece.* Baltimore: Johns Hopkins University Press, 2001.

Baumann, Hellmut. *The Greek Plant World in Myth, Art, and Literature.* Portland, OR: Timber Press, 1993.

Baynes, N. H. "Decline of the Roman Empire in Western Europe: Some Modern Explanations." *Journal of Roman Studies* 33 (1943): 29–35.

Baziotopoulou-Valavani, E. "A Mass Burial from the Cemetery of Kerameikos." In *Excavating Classical Culture: Recent Archaeological Discoveries in Greece.* Studies in Classical Archaeology 1, edited by M. Stamatopoulou and M. Yeroulanou, 187–201. Oxford: Beazley Archive and Archaeopress, 2002.

Bender, Helmut. "Historische Umweltforschung aus der Sicht der provinzialrömischen Archäologie." In *Siedlungsforschung: Archäologie-Geschichte-Geographie*, edited by Klaus Fehn et al., Band 6. Bonn: Verlag Siedlungsforschung, 1988.

Bergquist, Birgitta. *The Archaic Greek Temenos: A Study of Structure and Function.* Lund: Gleerup, 1967.

Bernard, Michelle. "Recent Advances in Research on the Zooplankton of the Mediterranean Sea." *Oceanography and Marine Biology* 5 (1967): 231–56.

Bernardo, Aurelio. "The Economic Problems of the Roman Empire." *Studia et Documenta Historiae et Juris* 31 (1965) 110–70.

Beug, Hans-Juergen. "On the Forest History of the Dalmatian Coast." *Review of Paleobotany and Palynology* 2 (1967): 271–79.

Biel, Erwin R. *Climatology of the Mediterranean Area.* University of Chicago, Institute of Meteorology: Miscellaneous reports, no. 13. Chicago: University of Chicago Press, 1944.

Biese, Alfred. *Die Entwicklung des Naturgefühls bei den Griechen und Römern.* 2 vols. Kiel: Lipsius and Tischer, 1882–84.

Billiard, Raymond. *La vigne dans l'antiquité*. Lyon: H. Lardanchet, 1913.

Birge, Darice Elizabeth. "Sacred Groves in the Ancient Greek World." Ph.D. diss., University of California, Berkeley, 1982.

———. "Trees in the Landscape of Pausanias' *Periegesis*." In *Placing the Gods: Sanctuaries and Sacred Space in Ancient Greece*, edited by Susan E. Alcock and Robin Osborne, 231–45. Oxford: Clarendon Press, 1994.

Birot, Pierre, Piere Gabert, and Jean Dresch. *La Méditeranée et le Moyen Orient*. 2 vols. Paris: Presses Universitaires de France, 1964.

Blake, Marion E. *Ancient Roman Construction in Italy from the Prehistoric Period to Augustus*. Washington, DC: Carnegie Institution, 1947.

———. *Ancient Roman Construction in Italy from Tiberius through the Flavians*. Washington, DC: Carnegie Institution, 1959.

———. *Ancient Roman Construction in Italy from Nerva through the Antonines*. Philadelphia: American Philosophical Society, 1973.

Blondel, Jacques. "Man as 'Designer' of Mediterranean Landscapes: A Millennial Story of Humans and Ecological Systems during the Historic Period." *Human Ecology* 34 (2006): 713–29.

Blondel, Jacques, and James Aronson. *Biology and Wildlife of the Mediterranean Region*. Oxford: Oxford University Press, 1999.

Blondel, Jacques, James Aronson, Jean-Yves Bodiou, and Gilles Boeuf. *The Mediterranean Region: Biological Diversity in Space and Time*. 2nd ed. Oxford: Oxford University Press, 2010.

Boak, Arthur E. R. *Manpower Shortage and the Fall of the Roman Empire in the West*. Ann Arbor: University of Michigan Press, 1955.

Bokser, Baruch M. "Approaching Sacred Space." *Harvard Theological Review* 78 (1985): 279–99.

Bolkestein, Hendrik, ed. *Economic Life in Greece's Golden Age*. Leiden: E. J. Brill, 1958.

Bolle, Hans-Jurgen, ed. *Mediterranean Climate: Variability and Trends*. Berlin: Springer-Verlag, 2003.

Borgeaud, Philippe. *The Cult of Pan in Ancient Greece*. Chicago: University of Chicago Press, 1988.

Bottema, Sietse. *Late Quaternary Vegetation History of Northwestern Greece*. Groningen: V. R. B. Offsetdrukkerij, 1974.

Bötticher, C. Über den Baumkultus der Hellenen und Römer. Berlin: Weidmannsche Buchhandlung, 1856.

Bourne, F. C. "Reflections on Rome's Urban Problems." *Classical World* 62 (1969): 205–9.

Bradford, Ernle. *Mediterranean: Portrait of a Sea*. London: Hodder and Stoughton, 1971.

Bradford, John. *Ancient Landscapes in Europe and Asia*. London: G. Bell and Sons, 1957.

Braudel, Fernand. *La Méditerranée et le Monde Méditerranéen À l'époque de Philippe II*. 2 vols. Paris: Armand Colin, 1966.

Brice, William Charles. "The History of Forestry in Turkey." *Istanbul Üneversitesi Orman Facültesi Dergisi*, ser. A, 20 (1955): 29–38.

———, ed. *Environmental History of the Near and Middle East since the Last Ice Age*. New York: Academic Press, 1978.

Bromehead, Cyril Edward Nowell. "The Early History of Water Supply." *Classical Journal* 99 (1942): 142–51, 183–96.

Brothwell, Don R. "Foodstuffs, Cooking, and Drugs." In *Civilization of the Ancient Mediterranean*, edited by Michael Grant and Rachel Kitzinger, 1:247–64. New York: Charles Scribner's Sons, 1988.

Brothwell, Don R., and Patricia Brothwell. *Food in Antiquity: A Survey of the Diet of Early Peoples*. New York: Praeger, 1969.

Brown, John Pairman. *Israel and Hellas*. Vol. 3. *The Legacy of Iranian Imperialism and the Individual*. Berlin: Walter de Gruyter, 2001.

Browning, Robert. *Justinian and Theodora*. New York: Praeger, 1971.

Brumbaugh, Robert Sherrick. *Ancient Greek Gadgets and Machines*. New York: Crowell, 1966.

Bryson, R. A., and T. J. Murray. *Climates of Hunger: Mankind and the World's Changing Weather*. Madison: University of Wisconsin Press, 1977.

Buck, Robert John. "Agriculture and Agricultural Practice in Roman Law." In *Historia; Einzelschriften*, Heft 45. Wiesbaden: F. Steiner, 1983.

Bulliet, Richard W. *The Camel and the Wheel*. New York: Columbia University Press, 1990.

Bunting, Brian T. "Soils of Mediterranean and Humid Subtropical Areas." In *The Geography of Soil*, 179–86. Chicago: Aldine, 1965.

Burford, Alison. "Heavy Transport in Classical Antiquity." *Economic History Review* 13 (1960): 1–18.

———. *Craftsmen in Greek and Roman Society*. Ithaca, NY: Cornell University Press, 1972.

———. "Crafts and Craftsmen." In *Civilization of the Ancient Mediterranean: Greece and Rome*, edited by Michael Grant and Rachel Kitzinger, 1:367–88. New York: Charles Scribner's Sons, 1988.

Burns, A. "Ancient Greek Water Supply." *Technology and Culture* 15 (1974): 389–412.

Burroughs, William J. *Climate Change in Prehistory: The End of the Reign of Chaos*. Cambridge: Cambridge University Press, 2005.

Butler, Alfred Joshua. *Sport in Classic Times*. Los Altos, CA: W. Kaufmann, 1975.

Butzer, Karl W. *Environment and Archaeology*. Chicago: Aldine, 1964.

———. *Early Hydraulic Civilization in Egypt: A Study in Cultural Ecology*. Chicago: University of Chicago Press, 1976.

———. "Long-Term Nile Flood Variation and Political Discontinuities in Pharaonic Egypt." In *From Hunters to Farmers: The Causes and Consequences of Food Production in Africa*, edited by J. Desmond Clark and Steven A. Brandt, 102–12. Berkeley: University of California Press, 1984.

Caputo, M., and L. Pieri. "Eustatic Sea Variation in the Last 2000 Years in the Mediterranean." *Journal of Geophysical Research* 81, no. 33 (1976): 5787–90.

Carcopino, Jerome. *Daily Life in Ancient Rome*. Edited by Henry T. Rowell. Translated by E. O. Lorimer. New Haven, CT: Yale University Press, 1940.

Carney, Elizabeth. "Hunting and the Macedonian Elite: Sharing the Rivalry of the Chase." In *The Hellenistic World: New Perspectives*, edited by Daniel Ogden, 59–80. London: Gerald Duckworth, 2002.

Carpenter, Rhys. *Discontinuity in Greek Civilization*. Cambridge: Cambridge University Press, 1966.

Carrington, Richard. *The Mediterranean: Cradle of Western Culture*. New York: Viking Press, 1971.

Carter, Francis W., ed. *An Historical Geography of the Balkans*. New York: Academic Press, 1977.

Cartledge, Paul. *Sparta and Lakonia: A Regional History, 1300–362 B.C.* London: Routledge, 1979.

Cartwright, Frederick Fox. *Disease and History*. New York: Crowell, 1972.

Cary, Max. *The Geographic Background of Greek and Roman History*. Oxford: Clarendon Press, 1949.

Casson, Lionel. *Travel in the Ancient World*. London: Allen and Unwin, 1974.

Casson, Stanley. *Macedonia, Thrace, and Illyria: Their Relations to Greece from the Earliest Times Down to the Time of Philip, Son of Amyntas*. Oxford: Oxford University Press, 1926.

Castagnoli, F. *Ippodamo di Mileto e l'urbanistica a pianta ortogonale*. Rome: De Luca, 1956.

Chabal, Lucie, and Fanette Laubenheimer. "L'atelier gallo-romain de Sallèles d'Aude: Les potiers et le bois." In *Terre Cuite et Société, la Céramique, Document Technique, Économique et Culturel* (XIVes Recontres Internationales d'Archéologie et d'Histoire d'Antibes), 99–129. Juan les Pins: Centre National de la Recherche Scientifique, 1994.

Chamberlin, J. Edward. *Horse: How the Horse Has Shaped Civilizations*. New York: BlueBridge, 2006.

Chandran, M., D. Subash, and J. Donald Hughes. "Sacred Groves and Conservation: The Comparative History of Traditional Reserves in the Mediterranean Area and in South India." *Environment and History* 6, no. 2 (May 2000): 169–86.

Chappell, J. E. "Climatic Change Reconsidered: Another Look at the 'Pulse of Asia.'" *Geographic Review* 60 (1970): 347–73.

Charlesworth, M. P. *Trade Routes and Commerce of the Roman Empire*. Cambridge: Cambridge University Press, 1924.

Cheyette, Fredric L. "The Disappearance of the Ancient Landscape and the Climatic Anomaly of the Early Middle Ages: A Question to be Pursued." *Early Medieval Europe* 16, no. 2 (2008): 127–65.

Chloros, N. "Forstwissenschaftliche Leistungen der Altgriechen." *Forstwissenschaftliches Centralblatt* 5 (1885): 15–23.

Cioni, Raffaello, Lucia Gurioli, Alessandro Sbrana, and Georges Vougioukalakis. "Precursory Phenomena and Destructive Events Related to the Late Bronze Age Minoan (Thera, Greece) and AD 79 (Vesuvius, Italy) Plinian Eruptions: Inferences from the Stratigraphy in the Archaeological Areas." In *The Archaeology of Geological Catastrophes*. Special Publications 171, edited by William J. McGuire, D. R. Griffiths, P. L. Hancock, and I. S. Stewart, 123–42. London: Geological Society, 2000.

Claiborne, Robert. *Climate, Man, and History*. New York: Norton, 1970.

Clark, John Graham Desmond. "Water in Antiquity." *Antiquity* 18 (1944): 1–15.

Clark, Kenneth. *Animals and Men*. New York: William Morrow, 1977.

Clausing, Roth. "The Roman Colonate: The Theories of Its Origin." (Studies in History, Economics and Public Law 117, no. 1; whole no. 260, edited by Faculty of Political Science of Columbia University.) New York: Columbia University, 1925.

Cloudsley-Thompson, J. L. *Insects and History*. New York: St. Martin's Press, 1976.

Cockle, Helen. "Pottery Manufacture in Roman Egypt: A New Papyrus." *Journal of Roman Studies* 71 (1981): 87–97.

Cohen, Mark Nathan. *Health and the Rise of Civilization*. New Haven, CT: Yale University Press, 1989.

Collingwood, R. G. *The Idea of Nature*. New York: Oxford University Press, 1945.

Collis, John Stewart. *The Triumph of the Tree*. New York: Viking Press, 1954.

Conophagos, Constantin E. *Le Laurium antique et la technique grecque de la production de l'argent*. Paris: Olympe, 1980.

Coulton, J. J. "Lifting in Early Greek Architecture." *Journal of Hellenic Studies* 94 (1974): 1–19.

———. "Greek Building Techniques." In *Civilization of the Ancient Mediterranean: Greece and Rome*, edited by Michael Grant and Rachel Kitzinger, 1:277–98. New York: Charles Scribner's Sons, 1988.

Counts, Derek B., and Bettina Arnold. *The Master of Animals in Old World Iconography*. Budapest: Archaeolingua Alapítvány, 2010.

Crawford, Dorothy J. "Food: Tradition and Change in Hellenistic Egypt." *World Archaeology* 11 (1979): 136–46.

Crouch, Dora P. *Water Management in Ancient Greek Cities*. Oxford: Oxford University Press, 1993.

Crumley, Carole L. *Historical Ecology: Cultural Knowledge and Changing Landscapes*. Santa Fe, NM: School of American Research Press, 1994.

Cunliffe, Barry W. *Fishbourne: A Roman Palace and Its Garden*. Baltimore: Johns Hopkins University Press, 1971.

Dale, Tom, and Vernon Gill Carter. *Topsoil and Civilization*. Norman: University of Oklahoma Press, 1955.

Dallman, Peter R. *Plant Life in the World's Mediterranean Climates: California, Chile, South Africa, Australia, and the Mediterranean Basin*. Berkeley: University of California Press, 1998.

Darby, H. C. "The Clearing of the Woodland in Europe." In *Man's Role in Changing the Face of the Earth*, edited by William L. Thomas, 183–216. Chicago: University of Chicago Press, 1956.

Darley, Gillian. *Vesuvius*. London: Profile Books, 2011.

Davies, Oliver. *Roman Mines in Europe*. Oxford: Oxford University Press, 1935.

Davies, R. W. "The Roman Military Diet." *Britannia* 2 (1971): 122–42.

Davis, Diana K. *Resurrecting the Granary of Rome: Environmental History and French Colonial Expansion in North Africa.* Athens: Ohio University Press, 2007.

Davis, J. L., ed. *Sandy Pylos: An Archaeological History from Nestor to Navarino.* Austin: University of Texas Press, 1998.

Deacon, Margaret. "The Ancient World." In *Scientists and the Sea*, 3–19. London: Academic Press, 1971.

De Boer, Jelle Zeilinga, and Donald Theodore Sanders. *Volcanoes in Human History: The Far-Reaching Effects of Major Eruptions.* Princeton, NJ: Princeton University Press, 2002

De Camp, L. Sprague. *The Ancient Engineers.* Cambridge, MA: MIT Press, 1970.

De Carolis, Ernesto, and Giovanni Patricelli. *Vesuvius, A.D. 79: The Destruction of Pompeii and Herculaneum.* Los Angeles: Getty Publications, 2003.

Decker, Frank Norton. *Historical Background: Arts, Skills and Needs of Ancient and Modern Farming.* Syracuse, NY: Syracuse University Press, 1961.

Dembeck, Hermann. *Animals and Men.* Garden City, NY: Natural History Press, 1965.

De Neeve, P. W. *Peasants in Peril: Location and Economy in Italy in the Second Century B.C.* Amsterdam: J. C. Gieben, 1984.

Detienne, Marcel, and Jean-Pierre Vernant. *The Cuisine of Sacrifice among the Greeks.* Translated by Paula Wissing. Chicago: University of Chicago Press, 1989.

Dewey, J. F., W. C. Pitman III, W. B. F. Ryan, and J. Bonnin. "Plate Tectonics and the Evolution of the Alpine System." *Geological Society of America Bulletin* 84 (1973): 3137–80.

Di Castri, Francesco. "Mediterranean-Type Shrublands of the World." In *Ecosystems of the World 11: Mediterranean-Type Shrublands*, edited by Francesco di Castri, David W. Goodall, and Raymond L. Specht, 1–52. Amsterdam: Elsevier, 1981.

Di Castri, Francesco, and Harold A. Mooney. *Mediterranean Type Ecosystems: Origin and Structure.* Heidelberg: Springer-Verlag, 1973.

Dilke, Oswald Ashton Wentworth, and Margaret S. Dilke. "Terracina and the Pomptine Marshes." *Greece and Rome*, 2nd ser., 8 (1961): 172–82.

Dombrowski, Daniel A. *The Philosophy of Vegetarianism.* Amherst: University of Massachusetts Press, 1984.

Doxiadis, Konstantinos Apostolou. *Architectural Space in Ancient Greece.* Translated and edited by Jacqueline Tyrwhitt. Cambridge, MA: MIT Press, 1972.

———. *The Method for the Study of the Ancient Greek Settlements.* Athens: Athens Center of Ekistics, 1972.

Drachmann, Aage Gerhardt. *Ktesibios, Philon, and Heron.* Copenhagen: E. Munksgaard, 1948.

———. *The Mechanical Technology of Greek and Roman Antiquity: A Study of the Literary Sources.* Madison: University of Wisconsin Press, 1963.

Dumezil, Georges. *Camillus: A Study of Indo-European Religion as Roman History.* Edited by Udo Strutynski. Berkeley: University of California Press, 1980.

Dunbabin, K. M. D. *The Mosaics of Roman North Africa.* Oxford: Oxford University Press, 1978.

Duncan-Jones, Richard P. *The Economy of the Roman Empire: Quantitative Studies.* 2nd ed. Cambridge: Cambridge University Press, 1982.

———. *Structure and Scale in the Roman Economy.* Cambridge: Cambridge University Press, 1990.

Eck, Diana L. "The City as a Sacred Center." *Journal of Developing Societies* 2 (1986): 149–281.

Edgerton, W. Dow. "Sacred Space (Thematic Issue)." *Chicago Theological Seminary Register* 75 (1985): 1–19.

Egerton, Frank N. *Roots of Ecology: Antiquity to Hegel.* Berkeley: University of California Press, 2012.

Ehrenberg, Victor. *The People of Aristophanes.* Oxford: B. Blackwell, 1951.

Ehrlich, Anne H., and Paul R. Ehrlich. *Earth.* New York: Franklin Watts, 1987.

Emberger, L. "La Végétation de la région Méditerranéenne." *Revue Generale Botanique* 32 (1930): 461–662, 705–21.

Erim, Kenan T. *Aphrodisias: City of Venus Aphrodite*. New York: Facts on File, 1986.

Erman, Adolf, ed. *The Ancient Egyptians: A Sourcebook of Their Writings*. London: Methuen, 1927. Reprint. New York: Harper and Row, 1966.

———. *Life in Ancient Egypt*. London: Macmillan, 1894. Reprint. New York: Dover, 1971.

Eubanks, J. "Navigation on the Tiber." *Classical Journal* 25 (1930): 683–95.

Evans, J. K. "Wheat Production and Its Social Consequences in the Roman World." *Classical Quarterly* 31 (1981): 428–42.

Evenari, Michael, Leslie Shanan, and Naphtali Tadmor. *The Negev: The Challenge of a Desert*. 2nd ed. Cambridge, MA: Harvard University Press, 1982.

Fairclough, Henry Rushton. *The Attitude of the Greek Tragedians toward Nature*. Toronto: Rowsell, 1897.

———. *Love of Nature among the Greeks and Romans*. New York: Longmans, Green, 1930.

Farnell, Lewis Richard. *The Cults of the Greek States*. 5 vols. Oxford: Clarendon Press, 1896.

Faure, Gabriel. *Gardens of Rome*. London: N. Kaye, 1960.

Faust, Dominick, Christoph Zielhofer, Rafael Baena Escudero, and Fernando Diaz del Olmo. "High-Resolution Fluvial Record of Late Holocene Geomorphic Change in Northern Tunisia: Climatic or Human Impact?" *Quaternary Science Reviews* 23 (2004): 1757–75.

Fernow, Bernhard E. *A Brief History of Forestry in Europe, the United States, and Other Countries*. Toronto: Toronto University Press, 1907.

Finley, Moses I. *Studies in Land and Credit in Ancient Athens, 500–200 B.C.* New Brunswick, NJ: Rutgers University Press, 1952.

———, ed. *Studies in Roman Property*. Cambridge: Cambridge University Press, 1976.

———. "The Ancient City from Fustel de Coulanges to Max Weber and Beyond." *Comparative Studies in Society and History* 19 (July 1977): 305–27.

———. *Economy and Society in Ancient Greece*. New York: Viking Press, 1982.

———. *The Ancient Economy*. 2nd ed. Berkeley: University of California Press, 1985.

Fischer-Hansen, Tobias, and Birte Poulson. *From Artemis to Diana: The Goddess of Man and Beast*. Copenhagen: Museum Tusculanum Press, 2009.

Fisher, Elizabeth A., and Robert A. Hadley. "Two Ancient Accounts of the Eruption of Vesuvius in A.D. 79." In *Pompeii and the Vesuvian Landscape: Papers of a Symposium Sponsored by The Archaeological Institute of America, Washington Society and The Smithsonian Institution*, 9–15. Washington, DC: Archaeological Institute of America, 1979.

Fisher, R. V., G. Heiken, and J. B. Hulen, *Volcanoes: Crucibles of Change*. Princeton, NJ: Princeton University Press, 1997.

Flemming, N. C. *Archaeological Evidence for Eustatic Change of Sea Level and Earth Movements in the Western Mediterranean during the Last 2000 Years*. Special Paper 109. Boulder, CO: Geological Society of America, 1969.

———. "Holocene Earth Movements and Eustatic Sea Level Change in the Peloponnese." *Nature* 217 (1968): 1031–32.

Fontenrose, Joseph. *Orion: The Myth of the Hunter and the Huntress*. Classical Studies 23. Berkeley: University of California Press, 1981.

Forbes, H. A., and H. A. Koster. "Fire, Axe and Plow: Human Influence in Local Plant Communities in the Southern Argolid." *Annals of the New York Academy of Sciences* 268 (1976): 109–26.

Forbes, Hamish. "The Uses of the Uncultivated Landscape in Modern Greece: A Pointer to the Value of the Wilderness in Antiquity?" In *The Greek World*, edited by Anton Powell, 68–97. London: Routledge, 1995.

Forbes, Robert J. *Studies in Ancient Technology*. 9 vols. Leiden: E. J. Brill, 1955–64.

———. "Land Transport and Road-Building." In *Studies in Ancient Technology*, edited by Robert J. Forbes, 2:126–86. Leiden: E. J. Brill, 1955.

————. "Water Supply." In *Studies in Ancient Technology*, edited by Robert J. Forbes, 1:145–89. Leiden: E. J. Brill, 1955.

————. "Hydraulic Engineering and Sanitation." In *A History of Technology*, edited by Charles Singer, E. J. Holmyard, and A. R. Hall, 2:663–94. London: Oxford University Press, 1956.

Forster, E. S. "Trees and Plants of Herodotus." *Classical Review* 56 (1942): 57–63.

Fowler, W. Warde. *The City-State of the Greeks and Romans*. London: Macmillan, 1893.

————. *Social Life at Rome in the Age of Cicero*. London: Macmillan, 1908.

Foxhall, Lynn, and H. A. Forbes. "Sitometreia: The Role of Grain as a Staple Food in Classical Antiquity." *Chiron* 12 (1982): 41–90.

Fraser, P. M. *Ptolemaic Alexandria*. 3 vols. Oxford: Clarendon Press, 1972.

Frazer, James George. *The Golden Bough: A Study in Magic and Religion*. 3rd ed. 2 vols. New York: Macmillan, 1935.

Freeman, Kathleen. *Greek City-States*. New York: W. W. Norton, 1950.

Friedländer, Ludwig. *Roman Life and Manners under the Early Empire*. 4 vols. London: George Routledge and Sons, 1909–13.

Fuchs, Markus. "Mensch und Umwelt der Antike Südgriechenlands." *Geographische Rundschau* 58, no. 4 (April 2006): 4–11.

Fussell, George Edwin. "Farming Systems of the Classical Era." *Technology and Culture* 8 (1967): 16–44.

Fustel de Coulanges, Numa Denis. *La Cité Antique*. Paris: Librairie Hachette, 1864.

Gage, Jean. "Sur les origines du culte de Janus [Trees in Religion]." *Revue de l'Histoires des Religions* 195 (1979): 3–33.

Gale, N. H., and Z. A. Stos-Gale. "The Sources of Mycenaean Silver and Lead." *Journal of Field Archaeology* 9 (1982): 467–85.

Gallant, Thomas W. *Risk and Survival in Ancient Greece: Reconstructing the Rural Domestic Economy*. Stanford, CA: Stanford University Press, 1991.

Gamulin-Brida, Helena. "The Benthic Fauna of the Adriatic Sea." *Oceanography and Marine Biology* 5 (1967): 535–68.

Garnsey, Peter D. A. "Peasants in Ancient Roman Society." *Journal of Peasant Studies* 3 (1976): 221–35.

————. *Famine and Food Supply in the Greco-Roman World*. Cambridge: Cambridge University Press, 1988.

Garnsey, Peter D. A., K. Hopkins, and C. R. Whittaker, ed. *Trade in the Ancient Economy*. Berkeley: University of California Press, 1983.

Gates, Lydia Dümenil, and Stefan Liess. "Impacts of Deforestation and Afforestation in the Mediterranean Region as Simulated by the MPI Atmospheric GCM." *Global and Planetary Change* 30 (2001): 309–28.

Geikie, Archibald. *The Love of Nature among the Romans*. London: John Murray, 1912.

Gerasimidis, Achilleas M. *Stathmologikes Sinthikes kai Metapagetodis Exelixi tis Blastisis sta Dasi Laila Serron kai Kataphigiou Pierion*. Thessaloniki: Aristotelian University of Thessaloniki (*Didaktoriki Diatribi*), 1985.

Gilding, Paul. *The Great Disruption: Why the Climate Crisis Will Bring On the End of Shopping and the Birth of a New World*. New York: Bloomsbury Press, 2011.

Gilfillan, S. Colum. "Roman Culture and Dysgenic Lead Poisoning." *Mankind Quarterly* 5 (1965): 3–20.

Gilliam, J. F. "The Plague under Marcus Aurelius." *American Journal of Philology* 82 (1961): 225–51.

Glacken, Clarence J. *Traces on the Rhodian Shore*. Berkeley: University of California Press, 1967.

Glotz, Gustave. *Ancient Greece at Work: An Economic History of Greece from the Homeric Period to the Roman Conquest*. London: Kegan Paul, 1930.

Glover, Terrot R. *The Challenge of the Greek and Other Essays*. Freeport, NY: Books for Libraries Press, 1972.

Godwin, H., and A. G. Tansley. "Prehistoric Charcoals as Evidence of Former Vegetation, Soil and Climate." *Journal of Ecology* 29 (1941): 117–26.

Goldberg, Neil J., and Frank J. Findlow. "A Quantitative Analysis of Roman Military Operations in Britain, circa A.D. 43 to 238." In *Warfare, Culture, and Environment*, edited by R. Brian Ferguson, 376. Orlando, FL: Academic Press, 1984.

Gothein, Marie Luise. "Der griechische Garten." *Mitteilungen des deutschen archäologischen Instituts, Athenische Abteilung* 34 (1909): 100–144.

———. *A History of Garden Art*. Edited by Walter P. Wright. Translated by M. A. Archer-Hind. London: J. M. Dent and Sons, 1928.

Goulandris, Niki A., and Constantine M. Goulimis. *Wild Flowers of Greece*. Edited by W. T. Stearn. New York: Academic Press, 1969.

Gow, Andrew Sydenham Farrer. "The Ancient Plough." *Journal of Hellenic Studies* 34 (1914): 249–75.

Gräber, H. *Die Wasserleitungen von Pergamon*. Berlin: Abhandlung Akademischer Wissenschaften, 1887.

Graham, A. J. *Colony and Mother City in Ancient Greece*. Manchester: Manchester University Press, 1964.

Graham, J. W. "The Greek House and the Roman House." *Phoenix* 20 (1966): 3–31.

Grant, Michael. *Roman History from Coins*. Cambridge: Cambridge University Press, 1968.

———. *The Ancient Mediterranean*. New York: Charles Scribner's Sons, 1969.

———. *The Roman Forum*. New York: Macmillan, 1970.

———. *Cities of Vesuvius: Pompeii and Herculaneum*. New York: Macmillan, 1971.

Greene, Kevin. *The Archaeology of the Roman Economy*. Berkeley: University of California Press, 1990.

Grieg, J. R. A., and J. Turner. "Some Pollen Diagrams from Greece and Their Archaeological Significance." *Journal of Archaeological Science* 1 (1974): 177–94.

Grimal, Pierre. *Les Jardins Romains*. 2nd ed. Paris: Presses Universitaires de France, 1969.

———. *Roman Cities*. Translated and edited by G. Michael Woloch. Madison: University of Wisconsin Press, 1983.

Grmek, Mirko Drazen. *Diseases in the Ancient Greek World*. Baltimore: Johns Hopkins University Press, 1989.

Guggisberg, C. A. W. *Man and Wild Life*. London: Evans Brothers, 1970.

Guidoboni, E. *Catalogue of Ancient Earthquakes in the Mediterranean Area up to the 10th Century*. Rome: Istituto Nazionale di Geofisica, 1994.

Guthrie, W. K. C. *In the Beginning: Some Greek Views on the Origins of Life and the Early State of Man*. Ithaca, NY: Cornell University Press, 1957.

Haeckel, Ernst. *Generelle Morphologie der Organismen*. Berlin: Georg Reimer, 1866.

Hammond, Mason. *The City in the Ancient World*. Cambridge, MA: Harvard University Press, 1972.

Hansen, Mogens Herman. *Demography and Democracy: The Number of Athenian Citizens in the Fourth Century B.C.* Herning, Denmark: Systime, 1986.

Hanson, Victor Davis. *The Western Way of War*. New York: Knopf, 1989.

———. *Warfare and Agriculture in Classical Greece*. Berkeley: University of California Press, 1998.

———. *A War Like No Other: How the Athenians and Spartans Fought the Peloponnesian War*. New York: Random House, 2005.

Harries, Kent A. "Earthquake Resistant Construction in Classical Rome." Paper No. 448. New York: Elsevier, 1996.

Harris, Tegwyn. *The Natural History of the Mediterranean*. London: Pelham Books, 1982.

Harris, William V., ed. *The Ancient Mediterranean Environment between Science and History*. Leiden: Brill, 2012.

Harrison, Fairfax, ed. and trans. *Roman Farm Management: The Treatises of Cato and Varro Done into English, with Notes of Modern Instances, by a Virginia Farmer.* New York: Macmillan, 1913.

Hartwell, Kathleen. "Nature in Theocritus." *Classical Journal* 17 (1922): 181–90.

Hasebröck, Johannes. *Griechische Witschafts- und Gesellschaftsgeschichte bis zur Perserzeit.* Tübingen: J. C. B. Mohr, 1931.

Hauck, George F. W. "The Roman Aqueduct of Nimes." *Scientific American* 260 (March 1989): 98–104.

Haywood, Richard Mansfield. *The Myth of Rome's Fall.* New York: Crowell, 1958.

Healy, John F. *Mining and Metallurgy in the Greek and Roman World.* London: Thames and Hudson, 1978.

———. "Mining and Processing Gold Ore in the Ancient World." *Journal of Metals* 31 (1979): 11–16.

———. "Pliny the Elder and Ancient Mineralogy." *Interdisciplinary Science Reviews* 6 (1981): 166–80.

———. "Mines and Quarries." In *Civilization of the Ancient Mediterranean: Greece and Rome,* edited by Michael Grant and Rachel Kitzinger, 2:779–94. New York: Charles Scribner's Sons, 1988.

Heitland, William Emerton. *Agricola: A Study of Agriculture and Rustic Life in the Greco-Roman World from the Point of View of Labour.* Cambridge: Cambridge University Press, 1921.

Henrichs, A. "Thou Shalt Not Kill a Tree: Greek, Manichaean and Indian Tales." *Bulletin of the American Society of Papyrologists* 16 (1979): 85–108.

Hill, Ida Carleton Thallon. *The Ancient City of Athens: Its Topography and Monuments.* Chicago: Argonaut, 1969.

Hodder, Ian. *The Leopard's Tale: Revealing the Mysteries of Çatalhöyük.* London: Thames and Hudson, 2006.

Hodges, Henry. *Technology in the Ancient World.* London: Allen Lane, 1970.

Hoffman, Michael A. *Egypt before the Pharaohs: The Prehistoric Foundations of Egyptian Civilization.* New York: Knopf, 1979.

Hohlfelder, Robert L. "Sebastos, the Harbor Complex of Caesarea Maritima, Israel." In *Oceanography: The Past,* edited by Mary Sears and Daniel Merriman, 765–79. New York: Springer-Verlag, 1980.

Holland, Leicester B. "Colophon." *Hesperia* 13 (1944): 91–171.

Holum, Kenneth G., Robert L. Hohlfelder, Robert J. Bull, and Avner Raban. *King Herod's Dream: Caesarea on the Sea.* New York: W. W. Norton, 1988.

Hong, Sungmin, Jean-Pierre Candelone, Clair C. Patterson, and Claude F. Boutron. "Greenland Ice Evidence of Hemispheric Lead Pollution Two Millennia Ago by Greek and Roman Civilizations." *Science* 265, no. 5180 (1994): 1841–43.

Hopkins, Keith. "Roman Trade, Industry, and Labor." In *Civilization of the Ancient Mediterranean: Greece and Rome,* edited by Michael Grant and Rachel Kitzinger, 2:753–78. New York: Charles Scribner's Sons, 1988.

Hopper, Robert J. *Trade and Industry in Classical Greece.* London: Thames and Hudson, 1979.

Horden, Peregrine, and Nicholas Purcell. *The Mediterranean World: Man and Environment in Antiquity and the Middle Ages.* Oxford: Basil Blackwell, 1988.

Horle, Josef. *Catos Hausbucher: Analyse seiner Schrift De Agricultura nebst Wiederherstellung seines Kelterhauses und Gutshofes.* (Studien zur Geschichte und Kultur des Altertums, 15 Bd., 3. und 4. Hft.) Paderborn, Germany: F. Schoningh, 1929. Reprint. New York: Johnson Reprint Corp., 1968.

Horn, R. C. "The Attitude of the Greeks toward Natural Scenery." *Classical Journal* 11 (1916): 302–18.

Houston, James Macintosh. *The Western Mediterranean World: An Introduction to Its Regional Landscapes.* London: Longmans, Green, 1964.

Howe, Timothy. *Pastoral Politics: Animals, Agriculture and Society in Ancient Greece.* Publications of the Association of Ancient Historians 9. Claremont, CA: Regina Books, 2008.

Hubbell, Harry M. "Ptolemy's Zoo." *Classical Journal* 31 (1935): 68–76.

Hughes, J. Donald. "Ecology in Ancient Greece." *Inquiry* 18 (Summer 1975): 115–25.

————. "The Effect of Classical Cities on the Mediterranean Landscape." *Ekistics* 42 (1976): 332–42.

————. "The Environmental Ethics of the Pythagoreans." *Environmental Ethics* 2 (Fall 1980): 195–213.

————. "Early Greek and Roman Environmentalists." In *Historical Ecology: Essays on Environment and Social Change*, edited by Lester J. Bilsky, 45–59. Port Washington, NY: National University Publications, Kennikat Press, 1980. Reprinted in *The Ecologist* 11 (January 1981): 24–35.

————. "Gaia: Environmental Problems in Chthonic Perspective." *Environmental Review* 6 (December 1982): 92–104. Reprinted in *The Ecologist* (1982): 54–60; in a shorter version in *Omnibus* 8 (1984): 15–18; in a special issue of *Omnibus* (Autumn 1991): 60–63; and in *Environmental History: Critical Issues in Comparative Perspective,* edited by Kendall E. Bailes, 64–82. Lanham, MD: University Press of America, 1985.

————. "How the Ancients Viewed Deforestation." *Journal of Field Archaeology* 10 (1983): 437–45.

————. "Sacred Groves: The Gods, Forest Protection, and Sustained Yield in the Ancient World." In *History of Sustained-Yield Forestry: A Symposium,* edited by Harold K. Steen, 331–43. Durham, NC: Forest History Society, 1984.

————. "Theophrastus and the Mountain Forests of the Ancient Mediterranean." In *History of Forest Utilization and Forestry in Mountain Regions*. Beiheft zur Schweizerischen Zeitschrift für Forstwesen 74, edited by Anton Schuler, 7–20. Zürich: International Union of Forest Research Organizations, 1985.

————. "An Ecological Paradigm of the Ancient City." In *Human Ecology: A Gathering of Perspectives,* edited by Richard J. Borden, 214–20. College Park: University of Maryland and Society for Human Ecology, 1986.

————. "Pan: Environmental Ethics in Classical Polytheism." In *Religion and Environmental Crisis,* edited by Eugene C. Hargrove, 7–24. Athens: University of Georgia Press, 1986.

————. "Forests and Cities in the Classical Mediterranean." In *Perspectives in Urban Geography*. Vol. 10. *Morphology of Towns,* edited by C. S. Yadav, 203–23. New Delhi: Concept, 1987.

————. "The View from Etna: A Search for Ancient Landscape Appreciation." *Trumpeter: Journal of Ecosophy* 4 (Fall 1987): 7–13.

————. "Land and Sea." In *Civilization of the Ancient Mediterranean: Greece and Rome,* edited by Michael Grant and Rachel Kitzinger, 1:89–133. New York: Charles Scribner's Sons, 1988.

————. "Theophrastus as Ecologist." In *Theophrastean Studies: Fifteen Papers on Natural Science, Physics and Metaphysics, Ethics, Religion and Rhetoric,* edited by William W. Fortenbaugh and Robert W. Sharples, 67–75. New Brunswick, NJ: Transaction, 1988.

————. "Mencius' Prescriptions for Ancient Chinese Environmental Problems." *Environmental Review* 13 (1989): 15–27.

————. "Artemis: Goddess of Conservation." *Forest and Conservation History* 34 (October 1990): 191–97.

————. "Sustainable Agriculture in Ancient Egypt." *Agricultural History* 66 (1992): 12–22.

————. "Les Grecs, l'Orient et le savoir Écologique [The Greeks, the East, and Ecological Knowledge]," Écologie Politique 8 (Autumn 1993): 87–99.

————. "Forestry and Forest Economy in the Mediterranean Region in the Time of the Roman Empire in the Light of Historical Sources." In *Evaluation of Land Surfaces Cleared from Forests in the Mediterranean Region during the Time of the Roman Empire,* edited by Burkhard Frenzel, 1–14. Stuttgart: Gustav Fischer Verlag, 1994. (*Paläoklimaforschung / Palaeoclimate Research;* Vol. 10: European Science Foundation Project "European Palaeoclimate and Man," Special Issue 5), 1–14.

————. "The Hunters of Euboea: Mountain Folk in the Classical Mediterranean." *Mountain Research and Development* 16, no. 2 (May 1996): 91–100.

277

———. "Sacred Groves Around the Earth: An Overview," by J. Donald Hughes and M.D. Subash Chandran; (2) "Sacred Groves of the Ancient Mediterranean Area: Early Conservation of Biological Diversity," by J. Donald Hughes; (3) "Sacred Groves of the Western Ghats of India," by M.D. Subash Chandran, Madhav Gadgil, and J. Donald Hughes, in *Conserving the Sacred for Biodiversity Management*, edited by P.S. Ramakrishnan, K.G. Saxena, and U.M. Chandrashekara. UNESCO. Enfield, NH: Science Publishers Inc., and New Delhi and Calcutta: Oxford & IBH Publishing Co. Pvt. Ltd., 1998, (1) 69–86, (2) 101–122; (3) 211–232.

———. "Paraísos no Mundo Antigo: Dos Bosques Sagrados às Ilhas Afortunadas" [Paradises in the Ancient World: From Sacred Groves to the Isles of the Blessed]." In *História e Meio-ambiente: O Impacto da Expansão Europeia* [Environmental History: The Impact of European Expansion]. Colecção Memórias 26, edited by Alberto Vieira, 125–40. Funchal, Portugal: Centro de Estudos de História do Atlántico, 1999.

———. "Europe as Consumer of Exotic Biodiversity: Greek and Roman Times." *Landscape Research* 28, no. 1 (January 2003): 21–31.

———. "Preface: Beginning with Rome." In "The Nature of G. P. Marsh: Tradition and Historical Judgement," special issue, *Environment and History* 10, no. 2 (May 2004): 123–25.

———. *The Mediterranean: An Environmental History*, Santa Barbara, CA: ABC-CLIO, 2005.

———. "The Natural Environment." In *A Companion to the Classical Greek World*, edited by Konrad H. Kinzl, 227–44. Oxford: Blackwell, 2006.

———. "Environmental Impacts of the Roman Economy and Social Structure: Augustus to Diocletian." In *Rethinking Environmental History: World-System History and Global Environmental Change*, edited by Alf Hornborg, J. R. McNeill, and Joan Martinez-Allier, 27–40. Lanham, MD: Altamira Press, 2007.

———. "Hunting in the Ancient Mediterranean World." In *A Cultural History of Animals in Antiquity*, edited by Linda Kalof, 47–70. Oxford: Berg, 2007.

———. "Environmental Philosophy: I. Ancient Philosophy." In *Encyclopedia of Environmental Ethics and Philosophy*, edited by J. Baird Callicott, 1:355–59. New York: Macmillan, 2008.

———. *An Environmental History of the World: Humankind's Changing Role in the Community of Life*. 2nd ed. London: Routledge, 2009.

———. "Ancient Deforestation Revisited." *Journal of the History of Biology* 44, no. 1 (April 2011): 43–57.

———. "Ta iera temeni stin arhea Ellada ke i pikilia ton ikosistimaton tous [Sacred Groves in Ancient Greece and the Diversity of Their Ecosystems]." In *Perivallontiki Istoria: Meletes ya tin arhea ke ti sinhroni Ellada* [Environmental History: Essays on Ancient and Modern Greece], edited by Chloe Vlassopoulou and Georgia Liarakou, 25–58. Athens: Pedio Press, 2011. A previous version was published in 2010 by Ellinika Grammata, 25–67.

———. "The Ancient World, c. 500 BCE to 500 CE." In *A Companion to Global Environmental History*, edited by J. R. McNeill and Erin Stewart Mauldin, 18–38. Chichester: Wiley-Blackwell, 2012.

———. "Sustainability and Empire." *Hedgehog Review* 14, no. 2 (Summer 2012): 26–36.

———. "Responses to Natural Disasters in the Greek and Roman World." In *Forces of Nature and Cultural Responses*, edited by Katrin Pfeifer and Niki Pfeifer, 111–37. Dordrecht: Springer, 2013.

———. "Warfare and Environment in the Ancient World." In *The Oxford Handbook of Warfare in the Classical World*, edited by Brian Campbell and Lawrence A. Tritle, 128–39. New York: Oxford University Press, 2013.

Hughes, J. Donald, and Jim Swan. "How Much of the Earth is Sacred Space?" *Environmental Review* 10 (1986): 247–59.

Hughes, J. Donald, and J. V. Thirgood. "Deforestation, Erosion, and Forest Management in Ancient Greece and Rome." *Journal of Forest History* 26 (1982): 60–75.

Hull, Denison Bingham. *Hounds and Hunting in Ancient Greece*. Chicago: University of Chicago Press, 1964.

Hultkrantz, Üke. "The Owner of the Animals in the Religion of the North American Indians." In *Belief and Worship in Native North America*, edited by Christopher Vecsey, 135–46. Syracuse, NY: Syracuse University Press, 1981.

Humphreys, Sarah C. *Anthropology and the Greeks*. London: Routledge, 1978.

Humphries, Rolfe, trans. *The Satires of Juvenal*. Bloomington: Indiana University Press, 1958.

———. *The Way Things Are*. Bloomington: Indiana University Press, 1968.

Hunt, A. S., and C. C. Edgar. *Select Papyri*. 2 vols. London: Harvard-Heinemann, 1934.

Huntington, Ellsworth. "Climatic Changes and Agricultural Decline as Factors in the Fall of Rome." *Quarterly Journal of Economics* 31 (1917): 173–208.

Huntley, Brian J., and Harry John Betteley Birks. *An Atlas of Past and Present Pollen Maps for Europe: 0–13,000 Years Ago*. Cambridge: Cambridge University Press, 1983.

Huxley, A. J. *Flowers in Greece: An Outline of the Flora*. London: Royal Horticultural Society, 1965.

Hyams, Edward. *Soil and Civilization*. London: Thames and Hudson, 1952.

Hyde, W. W. "The Ancient Appreciation of Mountain Scenery." *Classical Journal* 11 (1915): 70–84.

Imhof-Blumer, Friedrich, and Otto Keller. *Tier- und Pflanzenbilder auf Münzen und Gemmes des klassischen Altertums*. Leipzig: B. G. Teubner, 1889.

Isaac, Erich. *The Geography of Domestication*. Englewood Cliffs, NJ: Prentice-Hall, 1970.

Jacobsen, Thorkild, and Robert M. Adams. "Salt and Silt in Ancient Mesopotamian Agriculture." *Science* 128 (1958): 1251–58.

James, Edwin Oliver. *From Cave to Cathedral: Temples and Shrines of Prehistoric, Classical, and Early Christian Times*. New York: F. A. Praeger, 1965.

———. *The Tree of Life: An Archaeological Study*. Leiden: E. J. Brill, 1966.

Jameson, Michael H. "Agriculture and Slavery in Classical Athens." *Classical Journal* 73 (1977): 122–45.

Jashemski, Wilhelmina Mary Feemster. *The Gardens of Pompeii: Herculaneum and the Villas Destroyed by Vesuvius*. New Rochelle, NY: Caratzas Bros., 1979.

———. "Pompeii and Mount Vesuvius, A.D. 79." In *Volcanic Activity and Human Ecology*, edited by Payson D. Sheets and Donald K. Grayson, 587–613. New York: Academic Press, 1979.

Jasny, Naum. "Competition among Grains in Classical Antiquity." *American Historical Review* 47, no. 4 (1941): 747–64.

———. "The Daily Bread of the Ancient Greeks and Romans." *Osiris* 9 (1950): 227–53.

Jenkins, Patricia. *The Environment and the Classical World*. London: Bristol Classical Press, 1998.

Jennison, George. *Animals for Show and Pleasure in Ancient Rome*. Manchester: Manchester University Press, 1937.

Johanson, Donald C., and James Shreeve. *Lucy's Child: The Search for Our Beginnings*. New York: Morrow, 1989.

Johnson, Allan Chester. "Ancient Forests and Navies." *Transactions and Proceedings of the American Philological Association* 58 (1927): 199–209.

Jones, Arnold Hugh Martin. *Ancient Economic History*. London: H. K. Lewis, 1948.

———. *The Later Roman Empire*. 2 vols. Oxford: Oxford University Press, 1964.

———. *The Decline of the Ancient World*. New York: Holt, Rinehart, and Winston, 1966.

———. *The Greek City from Alexander to Justinian*. Oxford: Clarendon Press, 1967.

———. *The Roman Economy: Studies in Ancient Economic and Administrative History*. Edited by P. A. Brunt. Totowa, NJ: Rowman and Littlefield, 1974.

Jones, C. P. *The Roman World of Dio Chrysostom*. Cambridge, MA: Harvard University Press, 1978.

Jones, John Ellis. "The Laurion Silver Mines: A Review of Recent Researches and Results." *Greece and Rome*, 2nd ser. 29, no. 2 (1982): 169–83.

Jones, Karen R., and John Wills. *The Invention of the Park from the Garden of Eden to Disney's Magic Kingdom*, Cambridge: Polity, 2005

Jones, Nicholas F. *Public Organization in Ancient Greece: A Documentary Study*. Philadelphia: American Philosophical Society, 1987.

Jones, William Henry Samuel. *Malaria: A Neglected Factor in the History of Greece and Rome*. Cambridge: Macmillan and Bowes, 1907.

———. *Malaria and Greek History*. Manchester: University Press, 1909.

Jordan, Borimir, and John Perlin. "On the Protection of Sacred Groves." In *Studies Presented to Sterling Dow on His Eightieth Birthday*, edited by Alan L. Boegehold, 153–61. Durham, NC: Duke University Press, 1984.

Judson, Sheldon. "Erosion and Deposition of Italian Stream Valleys during Historic Time." *Science* 140 (1963): 898–99.

———. "Stream Changes during Historic Time in East-Central Sicily." *American Journal of Archaeology* 67 (1963): 287–89.

———. "Erosion Rates near Rome, Italy." *Science* 160 (1968): 1444–46.

Kagan, Donald. *The Peloponnesian War*. New York: Viking, 2003.

Kahil, Lilly. "The Mythological Repertoire of Brauron." In *Ancient Greek Art and Iconography*, edited by Warren G. Moon, 231–44. Madison: University of Wisconsin Press, 1983.

Kees, Herrmann. *Ancient Egypt: A Cultural Topography*. Chicago: University of Chicago Press, 1961.

Kehoe, Dennis P. *The Economics of Agriculture on Roman Imperial Estates in North Africa*. Gottingen: Vanderhoeck and Ruprecht, 1988.

Keller, Otto. *Die antike Tierwelt*. 2 vols. Leipzig: Wilhelm Engelmann, 1909–13.

Kemp, Barry J. *Ancient Egypt: Anatomy of a Civilization*. London: Routledge, 1989.

Kerenyi, Karl. "Il Dio Cacciatore." *Dioniso* 15 (1952): 131–42.

Kiechle, Franz. *Sklavenarbeit und technischer Fortschritt im römischen Reich*. Wiesbaden: F. Steiner, 1969.

King, Anthony. *Roman Gaul and Germany*. Berkeley: University of California Press, 1990.

Körner, Otto. *Die Homerische Thierwelt: Ein Beitrag zur Geschichte der Zoologie*. Berlin: Kessinger, 1880.

Koster, H. A., and H. A. Forbes. "The Commons and the Market." Paper presented at the Deforestation, Erosion, and Ecology in the Ancient Mediterranean and Middle East symposium, National Museum of Natural History, Smithsonian Institution, Washington, DC, April 19, 1978.

Koster, H. A., H. A. Forbes, and L. Foxhall. "Terrace Agriculture and Erosion: Environmental Effects of Population Instability in the Mediterranean." Paper presented at the Deforestation, Erosion, and Ecology in the Ancient Mediterranean and Middle East symposium, National Museum of Natural History, Smithsonian Institution, Washington, DC, April 19, 1978.

Kounas, Dionysios A., ed. *Studies on the Ancient Silver Mines at Laurion*. Lawrence, KS: Coronado Press, 1972.

Koutsoyiannis, D., N. Zarkadoulas, A. N. Angelakis, and G. Tchobanoglous. "Urban Water Management in Ancient Greece: Legacies and Lessons." *Journal of Water Resources Planning and Management* (January/February 2008): 45–54.

Kraft, John. "The General Picture of Erosion in the Mediterranean Area." Paper presented at the Deforestation, Erosion, and Ecology in the Ancient Mediterranean and Middle East symposium, National Museum of Natural History, Smithsonian Institution, Washington, DC, April 19, 1978.

Kreissig, Heinz. *Wirtschaft und Gesellschaft im Seleukidenreich*. Berlin: Akademie-Verlag, 1978.

Kriesis, Anthony. *Greek Town Building*. Athens: National Technical University, 1965.

Kuhnholtz-Lordat, G. "La silva, les saltus, et l'ager de Garrigue." *Annales de l'Ecole Nationale d'Agriculture de Montpellier* 26 (1945): IV.

Kuniholm, Peter I. "Dendrochronology." In *Handbook of Archaeological Sciences*, edited by D. Brothwell and A. M. Pollard, 35–46. London: Wiley, 2001.

Lamb, Hubert H. *The Changing Climate*. London: Methuen, 1966.

———. "The Climatic Background to the Birth of Civilization." *Advancement of Science* (September 1968): 103–20.

———. *Climate: Present, Past and Future*. 2 vols. London: Methuen, 1972–77.

———. "Climate, Vegetation, and Forest Limits in Early Civilized Times." *Philosophical Transactions of the Royal Society A* 276 (1974): 193–230.

———. *Climate, History, and the Modern World*. New York: Methuen, 1982.

Lamb, Hubert H., U. Eicher, and V. R. Switsur. "An 18,000 Year Record of Vegetation, Lake-Level, and Climatic Change from Tigalmamine, Middle Atlas, Morocco." *Journal of Biogeography* 16 (1989): 65–74.

Lanciani, Rodolfo Amadeo. *Ancient and Modern Rome*. New Haven, CT: Yale University Press, 1940.

Landels, John G. *Engineering in the Ancient World*. Berkeley: University of California Press, 1978.

———. "Engineering." In *Civilization of the Ancient Mediterranean: Greece and Rome*, edited by Michael Grant and Rachel Kitzinger, 1:323–52. New York: Charles Scribner's Sons, 1988.

Lang, A., trans. *Theocritus, Bion and Moschus*. London: Macmillan, 1901.

Lang, Mabel. *Waterworks in the Athenian Agora*. Excavations of the Athenian Agora Picture Book 11. Princeton, NJ: American School of Classical Studies at Athens, 1968.

Lapham, Janice T. "Greek Agriculture and Religion." PhD diss., University of Denver, 1972.

Laubenheimer, Fanette. *20 Ans de Recherches à Sallèles d'Aude: Le Monde des Potiers Gallo-Romans*. Besançon: Presses Universitaires de Franche-Comté, 2001.

Leakey, Richard E., and Roger Lewin. *Origins*. New York: E. P. Dutton, 1977.

Lee, Doug. "Military History in Late Antiquity: Changing Perspectives and Paradigms." In *Recent Directions in the Military History of the Ancient World*. Publications of the Association of Ancient Historians 10, edited by Lee L. Brice and Jennifer T. Roberts, 145–66. Claremont, CA: Regina Books, 2011.

Lee, Norman E. *Harvests and Harvesting through the Ages*. Cambridge: Cambridge University Press, 1960.

Le Gall, J. C. *Le Tibre dans l'Antiquité*. Paris: Presses Universitaires de France, 1953.

Legon, R. P. "The Megarian Decree and the Balance of Greek Naval Power." *Classical Philology* 68 (1973): 161–71.

Le Houérou, H. N. "The Impact of Man and His Animals on Mediterranean Vegetation." In *Ecosystems of the World*, edited by F. di Castri et al., 479–521. Amsterdam: Elsevier, 1981.

Lehoux, Daryn. "Observation and Prediction in Ancient Astrology." *Studies in the History and Philosophy of Science* 35, no. 2 (2004): 227–46.

Lenz, Harald Othmar. *Botanik der alten Griechen und Römer*. Wiesbaden: Martin Sändig, 1966.

Lepper, Frank, and Sheppard Frere. *Trajan's Column: A New Edition of the Cichorius Plates*. Gloucester: Alan Sutton, 1988.

Lionello, P., P. Malanotte-Rizzoli, and R. Boscolo, ed. *Mediterranean Climate Variability*. Amsterdam: Elsevier, 2006.

Lloyd, R. B. "Three Monumental Gardens on the Marble Plan." *American Journal of Archaeology* 86 (1982): 91–100.

Lloyd-Jones, Hugh. "Artemis and Iphigeneia." *Journal of Hellenic Studies* 103 (1983): 87–102.

Loisel, Gustave. *Histoire des menageries de l'antiquité á nos jours*. 3 vols. Paris: Kessinger, 1912.

Lonsdale, Steven. *Animals and the Origins of Dance*. London: Thames and Hudson, 1981.

Lord, Russell. *The Care of the Earth*. New York: Thomas Nelson and Sons, 1962.

Lovelock, James. *The Ages of Gaia: A Biography of Our Living Earth*. New York: W. W. Norton, 1988.

Lowdermilk, Walter C. "Lessons from the Old World to the Americas in Land Use." In *Annual Report of the Board of Regents of the Smithsonian Institution for 1943*, 413–27. Washington, DC: Government Printing Office, 1944.

———. *Conquest of the Land through 7,000 Years*. U.S. Department of Agriculture Information Bulletin 99. Washington, DC: Government Printing Office, 1953.

Lowry, S. T. "The Classical Greek Theory of Natural Resource Economics." *Land Economics* 41 (1965): 292–98.

Ludwig, Emil. *The Mediterranean: Saga of a Sea*. New York: McGraw-Hill, 1942.

Luginbill, Robert D. *Author of Illusions: Thucydides' Rewriting of the History of the Peloponnesian War*. Newcastle upon Tyne: Cambridge Scholars, 2011.

Lukermann, F. "The Concept of Location in Classical Geography." *Annals of the Association of American Geographers* 51 (1961): 194–210.

MacArthur, William. "The Athenian Plague: A Medical Note." *Classical Quarterly* 48 (1954): 171–74.

MacDougall, Elisabeth Blair, ed. *Ancient Roman Villa Gardens: Dumbarton Oaks Symposium on Ancient Roman Gardens*. Washington, DC: Dumbarton Oaks Research Library and Collection, 1987.

Maddin, Robert, ed. *The Beginning of the Use of Metals and Alloys*. Cambridge, MA: MIT Press, 1988.

Majno, Guido. *The Healing Hand: Man and Wound in the Ancient World*. Cambridge, MA: Harvard University Press, 1975.

Makkonen, Olli. "Ancient Forestry: An Historical Study." *Acta Forestalia Fennica* 82 (1968): 1–84; 95 (1969): 1–46.

Malinowski, Roman. "Ancient Mortars and Concretes: Aspects of Their Durability." *History of Technology* 7 (1982): 89–100.

Mannhardt, Wilhelm. *Wald- und Feldkulte*. 2 vols. Berlin: Gebrüder Borntråger, 1875–77.

Manning, Sturt W., and Mary Jaye Bruce, ed. *Tree-Rings, Kings, and Old World Archaeology and Environment: Papers Presented in Honor of Peter Ian Kuniholm*. Oxford: Oxbow Books, 2009.

Manns, O. Jagd. "Über die Jagd bei den Griechen." *Progr. Cassel* (1888): 7–38; (1889): 3–20; (1890): 3–21.

Manten, A. A. "Lennart von Post and the Foundation of Modern Palynology." *Review of Palaeobotany and Palynology* 1 (1967): 11–22.

Marquardt, Karl Joachim, and Theodor Mommsen, ed. *Handbuch der römischen Alterthumer*. Vol. 5. *Römische Staatsverwaltung*. 2nd ed. Leipzig: S. Hirzel, 1881.

Marres, P. "Les Garrigues Languedociennes: Le Mileu et l'Homme." In *Actes du 86eme Congrès Nationale des Sociétés Savantes*, 201–16. Montpellier: Impr. Nationale, 1961.

Marsh, George Perkins. *Man and Nature*. New York: Scribner, 1864. Reprint edited by David Lowenthal. Cambridge, MA: Harvard University Press, 1965.

Martinengo-Cesaresco, Evelyn Lilian Hazeldine Carrington. *The Outdoor Life in Greek and Roman Poets, and Kindred Studies*. London: Macmillan, 1911.

Matthen, Mohan. "The Organic Unity of Aristotle's World." In *The Greeks and the Environment*, edited by Laura Westra and Thomas M. Robinson, 133–48. Lanham, MD: Rowan and Littlefield, 1997.

Matthews, Kenneth D. *Cities in the Sand, Leptis Magna and Sabratha in Roman Africa*. Philadelphia: University of Pennsylvania Press, 1957.

Mayor, Adrienne. *The First Fossil Hunters: Paleontology in Greek and Roman Times*. Princeton, NJ: Princeton University Press, 2000.

———. *Greek Fire, Poison Arrows, and Scorpion Bombs: Biological and Chemical Warfare in the Ancient World*. Woodstock, NY: Overlook Duckworth, 2009.

McDonald, William A., and George R. Rapp Jr., ed. *The Minnesota Messenia Expedition: Reconstructing a Bronze Age Regional Environment*. Minneapolis: University of Minnesota Press, 1972.

McNeill, J. R. *The Mountains of the Mediterranean World: An Environmental History*. Cambridge: Cambridge University Press, 1992.

McNeill, William Hardy. *Plagues and Peoples*. Garden City, NY: Anchor Press, 1976.

Meier, Mischa. "Roman Emperors and 'Natural Disasters' in the First Century A.D." In *Historical Disasters in Context: Science, Religion, and Politics*, edited by Andrea Janku, Gerritt J. Schenk, and Franz Mauelshagenitors, 15–30. New York: Routledge, 2012.

Meiggs, Russell. *Roman Ostia*. Oxford: Clarendon Press, 1960.

———. "Sea-borne Timber Supplies to Rome." *Memoirs of the American Academy in Rome* 36 (1980): 185–96.

———. *Trees and Timber in the Ancient Mediterranean World*. Oxford: Clarendon Press, 1982.

Mellaart, James. *Çatal Hüyük: A Neolithic Town in Anatolia*. London: Thames and Hudson, 1967.

Michell, Humfrey. *The Economics of Ancient Greece*. Cambridge: Cambridge University Press, 1963.

Mikesell, Marvin W. "The Deforestation of Mt. Lebanon." *Geographical Review* 59 (1969): 1–28.

Milankovitch, Milutin. *Canon of Insolation and the Ice-age Problem*. Jerusalem: Program for Scientific Translations, 1969. Reprint 1998.

Mitchell-Boyask, Robin. *Plague and the Athenian Imagination: Drama, History and the Cult of Asclepius*. Cambridge: Cambridge University Press, 2008.

Moritz, L. Alfred. *Grain-Mills and Flour in Classical Antiquity*. New York: Arno Press, 1979.

Morris, Anthony Edwin James. *History of Urban Form: Before the Industrial Revolutions*. 2nd ed. New York: Wiley, 1979.

Mossé, Claude. *The Ancient World at Work*. New York: Norton, 1969.

Mumford, Lewis. *The City in History: Its Origins, Its Transformations, and Its Prospects*. New York: Harcourt, Brace and World, 1961.

Murphey, R. "The Decline of North Africa Since the Roman Occupation: Climatic or Human?" *Annals of the Association of American Geographers* 41 (1951): 116–32.

Nash, Ernest. *A Pictorial Dictionary of Ancient Rome*. 2nd ed. 2 vols. London: Thames and Hudson, 1968.

Neev, David. *The Geology of the Southeastern Mediterranean Sea*. Jerusalem: Geological Survey of Israel, 1976.

Neumann, K. "The Contribution of Anthracology to the Study of the Late Quaternary Vegetation History of the Mediterranean Region and Africa." *Bulletin de la Société Botanique de France* 139 (1992): 421–40.

Newbigin, Marion Isabel. *The Mediterranean Lands*. London: Christophers, 1924.

———. *Southern Europe*. 3rd ed. London: Methuen, 1949.

Newbold, R. F. "The Reporting of Earthquakes, Fires and Floods by Ancient Historians." *Proceedings of the African Classical Associations* 16 (1982): 28–36.

Noble, Joseph Veach. *The Techniques of Painted Attic Pottery*. New York: Thames and Hudson, 1988.

North, John A. "The Afterlife: Rome." In *Civilization of the Ancient Mediterranean*, edited by Michael Grant and Rachel Kitzinger, 2:1001–2. New York: Charles Scribner's Sons, 1988.

Nostro, Concetta, Ross S. Stein, Massimo Cocco, Maria Elina Belardinelli, and Warner Marzocchi. "Two-Way Coupling between Vesuvius Eruptions and Southern Apennine Earthquakes, Italy, by Elastic Stress Transfer." *Journal of Geophysical Research* 103 (1998): 24,487–524.

Oleson, John Peter. *Greek and Roman Mechanical Water-Lifting Devices: The History of a Technology*. Toronto: University of Toronto Press, 1984.

———. *Bronze Age, Greek, and Roman Technology: A Select, Annotated Bibliography*. New York: Garland, 1986.

Ölschlager, Max. *The Idea of Wilderness: From Prehistory to the Age of Ecology*. New Haven, CT: Yale University Press, 1991.

Olson, L. "Cato's Views on the Farmer's Obligation to the Land." *Agricultural History* 19 (1945): 129–32.

Olson, S. Douglas. "Firewood and Charcoal in Classical Athens." *Hesperia* 60, no. 3 (1991): 411–20.

Osborn, Fairfield. *The Limits of the Earth*. Westport, CT: Greenwood Press, 1971.

Packer, James E. "Roman Building Techniques." In *Civilization of the Ancient Mediterranean: Greece and Rome*, edited by Michael Grant and Rachel Kitzinger, 1:299–322. New York: Charles Scribner's Sons, 1988.

Palgrave, Francis T. *Landscape in Poetry from Homer to Tennyson*. London: Macmillan, 1897.

Palmer, R. E. "Notes on Some Ancient Mine Equipment and Systems." *Transactions of the Institute of Mining and Metallurgy* 36 (1926): 299–310.

———. "Jupiter Blaze, Gods of the Hills, and the Roman topography of CIL VI 377." *American Journal of Archaeology* 80 (1976): 43–56.

Papadopoulos, G. A., and B. J. Chalkis. "Tsunamis Observed in Greece and the Surrounding Area from Antiquity up to the Present Times." *Marine Geology* 56 (1984): 309–17.

Papagrigorakis, Manolis J., Christos Yapijakis, Philippos N. Synodinos, and Effie Baziotopoulou-Valavani. "DNA Examination of Ancient Dental Pulp Incriminates Typhoid Fever as a Probable Cause of the Plague of Athens." *International Journal of Infectious Diseases* 10 (2006): 206–14.

Papanastasis, Vasilios P. "Integrating Goats into Mediterranean Forests." Unasylva No. 154, Corporate Document Repository, Food and Agriculture Organization of the United Nations, Rome, 1985. http://www.fao.org/docrep/50630e/50630e06.htm.

Paris, Ginette. "Artemis and Ecology." In *Pagan Meditations*, 109–10. Dallas: Spring Publications, 1986.

Park, Robert E., Ernest W. Burgess, and Roderick D. McKenzie. *The City*. Chicago: University of Chicago Press, 1925.

Parker, Robert. *Miasma: Pollution and Purification in Early Greek Religion*. Oxford: Clarendon Press, 1983.

Parry, Adam M. "Landscape in Greek Poetry." *Transactions of the American Philological Association* 87 (1956): 1–29. Reprinted in *The Language of Achilles and Other Papers*, 8–35. Oxford: Clarendon Press, 1989.

Patey, Katherine. "Endangered Forests." *The Athenian* (November 1987): 18–22.

Patterson, Clair C., C. Boutron, and R. Flegal. "Present Status and Future of Lead Studies in Polar Snow." In *Greenland Ice Core: Geophysics, Geochemistry, and the Environment*, edited by C. C. Langway Jr., H. Oeschger, and W. Dansgaard, 101–4. Washington, DC: American Geophysical Union, 1985.

Patterson, Clair C., Tsaihwa J. Chow, and Masayo Murozumi. "The Possibility of Measuring Variations in the Intensity of Worldwide Lead Smelting during Medieval and Ancient Times Using Lead Aerosol Deposits in Polar Snow Strata." In *Scientific Methods in Medieval Archaeology*, edited by Rainer Berger, 339–50. Berkeley: University of California Press, 1970.

Patterson, Helen, ed. *Bridging the Tiber: Approaches to Regional Archaeology in the Middle Tiber Valley*. Archaeological Monograph 13. Rome: British School at Rome, 2004.

Pavlovskis, Zoja. *Man in an Artificial Landscape: The Marvels of Civilization in Imperial Roman Literature*. Leiden: Brill, 1973.

Pearson, Charlotte L., Darren S. Dale, Peter W. Brewer, Peter I. Kuniholm, Jeffrey Lipton, and Sturt W. Manning. "Dendrochemical Analysis of a Tree-Ring Growth Anomaly Associated with the Late Bronze Age Eruption of Thera." *Journal of Archaeological Science* 36, no. 6 (2009): 1206–14.

Peck, Harry Thurston ed. *Harper's Dictionary of Classical Literature and Antiquities*. New York: American Book Co., 1923.

Pérès, J. M. "The Mediterranean Benthos." *Oceanography and Marine Biology* 5 (1967): 449–534.

Perlin, John. *A Forest Journey: The Role of Wood in the Development of Civilization*. New York: W. W. Norton, 1989.

Perlman, Paula. "Plato Laws 833C-834D and the Bears of Brauron." *Greek, Roman, and Byzantine Studies* 24 (1983): 115–30.

Perry, Allen. "Mediterranean Climate." In *The Mediterranean: Environment and Society*, edited by Russell King, Lindsay Proudfoot, and Bernard Smith, 30–44. London: Arnold, 1997.

Philippson, Alfred. *Das Mittelmeergebiet: Seine Geographische und Kulturelle Eigenart*. 2nd ed. Leipzig: Teubner, 1907.

Philpot, J. H. *The Sacred Tree, or the Tree in Religion and Myth*. New York: Macmillan, 1897.

Pinto, Bruno, Carlos Aguiar, and Maria Partidário. "Brief Historical Ecology of Northern Portugal during the Holocene." *Environment and History* 16, no. 1 (February 2010): 3–42.

Pirazzoli, P. A. "Sea Level Variation in the Northeastern Mediterranean during Roman Times." *Science* 194 (1976): 519–21.

Platner, Samuel Ball. *Topography and Monuments of Ancient Rome*. Boston: Allyn and Bacon, 1911.

Platner, Samuel Ball, and Thomas A. Ashby. *A Topographical Dictionary of Ancient Rome*. Oxford: Oxford University Press, 1929.

Plato. *Timaeus and Critias*. Translated by Robin Waterfield. Oxford: Oxford University Press, 2008.

Pollard, John Richard Thornhill. *Birds in Greek Life and Myth*. London: Thames and Hudson, 1977.

Polunin, Oleg, and Anthony Huxley. *Flowers of the Mediterranean*. Boston: Houghton Mifflin, 1966.

Polunin, Oleg, and B. E. Smythies. *Flowers of Southwest Europe*. London: Oxford University Press, 1973.

Pons, A. "The History of the Mediterranean Shrublands." In *Ecosystems of the World 11: Mediterranean-Type Shrublands*, edited by Francesco di Castri, David W. Goodall, and Raymond L. Specht, 131–38. Amsterdam: Elsevier, 1981.

Porteous, Alexander. *Forest Folklore, Mythology, and Romance*. London: Allen and Unwin, 1928.

Prager, Frank D. "Vitruvius and the Elevated Aqueducts." *History of Technology* 3 (1978): 105–21.

Preus, Anthony. *Science and Philosophy in Aristotle's Biological Works*. Hildesheim: Georg Olms Verlag, 1975.

Price, Derek John de Solla. "Gears from the Greeks." *Transactions of the American Philosophical Society*, n.s., 64, pt. 7 (1974): 5–68.

Ptolemy, Claudius. *Geography of Claudius Ptolemy*. Translated and edited by Edward Luther Stevenson. New York: New York Public Library, 1932.

Pyne, Stephen J., *Fire: A Brief History*. Seattle: University of Washington Press, 2003.

Raban, Avner. "The Siting and Development of Mediterranean Harbors in Antiquity." In *Oceanography: The Past*, edited by Mary Sears and Daniel Meriman, 750–64. New York: Springer-Verlag, 1980.

Rackham, Oliver. "Land-Use and the Native Vegetation of Greece." In *Archaeological Aspects of Woodland Ecology*. Symposia of the Association for Environmental Archaeology 2, edited by Martin Bell and Susan Limbrey, 177–98. Oxford: British Archeological Reports, 1982.

———. "Observations on the Historical Ecology of Boeotia." *Annual of the British School at Athens* 78 (1983): 291–351.

Radcliffe, William. *Fishing from the Earliest Times*. London: J. Murray, 1921.

Ramage, Edwin S. "Urban Problems in Ancient Rome." In *Aspects of Graeco-Roman Urbanism: Essays on the Classical City*, edited by Ronald T. Marchese, 61–92. Oxford: British Archaeological Reports, 1983.

Ramakrishnan, P. S., K. G. Saxena, and U.M. Chandrashekara, ed. *Conserving the Sacred for Biodiversity Management*. Enfield, NH: Science Publishers, 1998.

Randsborg, Klavs. *The First Millennium A.D. in Europe and the Mediterranean: An Archaeological Essay*. Cambridge: Cambridge University Press, 1991.

Rawlinson, H. H. *Intercourse between India and the Western World from the Earliest Times to the Fall of Rome*. Cambridge: University of Cambridge Press, 1926.

Reale, Oreste, and Paul Dirmeyer. "Modeling the Effects of Vegetation on Mediterranean Climate during the Roman Classical Period. I: Climate History and Model Sensitivity." *Global and Planetary Change* 25 (2000): 163–84.

Reale, Oreste, and Jagadish Shukla. "Modeling the Effects of Vegetation on Mediterranean Climate during the Roman Classical Period. II: Model Simulation." *Global and Planetary Change* 25 (2000): 185–214.

Reckford, Kenneth J. "Some Trees in Virgil and Tolkien." In *Perspectives of Roman Poetry: A Classics Symposium*, edited by G. Karl Galinsky, 57–91. Austin: University of Texas Press, 1974.

Regnault, Félix. "La décadence de la Grèce expliquée par la déforestation et l'impaludisme." *Presse Médicale* (1909): 729–31.

———. "Du rôle du dépeuplement, du déboisement et de la malaria dans la décadence de certaines nations." *Revue Scientifique* 52 (1914): 46–59.

Rendell, Helen. "Earth Surface Processes in the Mediterranean." In *The Mediterranean: Environment and Society*, edited by Russell King, Lindsay Proudfoot, and Bernard Smith, 52–77. London: Arnold, 1997.

Renfrew, Colin. "Erosion in Melos and the Question of the Younger Fill." Paper presented at the Deforestation, Erosion, and Ecology in the Ancient Mediterranean and Middle East symposium, National Museum of Natural History, Smithsonian Institution, National Museum of Natural History, Washington, DC, April 19, 1978.

Rice, E. E. *The Grand Procession of Ptolemy Philadelphus*. Oxford: Oxford University Press, 1983.

Richmond, John Anthony. *Chapters on Greek Fish-lore*. Hermes Zeitschrift fur klassische Philologie. Einzelschriften Heft 28. Wiesbaden: F. Steiner, 1973.

Rickman, Geoffrey E. *Roman Granaries and Store Buildings*. Cambridge: Cambridge University Press, 1971.

———. *The Corn-Supply of Ancient Rome*. Oxford: Clarendon Press, 1980.

Rikli, Martin Albert. *Das Pflanzenkleid der Mittelmeerländer*. 3 vols. Bern: Hans Huber, 1943.

Robin, G. de Q., ed. *The Climatic Record in Polar Ice Sheets: A Study of Isotopic and Temperature Profiles in Polar Ice Sheets Based on a Workshop Held in the Scott Polar Research Institute, Cambridge*. Cambridge: Cambridge University Press, 1983.

Robinson, Henry Schroeder. *The Urban Development of Ancient Corinth*. Athens: American School of Classical Studies, 1965.

Rossi, Lino. *Trajan's Column and the Dacian Wars*. Ithaca, NY: Cornell University Press, 1971.

Rostocker, W., and E. Gebhard. "The Reproduction of Roof Tiles for the Archaic Temple of Poseidon at Isthmia, Greece." *Journal of Field Archaeology* 8 (1981): 211–17.

Rostovtzeff, Mikhail Ivanovich. *A Large Estate in Egypt in the Third Century B.C.* New York: Arno Press, 1979.

———. *The Social and Economic History of the Hellenistic World*. 3 vols. Oxford: Clarendon Press, 1941.

———. *The Social and Economic History of the Roman Empire*. 2nd ed. 2 vols. Oxford: Clarendon Press, 1957.

Rouner, Leroy S., ed. *On Nature*. Notre Dame, IN: University of Notre Dame Press, 1984.

Roux, Georges. *Ancient Iraq*. London: Allen and Unwin, 1964.

Royds, Thomas Fletcher. *The Beasts, Birds, and Bees of Virgil: A Naturalist's Handbook to the Georgics*. Oxford: Blackwell, 1914.

Ruck, Carl A. P. "The Wild and the Cultivated in Greek Religion." In *On Nature*, edited by Leroy S. Rouner, 79–95. Notre Dame, IN: University of Notre Dame Press, 1984.

Ruddiman, William F. *Plows, Plagues and Petroleum: How Humans Took Control of Climate*. Princeton, NJ: Princeton University Press, 2005.

Runnels, Curtis N. "Environmental Degradation in Ancient Greece." *Scientific American* 272, no. 3 (March 1995): 96–99.

Rykwert, Joseph. *The Idea of a Town: Anthropology of Urban Form in Rome, Italy and the Ancient World*. Cambridge, MA: MIT Press, 1988.

Sagan, Dorion, and Lynn Margulis. "Gaia and Philosophy." In *On Nature*, edited by Leroy S. Rouner, 60–75. Notre Dame, IN: University of Notre Dame Press, 1984.

Salisbury, K. J., and F. W. Jane. "Charcoals from Maiden Castle and Their Significance in Relation to the Vegetation and Climatic Conditions in Prehistoric Times." *Journal of Ecology* 28 (1940): 310–25.

Sallares, Robert. *The Ecology of the Ancient Greek World*. Ithaca, NY: Cornell University Press, 1991.

———. *Malaria and Rome: A History of Malaria in Ancient Italy*. Oxford: Oxford University Press, 2002.

Sandars, N. K., trans. *The Epic of Gilgamesh*. Harmondsworth, UK: Penguin, 1960.

Sarton, George. *Introduction to the History of Science*. 3 vols., 1:107. Washington, DC: Krieger, 1927.

———. *A History of Science: Ancient Science through the Golden Age of Greece*. 2 vols. Cambridge, MA: Harvard University Press, 1952.

Sauer, Carl O., Marston Bates, and Lewis Mumford, ed. *Man's Role in Changing the Face of the Earth*. Chicago: University of Chicago Press, 1956.

Sawyer, J. S., ed. *World Climate from 8000 to 0 B.C.* London: Royal Meteorological Society, 1966.

Scarborough, John. "The Myth of Lead Poisoning among the Romans: An Essay Review." *Journal of the History of Medicine and Allied Sciences* 39 (1984): 469–75.

Scarth, Alwyn. *Vesuvius: A Biography*. Princeton, NJ: Princeton University Press, 2009.

Schiavone, Aldo. *The End of the Past: Ancient Rome and the Modern West*. Cambridge, MA: Harvard University Press, 2002.

Schibli, Hermann S. *Pherekydes of Syros*. Oxford: Clarendon Press, 1990.

Schiöler, Thorkild. "Bronze Roman Piston Pumps." *History of Technology* 5 (1980): 17–38.

Schlebeker, J. T. "Farmers and Bureaucrats: Reflections on Technological Innovation in Agriculture." *Agricultural History* 51 (1977): 641–55.

Schopf, Thomas J. M. *Paleoceanography*. Cambridge, MA: Harvard University Press, 1980.

Scullard, Howard Hayes. *The Etruscan Cities and Rome*. Ithaca, NY: Cornell University Press, 1967.

———. *The Elephant in the Greek and Roman World*. Ithaca, NY: Cornell University Press, 1974.

Scully, Vincent Joseph. *The Earth, the Temple, and the Gods: Greek Sacred Architecture*. New Haven, CT: Yale University Press, 1962.

Sears, Paul Bigelow. *Deserts on the March*. Norman: University of Oklahoma Press, 1935.

Sebesta, Judith Lynn. "Vesuvius in Classical Literature." *New England Classical Journal* 33, no. 2 (2006): 99–111.

Seidensticker, August. *Waldgeschichte des Alterthums*. 2 vols. Frankfurt: Trowitzsch und Sohn, 1886.

Sellin, Robert H. J. "The Large Roman Watermill at Barbegal (France)." *History of Technology* 8 (1983): 91–109.

Semple, Ellen Churchill. *The Geography of the Mediterranean Region: Its Relation to Ancient History*. New York: Henry Holt, 1931.

Sereni, Emilio. *Storia del paesaggio agrario italiano*. Bari: Laterza, 1961.

Sessions, George. "Spinoza and Jeffers: An Environmental Perspective." *Inquiry* 20 (1977): 481–528.

Sharples, R. W. "Theophrastus: *On Fish*." In *Theophrastus: His Psychological, Doxographical, and Scientific Writings*, edited by W. W. Fortenbaugh and D. Gutas, 347–85. New Brunswick, NJ: Transaction, 1992.

Sheets, Payson D., and Donald K. Grayson, ed. *Volcanic Activity and Human Ecology*. New York: Academic Press, 1979.

Shepard, Paul. *Man in the Landscape*. New York: Knopf, 1967.

Shepard, Paul, and Barry Sanders. *The Sacred Paw: The Bear in Nature, Myth, and Literature*. New York: Viking, 1985.

Shrewsbury, J. F. D. "The Plague of Athens." *Bulletin of the History of Medicine* 24 (1950): 1–25.

Sigurdsson, Haraldur. *Melting the Earth: The History of Ideas on Volcanic Eruptions*. New York: Oxford University Press, 1999.

———. "Mount Vesuvius before the Disaster." In *The Natural History of Pompeii*, edited by Wilhelmina Feemster Jashemski and Frederick G. Meyer, 29–36. Cambridge: Cambridge University Press, 2002.

Simkhovitch, Vladimir Grigorievitch. "Rome's Fall Reconsidered." In *Toward the Understanding of Jesus and Other Historical Studies*, 84–139. New York: Macmillan, 1921.

Singer, Charles, E. J. Holmyard, and A. R. Hall, ed. *A History of Technology*. vol. 2. Oxford: Oxford University Press, 1956.

Singh, Purushottam. *Neolithic Cultures of Western Asia*. London: Seminar Press, 1974.

Sjoberg, Gideon. *The Preindustrial City: Past and Present*. New York: Free Press, 1960.

Sklawunos, K. G. "Über die Holzversorgung Griechenlands in Altertum." *Forstwissenschaftliches Zentralblatt* 52 (1930): 868–91.

Smith, Catherine Delano. *Western Mediterranean Europe*. London: Academic Press, 1979.

Smith, Norman A. F. "Attitudes to Roman Engineering and the Question of the Inverted Siphon." *History of Technology* 1 (1976): 45–71.

Snell, Leonard J. "Effects of Sedimentation on Ancient Cities of the Aegean Coast, Turkey." *Bulletin of the International Association of Scientific Hydrology* 8 (1963): 71–73.

Sokolowski, F. "On the Episode of Onchestus in the Homeric Hymn to Apollo." *Transactions and Proceedings of the American Philological Association* 91 (1960): 376–80.

Sonnenfeld, Peter, ed. *Tethys: The Ancestral Mediterranean*. Stroudsburg, PA: Hutchinson Ross, 1981.

Sourvinou-Inwood, Christiane. "Myths of the First Temples at Delphi." *Classical Quarterly*, n.s. 29 (1979): 231–51.

———. *Studies in Girls' Transitions: Aspects of the Arkteia and Age Representation in Attic Iconography*. Athens: Kardamitsa, 1988.

Soutar, George. *Nature in Greek Poetry*. London: Oxford University Press, 1939.

Spain, Robert J. "The Second-Century Romano-British Watermill at Ickham, Kent." *History of Technology* 9 (1984): 143–80.

Spindler, Konrad. *The Man in the Ice: The Preserved Body of a Neolithic Man Reveals the Secrets of the Stone Age*. London: Phoenix, 2001.

Spurr, Stephen. "The Cultivation of Millet in Roman Italy." *Papers of the British School at Rome* 51 (1983): 1–15.

———. *Arable Cultivation in Roman Italy*. Journal of Roman Studies Monographs, no. 3. London: Society for the Promotion of Roman Studies, 1986.

Stadter, Philip A. *Arrian of Nicomedia*. Chapel Hill: University of North Carolina Press, 1980.

Stambaugh, John E. *The Ancient Roman City*. Baltimore: Johns Hopkins University Press, 1988.

Stanley, Daniel J., ed. *The Mediterranean Sea: A Natural Sedimentation Laboratory*. Stroudsburg, PA: Dowden, Hutchinson, and Ross, 1972.

Starr, Chester G. *The Economic and Social Growth of Early Greece, 800–500 B.C.* New York: Oxford University Press, 1977.

Stefani, Grete. *Man and the Environment in the Territory of Vesuvius: The Antiquarium of Boscoreale*. Pompeii: Flavius, 2010.

Stevens, Courtenay Edward. "Agriculture and Rural Life in the Later Empire." In *Cambridge Economic History of Europe*. 2nd ed. 6 vols., 1:92–124. Cambridge: Cambridge University Press, 1966.

Stiros, Stathis C. "The AD 365 Crete Earthquake and Possible Seismic Clustering during the Fourth to Sixth Centuries AD in the Eastern Mediterranean: A Review of Historical and Archaeological Data." *Journal of Structural Geology* 23 (February 2001): 545–62.

Storoni Mazzolani, Lidia. *The Idea of the City in Roman Thought: From Walled City to Spiritual Commonwealth*. Translated by S. O'Donnell. Bloomington: Indiana University Press, 1970.

Stothers, Richard B. "The Case for an Eruption of Vesuvius in 217 BC." *Ancient History Bulletin* 16, no. 3–4 (2002): 182–85.

Strassler, Robert B., ed. *The Landmark Thucydides: A Comprehensive Guide to the Peloponnesian War*. Rev. ed. Translated by Richard Crawley. New York: Free Press, 1996.

Strong, Donald Emrys. *Greek and Roman Gold and Silver Plate*. Ithaca, NY: Cornell University Press, 1966.

Strong, Donald Emrys, and David Brown, ed. *Roman Crafts*. New York: New York University Press, 1976.

Sulpizio, R., R. Bonasia, P. Dellino, D. Mele, M. A. Di Vito, and L. La Volpe. "The Pomici di Avellino Eruption of Somma–Vesuvius (3.9 ka BP). II: Sedimentology and Physical Volcanology of Pyroclastic Density Current Deposits." Abstract. *Bulletin of Volcanology* 72 (2010): 559.

Tarn, W. W., and G. T. Griffith. *Hellenistic Civilization*. London: Arnold, 1952.

Tassios, T. P. "Selected Topics of Water Technology in Ancient Greece." In *Proceedings of the 1st IWA International Symposium on Water and Wastewater Technologies in Ancient Civilizations*, edited by A. N. Angelakis and D. Koutsoyiannis, 3–26. London: International Water Association, 2006.

———. "Water Supply of Ancient Greek Cities." *Water Science and Technology: Water Supply* 7, no. 1 (2007): 165–72.

Taylor, A. E., trans. *The Collected Dialogues of Plato*. Edited by Edith Hamilton and Huntington Cairns. Princeton, NJ: Princeton University Press, 1961.

Taylor, Lily Ross. "Caesar's Agrarian Legislation and His Municipal Policy." In *Studies in Roman Economic and Social History in Honor of Allan Chester Johnson*, edited by P. R. Coleman-Norton, 68–78. Princeton, NJ: Princeton University Press, 1951.

Tcherikover, Avigdor. *Die hellenistischen Städtegrundungen von Alexander dem Grossen bis auf die Römerzeit*. New York: Arno Press, 1973.

Tengstrom, Emin. *Bread for the People: Studies of the Corn-Supply of Rome during the Late Empire*. Lund, Sweden: P. Astrom, 1974.

Thirgood, J. V. *Man and the Mediterranean Forest: A History of Resource Depletion*. London: Academic Press, 1981.

Thommen, Lukas. *An Environmental History of Ancient Greece and Rome*. Cambridge: Cambridge University Press, 2012.

Thompson, D'Arcy Wentworth. *A Glossary of Greek Birds*. Oxford: Oxford University Press, 1936.

Thomson, J. Oliver. *History of Ancient Geography*. Cambridge: Cambridge University Press, 1948.

Thucydides and Robert B. Strassler, ed. *The Landmark Thucydides: A Comprehensive Guide to the Peloponnesian War*. rev. ed. Translated by Richard Crawley. New York: Free Press, 1996.

Tod, Marcus Niebuhr. *A Selection of Greek Historical Inscriptions*. 2 vols. Oxford: Clarendon Press, 1933.

Tomlinson, Richard Allan. *Greek Sanctuaries*. New York: St. Martin's Press, 1976.

Toutain, Jules Francois. *The Economic Life of the Ancient World*. Translated by M. R. Dobie. New York: Barnes and Noble, 1951.

Toynbee, Arnold J. "The Roman Revolution from the Flora's Point of View." In *Hannibal's Legacy: The Hannibalic War's Effects on Roman Life*, 2:585–99. London: Oxford University Press, 1965.

Toynbee, Jocelyn M. C. *Animals in Roman Life and Art*. Ithaca, NY: Cornell University Press, 1973.

Tozer, Henry Fanshawe. *A History of Ancient Geography*. 2nd ed. Cambridge: Cambridge University Press, 1897. Reprint. New York: Biblo and Tannen, 1964.

———. *Lectures on the Geography of Greece*. London: John Murray, 1873. Reprint. Chicago: Ares, 1974.

Triat-Laval, H. "Contribution Pollenanalytique à l'Histoire Tardi-et Postglaciare de la Basse Vallée du Rhône." PhD diss., University of Aix-Marseilles III, 1978.

Trotta-Treyden, Hans von. "Die Entwaldung in den Mittelmeerländern, mit einem Anhang über den heutigen Waldstand." In *Petermann's Geographische Mitteilungen aus Justus Perthes Geographischer Anstalt*, 248–53. Gotha, Germany: Petermann, 1916.

Tsoumis, George. "Depletion of Forests in the Mediterranean Region: A Historical Review from Ancient Times to the Present." *Scientific Annals of the Department of Forestry and Natural Environment* 28 (1988): 283–300.

Turrill, W. B. *The Plant-Life of the Balkan Peninsula*. Oxford: Clarendon Press, 1929.

United Nations Educational, Scientific and Cultural Organization. *Mediterranean Forests and Maquis: Ecology, Conservation, and Management*. Paris: UNESCO, 1977.

Urbainczyk, Theresa. *Slave Revolts in Antiquity*. Berkeley: University of California Press, 2008.

Usher, Abbott Payson. *A History of Mechanical Inventions*. 2nd ed. Cambridge, MA: Harvard University Press, 1954.

Van Andel, Tjeerd H., and Curtis N. Runnels. *Beyond the Acropolis: A Rural Greek Past*. Stanford, CA: Stanford University Press, 1987.

Van Andel, Tjeerd H., Curtis N. Runnels, and Kevin O. Pope. "Five Thousand Years of Land Use and Abuse in the Southern Argolid, Greece." *Hesperia* 55 (1986): 103–28.

Vermeule, Emily. "The Afterlife: Greece." In *Civilization of the Ancient Mediterranean*, edited by Michael Grant and Rachel Kitzinger, 2:993–94. New York: Charles Scribner's Sons, 1988.

Vernet, Jean-Louis. "Reconstructing Vegetation and Landscapes in the Mediterranean: The Contribution of Anthracology." In *Environmental Reconstruction in Mediterranean Landscape Archaeology*, edited by Philippe Leveau, Frédéric Trément, Kevin Walsh, and Graeme Barker, 25–36. Oxford: Oxbow Books, 1999.

Vidal-Naquet, Pierre. *The Black Hunter: Forms of Thought and Forms of Society in the Greek World*. Baltimore: Johns Hopkins University Press, 1983.

Vita-Finzi, Claudio. "Roman Dams in Tripolitania." *Antiquity* 35 (1961): 77–95.

———. *The Mediterranean Valleys: Geological Changes in Historical Times*. Cambridge: Cambridge University Press, 1969.

Vittori, Eutizio, Sabina Fulloni, and Luigi Piccardi. "Environment and Natural Hazards in Roman and Medieval Texts: Presentation of the Clemens Database Project." In *Myth and Geology*. Special Publications 273, edited by Luigi Piccardi and W. Bruce Masse, 51–59. London: Geological Society, 2007.

Vött, Andreas, and Helmut Brückner. "Versunkene Häfen im Mittelmeerraum." *Geographische Rundschau* 58, no. 4 (April 2006): 12–21.

Wacher, J. S. *The Towns of Roman Britain*. Berkeley: University of California Press, 1975.

Walker, Donald S. *The Mediterranean Lands*. London: Methuen, 1965.

Ward-Perkins, John B. *Landscape and History in Central Italy*. Oxford: Blackwell, 1964.

———. *Quarrying in Antiquity: Technology, Tradition, and Social Change*. Oxford: Oxford University Press, 1972.

———. *Cities of Ancient Greece and Italy: Planning in Classical Antiquity*. New York: George Braziller, 1974.

Waterfield, Robin, trans. *Plato: Timaeus and Critias*. Oxford: Oxford University Press, 2008.

Weber, Max. *The City*. New York: Free Press, 1958.

———. *The Agrarian Sociology of Ancient Civilizations*. Translated by R. I. Frank. Atlantic Highlands, NJ: Humanities Press, 1976.

———. *Römische Agrargeschichte in ihrer Bedeutung für das Staats- und Privatrecht*. New York: Arno Press, 1979.

Wedeck, Harry Ezekiel. *Humor in Varro, and Other Essays*. Oxford: B. Blackwell, 1929.

Wegener, Wilhelm. *Die Tierwelt bei Homer*. Königsberg: Hartung, 1887.

Wertime, Theodore A. "The Furnace versus the Goat: The Pyrotechnologic Industries and Mediterranean Deforestation in Antiquity." *Journal of Field Archaeology* 10 (1983): 445–52.

Wertime, Theodore A., and James D. Muhly, ed. *The Coming of the Age of Iron*. New Haven, CT: Yale University Press, 1980.

Wertime, Theodore A., and S. Wertime, ed. *Early Pyrotechnology: The Evolution of the Fire Using Industries*. Washington, DC: Smithsonian Institution, 1982.

Wheeler, R. E. M. *Rome beyond the Imperial Frontiers*. London: G. Bell and Sons, 1954.

White, Kenneth D. "Wheat-Farming in Roman Times." *Antiquity* 37 (1963): 207–12.

———. *Agricultural Implements of the Roman World*. London: Cambridge University Press, 1967.

———. *A Bibliography of Roman Agriculture*. Reading: Institute of Agricultural History, University of Reading, 1970.

———. *Roman Farming*. Ithaca, NY: Cornell University Press, 1970.

———. *Farm Equipment of the Roman World*. Cambridge: Cambridge University Press, 1975.

———. "Food Requirements and Food Supplies in Classical Times in Relation to the Diet of the Various Classes." *Progress in Food and Nutritional Science* 2, no. 4 (1976): 143–91.

———. *Greek and Roman Technology*. Ithaca, NY: Cornell University Press, 1984.

———. "Farming and Animal Husbandry." In *Civilization of the Ancient Mediterranean*, edited by Michael Grant and Rachel Kitzinger, 1:211–46. New York: Charles Scribner's Sons, 1988.

Wigley, T. M. L., M. J. Ingram, and G. Farmer, ed. *Climate and History: Studies in Past Climates and Their Impact on Man*. Cambridge: Cambridge University Press, 1981.

Wilhelm, Adolf. "Die Pachturkunden der Klytiden." *Jahresheft des Österreichischen Archäologischen Institutes in Wien* 28 (1933): 197–221.

Willcox, George H. "A History of Deforestation as Indicated by Charcoal Analysis of Four Sites in Eastern Anatolia." *Anatolian Studies* 24 (1974): 117–33.

———. "Charcoal Analysis and Holocene Vegetation History in Southern Syria." *Quaternary Science Reviews* 18, no. 4–5 (April 1999): 711–16.

Wilsdorf, Helmut. *Bergleute und Hüttenmännern im Altertum bis zum Ausgang der römischen Republik*. Berlin: Freiburger Forschungshefte, 1952.

Wilson, John A. *The Culture of Ancient Egypt*. Chicago: University of Chicago Press, 1951.

Windley, Brian F. *The Evolving Continents*. London: John Wiley and Sons, 1977.

Winiwarter, Verena. "Prolegomena to a History of Soil Knowledge in Europe." In *Soils and Societies: Perspectives from Environmental History*, edited by J. R. McNeill and Verena Winiwarter, 177–215. Isle of Harris, UK: White Horse Press, 2006.

Winters, Robert K. *The Forest and Man*. New York: Vantage Press, 1974.

Wittfogel, Karl. *Oriental Despotism: A Comparative Study of Total Power*. New Haven, CT: Yale University Press, 1957.

Wright, H. E., Jr. "Vegetation History." In *The Minnesota Messenia Expedition: Reconstructing a Bronze Age Regional Environment*, edited by William A. McDonald and George R. Rapp Jr. Minneapolis: University of Minnesota Press, 1971.

Wycherley, R. E. *How the Greeks Built Cities*. New York: Macmillan, 1962.

———. *The Stones of Athens*. Princeton, NJ: Princeton University Press, 1978.

Yeo, Cedric A. "The Overgrazing of Ranch Lands in Ancient Italy." *Transactions and Proceedings of the American Philological Association* 79 (1948): 275–307.

Yoshino, Masatoshi M., ed. *Local Wind Bora*. Tokyo: University of Tokyo Press, 1976.

Young, Rodney. "An Industrial District of Ancient Athens." *Hesperia* 20 (1951): 135–288.

Zeuner, Frederick E. *A History of Domesticated Animals*. New York: Harper and Row, 1963.

Zielhofer, Christoph. "Römische Landnutzung und deren Einfluss auf die antike Umwelt in Nordtunisien." *Geographische Rundschau* 58, no. 4 (April 2006): 22–29.

Zielhofer, Christoph, and D. Faust. "Palaeoenvironment and Morphodynamics in the mid-Medjerda Floodplain (Northern Tunisia) between 12,000 and 2000 BP: Geoarchaeological and Geomorphological Findings." In *Alluvial Archaeology in Europe*, edited by Andy J. Howard, Mark G. Macklin, and David G. Passmore, 203–16. Lisse, Netherlands: A. A. Balkema, 2000.

Zimmern, Alfred. *The Greek Commonwealth: Politics and Economics in Fifth Century Athens*. 5th ed. Oxford: Oxford University Press, 1931.

Zinsser, Hans. *Rats, Lice and History*. Boston: Little, Brown, 1935.

Index

ANCIENT SOCIETY AND HISTORY

The series Ancient Society and History offers books, relatively brief in compass, on selected topics in the history of ancient Greece and Rome, broadly conceived, with a special emphasis on comparative and other nontraditional approaches and methods. The series, which includes both works of synthesis and works of original scholarship, is aimed at the widest possible range of specialist and nonspecialist readers.

Tim G. Parkin, *Old Age in the Roman World: A Cultural and Social History*
Thomas S. Burns, *Rome and the Barbarians, 100 B.C.–A.D. 400*
Michael Kulikowski, *Late Roman Spain and Its Cities*
Gregory S. Aldrete, *Floods of the Tiber in Ancient Rome*
Stephen L. Dyson, *Rome: A Living Portrait of an Ancient City*
Elaine Fantham, *Roman Literary Culture: From Plautus to Macrobius*, 2nd edition
J. Donald Hughes, *Environmental Problems of the Greeks and Romans: Ecology in the Ancient Mediterranean*, 2nd edition
Mark Golden, *Children and Childhood in Classical Athens*, second edition